Event-Driven Trading Systems

Queues, State, and Reliable Processing in Practice

Thomas V. Trex

Published by NobleTrex Press

For permissions and other inquiries, write to:
P.O. Box 3132, Framingham, MA 01701, USA

Contents

Introduction

Electronic markets are systems of events. Quotes update, orders arrive, trades print, sessions flap, clocks drift, and capital is exposed to all of it. This book takes that stream of facts as its starting point and treats event flow-not threads, not RPCs-as the primitive around which reliable trading systems are engineered. The premise is simple: if you can name your events precisely, move them predictably, and persist them durably, then you can recover from almost anything that live markets will do to you.

The chapters that follow build a coherent, end-to-end architecture for event-driven trading. We begin with foundations: the market landscape, order lifecycles, and the latency economics that turn microseconds into queue position and, ultimately, PnL. Alongside this domain grounding, we adopt distributed-systems mental models-partial failure, replication, and CAP trade-offs-that are indispensable when correctness and speed are in tension. We establish a vocabulary that will recur throughout: events as immutable facts, commands as intent, and streams as the boundaries across which services coordinate.

With that vocabulary in hand, we construct the messaging and streaming backbone that carries the business. You will see how pub/sub and queueing patterns enable fan-out and parallelism, and why a distributed log becomes the spine of the architecture when replay, ordering, and backfill matter. We contrast logs with message queues for low-latency workflows, delve into schema management as a discipline of contracts over time, and treat partitioning and backpressure as first-class design problems. The goal is not to promote a specific product but to make the trade-offs legible: durability versus throughput, ordering versus scalability, independence of teams versus coherence of data.

State is where events come to rest. The middle of the book explores consistency models in the context of trading constraints: how to preserve correctness when linearizability is expensive and eventual consistency is insufficient for certain risk checks. We examine transactions and sagas with an eye to cross-service workflows, introduce the outbox pattern to avoid dual writes, and explore event sourcing and CQRS when an auditable history is the system of record. Stateful stream processing then shows how keyed state, timers, snapshots, and exactly-once effects can be composed to compute risk, PnL, and analytics in real time without losing determinism.

Time and ordering deserve their own treatment in markets where clocks disagree and packets arrive out of order. We separate event time from processing time, motivate watermarks and allowed lateness, and show how reordering buffers and per-key guarantees keep aggregations correct under jitter. Clock synchronization and regulatory accuracy are addressed pragmatically, including the operational realities of hardware timestamping and monitoring. Reliability patterns-retries with backoff and jitter, dead-letter queues, circuit breakers, rate limits, and kill switches-are presented not as checklists but as budgets: how much failure you can absorb before capital is at risk.

Performance is the art of removing variance. We move down the stack to networking and OS fundamentals, kernel and NIC tuning, memory management and GC strategies, and the details of batching, vectorization, and zero-copy serialization. Concurrency is approached with lock-free and asynchronous patterns suited to bursty, latency-sensitive workloads. Throughout, we emphasize measurement over myth: realistic workload generation, tail latency profiling, and tracing that ties a user-observable symptom back to the exact event path.

Having established principles and infrastructure, we map the core components of a trading platform: market data ingestion and normalization, the order management system as the authoritative state machine, the risk and limits engine that must fail closed, the execution management system that speaks to venues and enforces cancel-on-disconnect, and the pipelines that keep PnL, positions, and reconciliations both real-time and auditable. Safety controls-operator and automated-are treated as products in their own right, not as afterthoughts.

Finally, good systems are run, not just built. We close with testing, observability, security, and operations. Deterministic record/replay enables forensics and backtesting. Property-based and chaos testing expose invariants and weak links. Logging, metrics, tracing, and SLO management provide the nervous system for live trading hours. Effective alerting, runbooks, and incident response reduce time-to-mitigate when seconds matter. Least-privilege access, encryption, lineage, and data governance satisfy not only regulators but your own need for trust in what the machines are doing. Deployment, orchestration, and capacity planning tie it together so that change can happen continuously without jeopardizing stability.

This is a practitioner's book. You will find patterns, failure modes, and design heuristics you can apply immediately, whether you are building a greenfield OMS, hardening a risk service, or refactoring a market data pipeline. The unifying theme is disciplined event thinking: name your facts, bound your streams, measure your tails, and insist on replayability. Markets will surprise you. Your systems should not.

Chapter 1

Foundations of Event-Driven Trading

In a modern electronic market, every microsecond is an opinionated design decision. Before we touch queues, state machines, or stream processors, we need a clear mental picture of what a trading system is actually fighting against: fragmented venues, hostile microstructure, unforgiving latency economics, and the ever-present risk of partial failure. This chapter traces a single order from strategy to venue and back again, revealing how market structure and distributed-systems constraints conspire to make event-driven architectures not a stylistic choice, but a survival mechanism. By the end, you'll see 'events, commands, and streams' not as buzzwords, but as the natural language of real-world trading systems.

1.1 Market Landscape and System Goals

Event-driven trading systems do not live in isolation. They sit in the middle of a busy ecosystem of humans, algorithms, brokers, exchanges, and regulators, all exchanging messages at high speed and under tight constraints. Before we can design queues, state machines, or recovery mechanisms, we need a concrete picture of this landscape and of what the business actually needs the system to accomplish.

This section has three aims:

- To sketch the front-to-back path of a trade, from idea to post-trade reporting.
- To introduce the main actors in that path and how they interact.
- To show how business constraints crystalize into four system-level objectives: low latency, high reliability, strong observability, and tight control of risk.

Throughout, keep one question in mind: *if this system misbehaves for 30 seconds at 10:17:30, what happens in the real world?* The answer is always expressed in business terms—lost P&L, regulatory exposure, client damage, or missed opportunity—and it is those terms that should drive our technical design.

The Front-to-Back Trading Flow

At the highest level, almost every electronic trade passes through the same logical stages:

- A trading *idea* or *signal* is produced.
- That idea is turned into one or more *orders*.
- Orders are checked against *constraints* (regulation, risk limits, client instructions).
- Valid orders are *routed* to one or more trading venues.
- Venues respond with *acknowledgements*, *fills*, and *cancels*.
- Trades are *allocated*, *confirmed*, and sent into *post-trade* workflows: clearing, settlement, and reporting.

This path is often called "front-to-back":

- The *front office* focuses on trading and execution: traders, algos, and smart order routers.
- The *middle office* focuses on risk, compliance, and trade support.
- The *back office* handles confirmations, settlement, accounting, and regulatory reporting.

From an event-driven perspective, each step is both a consumer and a producer of events. A strategy consumes market data and risk views, and produces order instructions. A risk engine consumes proposed orders and current exposures, and produces approvals or rejections. Venues consume orders and produce execution reports.

To keep things concrete, imagine a simple example:

> A quantitative equities fund runs a strategy that buys stocks that just had a positive earnings surprise. When company XYZ reports better-than-expected earnings at 10:00:00, the strategy calculates a target to buy 100,000 shares, sends orders to the market, receives fills over the next few seconds, and then the firm reports the executed trade to the client and the regulator.

Even this plain scenario touches most components of a modern trading stack. We will introduce them now, then return to this flow when discussing system goals.

A Swim-Lane View of the Value Chain

It is often helpful to visualize the trading value chain as a set of horizontal "swim lanes" representing major functional areas. Messages travel left-to-right across lanes as an order progresses from idea to settlement, while information about executions flows back.

Immediately after introducing the logical flow above, we can depict it as follows:

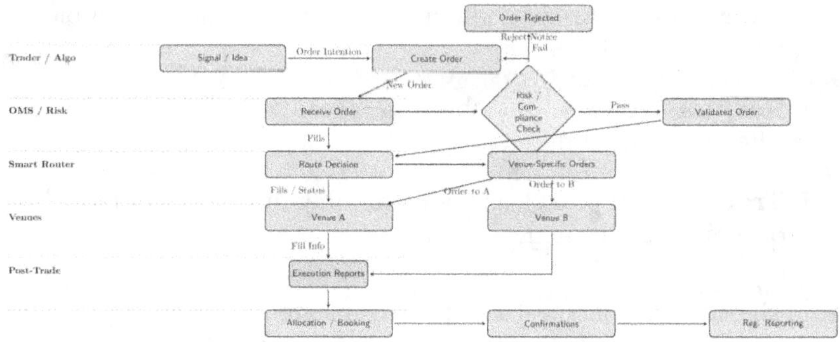

This diagram is not meant to capture every edge case; its purpose is to anchor our discussion. Each box is a subsystem that will, in an event-driven design, have its own input streams, output streams, internal queues, and state. The arrows suggest which components must interact under tight latency constraints and which can tolerate more relaxed, batch-oriented processing.

Key Actors in the Electronic Trading Ecosystem

With the high-level flow in mind, we can identify the main actors and what they care about. These priorities eventually appear as non-functional requirements on our systems.

Clients and Traders

At the top of the chain are the ultimate decision-makers:

- *Institutional clients* such as asset managers, hedge funds, and pension funds.
- *Sell-side desks* and *proprietary trading firms* trading on their own accounts.
- *Algorithms and strategies* that automate decision-making.

They care about:

- **Execution quality**: good prices, low market impact, stable behavior under stress.
- **Responsiveness**: the ability to get into and out of positions when the market moves.
- **Transparency**: a clear understanding of where and how their orders were executed.

From the system's perspective, these translate into latency and reliability requirements on the path from strategy output to venue order, and into observability requirements around what actually happened to each order.

Brokers and Execution Platforms

Brokers sit between clients and venues, providing connectivity, credit, risk controls, and algorithms. Their priorities include:

- **Risk containment**: never allowing a client or strategy to exceed agreed limits.
- **Regulatory compliance**: enforcing market rules on message rates, order types, and trading halts.
- **Service quality**: providing stable uptime across many clients and venues.

Brokers implement much of this via pre-trade and post-trade risk checks, smart order routing, and monitoring infrastructure. Event-driven architecture becomes necessary to coordinate these functions across many independent streams of orders.

Venues: Exchanges, Dark Pools, and ECNs

Venues offer order books or matching engines where trades occur. Examples include:

- *Exchanges* with central limit order books and transparent prices.
- *Dark pools* that match orders without displaying quotes.

- *Electronic Communication Networks (ECNs)* that route and match orders electronically.

Venues care about:

- **Fair and orderly markets**: correct matching, priority rules, and surveillance.
- **Capacity and stability**: handling peak message loads without breakdowns.

They expose their world as streams of market data and execution reports. Your system must consume and interpret these streams, and must also respect their constraints: throttling limits, session resets, and protocol rules.

Clearing Houses and Custodians

Once trades are executed, clearing houses stand between buyers and sellers to manage counterparty risk, while custodians hold client assets. They care about:

- **Accurate positions and cash**: no missing or duplicated trades.
- **Timely settlement**: ensuring obligations are met by deadlines.

The front office often treats this as "someone else's problem," but from an event-driven perspective, front and back office are connected by a chain of events. If execution-level events are unreliable, everything downstream from positions to regulatory reports is at risk.

Regulators

Regulators oversee markets and market participants. They are less interested in microseconds and more in:

- **Integrity and fairness**: no manipulative trading, no abuse of clients.
- **Traceability**: detailed audit trails of who did what, when, and why.

This is where your design choices on event logging, ordering, and state reconstruction become directly relevant to legal obligations.

With these actors in mind, we can now follow an individual order more concretely and see where system goals emerge.

Walking an Order Through the Stack

Return to our simple example: the strategy wants to buy 100,000 shares of XYZ.

1. Idea and Order Creation

The strategy's logic—running on a research or production platform—decides that XYZ should be bought. It translates this into an order: side (buy), quantity, optional price limit, and other parameters.

At this point:

- **Latency** matters because market conditions may be changing rapidly. A delay of even tens of milliseconds can move you down the venue's queue or into a worse price environment.
- **Risk** matters because the strategy may be wrong or may misbehave; limits on notional, volume, and leverage should already influence what it attempts to do.

The system must quickly transform a high-level idea into concrete orders without introducing unnecessary delay, but also without trusting the strategy blindly.

2. Order Management and Risk Checks

The order enters an Order Management System (OMS) or a front-office risk layer. Here, several things happen:

- The order is checked against client-specific instructions (for example, whether it is allowed to trade this instrument or venue).
- Pre-trade risk checks evaluate whether this order would breach exposure, notional, or concentration limits.

- The order might be combined with or split into child orders to execute across time and venues.

This stage is our first encounter with an important tension:

- *We must be fast enough* that the trader does not lose the market opportunity.
- *We must be cautious enough* that a single bug or fat-finger event cannot sink the firm.

Practically, this means optimizing risk checks in the critical path, pre-computing exposures where possible, and designing state representations that can be updated and queried quickly. It also means putting guard rails around the system so that, under failure, orders are blocked or slowed rather than unleashed without controls.

3. Smart Order Routing and Venue Connectivity

Once approved, the order reaches the smart order router. Its job is to decide:

- Which venues to target.
- How to slice the order across those venues.
- At what pace to send orders so as not to move the price too aggressively.

Here, latency and market microstructure interact directly: a route that reaches the best venue 1 millisecond earlier may secure better queue position and therefore better fill quality. At the same time, the router must obey venue-specific rules: message rate caps, valid order types, and connectivity limits.

From an event-driven design standpoint, this stage is characterized by many small, fast decisions reacting to a high rate of incoming market data and execution events, all feeding back into routing choices.

4. Execution at Venues

At the venues, your orders compete with those from the entire market. The venue sends back:

- *Acknowledgements*: confirming that the order was accepted into the book.
- *Partial or full fills*: when all or part of the order trades.
- *Cancellations or rejects*: if the order is withdrawn or invalid.

These messages must be correlated with your internal order state. If the system mislabels a venue response or fails to see it at all, your notion of position and risk will diverge from reality. This is a reliability and observability concern: the flows are fast and frequent, but they must be processed correctly and durably.

5. Allocation, Booking, and Post-Trade

Once executions accumulate, they are:

- *Allocated* to client accounts or internal books.
- *Booked* into the firm's ledger as positions and P&L.
- *Reported* to clients, regulators, and clearing houses.

This part of the flow is typically less latency-sensitive in the microsecond sense, but it is crucial for reliability and control of risk. Mis-booked trades lead to wrong positions, which in turn drive wrong future decisions and risk calculations. Regulatory mis-reporting can result in fines and reputational damage.

Event-driven systems can help here by providing a consistent, append-only record of all changes, from which positions and reports can be derived in a transparent way.

With the full journey in view, we can now extract the core system objectives that underpin a robust event-driven trading architecture.

From Business Constraints to System Objectives

Across all actors and stages, four recurring themes emerge:

- **Latency**: how quickly the system reacts along the critical trading path.

- **Reliability**: whether it behaves correctly and predictably under normal and stressed conditions.
- **Observability**: whether we can see, understand, and explain what the system is doing.
- **Control of risk**: whether losses and exposures are bounded even when things go wrong.

These are not abstract technical virtues; they are direct responses to business constraints.

Latency: Speed Where It Matters

Latency is the end-to-end time between an input arriving and the corresponding action leaving your system. But not all latency is equally important.

Critical Path vs. Non-Critical Path

On the critical path—from market data to strategy decision to order at the venue gateway—small delays can have meaningful economic impact:

- Your order may end up deeper in the queue, reducing the probability of a favorable fill.
- Prices may move away, turning a profitable trade into a loss or missed opportunity.

In contrast, many other processes tolerate much higher latencies:

- End-of-day batch reports.
- Certain analytics and dashboards.
- Archival and backup processes.

A key design discipline in event-driven trading is to *separate* these paths. The critical path should be as lean and non-blocking as possible, often avoiding disk I/O and heavy computation. Non-critical tasks should be decoupled via queues and streams so they do not slow down trading decisions.

Business-Driven Latency Budgets

Rather than chasing "the lowest possible latency," it is more useful to ask:

> What is the maximum acceptable delay in each stage before execution quality degrades in a measurable way?

For some strategies, a few hundred microseconds may matter; for others, tens of milliseconds are fine. These budgets then guide architectural choices: where to colocate, what technologies to use, and where to introduce asynchronous processing.

Reliability: Correctness Under Stress

Reliability is about more than uptime. It asks: does the system continue to do the right thing when faced with:

- Component failures (a crashed process, a stuck risk engine).
- External problems (a venue outage, a network partition).
- Internal bugs (a strategy sending malformed orders).

In trading, failures are not just inconvenient; they can be expensive or even catastrophic.

Bounded Loss Under Failure

A central goal is to design systems such that, even when they malfunction, the financial damage is bounded and knowable. This may involve:

- Hard caps on order sizes and daily notional limits enforced by independent components.
- Automatic kill-switches that stop trading when inconsistencies are detected.
- Conservative defaults when in doubt: for example, block orders rather than let them pass if risk state is stale.

These mechanisms rely on clear event flows and state representations. If it is ambiguous which orders are outstanding or what the current exposure is, it becomes difficult to design safe failure behavior.

Deterministic Recovery

After a failure, we need to reconstruct the exact state of the world:

- Which orders are still live at each venue?
- What positions and P&L should we recognize?
- Which risk checks have already been applied?

Event-driven architectures, especially those that log all state-changing events, enable deterministic recovery by replay: by processing the event history in order, we can rebuild a consistent view. This is a major reason why clear definitions of events and streams are so important later in the book.

Observability: Seeing and Explaining Behavior

Observability means being able to answer questions about the system's internal state and history *without* stopping it or guessing. In trading, natural questions include:

- Why did this order get rejected?
- Why did the strategy stop trading at 10:17:30?
- What was our exposure to XYZ at 10:00:05 when we sent this order?

To answer these, the system needs:

- **Structured logs and events** with consistent identifiers tying orders, fills, and risk checks together.
- **Metrics and traces** capturing latencies, queue lengths, and error rates.
- **Audit trails** that are immutable and time-stamped.

Observability has a feedback loop with reliability and risk. You cannot control what you cannot see. Without good visibility into event flows and state transitions, you will struggle to enforce limits, detect anomalies, or convince regulators you are in control.

Control of Risk: Guard Rails Around Speed

Control of risk is the thread that connects all other objectives. It answers the question:

> Given that we operate at speed, how do we prevent rare events from turning into existential crises?

This involves several layers:

Pre-Trade Controls

Before orders leave the building, controls can:

- Enforce position and notional limits.
- Block trading in forbidden instruments or venues.
- Apply credit and leverage constraints.

These must be fast and always-on, which is why their data dependencies and state management are central to an event-driven design.

In-Flight Controls

While orders are active:

- Strategies may adapt sizes or cancel orders based on partial fills.
- Risk systems may tighten limits in response to market stress.
- Kill-switches may pull existing orders under extreme conditions.

These actions require up-to-date knowledge of outstanding orders and exposures, derived from the same streams of events that drive trading decisions.

Post-Trade Controls

After execution:

- Reconciliation checks compare internal records with venue and clearing data.
- Exception processes investigate breaks or unusual trades.
- Historical analysis feeds into future limit settings and model risk assessments.

Again, a clean event history and reconstructable state make these tasks feasible and auditable.

In sum, control of risk is not a single component but an emergent property of how events are generated, processed, and recorded across the entire front-to-back flow.

Common Failure Modes and Their Lessons

To cement the link between business reality and system objectives, it is useful to briefly catalog a few typical failure modes:

Stale Risk Limits

If a risk engine lags behind reality, it may approve orders that should have been blocked. This is a breakdown of both latency (risk views not refreshed in time) and reliability (no mechanism detected or compensated for the staleness).

Runaway Algorithms

A buggy strategy might start sending orders in a tight loop. Without independent limit checks and rate controls, this can quickly accumulate dangerous positions. Here, weak control of risk and poor observability (no immediate detection of abnormal activity) combine into a serious incident.

Stuck Order Queues

A downstream component (for example, a post-trade system) may slow down and cause queues upstream to grow, eventually impacting trading. This is a case where lack of backpressure management and poor throughput planning compromise both latency and reliability.

Venue Outages or Glitches

An exchange might go down or send inconsistent messages. If your system assumes the venue is always correct and available, this can freeze trading or result in inconsistent state. Designing for partial failure—gracefully degrading trading behavior and isolating faults—is central to reliability.

Each of these examples illustrates why event-driven thinking matters. When messages, states, and transitions are explicit, you can design systems that fail in controlled ways, that can be observed and audited, and that target low latency where it is economically justified.

Where This Leaves Us

We now have a conceptual map of the trading landscape:

- A front-to-back flow from idea to post-trade reporting.
- A set of actors with distinct but interacting priorities.
- A chain of events whose correctness and timing directly affect P&L, clients, and regulators.

From this map, we distilled four core system objectives: latency, reliability, observability, and control of risk. These are the lenses through which we will evaluate architectural choices in the rest of the book.

In the next sections, we will zoom in further: first to the lifecycle of a single order and its interaction with venues, then to the microstructure of markets and the economic value of latency, and finally to the distributed-systems concepts that underpin robust event-driven designs. By grounding those technical discussions in the landscape sketched here, we can keep our focus on what ultimately matters: building trading systems that do the right thing, fast enough, even when the world around them is failing.

1.2 Order Lifecycle and Venue Connectivity

In the previous section we stepped back and looked at the entire front-to-back trading value chain. We saw how an idea becomes an order, how that order travels through risk checks and routing, how venues execute it, and how post-trade systems record and report the result. We also identified four system-level objectives: latency, reliability, observability, and control of risk.

We now zoom in on a single thread running through that tapestry: the lifecycle of *one* order.

Understanding this lifecycle has three purposes:

- It gives a clear vocabulary for order states and transitions, which later chapters will use when discussing queues and event sourcing.
- It shows how venue rules and connectivity protocols shape what your gateway and routing logic must do.
- It highlights where and how you must manage state carefully to keep your internal view aligned with the external world.

Think of this as dissecting the "cell biology" of trading: once you understand how an order lives, changes, and dies, the behavior of larger systems becomes easier to reason about.

Core Order Semantics

Before following an order through time, we need to clarify what we mean by an "order". At its core, an order is an instruction to trade a financial instrument, under certain conditions, at a venue. Regardless of asset class or venue, a few elements are almost always present.

Side

The simplest property is the *side*:

- **Buy**: acquire the instrument.
- **Sell**: dispose of the instrument.

All other fields are interpreted in light of the side. For example, a price is a maximum for a buy and a minimum for a sell.

Quantity

The *quantity* specifies how much you want to trade: number of shares, contracts, lots, and so on. This may be split into smaller slices internally, but at the venue level each order has an explicit size.

Price and Order Type

Orders can behave differently depending on how price is specified:

- **Market order**: no explicit limit price. The order trades immediately against the best available prices in the order book, subject to venue protections.
- **Limit order**: specifies a maximum price to pay (for a buy) or minimum price to receive (for a sell). The order rests in the book until it is either filled, canceled, or expired.

On top of these basics, venues offer many variants:

- **Immediate-or-cancel (IOC)**: whatever quantity can be filled immediately is traded; the remainder is canceled.
- **Fill-or-kill (FOK)**: either the full quantity is executed immediately, or the entire order is canceled.
- **Pegged orders**: prices that track some reference, such as the best bid or midpoint.
- **Hidden and iceberg orders**: orders that are fully or partially invisible in the public book.

From a system design perspective, these details matter because they determine what states an order can go through and what events you will see back from the venue.

Time-in-Force

Time-in-force (TIF) specifies how long the order remains active:

- **Day**: active until the end of the trading day.
- **Good-till-date / good-till-cancel**: active until a specified time or until canceled.
- **IOC / FOK**: essentially a lifetime of a few microseconds; the order either trades or disappears immediately.

The TIF influences the order's possible transitions: a day order can eventually expire; an IOC order never becomes a resting order.

Routing and Venue Instructions

Finally, orders may include instructions such as which venue to use, which broker to go through, whether to allow internal crossing, and so on. In some architectures, these are added by the smart order router rather than the trading strategy.

All of these fields define the *intended behavior* of the order. The lifecycle we study next shows how that intention is realized—or not—in the real world.

From Intention to External Order: Internal vs. External Views

In an event-driven trading system, it is helpful to distinguish between two notions of an order:

- An **internal order**, which is the system's logical representation of the trading intent: what the strategy or trader wants to achieve.
- One or more **external orders**, which are the concrete messages sent to venues to realize that intent.

For example, a strategy might decide to buy 100,000 shares of XYZ over the next five minutes. Internally, you may represent this as a single parent order. The smart router then breaks this into many child orders across venues and time. Each child order has its own lifecycle at its venue, but they all roll up to the state of the parent.

In this section we will mostly talk about the lifecycle at the child (venue) level, since that is where connectivity and protocol details come into play. However, keep in mind that your system must maintain both levels of state and keep them consistent.

Order States: A Conceptual Map

Now we can outline the main states an order may pass through between birth and death. Different firms and venues use different labels, but a typical high-level set is:

- **Created**: the order has been created internally but not yet sent for validation or routing.
- **Validated / Risk-Checked**: internal checks have accepted the order.
- **Pending Venue**: the order has been sent to the venue, but no acknowledgement has been received yet.
- **Active**: the order is accepted by the venue and capable of generating fills.
- **Partially Filled**: some quantity has traded; the remainder is still active.
- **Filled**: the order quantity has been completely traded.
- **Canceled**: the remaining quantity has been withdrawn.
- **Rejected**: the order was not accepted at all.
- **Expired**: the order reached its time limit and was removed by the venue.

These are logical states from your system's perspective. The venue may expose its own set of statuses, which you must translate into your internal model.

To avoid confusion, note that *"pending venue"* and *"active"* differ in an important way: pending venue orders exist only in your system, based on the fact that you *sent* a message; active orders exist at the venue, based on the fact that you *received* confirmation.

This distinction becomes critical when dealing with network glitches and sequence gaps.

State Transitions: Commands vs. Events

States change in response to two broad categories of stimuli:

- **Internal commands**: actions your system initiates, such as *submit order*, *cancel order*, or *modify order*.
- **External events**: messages coming back from venues, such as *order acknowledged*, *trade executed*, or *order canceled by venue*.

Thinking in these terms aligns well with event-driven architectures and will be used throughout the book.

Internal Commands

Common internal commands include:

- *New order* command: instructs the gateway to send a new order to a venue.
- *Cancel* command: instructs the venue to cancel an existing order.
- *Replace / modify* command: update price, quantity, or other fields, often implemented as a cancel-plus-new at the venue.

These commands represent *intent* but do not guarantee that the external world will comply. For example, a cancel command may be rejected if the order already traded.

External Venue Events

In response, the venue emits events such as:

- *New order acknowledgement*: confirms the order was accepted and is now live.
- *New order reject*: indicates the order was not accepted, often with an error code.
- *Execution report*: indicates a partial or full fill.
- *Cancel acknowledgement*: confirms the order has been removed.
- *Cancel reject*: indicates that the cancel could not be processed.
- *Order expiration*: indicates removal due to TIF.

Your system consumes these events and updates its internal state machine for the order.

A crucial design principle is to ensure that internal commands and external events are clearly separated in your architecture. Commands are usually sent once and may be retried with care; events must be processed idempotently, since duplicates or out-of-order delivery can occur.

A Canonical Order State Machine

To make all of this concrete, let us describe a typical state machine for a single venue-level order. We will then present a diagram to serve as a reference.

Start in **Created**: the order exists internally but has not yet passed risk checks.

- On a *risk-approved* internal command, it moves to **Validated** and the system generates a *new order* command to the gateway.
- If validation fails (for example, limit exceeded), it moves directly to **Rejected** (internal).

From **Validated**, the gateway sends the order to the venue and the state becomes **Pending Venue**.

- On *venue acknowledgement*, it moves to **Active**.
- On *venue reject*, it moves to **Rejected** (external).

In the **Active** state, several transitions are possible:

- On a *fill* event:
  - If cumulative filled quantity remains less than the order quantity, the state becomes **Partially Filled**.
  - If cumulative filled quantity equals the order quantity, the state becomes **Filled**.
- On a *cancel acknowledgement* (after a cancel command), the state becomes **Canceled**.
- On an *expiry* event from the venue, the state becomes **Expired**.

From **Partially Filled**, similar transitions apply:

- Additional fills can leave it in **Partially Filled** or move it to **Filled**.
- A cancel acknowledgement can move it to **Canceled**, with any remaining quantity untraded.
- Expiry can move it to **Expired**.

Once in **Filled**, **Canceled**, **Rejected**, or **Expired**, the order is *terminal*: no further state transitions should occur, except perhaps the processing of late, conflicting events, which must be handled carefully.

We can now visualize this state machine as a reference figure.

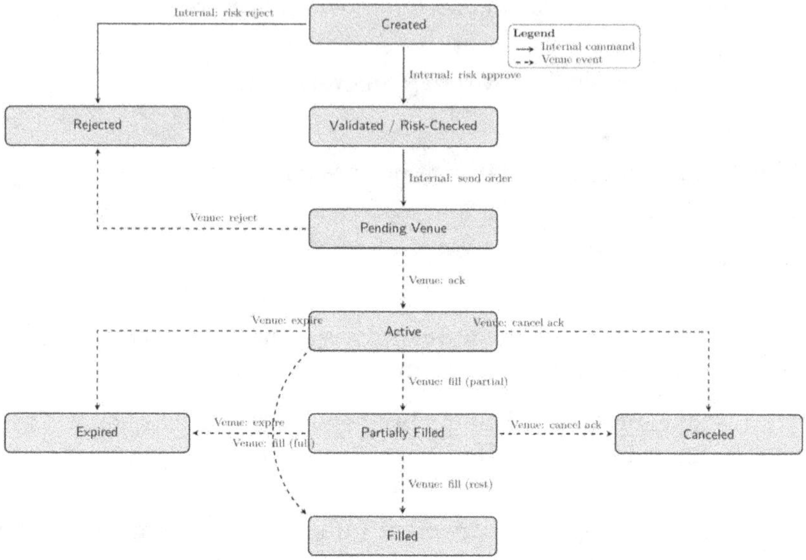

This diagram is a simplification, but it captures the essential points:

- Internal commands move the order forward inside your system and request changes in the external world.
- External events confirm or deny those changes and advance the order toward a terminal state.

Later, when we discuss queues and recovery, this simple picture will help us reason about what can and cannot happen.

Venue Rules and Their Impact on the Lifecycle

Real venues introduce additional complexity that influences your state machine and connectivity logic.

Order Priority and Modifications

Most electronic order books use price-time priority: better price wins; for equal prices, earlier orders are prioritized. Many venues treat a price modification as a new order from a priority standpoint. This has two consequences:

- Your router may need to implement replaces as cancel-plus-new at the venue, resulting in a temporary state where the order is not active.
- Your internal state machine must handle transitions where one internal order maps to multiple external order identifiers over time.

This is a good example of venue rules shaping your internal models: an apparently simple action—changing a limit price—can involve complex state transitions.

Partial Fills and Minimum Quantities

Some venues and order types support minimum execution sizes. An order might specify that it only wants fills above a certain threshold. This may lead to more complicated patterns of partial fills and cancellations, especially when liquidity is fragmented.

Your system's order state must therefore track not only remaining quantity but also conditions under which it can be filled, since these affect both risk and routing decisions.

Venue-Specific Rejects and Error Codes

Venues reject orders for a variety of reasons:

- Syntax errors or invalid field combinations.
- Breach of venue-specific limits, such as message rates or maximum order size.
- Market status (for example, the instrument is halted).

From a lifecycle perspective, all of these yield a transition to some form of **Rejected** state, but *why* the rejection occurred may influence:

- Whether the system should retry or adjust and resend.

- Whether the incident should trip broader controls (for example, kill-switches).

This suggests that your internal state machine should not just have a generic rejected state, but also record structured reasons tied to venue codes, which improves observability and automates responses.

Session Management and Resets

Many venues organize activity into sessions with their own sequence numbering and reset semantics. At the start of the day, for example, you may have to re-establish all connections and, in some cases, re-request the status of live orders.

This directly affects lifecycle handling:

- On session restart, your gateway must reconcile internal order states with the venue's view.
- During a session gap, you may not receive some events; your system must detect and correct such mismatches.

This is where good state management and careful use of sequence numbers and correlation identifiers come into play.

Connectivity Patterns: Gateways and Normalization

The order lifecycle we just described unfolds across a connectivity layer that carries messages between your systems and venues. The design of this layer shapes how you implement state transitions.

Per-Venue Gateways

Most architectures use per-venue *gateways*:

- Each gateway encapsulates the protocol details of a venue (for example, FIX or a native binary protocol).
- The rest of the trading system deals with a normalized internal representation of orders and execution reports.

From an event-driven perspective, each gateway is an event processor:

- It consumes internal commands (new, cancel, modify).
- It translates them into venue-specific messages and sends them on the wire.
- It receives venue events, normalizes them, and emits internal events to update order state.

The gateway thus sits directly on the critical latency path and the critical correctness path.

Normalization and Enrichment

Venues differ in field names, units, status codes, and error semantics. Normalization means mapping all of these into a common internal schema. Enrichment means attaching additional information that downstream systems need but the venue did not provide, for example:

- Internal order identifiers and client account IDs.
- Strategy or algo identifiers.
- Risk and routing metadata.

Normalization and enrichment should be implemented carefully:

- They must be fast enough not to add meaningful latency to the path.
- They must be deterministic and well-documented, since they define how your logical state relates to raw external messages.

Backpressure and Throttling

Venues impose rate limits: too many messages in a short window may trigger throttling or disconnects. Gateways must therefore:

- Track outgoing message rates.
- Queue or reject internal commands when limits are approached.

- Handle venue-side throttling responses gracefully (for example, slow down, retry later).

Backpressure from gateways can propagate upstream: routers and strategies may need to slow down or adapt when certain venues are congested. This dynamic interaction is a core concern of event-driven system design and will be revisited in later chapters.

Correlation, Idempotency, and State Management

We now turn to three subtle but crucial concepts for managing order state correctly: correlation, idempotency, and durable state.

Correlation Keys

Every order needs a way to tie together:

- Internal commands (new, cancel, modify).
- External identifiers assigned by venues.
- Execution reports and other venue events over time.

A common pattern is:

- Generate a unique *client order ID* internally for each external order.
- Include this ID in all messages to the venue (when allowed).
- Store the venue's own order ID when you receive the first acknowledgement.

All subsequent events are then correlated using some combination of client and venue IDs. This mapping must be stable, durable, and easy to query, since virtually every part of the trading system relies on it.

Idempotent Processing

In real networks, messages may be duplicated or arrive out of order. An idempotent processor produces the same final state even if it processes the same event multiple times.

For order lifecycles, this means:

- A second copy of a fill event should not double-count the traded quantity.
- A late cancel acknowledgement received after you already marked the order as canceled should not cause confusion.

To support idempotency:

- Each event should carry a unique identifier or sequence number.
- Your state management should record which events have been applied.
- State updates should be designed to tolerate reapplication without changing the logical outcome.

These patterns integrate naturally with event-sourced architectures, where the source of truth is an ordered log of events; they also matter in more traditional database-centric systems.

Durable State and Recovery

Finally, order state is not just an in-memory convenience—it is a critical record that must survive process crashes, restarts, and even data-center failures.

Design questions include:

- Where is the authoritative state of each order kept: an in-memory engine, a database, a distributed log, or some combination?
- How do you atomically update state alongside emitting events or sending messages, to avoid inconsistencies?
- How do you reconstruct state after a failure: by replaying events, by reloading from a snapshot, or by re-querying venues for live orders?

Your answers will be shaped by latency targets, reliability needs, and the volume of orders handled. However, the order lifecycle state machine provides the structure into which these answers must fit. If you cannot consistently reconstruct which orders are in which states, you cannot reliably control risk or explain past behavior.

Implications for Event-Driven Design

We can now connect the dots between the detailed lifecycle we have explored and the broader themes of this book.

Queues and Backpressure

Every transition between states corresponds to at least one message passing between components. Queues—in gateways, routers, risk engines, and post-trade systems—buffer these messages. Their sizes, policies, and failure modes directly influence:

- Latency from command to external effect.
- How gracefully the system degrades when some part is slow or down.
- Whether internal state lags external reality, creating risk.

Understanding the order lifecycle helps you place queues intentionally: you know where loss or duplication of a message would be catastrophic and where it would merely delay non-critical reporting.

State and Consistency

The lifecycle also clarifies which pieces of state must be strongly consistent:

- The mapping between internal and venue order IDs.
- The cumulative filled quantity and remaining quantity for each order.
- The latest known status (active, canceled, filled, and so on).

Other derived views—aggregated positions, historical analytics—can often tolerate eventual consistency. This distinction will be important when we discuss distributed-systems trade-offs later in the chapter.

Reliable Processing

Finally, reliable processing is about ensuring that commands and events drive the order state machine in a single, coherent direction, even in the face of failures. The lifecycle states we defined give you a checklist:

- Can any order remain stuck indefinitely in **Pending Venue**? How will you detect and resolve that?
- Can an order be both **Filled** and **Canceled** in your internal view due to conflicting events? How would your system detect and correct such inconsistencies?
- What happens if a crash occurs between sending a cancel and receiving the acknowledgement? How do you decide the true state on restart?

All of these questions become more manageable when you have a precise order state model and a disciplined separation between internal commands and external events.

In the next section, we will connect this lifecycle to market microstructure. We will see how order book mechanics and queue position turn the abstract notion of "latency" into concrete P&L effects, and how that, in turn, justifies the engineering effort behind event-driven, low-latency architectures.

1.3 Market Microstructure and Latency Economics

In the previous section we treated orders as state machines: created, risk-checked, sent to venues, filled, canceled, or expired. We focused on how your system must track that lifecycle accurately and reliably.

We now ask a more economic question: *why* are we so concerned about shaving microseconds off the time between a market-data event and an order hitting the exchange? What exactly do we gain by being faster, and what do we lose by being slow?

To answer this, we need to connect the mechanics of order books and queue position to concrete measures of trading performance, especially realized P&L. Only then can we justify aggressive latency budgets and the engineering complexity of event-driven architectures.

Limit Order Books in Plain Terms

Most modern electronic markets for stocks, futures, and many other instruments are organized as *continuous limit order books*. Understanding them does not require advanced math, but it does require a precise picture.

Price Levels and Sides

The order book is split into two sides:

- The **bid** side: buy limit orders, each specifying how much someone is willing to buy and at what maximum price.
- The **ask** (or offer) side: sell limit orders, each specifying how much someone is willing to sell and at what minimum price.

On each side, orders are grouped by price level:

- At each price, there may be many orders from different participants.
- The *total quantity* at that price is the sum of all these orders.

The **best bid** is the highest buy price currently resting in the book; the **best ask** is the lowest sell price. The difference between them is the *spread*.

Price-Time Priority and Queue Position

At a given price level, orders are typically prioritized by:

- **Price**: better price gets executed before worse price.
- **Time**: among orders at the same price, earlier orders get executed first.

That "time" ordering is what creates a *queue* at each price level. If you submit a buy order at the best bid price, you join the back of the bid queue at that price. To get filled, one of two things must happen:

- Sellers hit the bid with market or aggressively priced sell orders, consuming the queue from the front.
- Other participants cancel their bids ahead of you, moving you closer to the front.

If you join the queue late, you stand behind existing volume. If you are slow by even a few milliseconds, thousands of shares may arrive ahead of you in that time. Your fill probability will be lower, and your realized trading performance may suffer.

This is the core link between latency and economics: *latency determines queue position, and queue position influences how often and at what quality you trade.*

How Actions Change the Book and Your Position

The order book is not static. Every action by any participant reshapes it in small ways. To understand latency economics, we need to look at how a few basic actions change both the book and your queue position.

Posting Liquidity

When you submit a limit order that does not cross the spread (for example, a buy at the bid or lower), you are *posting liquidity*. You are offering to trade if someone else is willing to cross the spread and accept your price.

- If you improve the price (for example, bid higher than the current best bid), you create a new front of the queue at that better price.

- If you join at the existing best price, you go to the back of the existing queue at that level.

Latency matters here in two ways:

- If many participants are competing to improve the quote, faster ones will get their better-priced orders in first and may capture more trade flow.
- If you are slow to join at the current best price, you may find a long line has already formed ahead of you.

Taking Liquidity (Sweeping the Book)

When you submit an order that crosses the spread (for example, a market buy or a limit buy above the current best ask), you are *taking liquidity*. Your order will trade immediately against resting orders on the opposite side, starting with the best price and moving up or down the book as needed.

Here, latency affects:

- **Price**: when prices are moving, a delayed market order may execute at worse prices than you anticipated.
- **Adverse selection**: if you are slower than informed traders, you may end up trading mostly when prices are moving against you.

Canceling and Re-Posting

Participants often cancel resting orders and re-post them at new prices. For example, a market maker might move quotes inward or outward in response to new information.

Cancel and re-post actions change the book and queues in several ways:

- If other participants cancel ahead of you, you move forward in the queue without doing anything.
- If you cancel and re-post at the same price, you lose your old queue position and start again at the back.

- If you re-post at a better price, you may jump ahead of the previous queue (at the old price), but now bear different fill and risk characteristics.

These dynamics mean that your system's reaction time to market data and venue events directly shapes how long you are willing to wait in queues, when you decide to cancel, and how you reposition your orders in response to risk or information.

From Latency to Queue Position

We can now focus explicitly on the link from latency to queue position.

Suppose the best bid in XYZ is 100.00, with 30,000 shares resting at that price ahead of you. Sellers occasionally hit the bid, but volume per hit is modest, say 1,000–3,000 shares at a time. Your algorithm wants to join that bid, thinking it is a fair price.

If you send your order now and it reaches the venue instantly, you might be, say, 30,000 shares back in the queue. If instead, due to network delay and processing time, your order reaches the venue 5 milliseconds later, and in that time other participants have joined the bid with 20,000 shares, you are now 50,000 shares back.

Your position in the queue is not solely under your control; it depends on:

- The speed at which you send orders relative to others.
- The arrival process of other orders and cancels at that price.
- The rate at which the opposite side hits or lifts the price.

However, all else equal, lower latency improves your expected queue position. If you consistently arrive earlier, you will more often be closer to the front of the queue, and you will capture a larger share of the available liquidity at that price level.

This is why trading teams pay close attention not just to mean latency but to tail latencies and jitter. A few delayed orders that fall far back in the queue can disproportionately reduce your realized fills.

Queue Position and Expected Fill Probability

Queue position only matters because it affects how likely and how quickly you are filled at a given price. We can think of a simple intuition:

- The more total volume ahead of you in the queue, the more opposite-side volume must arrive before you start getting filled.
- The higher the arrival rate of that opposite-side volume, the faster your place in the queue will be consumed.

If very little opposite-side volume ever hits that price, being further back in the queue means you may never trade at all. If a lot of volume sweeps through, you might get filled even from deep in the queue, but perhaps in more volatile conditions or with higher adverse selection risk.

In practice, firms estimate, explicitly or implicitly, the *expected fill probability* of their orders as a function of:

- Their queue position (for example, number of shares ahead).
- Time horizon (for example, within the next second, 100 milliseconds, or 10 seconds).
- Market regime (calm, busy, news-driven).

Latency improves these probabilities by nudging your orders forward in the queue, especially in highly contested, liquid instruments.

A Visual Link: Latency, Queue Position, and Fills

To make this concrete, we can visualize the relationship between arrival time, queue position, and fill probability at the best bid. On the left, imagine a stylized order book snapshot at a single instant. On the right, plot how expected fill probability declines as orders join the queue later and thus further back.

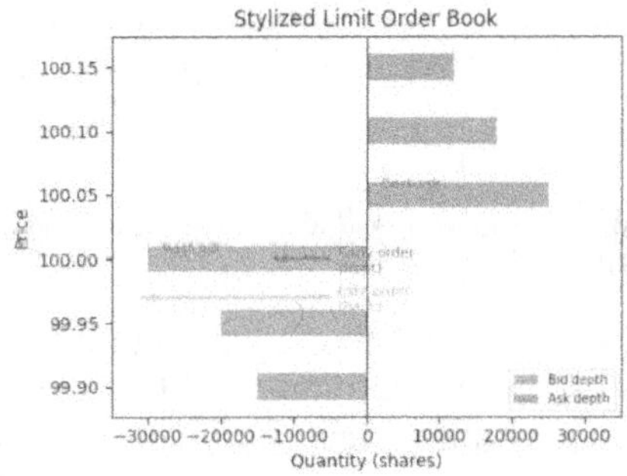

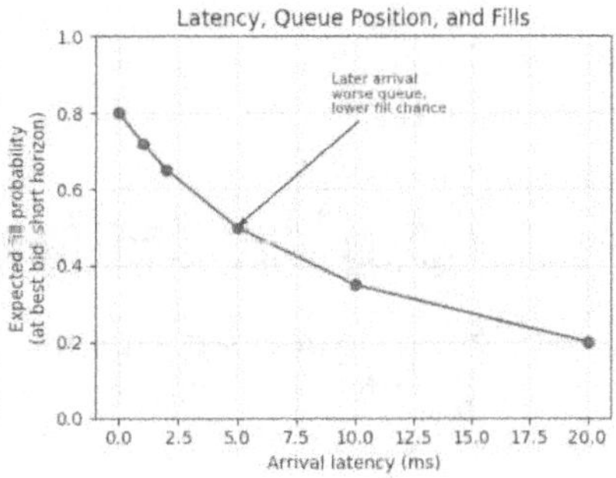

The exact numbers here are illustrative, but the shape is realistic: as latency increases, expected fill probability at the best price tends to fall, sometimes sharply. For strategies that rely on earning small edges repeatedly, this drop in fill probability can erase much of their theoretical profitability.

Latency and Adverse Selection

Queue position is not the only way latency affects P&L. Another key mechanism is *adverse selection.*

What Is Adverse Selection?

You are adversely selected when you tend to trade more often just before price moves against you. For example:

- You provide liquidity on the bid, and your orders are the ones that get hit when the next move is down.
- You take liquidity by buying at the ask, just before sellers drive prices lower.

If faster traders have better information or models, they may cancel their orders or reverse their positions just before you act. If your system is slower to react to news or order-book changes, you may become the "liquidity provider of last resort" at stale prices.

Latency, Information, and Who Trades First

Consider the timeline around a small but important piece of information: a sudden shift in the order book that suggests selling pressure is about to increase.

- Very fast participants detect this shift first and adjust: cancel bids, lower offers, or even go short.
- Slightly slower participants (perhaps you) see the change later; by the time your cancel reaches the venue, you might already have been hit at the old, now unfavorable price.

Here, the problem is not just that you are further back in a queue; it is that you are *still in the wrong queue* when others have already left. Your latency budget sets how long you linger at stale prices before you can react.

Event-driven architectures aim to minimize the time between an external event (for example, a change in the order book or a piece of news) and the corresponding internal decision and venue message. The tighter this loop, the less likely you are to carry outdated orders into a changed market.

Simple P&L Intuition for Latency

We can now translate these mechanics into intuitive P&L effects.

Suppose your strategy expects, on average, to earn a small edge of one tick (for example, one cent) per share when providing liquidity at the best bid or offer, over many trades. This edge might come from earning the spread, collecting rebates, or statistical signals.

Latency erosion shows up in at least three ways:

- **Lower fill rate at good prices**: if you are slower and thus often deeper in the queue, fewer of your orders are filled at the target price.
- **More fills at worse prices**: to achieve the same execution volume, your strategy may need to cross the spread more often (for example, send more market orders), sacrificing spread and incurring higher costs.

- **Higher adverse selection on filled orders**: when you do get filled, it may be disproportionately in situations where prices are about to move against you, because faster traders have already exited.

Even if each of these effects is small, they compound. For high-turnover strategies, a modest drop in average realized edge per trade can wipe out most of the P&L.

This is why trading teams invest heavily in understanding where latencies occur: network hops, serialization, queueing inside services, and so on. It is not latency for its own sake; it is an attempt to preserve the economic edge implied by their model in the face of competition.

Where Latency Optimization Matters Most

The connection between latency and P&L is not uniform across the trading stack. Some parts of your system can be relatively slow without much harm; others lie directly on the critical path from market event to order on the wire.

The Critical Path

Think of the following chain:

$$\text{Market data event} \rightarrow \text{internal book/feature update} \rightarrow \text{strategy decision} \rightarrow \text{risk check}$$
$$\rightarrow \text{order construction} \rightarrow \text{gateway send} \rightarrow \text{venue matching}$$

Delays anywhere in this chain directly worsen your queue position and increase adverse selection risk. This is where:

- Event-driven, non-blocking architectures.
- In-memory data structures.
- Carefully controlled serialization and network paths.

are most valuable.

Non-Critical Paths

Other paths, while important for reliability and compliance, do not need microsecond-level performance:

- Trade confirmations sent to clients.
- Regulatory reporting.
- Archival and analytics jobs.

These can tolerate higher, more variable latencies, provided they are still timely enough for their purposes. It would be wasteful to apply the same ultra-low-latency engineering everywhere.

A well-designed event-driven system makes this separation explicit:

- Critical-path services are tightly focused and optimized for speed and predictability.
- Non-critical services consume the same event streams but operate with looser latency budgets and more emphasis on robustness and flexibility.

Event-Driven Architectures as a Response to Latency Economics

We can now tie the microstructure story back to architecture. Event-driven designs are not just fashionable; they are a direct response to the economic pressures created by order books and competition.

Reducing Unnecessary Waiting

In a traditional, synchronous design, a trading decision might block while waiting for:

- A remote risk service to answer.
- A database to commit a record.
- Another service to acknowledge a request.

Each such wait adds latency, jitter, and failure dependencies. In contrast, an event-driven design:

- Minimizes blocking calls on the critical path.
- Uses queues and asynchronous messages to decouple fast and slow components.
- Allows critical-path services to continue processing even if downstream components lag, as long as risk and consistency constraints are met.

The result is a more predictable and lower end-to-end reaction time to market events.

Aligning State Updates with Events

To act quickly and safely, a trading system needs an up-to-date internal view of:

- The order book and recent trades.
- Current orders, positions, and risk utilizations.

Event-driven architectures maintain this view by streaming events—market data, order acknowledgements, fills, cancels—and updating local state incrementally in response. This is often faster and more predictable than repeatedly querying central databases or services.

In turn, this timely state drives better decisions about whether to join queues, cancel, or cross the spread, which directly influences queue position and adverse selection.

Handling Partial Failure Without Freezing

Markets do not stop when your systems misbehave. Event-driven architectures support graceful degradation:

- If a non-critical consumer of events (for example, a reporting service) falls behind, queues can absorb the backlog without slowing down the critical trading loop.

- If a venue connectivity problem arises, the system can continue trading on other venues, adjusting routing decisions in response.

Without such decoupling, a localized problem can freeze the entire trading platform, causing you to miss opportunities and lose your place in queues across the market. That is a direct, and often large, P&L hit.

Making Latency Visible and Measurable

Finally, event-driven systems lend themselves to detailed measurement:

- Each event can be time-stamped at multiple points: arrival at gateway, arrival at strategy, order send, venue acknowledgement, and so on.
- These time-stamps reveal where latency is spent and where variability creeps in.

Being able to see, for example, that 40% of your decision-to-order latency comes from a particular blocking call is the first step in improving it. Over time, you can correlate these latency metrics with realized queue position and fill statistics, closing the loop between engineering and trading performance.

Where This Leads

In this section we connected the mechanics of order books and queues to the economics of latency:

- Limit order books create queues at each price level, ordered by price and then time.
- Latency determines where in those queues your orders land and how long stale orders linger.
- Queue position and reaction speed influence your fill probabilities, prices, and exposure to adverse selection.

- These effects, accumulated over many trades, shape realized P&L and justify the considerable effort invested in low-latency, event-driven systems.

With this intuition, we can now approach distributed-systems concepts with a sharper sense of purpose. In the next section, we will unpack latency into its components—network, serialization, queueing, processing, I/O—and introduce the mental models of throughput, backpressure, partial failure, and consistency. Those concepts will help us design trading platforms that respect the economic value of microseconds while still behaving reliably under stress.

1.4 Distributed-Systems Mental Models

Up to this point, we have viewed trading systems through two lenses:

- The *business* lens: front-to-back flows, system goals, and risk control.
- The *microstructure* lens: order books, queue position, and how latency affects P&L.

We now add a third lens: the *distributed-systems* view. This is the set of conceptual tools you need to reason about a trading platform built from many interacting services, machines, and networks.

The goal of this section is not to teach distributed systems in full generality. Instead, we will build a compact mental toolkit tailored to electronic trading:

- How to think about **latency** and where it really comes from.
- How to reason about **throughput** and **backpressure**.
- How to live with **partial failure** rather than pretending it does not exist.
- How to understand **replication** and **consistency** at a level that is directly relevant to orders, risk, and positions.

These concepts will recur throughout the book whenever we weigh speed against safety or simplicity against robustness.

Latency as a Sum of Small Costs

In the previous section, latency appeared as a single number: time from market event to order arrival at the venue. To design a system, we must break that number down.

A useful mental model is to think of end-to-end latency as the sum of several smaller components:

- **Network propagation**: the time it takes signals to travel over fiber or wire between two physical locations.
- **Serialization and deserialization**: turning in-memory objects into bytes on the wire and back.
- **Queuing**: time spent waiting in internal queues before a component starts processing a message.
- **Processing**: the actual CPU work to parse, compute, update state, and make decisions.
- **Disk and storage I/O**: time to sync data to disk or a remote store, when that is on the critical path.
- **Cross-service hops**: each additional service boundary crossed adds its own network, serialization, and queuing overhead.

When you measure a 2-millisecond interval between receiving market data and sending an order, it is rarely dominated by a single thing. More often, it is 200 microseconds here, 100 microseconds there, and a few unpredictable spikes when queues or I/O get congested.

This decomposition matters because:

- Different components are optimized in different ways. You use different tools to reduce network delay than to reduce processing time.

- You want to be deliberate about which costs you are willing to pay on the critical path. For example, you might decide never to wait for disk on a hot trading loop, but to rely on later asynchronous persistence.

As you design an event-driven architecture, try to draw a simple chain from "market data received" to "order sent" and annotate it with approximate costs for each step. That mental picture helps you see where new features might quietly add latency and where you should resist the temptation to add more cross-service calls.

Throughput and Backpressure: Flow, Not Just Speed

Latency is about *how long* one message takes; **throughput** is about *how many* messages you can process per unit time. In trading, both matter:

- High throughput is needed to keep up with bursts of market data and order flow without falling behind.
- Good latency under light load is meaningless if the system collapses under heavy load.

A simple analogy is traffic on a highway:

- When there are few cars (low load), each car can go quickly.
- As more cars enter (higher throughput demand), the system may reach a point where adding more cars causes congestion, dramatically increasing travel time (latency).

In software, this congestion often appears as:

- Growing message queues in front of a busy service.
- Timeouts and retries that add even more load.

- Cascading slowdowns as upstream components wait for responses.

Backpressure

Backpressure is the system's way of saying "slow down":

- A gateway stops accepting new orders when its send buffer is full.
- A risk engine limits the number of concurrent requests it will process.
- A message broker applies quotas or sheds low-priority traffic under stress.

In a well-designed event-driven system, backpressure is intentional and visible. Producers know when consumers are struggling and can react:

- Slow down order submission to a congested venue.
- Temporarily drop non-critical analytics tasks.
- Trigger circuit breakers when lag exceeds safe thresholds.

Without explicit backpressure, components continue to accept work they cannot process in time. Queues grow silently until they hit limits; then messages are dropped or entire services fail. This is especially dangerous in trading, where delayed risk checks or stale market data can lead to incorrect decisions.

As you think about throughput, ask for each service:

- What is its realistic capacity under peak load?
- How does it signal to upstream components that it is overloaded?
- How do those upstream components respond?

Partial Failure: When Only Part of the System Breaks

In a centralized system, it's tempting to think in terms of two states: everything is up, or everything is down. Distributed systems rarely behave so cleanly. More often, you face **partial failure**: some components are slow, unreachable, or inconsistent, while others are fine.

In trading, typical partial failures include:

- A single venue gateway loses connectivity while others remain healthy.
- The risk engine becomes temporarily overloaded and responds slowly.
- A market data feed for one venue lags behind real time, while others stay current.
- A database node fails, triggering a failover that temporarily increases latency.

If your architecture assumes that all dependencies are either fully available or completely down, these partial failures can create strange behavior:

- Orders are held back firm-wide because one venue is having issues, even though others are still available.
- System components spin, retrying calls to a slow service, amplifying the overload.
- Different parts of the system have different views of which orders are live, because some events were delayed or lost.

Designing for Partial Failure

The key mental shift is to design assuming that:

- Any external call can fail, time out, or return late.

- Network partitions can make components temporarily invisible to each other.
- You may not immediately know whether a request succeeded or not.

From this starting point, you can ask:

- If the risk engine is slow, should trading stop completely, slow down, or continue with more conservative assumptions?
- If one venue is unreachable, does the router automatically shift flow elsewhere, or does it block until that venue is back?
- If an acknowledgement from a venue is lost, how will we discover the true state of the order and reconcile?

Event-driven designs help here by decoupling components via queues and explicit events. For instance:

- If a non-critical consumer fails, the queue can buffer events until it recovers, without blocking the producer.
- If a critical service becomes slow, upstream services can detect the growing lag in its input or output streams and take predefined action.

The aim is not to eliminate partial failure—that is impossible—but to *contain* it, so that a localized problem doesn't turn into a firm-wide trading halt or an uncontrolled risk event.

Replication: Many Copies of Important Things

Trading systems replicate data and services for two main reasons:

- **Availability and resilience**: if one copy fails, another can take over.
- **Performance**: local copies can serve reads faster and closer to where computation happens.

Examples abound:

- Market data feeds may have multiple independent receivers to avoid single points of failure.
- Order state may be stored both in an in-memory engine and in a replicated log or database.
- Risk and position views are often cached in several services for fast access.

Replication sounds like a pure good, but it introduces a new challenge: **keeping copies in sync**.

Synchronous vs Asynchronous Replication

A useful mental distinction is:

- **Synchronous replication**: a write is not considered successful until it has been applied to multiple replicas. This improves safety (less chance of losing data) but increases latency, because the caller waits for all replicas to confirm.
- **Asynchronous replication**: the primary copy acknowledges the write immediately and updates replicas in the background. This reduces latency but creates windows where replicas are out of date.

In trading, you rarely want full synchronous replication on the hottest parts of the critical path because it can add too much delay. Instead, you might:

- Keep the authoritative, low-latency state in a primary engine.
- Stream changes to one or more downstream replicas (for example, a database, a risk aggregation system, or an analytics platform).

This design accepts that different consumers see slightly different versions of the truth at different times. That leads us directly to consistency.

Consistency: How Aligned Must Views Be?

Consistency is about how quickly and how strictly different parts of your system agree on the same facts.

At one extreme is *strong consistency*: after a change, every reader sees the same, up-to-date value. At the other is *eventual consistency*: different readers may temporarily see different values, but if no new changes occur, they will eventually converge.

Trading systems use both, but for different kinds of data.

Where Strong Consistency Is Needed

Some facts are so critical that you want all key components to agree on them almost immediately:

- Whether a particular order has been acknowledged or canceled.
- The mapping between your internal order IDs and venue order IDs.
- The cumulative executed quantity on an order, which drives risk and routing decisions.

If one part of the system thinks an order is still active while another believes it was canceled, you can end up sending conflicting instructions or miscalculating exposure. For these kinds of facts, you typically choose designs that minimize the chance of divergence:

- A single authoritative owner of order state, which others query or subscribe to.
- Carefully designed update flows where all changes pass through a consistent pipeline (for example, an ordered log of events).

Where Eventual Consistency Is Acceptable

Other facts can be slightly out of date without causing immediate harm:

- Aggregated intraday positions used for analytics and reporting.

- Historical P&L views used for risk management and optimization, but not for per-trade limit checks.
- Some client-facing dashboards where a delay of a few seconds is acceptable.

For these, you can choose architectures that favor availability and performance over perfect synchronization:

- Multiple read replicas fed by an event stream.
- Caches that refresh periodically or in response to change events.

The key is to be explicit: for each category of data, decide how quickly and how reliably different components must agree, and design accordingly. Implicit assumptions about consistency are a common source of subtle, dangerous bugs.

Consistency vs Availability Under Failure

Sometimes, especially under partial failure, you must choose between:

- **Blocking** to preserve consistency: for example, refusing to trade when you cannot reliably read current risk state.
- **Continuing** with degraded or cached information: for example, allowing trading to proceed with stale positions when a risk database is temporarily unreachable.

Neither choice is universally correct. The right answer depends on your risk appetite, regulatory constraints, and business priorities. What matters is that you:

- Recognize these situations in advance.
- Define clear rules for how the system should behave.
- Implement those rules using events and state transitions that are observable and auditable.

Putting It Together: A Mental Model of a Trading Platform

We can now sketch a high-level mental model of an event-driven trading platform as a distributed system:

- A set of **services** (gateways, strategy engines, risk engines, routers, market data handlers, post-trade processors).
- Connected by **streams** and **messages** representing commands and events (submit order, order accepted, trade executed, risk updated).
- Each service maintains local **state**, some of which is authoritative and some derived.
- Data and services are **replicated** for resilience and performance, at the cost of potential inconsistency.
- The system experiences **latency**, **load**, and **partial failures** continuously; robustness involves managing, not avoiding, these realities.

The principles we have just discussed help you reason about this picture:

- Use the latency breakdown to decide where to place computation and which calls must be avoided on the critical path.
- Use throughput and backpressure thinking to design queues and limits that prevent overload from cascading.
- Use partial failure awareness to avoid brittle, all-or-nothing dependencies.
- Use replication and consistency thinking to decide which data must be strongly consistent and which can be eventually consistent.

These are not abstract academic notions. They show up in everyday questions like:

- Should the strategy engine synchronously call the risk service on every order, or should it consume a risk state stream and check limits locally?
- Should the gateway write orders to a database before sending them, or send first and persist asynchronously?
- How do we detect that a market data feed is lagging, and what should trading do in response?

Where This Takes Us Next

By now, you have three complementary views of event-driven trading:

- The *business view*: orders as the carriers of risk and P&L through the trading ecosystem.
- The *microstructure view*: how order books and queues translate latency into economic outcomes.
- The *distributed-systems view*: how latency, throughput, partial failure, replication, and consistency shape the behavior of the platform itself.

In the final section of this chapter, we will introduce the vocabulary that ties these views together in concrete designs: *commands*, *events*, and *streams*. That vocabulary will allow us to describe, precisely and concisely, how trading systems process information and change state, and it will serve as the foundation for later chapters on queues, state management, and reliable processing.

1.5 Events, Commands, and Streams Primer

We now have three perspectives on event-driven trading systems:

- The *business and market* view: orders, venues, and risk.

- The *lifecycle* view: how a single order moves through states.
- The *distributed-systems* view: latency, throughput, partial failure, replication, and consistency.

To connect these perspectives into a practical design language, we need precise, lightweight concepts for how information moves through the system and how state changes are represented. In this section we introduce three such concepts:

- **Commands**: requests to *change* the world.
- **Events**: records of *what has happened*.
- **Streams**: ordered sequences of related events and sometimes commands.

This vocabulary will underpin the rest of the book. It may sound abstract, but as we will see, it maps very naturally onto trading workflows.

Commands: Intent to Change the World

A **command** is a message that expresses *intent*. It is issued by one component to another, asking for some action to be taken. In our domain, commands typically represent:

- A trading decision: "Submit this order."
- A control action: "Cancel that order" or "Disable this strategy."
- An operational request: "Reload limits for this account."

Commands have several characteristic properties:

- They are **directional**: they go from a caller (for example, a strategy) to a callee (for example, a gateway).
- They can **succeed or fail**: the callee may or may not be able to carry out the requested action.

- They are usually **validated** and may be **rejected** by the receiver.

Trading Examples of Commands

Concrete command examples include:

- SubmitOrder: sent from a strategy engine to an order management system or gateway. It contains side, quantity, price, time-in-force, and routing instructions.
- CancelOrder: sent from a strategy or risk engine to cancel a specific active order.
- ReplaceOrder: request to modify the price or quantity of an existing order.
- UpdateRiskLimits: instructs a risk service to load a new set of constraints for an account or strategy.

When you see these as commands, an important design point becomes clear: a command is not yet a fact. It is a *proposal.* The fact is whatever happens *after* the system processes it, and that fact is captured by an event.

Events: Facts About What Happened

An **event** is a statement about something that *has already occurred.* Once an event is recorded, it should not be revised or retracted; instead, later events may clarify or supersede it.

Events differ from commands in several key ways:

- Events are **descriptive**, not prescriptive. They say "This order was accepted" or "This trade executed," not "Please accept this order."
- Events are **immutable** records. You should not change a past event; you add new events if corrections are needed.
- Events are often **broadcast** to many consumers, who may each react differently.

Trading Examples of Events

Typical event types in a trading system include:

- OrderAccepted: emitted when a gateway or OMS has successfully validated a SubmitOrder and possibly when the venue has acknowledged it.
- OrderRejected: indicates that a requested order was not accepted, with a reason code (for example, risk limit breach or venue error).
- OrderCanceled: emitted when an order has been successfully canceled at the venue.
- TradeExecuted: records a fill, including price, quantity, venue, and any fee or rebate information.
- RiskLimitBreached: indicates that a certain exposure or notional limit has been exceeded.
- PositionUpdated: reflects the impact of executions and other events on positions and P&L.

Notice the pattern: commands propose changes; events record outcomes. This separation has deep consequences for how we design stateful, reliable systems.

Why Distinguish Commands from Events?

At first glance, you might think: "Why not just treat every message as a generic thing and update state when it arrives?" Distinguishing commands from events brings several practical benefits.

Auditability and Explainability

Regulators, clients, and internal risk functions often ask:

- "Who asked for this order to be sent?"
- "What exactly did we send to the venue?"
- "When did the venue accept or reject the order?"

With a clear command/event separation, you can answer:

- SubmitOrder (command) from Strategy X at time t_1.
- OrderAccepted (event) from OMS at time t_2.
- OrderAcknowledgedByVenue (event) at time t_3.

You can reconstruct the full story: intent, decision, and outcome, with timestamps and reasons.

Reasoning About Side Effects

Commands are where side effects originate: sending a message to a venue, writing to a database, toggling a kill-switch. Events, by contrast, are often used as *inputs* to logic, not as instructions.

By treating events as facts, your processing functions can be written as "Given this prior state and this new event, what is the next state and what commands (if any) should we emit?" This discipline makes complex behaviors easier to reason about, test, and replay.

Idempotency and Retries

Failures happen. A command may be retried; an event may be delivered twice. Keeping them distinct helps you design idempotent processing:

- If SubmitOrder is sent twice by mistake, you do *not* want two identical venue orders. Your command handler should detect duplicates and either reject or merge them.
- If TradeExecuted is processed twice, your event handler must not double-count the fill. It should recognize that the event has already been applied to state.

A clean separation makes it easier to track which commands have been acted on and which events have been incorporated into state, which is central to reliability.

Composability of Services

Different services may see the same event but decide on very different commands. For example:

- A strategy engine sees TradeExecuted and reduces its target position.
- A risk engine sees the same event and recomputes exposures.
- A reporting service sees it and records it in a client report.

If you confused "this trade executed" (an event) with imperative instructions, you would quickly entangle unrelated services. Keeping the descriptive layer (events) separate from prescriptive layers (commands) encourages cleaner, composable designs.

Streams: Ordered Sequences of Facts

So far we have described individual commands and events. In reality, trading systems deal with *sequences* of them, often at high rates. A **stream** is an ordered sequence of related messages, typically events, that share some logical key.

A stream might be defined:

- Per order: all events related to a particular order ID.
- Per instrument: all trades and quotes for a given symbol.
- Per account or portfolio: all events affecting a client's exposure.
- Per venue connection: all messages sent to and received from a given exchange.

Thinking in terms of streams is central to event-driven design for three reasons.

Ordering

Within a stream, the *order* of events matters. For a single order, you need to know that:

- OrderAccepted happened before TradeExecuted.
- TradeExecuted happened before OrderCanceled.

If you process events out of order, you might temporarily believe that an order was canceled before it ever existed, or that a fill occurred on a rejected order. Ordering per stream allows you to maintain consistent, intuitive notions of state even when multiple streams are processed in parallel.

Partitioning and Parallelism

You cannot process all messages on a single thread if you are handling thousands of instruments and millions of events. Streams allow you to partition work:

- Each order-level stream can be processed independently, as long as its events are ordered.
- Instrument- or account-level aggregates can be computed by consuming from relevant streams.

This partitioning is key to scaling without losing consistency where it matters. For instance:

- You might assign different orders to different processing shards based on order ID.
- Each shard ensures local ordering for its orders, while the system as a whole processes many orders in parallel.

Durability and Replay

Streams are natural units for durable storage. If you append every event to a persistent log per stream, you can later:

- Rebuild the state of a single order from scratch by replaying its events.
- Recompute positions or P&L by scanning trade and cash-flow events.
- Debug incidents by reviewing exactly what happened and when.

This is the foundation of event sourcing and deterministic recovery, themes we will return to in later chapters.

Mapping Streams to Trading Workflows

Let us ground these ideas in concrete examples of stream boundaries.

Order-Level Streams

For each venue-level order, you can define a stream keyed by a unique order ID. It might contain:

- The internal command that created the order (for example, SubmitOrder).
- Events such as OrderValidated, OrderSentToVenue, OrderAcknowledged, TradeExecuted, OrderCanceled, and OrderExpired.

A service that wants to maintain the state machine for that order subscribes to this stream and processes events in order. At any point it can say: "Given the history so far, what is the current state?"

Instrument-Level Market Data Streams

Market data feeds naturally form streams per instrument or per venue:

- QuoteUpdated events that change best bid/ask and depth.
- TradePrinted events for executed trades.

Strategies subscribe to relevant instrument streams and transform incoming events into trading signals. Latency on these streams is critical, which leads to specific engineering trade-offs about how they are transported and processed.

Account- or Book-Level Risk Streams

Risk and P&L views often aggregate information from many orders and instruments. You can maintain them by consuming:

- Trade events from many order-level streams.
- Corporate action events (for example, splits, dividends).
- Cash movement events (for example, funding, fees).

These aggregated streams may tolerate slightly higher latency and can be processed by separate services, but their correctness still depends on the underlying event history.

From Single Events to End-to-End Narratives

To see how commands, events, and streams work together, let us walk through an end-to-end scenario for a single order. We will then illustrate it in a diagram.

Consider the following sequence:

1. A market-data event arrives: QuoteUpdated for stock XYZ.
2. A strategy processes this event and issues a command: SubmitOrder to buy 10,000 shares at a given limit price.
3. The order management service validates the command and emits an event: OrderAccepted.
4. The gateway sends the order to the venue and, upon venue acknowledgement, emits OrderAcknowledgedByVenue.
5. The venue matches part of the order and sends back fills, which the gateway turns into TradeExecuted events.
6. A risk service consumes these trade events and emits PositionUpdated and possibly RiskLimitUpdated events.

All of these messages travel on specific streams:

- Market data on an instrument-level stream for XYZ.
- Order lifecycle events on an order-level stream keyed by the order ID.
- Risk and P&L updates on an account-level stream.

Commands initiate transitions, events record what actually occurred, and streams tie related messages together in order. This narrative structure is what will allow us, in later chapters, to discuss queues, retries, and recovery without losing track of what is happening.

Diagram: Commands and Events Across Components

The following diagram summarizes the flow of commands and events between typical trading components for a single order. Commands are shown with solid arrows, events with dashed arrows. Streams are indicated by named channels.

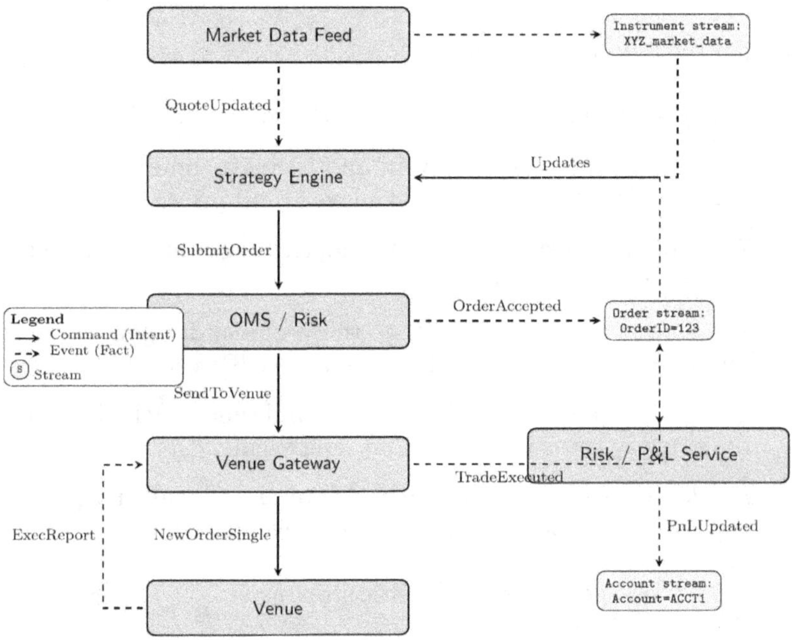

This diagram omits many real-world details (error handling, cancels, multiple venues), but it captures the core structural ideas:

- Commands flow mostly left-to-right, expressing intent to trade.
- Events flow in both directions, reporting outcomes and driving downstream logic.

- Streams act as shared, ordered channels of facts that multiple services can consume.

Why This Vocabulary Matters for the Rest of the Book

The distinction between events, commands, and streams is not just terminological. It will guide almost every architectural discussion that follows:

- When we talk about **queues**, we will ask: which queues carry commands and which carry events, and how does that affect error handling?
- When we talk about **state**, we will often think of it as a function of past events on one or more streams, updated in response to new events.
- When we talk about **reliable processing**, we will design mechanisms so that each command is either applied once or deterministically retried, and each event is processed idempotently.
- When we talk about **observability and audit**, we will lean on event logs and stream histories as the authoritative record of what occurred.

For now, it is enough that you can look at any trading workflow and rephrase it in these terms. For example:

> "A burst of market-data events (*events*) arrives on an instrument stream. The strategy reacts by sending one or more *commands* to submit or cancel orders. Those commands trigger order lifecycle *events* on order streams, which in turn drive risk and P&L updates on account streams."

If you can comfortably speak this language, you are ready for the next chapters, where we will design queues, state machines, and recovery mechanisms that respect the realities of markets while delivering the reliability and control demanded by modern trading.

Chapter 2

Messaging and Streaming Backbone

Every profitable trading idea eventually runs into a harder problem: moving messages reliably, in order, and fast enough that the market still cares. This chapter goes under the hood of your event highway-pub/sub buses, distributed logs, and low-latency queues-and shows how to shape topics, schemas, and flow control so that even at the chaos of the open, your system behaves less like a traffic jam and more like a well-timed conveyor belt.

2.1 Pub/Sub and Queueing Patterns

In the previous chapter we treated the trading system as an event-driven plant: exchanges, venues, and internal services emit a stream of events, and strategies react to those events to make decisions. To make that practical, we need a *messaging backbone* that carries these events between independent services without hard-wiring them to each other. This section explains the core messaging patterns you will use over and over again in such a backbone: publish/subscribe (pub/sub) fan-out, competing consumers, routing, and request–reply. We will see how each pattern behaves, where it fits in a trading architecture, and most importantly, how these patterns let you evolve strategy logic independently of market data, order management, and risk infrastructure.

From Point-to-Point to Publish/Subscribe

The simplest way to connect two components is point-to-point messaging: one sender knows the address of one receiver and sends messages directly to it. Conceptually, this is like a telephone call: the market data adapter "calls" the strategy engine every time a new tick arrives.

Point-to-point messaging is easy to understand but scales poorly in a trading plant:

- If you add a new strategy, you must reconfigure the sender to deliver to the new address.
- If the risk engine also needs the data, the sender now needs multiple connections and perhaps different formats.
- If you change the receiver (for example, you rewrite the strategy engine), you may have to change the sender to match.

Publish/subscribe flips this around. Instead of senders knowing receivers, both sides agree on *topics*. A *producer* (publisher) sends messages to a topic on a central message bus. One or more *consumers* (subscribers) express interest in that topic and receive copies of the messages.

Key abstractions:

- **Producer**: any service that emits messages (e.g., market data adapter, order manager, risk calculator).
- **Consumer**: any service that reads messages (e.g., strategy, risk engine, monitoring service).
- **Topic**: a named channel such as `md.equities.nyse` or `orders.submitted`.
- **Subscription**: a consumer's declaration that it wants to receive messages from a topic (perhaps with filters).

In this model the market data adapter only knows that it publishes to the md.equities.nyse topic. Strategies, risk controls, and recorders independently subscribe. The producer does not care who the subscribers are, and subscribers do not care how the producer is implemented. This *decoupling* is the foundation for flexible trading plants.

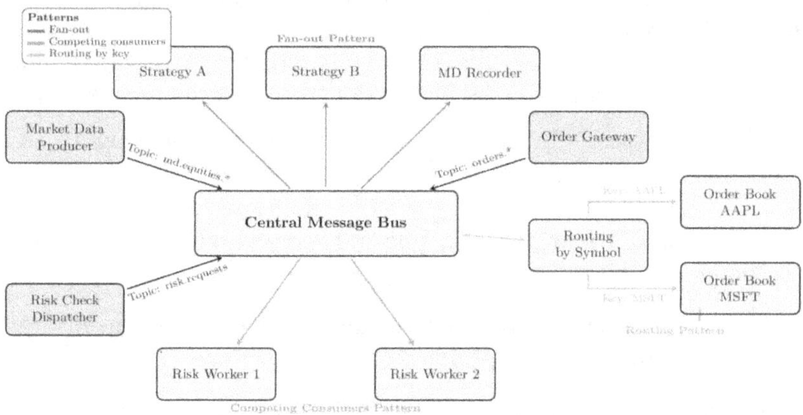

Fan-Out: Broadcasting Market and State Events

The most natural use of pub/sub in trading is *fan-out*: one producer, many independent consumers, each receiving a full copy of the event stream.

Typical examples:

- **Market data fan-out.** A single feed handler publishes trades and quotes for a venue. Multiple strategy engines, risk monitors, and recorders subscribe.
- **State change fan-out.** An order management system publishes events like "order accepted", "order filled", "order canceled". Strategy logic, P&L calculation, risk, and compliance consumers all react in their own way.
- **Reference data fan-out.** Updates to instruments, trading calendars, or configuration are broadcast to caches across the plant.

In a fan-out pattern:

- The producer emits each message once.
- The messaging backbone makes copies and delivers one copy to each subscriber.
- Consumers process messages at their own pace. One slow consumer does not necessarily slow down others, depending on the technology and configuration.

This is powerful because adding a new consumer is cheap. Suppose you want to add a new "volatility monitor" service that studies quote dynamics around macro events. With fan-out, you simply subscribe this new service to the existing market data and order event topics. No change is needed in the feed handler or the order management system.

Fan-out is a direct way to decouple *who reacts* from *who emits*. Traders and quants can experiment with new analytics, controls, or monitoring services without impacting the critical path components that publish the primary events.

There are two common caveats to keep in mind:

- **Multiplied load**. Every new consumer increases the total data volume leaving the bus, even if the producer sends the same number of messages. At high tick rates this can push the backbone or network limits if you add many subscribers.
- **Per-consumer state**. Each consumer maintains its own state and must handle loss, restart, and replay correctly. The messaging backbone keeps them independent, but that also means you need consistent conventions for identifiers, timestamps, and semantics across topics.

Despite these concerns, fan-out is the default pattern for distributing market events and state changes in a modern trading system.

Competing Consumers: Parallelizing Heavy Work

Fan-out delivers a full copy of each message to every subscriber. Sometimes that is exactly what you *do not* want. Consider per-order pre-trade risk checks that involve complex calculations. If you have a single risk worker and it cannot keep up with peak order rates, you will introduce dangerous latency.

In such cases you still want to decouple the order gateway from the specific risk workers, but you want *load sharing* rather than broadcasting. This is where the competing consumer pattern comes in.

In the competing consumer pattern:

- A producer publishes a stream of independent tasks or requests to a topic or queue.
- Multiple consumers subscribe in a coordinated way as a *group*.
- Each message is delivered to exactly one member of the group.

Within the group, the consumers *compete* to claim messages. Scaling is simple: you add more consumers (workers) to the group. The messaging system will distribute tasks among them, typically in a round-robin or balanced fashion.

Trading scenarios where this fits well:

- **Risk worker pool**. The order gateway publishes risk check requests. A pool of risk services consumes them as a group; each request is processed by one worker.
- **Valuation or analytics jobs**. A pricing service publishes jobs like "revalue portfolio X" or "compute risk Greeks". A farm of analytic workers shares the load.
- **Batch reconciliation or reports**. End-of-day processes that can be broken into many independent tasks are distributed across workers.

The decoupling benefit is similar to pub/sub fan-out: the order gateway does not know how many risk workers exist or where they run. However, the behavior of the messaging backbone is different:

- **Parallelism not duplication**. Unlike fan-out, you do not create multiple copies of the same risk request.

- **Throughput vs ordering**. Within a group, overall throughput rises with the number of workers, but ordering between tasks may change. You cannot assume that risk request $N + 1$ is processed after request N if they land on different workers.

This has implications for how you design your tasks. To use competing consumers safely:

- Make each task as independent as possible. Avoid hidden shared state that would require strict ordering.
- If you need ordering per entity (for example, per order or per account), group messages by key so that all tasks for one entity go to the same partition or worker. We will return to this idea when we discuss partitioning and routing.

Competing consumers are a way to scale *processing capacity* without changing producers. Operations teams can add or remove workers in response to load without coordinating with strategy developers.

Routing and Topic Hierarchies: Getting the Right Messages to the Right Place

Fan-out and competing consumers describe how many consumers see a message. Routing patterns describe *which* messages each consumer receives.

If every strategy subscribed to all market data for all symbols and venues, the volume would be enormous and filtering would be wasteful. Instead, you typically design routing so that each consumer only receives the subset of messages it cares about.

There are two complementary tools:

- **Topic hierarchies**. Topics are structured names that encode some routing information, such as md.equities.nyse.AAPL or orders.submitted.futures.cme.
- **Routing keys or filters**. Messages carry attributes (such as symbol, venue, account, or order type) that routing logic uses to decide where to send them.

With topic hierarchies, you can subscribe to entire branches or narrow leaves:

- A global equities strategy might subscribe to `md.equities.*` (all equities).
- A venue-specific strategy might subscribe to `md.equities.nyse.*`.
- A single-name strategy might subscribe only to `md.equities.nyse.AAPL`.

This allows coarse-grained routing without complex logic. However, fine-grained control still usually happens via routing keys or filters. For example:

- The order gateway publishes all new orders to `orders.submitted`.
- Each internal order book service subscribes to the topic, but only wants messages for its own symbol.
- A routing component (sometimes built into the broker, sometimes a separate microservice) inspects the symbol field and forwards the order to the right book.

Routing is where decoupling becomes very concrete for strategy teams:

- A new strategy for symbol X can be implemented as a new consumer that subscribes to all market data but uses filters to only process symbol X.
- If later you split the strategy into separate components (for signal generation and execution), the routing layer need not change. Both components subscribe to the same topics and use internal logic or message attributes to coordinate.
- Operationally, you can move a symbol from one strategy implementation to another by adjusting routing rules, not by changing all upstream producers.

The main design choices revolve around *how much meaning* you encode in topic names versus payload fields:

- If you encode everything in topics (for example, one topic per symbol), you may end up with hundreds of thousands of topics. Some brokers handle that poorly.
- If you encode everything in payload fields, topics become too coarse, and consumers have to filter a lot of irrelevant traffic.

A balanced approach is common: use topics for big, stable categories like asset class and venue; use routing keys and filters for finer-grained attributes such as symbol, account, or strategy group. Later sections on partitioning will revisit how these choices interact with performance and ordering.

Request–Reply: Synchronous Conversations over an Asynchronous Bus

Fan-out, competing consumers, and routing are all essentially one-way: producers send messages and do not wait for a direct response from consumers. Many trading workflows, however, are request–response in nature:

- A strategy submits an order and needs a confirmation or rejection quickly.
- A risk engine queries current exposure for an account.
- A monitoring tool fetches configuration or health information from a gateway.

You could handle these by calling remote services directly (for example, using a synchronous API). But there are advantages to reusing the messaging backbone: consistent auditing, unified security, and easier routing and failover.

The request–reply pattern emulates synchronous communication on top of asynchronous messaging:

1. The **client** sends a request message to a request topic, including a unique correlation identifier and often a "reply-to" topic or queue.

2. The **service** consumes the request, processes it, and sends a reply message to the indicated reply destination, carrying the same correlation identifier.

3. The client waits for a reply with the matching identifier, optionally with a timeout.

In a trading context, this pattern enables several important decouplings:

- **Order submission**. A strategy "client" sends an order request to an order gateway topic. The gateway processes it (including validations and risk checks) and sends back an acceptance or rejection. Strategies can change or move as long as they respect the message contract.

- **Configuration and reference data**. Strategies can ask configuration services for parameters, calendars, or instrument definitions via request–reply, rather than reading files or databases directly.

- **Health checks and warm-ups**. Upon startup, a strategy can send a "state snapshot" request to an order book or risk service and receive the latest view of positions or risk limits.

The messaging backbone becomes the fabric for both event-driven and request-driven communication. Importantly, you preserve the ability to observe, replay, and audit these conversations: request and reply messages can be logged in the same way as market data and orders.

Compared to direct remote calls, request–reply over a bus introduces a few considerations:

- **Latency**. Going through the bus may add overhead. For ultra-low-latency paths you might choose a dedicated point-to-point protocol instead, while still mirroring events onto the bus for audit and analytics.

- **Time-outs and retries**. Clients must handle cases where replies are slow or lost, which means being explicit about retry behavior and idempotency.

- **Correlation and state.** Clients maintain small amounts of transient state keyed by correlation IDs until replies arrive or time out.

Used thoughtfully, request–reply lets you keep the architectural advantages of the messaging backbone even for workflows that, at the business level, feel "synchronous."

Decoupling Strategy Logic from Infrastructure

It is helpful to tie these patterns back to the central goal: keeping strategy logic loosely coupled to market and risk infrastructure so that each can evolve at its own pace.

Independent lifecycles. With pub/sub fan-out, you can deploy a new strategy without touching the feed handlers or order gateways. With competing consumers, you can scale risk capacity without changing strategies. With routing, you can reorganize which service owns which symbol or account by changing configuration, not code interfaces. With request–reply, you can swap one implementation of an order gateway for another as long as the message contracts remain stable.

Testability and replay. When messaging patterns are used consistently, you can record topics for offline analysis. Strategies can be tested or replayed against historical event streams without running real gateways. Risk logic can be validated by feeding it exactly the same messages that production saw during a stress event.

Resilience. Decoupling via messaging allows components to fail and restart independently. A strategy process can crash and restart while the order gateway continues to operate, because their only dependency is on the bus. Risk workers in a competing-consumer pool can be drained and upgraded one by one. Routing can temporarily send certain flows to a fallback implementation.

Organizational separation. In many firms, infrastructure, risk, and strategy teams are distinct groups. A well-designed messaging backbone with clear patterns is a contract between these groups. The infrastructure team owns the bus and basic topics; the risk team owns risk service interfaces and semantics; the strategy team consumes events and emits orders and configuration changes. Each group can innovate without constantly rewriting integrations.

Choosing the Right Pattern

In practice, you will often combine these patterns:

- Market data is published to pub/sub topics and fanned out to strategies, recorders, and derived-data generators.
- Derived events (like per-symbol analytics) might be consumed by competing consumers that aggregate or re-price portfolios.
- Orders originating from strategies follow a request–reply path to an order gateway, which then publishes state-change events on pub/sub topics.
- Routing logic ensures each symbol or account is handled by the right service instance, while balancing load and preserving necessary ordering.

A simple way to select a pattern is to ask three questions for each flow:

1. **How many consumers should see each message?**
    - Many, independently: use fan-out pub/sub.
    - Exactly one from a pool: use competing consumers.
2. **Do I need a direct answer to each message?**
    - No: event-driven pub/sub is enough.
    - Yes: layer request–reply semantics over the bus or use a direct call for ultra-hot paths.
3. **Can consumers cheaply ignore irrelevant messages, or should routing avoid sending them?**
    - If volumes are modest, simple filtering on the consumer side may be fine.

- At higher scale, introduce routing via topic hierarchies and keys so each consumer only sees relevant traffic.

As the rest of this chapter unfolds, we will dig deeper into how these logical patterns are realized on concrete technologies such as distributed logs and message queues, and how choices like partitioning, retention, and acknowledgment modes impact latency, ordering, and reliability in a trading context. The concepts introduced here—fan-out, competing consumers, routing, and request–reply—are the vocabulary you will use to reason about nearly every messaging decision in an event-driven trading system.

2.2 Distributed Log Architecture

In the previous section we focused on *how* messages flow through a trading plant: fan-out, competing consumers, routing, and request–reply. We largely treated the messaging backbone as an abstract bus. In practice, most modern trading and risk systems implement this bus on top of a *distributed log*, typified by platforms such as Kafka and its relatives.

This section explains what a distributed log is and why it is such a good fit for trading workloads. We will unpack the core concepts—leaders and replicas, partitions and offsets, and retention—and show how they combine to form the durable spine of your trading events: trades, quotes, orders, fills, and risk snapshots.

From Messages to an Append-Only Log

Conceptually, a distributed log is an *append-only, ordered sequence of records* stored on a cluster of machines. You can think of it as a very long journal file that grows over time. New events are appended at the end; old events remain where they are and are never modified in place.

This is a slightly different mental model from the traditional "queue of messages" where messages are enqueued at the tail and then removed when consumers process them. In a log:

- Events are written once and kept for a configured period.
- Consumers do not remove events; instead, each consumer remembers how far it has read, using an *offset*.
- Multiple consumers can independently read the same events at different speeds, or even rewind and re-read history.

For a trading system, this is extremely attractive:

- You naturally want a complete, ordered history of important events such as trades, quotes, and orders.
- Many services—strategies, risk engines, recorders, analytics—need to consume the same events but process them in different ways.
- When something goes wrong, you want to replay what happened to understand, debug, and potentially backfill missing calculations.

The distributed log formalizes these needs in the core storage abstraction itself, rather than bolting audit and replay on as afterthoughts.

Topics, Partitions, and Leaders

Just as with pub/sub, events in a distributed log are grouped into *topics*. Each topic is a named stream dedicated to a category of events: md.equities, orders.submitted, orders.state, risk.snapshots, and so on.

To scale throughput and storage, each topic is split into one or more *partitions*. Each partition is itself a log: a fully ordered sequence of events, stored as a growing file (or set of files) on disk. Partitions are the primary unit of parallelism and distribution.

Within the cluster, each partition has:

- A single **leader replica**, which handles all writes and typically serves most reads.

- One or more **follower replicas**, which replicate the leader's data for durability and availability.

Leaders and followers for different partitions are spread across the cluster's machines. This means that while each partition is single-writer for ordering, the topic as a whole can achieve very high throughput by interleaving writes across many leaders on many nodes.

Formally, the log abstraction is simple:

- Each event written to a partition is assigned a monotonically increasing *offset* within that partition.

- Offsets serve as stable identifiers and positions in the log.

- The order of events within a partition is total and immutable.

For trading, you will typically choose partitioning schemes such that all events that must remain strictly ordered—for example, all order events for a given order ID or all book changes for a symbol—land on the same partition. We will return to these choices in the next section on partitioning and keys.

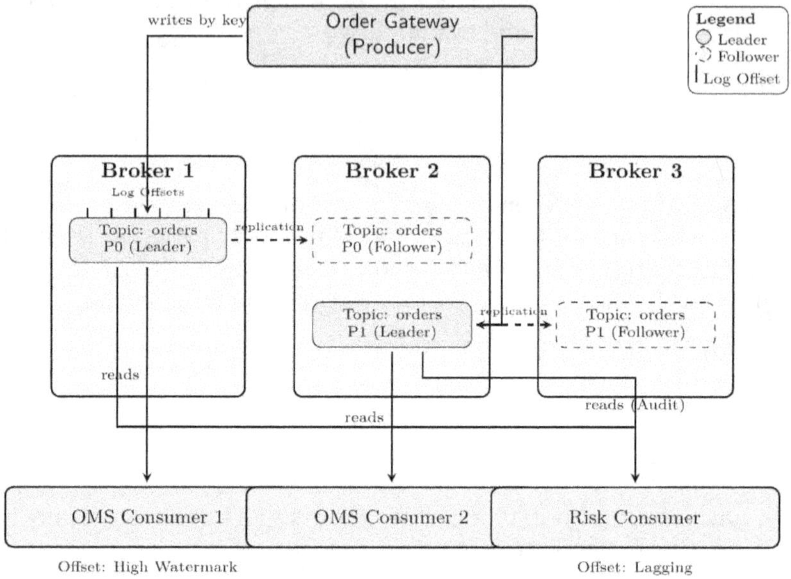

The Life of a Trading Event in the Log

Let us walk through what happens to a single trading event, say, an "order filled" update, from the moment a producer emits it to the moment various consumers process and replay it.

1. The producer appends the event. The order management system (OMS) or gateway acts as a producer. It creates a message containing the fill details: order ID, symbol, fill price, quantity, timestamps, and so on. It sends this message to the orders.state topic on the cluster.

The client library uses a partitioning strategy (for example, a hash of the order ID) to determine which partition within orders.state should receive this message. The message is then sent to the leader of that partition.

2. The leader writes and assigns an offset. The leader for that partition appends the message to its local log file. This is an efficient sequential disk write. At this moment, the message is internally assigned the next available offset in that partition, such as offset 10,538.

3. The event is replicated. To protect against machine failures, one or more follower replicas for the partition pull the new data from the leader and write it to their own local logs. Once enough followers (according to the configured replication factor and acknowledgment policy) have confirmed that they have written the event, the leader acknowledges the write back to the producer.

From the producer's perspective, the write is complete when the acknowledgement arrives. At this point you have:

- A durable copy of the event on the leader's disk.
- Redundant copies on follower disks, potentially on different racks or data centers depending on configuration.

4. Consumers see the event at their own pace. Multiple independent consumers may be subscribed to the `orders.state` topic:

- A P&L service that updates realized and unrealized P&L for the account.
- A risk service that updates exposures and limits.
- A compliance service that logs all fills for surveillance.
- Strategy engines that track their own order state.

Each consumer belongs to a *consumer group*. Within a group, partitions are divided among members using the competing-consumer pattern introduced earlier: each partition is consumed by exactly one member at a time. Across different groups, each group sees all events.

A consumer maintains its own *current offset* per partition: "I have processed events up to offset 10,537; the next one I need is 10,538." The messaging system delivers events starting from the consumer's current offset. After processing an event successfully, the consumer advances its offset and persists it (for example, in a coordination store or in the log itself).

5. Replay and catch-up. If a consumer is temporarily down, it simply stops advancing its offsets while the log continues to grow. When it comes back:

- It resumes from its last committed offsets.
- It reads all events that were appended while it was offline, in order, and catches up.

If a new consumer group is created—say, a new analytics service—it can start at:

- The *earliest* available offset (full replay from history), or
- The *latest* offset (only new events from now on).

This ability to treat the trading event stream as a persistent history, not just a transient queue, is central to how the distributed log becomes the "spine" of your system.

Offsets: Positions and Identities

Offsets do more than just track progress; they provide a stable, numeric coordinate system for your event streams.

Important properties of offsets:

- Within a partition, the offset of an event is immutable and strictly increasing.
- The pair (topic, partition, offset) uniquely identifies a specific event.
- Consumers can seek to a given offset to re-read starting at that point.

For trading, this has several practical consequences:

- **Deterministic replays.** If you want to replay a trading day for debugging a strategy, you can reset the strategy's consumer offsets to the start of the relevant window and feed events through in exactly the same order they occurred.

- **Auditability.** When investigating an incident, you can refer to specific offsets: "At offset 3,210 in partition 7 of `orders.state` the system received a cancel that caused..." This makes it easier to correlate logs across services.
- **Checkpointing.** Long-running calculations or analytics can periodically record "I have consumed up to offsets ..." so that they can restart and continue without duplication or loss.

Offsets are local to partitions, not globally across the topic. There is no global offset "42" that identifies the 42nd event in the whole topic; instead there is offset 42 in partition 0, offset 42 in partition 1, and so on. Global order across a whole topic is usually not required. Where strict ordering is necessary (for a symbol or order), you ensure that all relevant events share a partition and therefore share a consistent offset order.

Replication and Leader Failover

No trading system can afford to lose order or trade events. The distributed log achieves durability and availability primarily through replication.

Replication factor. For each topic (or sometimes per partition), you configure a replication factor such as 3. This means:

- Each partition has one leader and two followers.
- Every event written to that partition is stored on three different brokers.

Acknowledgment policies. When a producer writes an event, it can choose how many replicas must confirm receipt before the write is considered successful:

- **Leader-only acknowledgement.** Fastest but less durable. If the leader dies before followers catch up, some recently acknowledged writes may be lost.

- **Quorum acknowledgement.** Slower but safer. The write is only acknowledged once a majority (or all) replicas have written the event.

In trading systems, it is common to favor stronger durability for critical flows such as orders, even at some cost in latency, while using lighter settings for less critical analytics streams.

Leader failover. If a leader broker for a partition fails (hardware fault, network isolation, maintenance), the cluster's coordination service elects one of the up-to-date followers as the new leader. Producers and consumers automatically redirect their traffic to the new leader.

From the perspective of your trading services:

- Writes may pause briefly during the election.
- Once a new leader is in place, appends resume with correct ordering continuing from the last committed offset.

Careful configuration is required to avoid scenarios where a follower that is missing recent events becomes leader and "forgets" those events. Well-run clusters enforce that only fully caught-up replicas are eligible for leadership, or they accept a brief unavailability rather than risking inconsistency.

Understanding these trade-offs helps you reason about the rare but important corner cases: how many events could be lost in a catastrophic failure, and what does that imply for order idempotency, reconciliation with exchanges, and recovery procedures.

Retention: How Long Events Stay in the Log

Unlike a traditional message queue, a distributed log does not discard events once they are consumed. Instead, retention policies determine how long events remain available for reading.

Typical retention controls include:

- **Time-based retention.** Keep events for a configured duration such as 7 days, 30 days, or 1 year.

- **Size-based retention.** Keep events until the total log size reaches a threshold (for example, several terabytes), then delete oldest segments to stay within the limit.
- **Tiered storage.** Keep recent segments on fast local disks and move older segments to cheaper, slower storage while still allowing replay.

In a trading plant, different topics naturally require different retention:

- **Orders and fills.** Often retained for months or years for regulatory, audit, and backtesting purposes.
- **Raw tick-by-tick market data.** Very high volume; may be retained at full resolution for days or weeks, then downsampled or moved to specialized market data stores.
- **Risk snapshots and intraday analytics.** Medium volume; perhaps retained for weeks to support diagnostic and P&L explanations.

Choosing retention policies is not just about storage cost; it also shapes how you operate the plant:

- Long retention enables rich replays: new strategies can be tested against months of real event streams.
- Short retention requires more careful coordination with offline archives if you need to reproduce historical behavior.

As logs grow, the system organizes them into *segments* (chunks of the log file). When retention expires, entire old segments are deleted. Consumers that still hold offsets pointing into deleted segments are forced to jump forward to the earliest remaining offset. This is one reason why you should not allow critical services to lag indefinitely behind the head of the log.

Consumer Groups and At-Least-Once Processing

We have already touched on consumer groups as the way to combine pub/sub fan-out with competing-consumer parallelism. In the context of a distributed log, they also define the basic reliability story for event processing.

Within a consumer group: each partition of a topic is assigned to exactly one consumer instance. This achieves horizontal scaling: you add more consumers to the group to handle more partitions in parallel.

Across consumer groups: each group maintains its own offsets and sees all events. This is how you fan out events to independent services.

At-least-once delivery. The standard guarantee you get from a distributed log is at-least-once delivery:

- A consumer reads an event, processes it, and then commits a new offset.
- If the consumer crashes after processing but before committing, it will re-read the event on restart.

This means that an event may be processed more than once, but, if processing eventually completes and offsets are committed, it will not be silently dropped. For trading workloads, this is usually the right bias: avoid missing fills or orders, even if it means your consumers must be *idempotent* (able to handle duplicates without harm).

Building idempotent consumers often relies on business keys:

- Order ID and exchange execution ID to prevent double-booking fills.
- Trade ID to avoid duplicate P&L entries.
- Snapshot version numbers to ensure you apply updates in the right sequence.

Many log platforms also support transactional or "exactly-once" processing modes, which tighten these guarantees by coordinating offset commits and output writes. However, these come with additional latency and complexity. In practice, a combination of at-least-once delivery, idempotent business logic, and well-designed keys is usually sufficient for robust trading plants.

Why a Distributed Log is a Natural Trading Spine

Pulling the concepts together, we can now see why this architecture fits trading so well.

Ordered history for critical events. An append-only log naturally mirrors how we think about markets: as a time-ordered series of quotes, trades, orders, and risk states. This simplifies reasoning about causality: you can ask, "What did we know when we sent this order?" by replaying the relevant streams up to a point in time.

Many independent views. Strategies, risk, P&L, monitoring, and compliance all need to see the same base events but interpret them differently. The log's multi-consumer, offset-based model lets each of these services consume the stream at their own pace and even replay history independently.

Separation of concerns. Producers (gateways, OMS, risk data sources) focus on reliably appending events. Consumers focus on reacting to those events. The distributed log provides durable storage, replication, and basic delivery guarantees. This separation is especially valuable in organizations where infrastructure, trading, and risk teams are distinct.

Replay and evolution. Because history is retained, you can:

- Bring a new strategy online by backfilling it with historical events from the log.
- Recompute risk or P&L with corrected models by replaying fills and positions.
- Test new versions of services in "shadow" mode by feeding them a copy of real traffic and comparing outputs.

The log becomes both the live backbone and the historical record of your trading plant.

Scalable and fault-tolerant by design. Partitions let you scale throughput across many machines. Leaders and followers provide redundancy against failures. Consumer groups let you add and remove capacity without central coordination. All of these are built into the architecture rather than layered on later.

In the next section we will go deeper into how you choose partitioning keys, manage hot partitions, and use log compaction to keep long-lived streams efficient. Those design choices sit on top of the distributed log concepts you have just seen: leaders and replicas for durability and availability, offsets for ordering and replay, and retention as the knob that turns your event stream into a rich history of your trading system's behavior.

2.3 Partitioning, Keys, and Log Compaction

The previous section treated the distributed log as a single conceptual stream per topic, split into partitions for scalability. We saw that within a partition, events have a strict order, identified by offsets, and that replication and retention turn this into a durable spine for trading events.

We now move one level closer to design decisions you must actually make: *how* to partition your topics, *which keys* to use when publishing events, and *when* to apply log compaction. These choices directly affect:

- Whether events that logically belong together keep a consistent order.
- Whether load is evenly spread across your cluster or concentrated into hot spots.
- How much storage you burn, and how fast stateful services can recover or replay.

You can think of this section as the "geometry" of your event streams: how you slice them and shape them so they remain manageable under real trading loads.

Why Partitioning and Keys Matter

Recall that a topic is divided into multiple partitions, each with its own ordered log. When a producer sends an event, it chooses a partition (often via a key). That single routing decision has three important consequences:

- **Ordering scope.** Within a partition, events are totally ordered; across partitions, only a partial order exists. Any guarantee like "fills for an order arrive after its submit" only holds if those events share a partition.
- **Load distribution.** Each partition has its own leader and followers. If one partition receives far more events than others, it becomes a bottleneck: its broker can run hotter, and consumers assigned to it may lag behind.
- **Consumer parallelism.** Consumer groups process partitions in parallel, typically with one consumer instance per partition. The more partitions you have (and the more evenly they are loaded), the more parallelism you can exploit.

Key selection—the value you attach to a message so the client library can choose a partition—is how you tell the system which events belong together. In trading, keys are rarely arbitrary. They often encode business identity:

- Symbol or instrument ID.
- Order ID or execution ID.
- Account, portfolio, or strategy identifier.
- Venue or market segment.

Choosing good keys is one of the most important architectural decisions you will make about your event streams.

Partitioning Strategies: Hashing and Ranges

Distributed log platforms typically offer two broad families of partition assignment:

- **Hash-based partitioning.** The producer computes a hash of the key and takes it modulo the number of partitions. This spreads keys pseudo-randomly across partitions, assuming keys are not highly skewed.
- **Range-based partitioning.** The system maintains ordered ranges of keys per partition (for example, symbols from "A" to "F" in partition 0, "G" to "M" in partition 1, and so on). Events are routed by comparing their key against these ranges.

Hash-based partitioning. This is the default in many log systems because it is simple and usually balances load well. If you key by symbol and you have thousands of symbols trading with roughly similar activity, hashing will spread them evenly across partitions.

However, hashing hides the original order of keys inside partitions. You cannot easily ask, "Give me all symbols between A and F" by reading a single partition. More importantly, adding or removing partitions changes the mapping from keys to partitions unless you use additional techniques, so rebalancing may move a large fraction of keys at once.

Range-based partitioning. Range partitioning preserves some ordering in the key space. It can be attractive if you often work with key ranges (for example, by venue or ticker block) and want those to map to specific partitions. It also allows you to give more capacity (more or larger partitions) to hot ranges of keys.

The downside is that range boundaries must be chosen and adjusted carefully to keep load balanced. If you underestimate how active a range will become (for example, stocks starting with "S" become unusually hot), you can end up with a hot partition.

In practice, for trading events, hash-based partitioning is usually a good first choice because:

- You primarily care about per-key ordering (per order, per symbol, per account).

- You rarely need to process contiguous key ranges at the log level.
- You want automatic, near-even load spreading without constant manual tuning.

Range partitioning is more common in specialized data stores and analytical systems, or when you have explicit operational needs for controlling which machines handle which subsets of keys.

Choosing Keys: Ordering vs. Hotspots

The key you choose for a topic captures your main semantic requirement for ordering. In trading event streams, three patterns recur:

Per-Order Ordering

For topics like orders.state that carry the lifecycle of each order (submitted, acknowledged, partially filled, fully filled, canceled), it is often crucial that all events for a given order appear in the exact sequence they happened.

Here, a natural key is **order ID**. Hash-based partitioning by order ID ensures:

- All events for one order land in the same partition, preserving a strict order.
- Different orders are spread across partitions, enabling parallel processing.

Consumers that reconstruct order books, P&L, or strategy state per order can then rely on the per-order sequence.

Per-Symbol Ordering

For raw market data or per-symbol analytics, you often want all quotes and trades for a given symbol to arrive in the order they were published. While exchanges may not always provide perfect time ordering, you do not want your backbone to scramble events further.

Keying by **symbol** on topics like md.equities or analytics.per_symbol groups all events for the same symbol into one partition. This allows:

- Fast, localized order book construction.
- Deterministic replays of per-symbol price action.

However, there is a trade-off: some symbols are vastly more active than others. If you hash by symbol, a very hot symbol like an index ETF or a mega-cap stock might dominate its partition's volume, creating a *hot partition.*

Per-Account or Per-Strategy Ordering

Risk and P&L topics are often keyed by **account**, **portfolio**, or **strategy ID**. This ensures that all updates about a given account's positions, margin, or limits are applied in order.

For example, a risk.exposure topic might carry updates such as "account A's delta increased by 100" or "account B breached a limit." Keying by account maintains a clear narrative per account, which is critical for reconciliation and explanations.

Hot Partitions and Composite Keys

Even with hashing, real trading streams are skewed. A few symbols, strategies, or accounts may dominate volumes at certain times (often around the open, macro announcements, or during particular market events). If a hot key is mapped to a single partition, that partition's leader can become a bottleneck.

Common symptoms of hot partitions include:

- Increased end-to-end latency for messages destined for that partition.
- Consumers assigned to that partition lagging, while others are mostly idle.
- Higher CPU, disk, or network usage on the broker hosting that partition's leader.

To mitigate this, you can introduce *composite keys* or *key sharding.* Instead of keying solely by symbol, you might use:

- symbol + shard_id, where shard_id is a small integer.
- A hash of (symbol, side), so that buys and sells for the same symbol can be distributed.
- For very hot accounts, a key of (account, instrument group).

The idea is to split the load for one logical entity across multiple partitions, allowing:

- Producers to spread write load more evenly.
- Consumers to process different shards of the same entity in parallel, if their logic allows it.

The downside is that you *weaken* ordering guarantees. If you shard a single symbol across two partitions, you can no longer assume that all events for that symbol are totally ordered in a single log. You only preserve order *within each shard* (for example, within a given price band or level).

Whether that is acceptable depends on what consumers do:

- For full order book construction, you typically want strict per-symbol ordering and therefore avoid sharding individual books.
- For independent per-trade analytics or machine learning feature extraction, approximate or shard-level ordering may be fine, and the benefits of better load distribution outweigh the loss.

In other words, the "right" key is always conditional on downstream semantics. Before introducing composite or sharded keys, identify exactly which consumers rely on ordering and whether they can be adjusted.

Static vs. Dynamic Partition Counts

When you create a topic, you must choose its initial number of partitions. This is a capacity-planning decision:

- Too few partitions, and you will hit throughput or hot-partition limits.
- Too many partitions, and you pay overhead in open files, metadata, and consumer complexity, without gaining much.

Some platforms allow you to *increase* partition counts later. However, this is not free:

- For hash-based partitioning, increasing partitions changes the mapping from keys to partitions. New events for a key may go to a different partition than old events, breaking the "all events for a key are in one partition" assumption.
- Existing data is not reshuffled by default; you end up with historical events for a key in one partition and new events in another, unless you perform a separate re-partitioning job.

Because of this, it is often wise to:

- Over-provision partitions slightly at topic creation time for high-traffic flows like market data and orders.
- Accept that partition counts are relatively stable. When you need a significantly different slicing, you create a new topic and gradually migrate producers and consumers.

Dynamic schemes are possible—for example, using an extra routing layer or consistent hashing that isolates the effect of adding capacity—but they add complexity. For many trading plants, standard partitioning plus occasional topic migrations are a simpler operational trade-off.

Log Compaction: Storing State, Not Just History

So far we have treated the log as a complete history of every event. For some topics, this is exactly what you want: every trade, every order change, every tick of the market.

For other topics, however, what you really care about is the *current state per key*. For example:

- Latest reference data for an instrument (tick size, currency, listings).
- Current configuration settings for a strategy (thresholds, limits).
- Current account balances or risk limits.

Keeping every single update to these values forever can be wasteful. A popular stock's reference data might be updated a few times a year; that is fine. But a risk snapshot for an active account might be updated thousands of times per day. If you only need the latest state for most use cases, there is no reason to keep every intermediate update in hot storage indefinitely.

Log compaction is a mechanism that addresses this. Instead of deleting old messages purely based on time or size, the log periodically rewrites segments so that, for each key, only the most recent value is kept (plus some optional older records for safety). Conceptually:

- The log still receives every update as a normal append.
- In the background, the system scans segments from oldest to newest.
- For each key, if it finds multiple messages, it keeps only the latest one and discards the older ones.

After compaction, the topic behaves like a *materialized key-value store* backed by a log:

- New consumers can read the compacted log from the beginning to reconstruct a complete, up-to-date map of key → value.
- Storage usage is bounded by the number of keys, not the number of historical updates.

Compaction vs. Retention: Complementary Tools

Compaction and retention serve different, complementary purposes:

- **Retention** limits how far back in *time* you can replay events. Old segments beyond the retention window are deleted entirely.
- **Compaction** limits how many *versions per key* you keep within the retained window, collapsing them to the latest one.

You can combine them in several ways:

- A topic might have both a time-based retention (for example, two weeks) and compaction. Within those two weeks, only the latest update per key is stored; older ones within that window are thrown away during compaction.
- Alternatively, a topic might be purely compacted and not deleted for a long time. In this case, the log effectively stores the latest state per key as of the last compaction pass, potentially going back months or years.

For trading, a typical pattern is:

- Use **non-compacted** topics with longer retention for event histories you may want to replay in detail: orders, fills, raw market data.
- Use **compacted** topics for slowly changing state or state that is naturally keyed: reference data, configuration, risk limits, positions.

Sometimes, you maintain both:

- A non-compacted `orders.state` topic that records every state transition for audit and replay.
- A compacted `positions.by_account` topic that always holds the latest position per account, updated in response to those order events.

This separation mirrors how you think: detailed *event history* on one hand, concise *current state* on the other.

Designing Events for Safe Compaction

To use compaction safely, your message schemas must be designed with compaction in mind. The log will keep the latest message per key, so that message should fully describe the desired state for that key, or at least be *self-contained enough* that replaying the compacted log yields a correct state.

Potential pitfalls:

- **Partial updates.** If your messages say "increase limit by 10%" instead of "new limit is 1 000," compaction will keep only the last relative change and discard earlier ones. A new consumer replaying the compacted log will not see the full sequence and will compute the wrong limit.
- **Dependent fields.** If some fields are omitted assuming that consumers know defaults or previous values, a compacted log may not carry enough information to reconstruct the intended final state.

Better patterns include:

- For compacted topics, emit **full snapshots per key** whenever you update them: a complete record of an instrument, a full set of limits for an account, a full configuration for a strategy.
- Use partial updates only on non-compacted, purely event-style topics where you are not relying on compaction for long-term storage.

Additionally, consider how you model deletions. Compaction systems often interpret a special "tombstone" message (a message with a key and a null or empty value) as a signal to delete that key entirely during compaction. This can be useful, for example, when an instrument is delisted or an account is closed.

Impact on Recovery and Bootstrap Times

One practical motivation for compacted topics is that they make stateful services faster to start and recover. Consider a risk engine that maintains in-memory positions and exposures per account:

- If it reconstructs state purely from the raw event log of fills and orders, it may need to replay millions of events to catch up after a restart.
- If it can instead read a compacted topic of latest positions per account, it can load the current state with a small, bounded number of messages (one per account or per account-instrument pair).

A common architecture is:

- Maintain a non-compacted event topic such as `fills.executions`.
- Have a "position aggregator" service that continuously reads `fills.executions` and publishes updates to a compacted `positions.by_account` topic.
- On startup, risk engines read `positions.by_account` to initialize their in-memory state, then subscribe to `fills.executions` for real-time updates.

This arrangement combines the strengths of both approaches:

- Detailed history lives in the raw event log.
- Fast, bounded recovery is enabled by the compacted state topic.

The same pattern can be applied to order books, configuration, or any other derived state that multiple services need.

Putting It All Together: Practical Guidelines

To close the loop, let us summarize practical rules of thumb that link key selection, partitioning strategies, and compaction to the goals of ordering, load distribution, and storage efficiency.

1. Start from ordering requirements.

For each topic, ask:

- What must be strictly ordered? Per order, per symbol, per account, or something else?
- Which consumers rely on that ordering, and for what logic?

Choose keys so that all events involved in a critical ordering requirement share a key and therefore *can* share a partition. Avoid introducing sharding of hot keys unless you are certain consumers can tolerate weaker ordering.

2. Use hash-based partitioning by default.

Unless you have a clear reason to do otherwise:

- Partition based on a good business key (order ID, symbol, account).
- Let the system hash the key to assign partitions.

This tends to produce reasonable load distribution while preserving per-key ordering.

3. Monitor and respond to hot partitions.

Instrument your cluster and consumers so you can see:

- Per-partition throughput and lag.
- Per-broker CPU, disk, and network usage.

When you identify a hot partition caused by a few dominant keys, consider:

- Whether those keys can be split across composite keys without violating critical ordering requirements.
- Whether you should give them a dedicated topic or a different treatment (for example, separate infrastructure for an ultra-hot instrument).

4. Treat partition count as a semi-static capacity knob.

Plan for growth:

- Choose initial partition counts with headroom for expected traffic, especially for high-rate topics.
- Avoid frequent changes that re-map keys, unless you are prepared to migrate or rebuild state.

5. Reserve compaction for state-like topics.

Ask whether a topic is fundamentally about:

- A sequence of *events* (orders, trades, quote updates), or
- The evolving *state* of identified entities (accounts, instruments, configuration).

Use compaction primarily for the latter, and design messages as full snapshots per key. Leave event topics un-compacted with appropriate retention, and, when needed, derive compacted state topics from them.

6. Think in layers: raw events, derived state, and services.

Many robust trading architectures use a layered approach:

- **Raw event layer.** Non-compacted topics keyed for ordering, retaining enough history for replay and audit.
- **Derived state layer.** Compacted topics keyed by the entities that services care about, enabling fast bootstraps and queries.
- **Service layer.** Risk engines, strategies, P&L, monitoring, each consuming from both layers as appropriate.

Partitioning, keys, and compaction are the tools you use to shape each layer to its purpose, under real-world constraints of latency, throughput, and storage.

With these concepts in place, you can now reason more confidently about the structure of your event streams. In the following sections we will contrast distributed logs with classic message queues in the low-latency order path, and then return to cross-cutting concerns such as schema evolution and backpressure that affect both styles of backbone.

2.4 Message Queues for Low-Latency Workflows

So far we have treated the distributed log as the central spine of the trading plant. It gives us durable, replayable streams with many independent consumers. That is exactly what we want for market data, orders and fills history, and state streams such as risk or positions.

However, not every workflow in a trading system is best served by a log. Some paths are so latency-sensitive and so tightly controlled that the overheads and semantics of a log are not an ideal fit. In particular, the *hot order path*—from a strategy's decision to an order actually reaching the exchange gateway and being validated and risk-checked—often benefits from classic *message queues*.

This section explains where queues differ from logs, why queues are useful in low-latency paths, how acknowledgment semantics (ack/-nack) play into reliability, and how you can use queues for fine grained task dispatch without sacrificing the benefits of your log-based backbone.

Queues vs. Logs: Different Mental Models

A useful way to start is to contrast the data models.

A **distributed log**:

- Stores an append-only history of events.
- Retains events for some time, regardless of how many times they are read.
- Allows many independent consumers to read the same event at their own pace, using offsets.

A **message queue**, in its classic form:

- Holds a set of pending messages, each representing a unit of work or a request.
- Delivers each message to exactly one consumer.
- Removes the message once it has been successfully processed and acknowledged.

In a queue, the focus is not on maintaining a durable history for replay. The focus is on *getting work done as quickly and reliably as possible*:

- A message is something that must be handled once and then can be forgotten (e.g., "submit this order," "price this basket now").
- The system and its consumers are tuned to push these messages through with minimal overhead.

This difference in emphasis shapes everything: API design, acknowledgment semantics, batching, and how you scale out consumers.

Why Queues are Attractive for the Hot Order Path

The path from a strategy decision to an order reaching the matching engine often involves several steps:

1. The strategy decides to trade.
2. It sends an order to an internal gateway.
3. The gateway normalizes and enriches the order (for example, adding risk tags).
4. One or more pre-trade risk checks run.
5. If all is well, the order is transformed into the protocol required by the exchange and sent out.

You might implement all of this as calls over a distributed log: strategy publishes to an orders.requests topic, risk engines and gateways consume, and replies flow back via request–reply patterns.

But there are reasons to consider a dedicated queue for at least a portion of this path:

- **Lower per-message overhead.** Queues can be tuned to minimize disk touches (for example, using memory-backed queues with periodic persistence) and avoid the generality of a distributed log that supports many consumers and long retention.
- **Tighter control over task ownership.** In a queue, a task is "in flight" with exactly one consumer at a time. You can design the protocol so that if that consumer fails, the task is promptly re-queued and given to another worker.
- **Simpler semantics for one-off work.** Orders or risk checks along the hot path are often one-time actions where you care about whether the work is completed, not about replaying the exact sequence of messages later from this particular internal hop.

In practice, many firms use a hybrid:

- The *external* view of orders and fills—what you need for audit, replay, strategy evaluation, risk, and so on—lives in the distributed log.
- The *internal* hop between the strategy and a gateway or risk service, or between gateway and exchange, may use a high-performance queue that is optimized for minimal latency.

The two are linked by mirroring: the gateway writes order submissions and state changes to the distributed log, even if the immediate dispatch came through a queue.

Core Queue Semantics: Ack and Nack

The most important operational mechanism in a message queue is the notion of *acknowledgment* (ack) and its counterpart *negative ac-*

knowledgment (nack).

The basic dance looks like this:

1. A consumer fetches a message from the queue.
2. The queue marks the message as "in progress," often making it temporarily invisible to other consumers.
3. The consumer processes the message.
4. If processing succeeds, the consumer sends an **ack**. The queue then deletes the message permanently.
5. If processing fails or the consumer cannot complete it, the consumer may send a **nack**, or the queue may notice that the consumer has not acknowledged the message within a configured timeout. In either case, the queue makes the message visible again for another consumer to try.

This mechanism has several consequences:

- Messages are processed at-least-once by default. If a consumer dies mid-processing, another consumer will eventually pick up the message.
- You have direct control over when the system considers work "done": only after successful processing and ack.
- You can implement backpressure by limiting how many unacked messages a consumer can handle at the same time.

This is well-suited to the hot order path, provided your handlers are idempotent:

- Submitting the exact same order request twice must either be prevented outright (by rejecting duplicates using an order ID) or treated harmlessly.
- Similarly, a risk-check request might be retried; the risk service must avoid double-counting.

If your logic is idempotent, retries due to nacks or timeouts do not hurt correctness, and you gain resilience without sacrificing latency.

Delivery Guarantees: At-Most-Once, At-Least-Once, Effectively-Once

Queues—like logs—sit on a spectrum of delivery guarantees. On the order path you must consciously choose where to sit on that spectrum, because it affects both performance and failure behavior.

At-Most-Once Delivery

In at-most-once mode, messages are delivered *zero or one* times. The system does not retry if there is an error; it may even acknowledge to the producer before the consumer has completed processing.

This is sometimes achieved by:

- Automatically removing messages as soon as they are sent to consumers (no ack/nack).
- Or acknowledging to the producer when the message enters the queue, without guaranteeing successful consumption.

The advantage is minimal latency and overhead: no need to track in-flight messages, timeouts, or retries. The downside is the possibility of *silent loss*: a message that is never processed and never retried.

For trading orders, pure at-most-once semantics are dangerous. Lost cancel or replace messages can have large financial consequences. At-most-once may be acceptable only in non-critical analytics paths or for telemetry.

At-Least-Once Delivery

At-least-once mode ensures that every message is processed *one or more* times. The queue will retry delivering a message until some consumer acknowledges it. Nacks, consumer failures, or timeouts trigger redelivery.

This drives the design of your order and risk services:

- They must tolerate occasional duplicates.
- They should be able to recognize already-processed messages, often by a unique business key (such as client order ID plus timestamp).

At-least-once is usually the right default for order paths, because "double-handling" is easier to detect and correct than "never handled at all."

Effectively-Once Processing

Some queue systems and architectures aim at *effectively-once* or *exactly-once* behavior. In practice this means:

- The underlying queue may still deliver messages multiple times.
- But the combination of queue, consumer, and any side effects (database writes, log appends, outgoing orders) is structured so that the external effect occurs as if each message had been processed exactly once.

Achieving this usually requires:

- Idempotent handlers.
- Outbox or transactional patterns that tie message acknowledgment to durable recording of the effect (for example, record the order in a log and only then ack the queue).

On the hot path, you balance the complexity of such mechanisms against the latency and reliability requirements. Many trading systems implement the most safety-critical side effects (for example, order persistence and external communication) in a single tightly controlled component (the gateway), and keep its interface simple to avoid distributed transactions.

Fine-Grained Task Dispatch with Queues

Beyond the central hot order path, there are many smaller workflows in a trading plant that benefit from queues:

- Pricing a large basket of instruments for a client.
- Running bursty hedging calculations when exposure thresholds are crossed.

- Performing CPU-heavy analytics on snapshots of the order book.

These tasks share common traits:

- They can be decomposed into independent units of work.
- They may arrive in bursts.
- They do not necessarily define the global risk profile of the firm in the next few microseconds, so a bit more latency is acceptable compared to the direct trading path.

Queues shine here because:

- You can create a dedicated queue per type of task or per priority band.
- Multiple worker processes can pull tasks, forming a flexible pool that grows and shrinks with load.
- You can assign priorities, visibility timeouts, or rate limits per queue.

For example:

- A "pricing" queue feeds a farm of valuation workers. When a large client request arrives, the front-end breaks it into small tasks and enqueues them. The workers consume tasks in parallel, and the front-end aggregates results.
- A "hedging" queue carries tasks to adjust positions when delta or gamma thresholds are breached. Tasks may be prioritized so that the most urgent hedges are executed first.

Because queues remove messages once processed, there is no need to think about offsets or retention in this layer. The focus is on immediate throughput and fairness among workers.

Priority and Isolation in the Order Path

Queues also give you fine control over *which* messages get attention first when resources are tight.

Priority queues. Some message queue systems support built-in priority levels. Higher-priority messages (such as cancels or mass cancels) can jump ahead of lower-priority ones (such as new passive orders) in the dispatch order. This matters because they affect risk and exposure more immediately.

Even when the technology does not offer priority, you can emulate it:

- Use separate queues for different priorities: orders.cancel_high, orders.normal.
- Run more workers against the high-priority queue, or configure its consumers differently.

Isolation. Another virtue of queues is that you can isolate different activities so that a slow consumer in one area does not stall another.

Consider:

- A queue for handling normal order flow.
- A separate queue for heavy or experimental analytics triggered by those orders.

If the analytics workers fall behind, the main order path queue can still drain quickly, ensuring that trading remains responsive. Contrast this with a naive use of a single shared log partition where one slow consumer can create backpressure for all consumers unless the system supports fully independent consumption.

Queues vs. Logs: Latency Trade-offs

It is tempting to think that queues are always faster than logs, but this is not automatically true. The trade-offs depend on configuration and workload.

Factors that often make queues lower-latency on the hot path include:

- **Short-lifetime messages.** Queues are optimized for quick disposal of messages once processed. There is no need to manage a long history or support replayable offsets.
- **Simpler replication policies.** Some queues may be configured with lighter durability guarantees on the hot path (for example, in-memory replication across a small cluster) compared to the stronger disk-based replication of a log.
- **Less batching.** Distributed logs often batch writes and acknowledgments to improve throughput, which can introduce small but noticeable latency. Queues may run with smaller batches or even single-message writes on the hot path.

On the other hand, logs can be surprisingly efficient when configured well, especially if:

- You use asynchronous producers that batch writes.
- You keep a small replication factor for certain non-critical topics.
- Consumers read sequentially, which is cache- and disk-friendly.

The practical conclusion is:

- Use your distributed log wherever you benefit from durable history, multi-consumer fan-out, and replay.
- Use queues where you have tightly bounded, point-to-point or one-to-many *task dispatch* that is extremely sensitive to per-message overhead, and where you do not need full log semantics.

Measure both in the context of your actual workloads; do not rely solely on intuition.

Hybrid Designs: Hot Path on Queues, Spine on Logs

A robust architecture often combines both abstractions:

- The **hot path** from strategy to gateway and across internal risk checks may use queues:
  - The strategy places an order by enqueuing a message in a low-latency queue.
  - A gateway process takes the message, runs validations and risk checks (potentially via further internal task queues), and forwards the order to the exchange.
- In parallel, the gateway writes:
  - The received order request to a log topic like orders.submitted.
  - Subsequent state changes (acknowledged, partially filled, filled, canceled) to orders.state.

This gives you:

- Low latency in the immediate order transmission, tuned via queues.
- Complete, ordered, and replayable history in the log for all other consumers.

Similarly, a risk service might:

- Use a queue to dispatch individual risk calculations or limit checks to worker processes quickly.
- Publish the resulting risk state or limit changes to compacted log topics for downstream services.

The key is to define clear boundaries:

- Queues are inside the "engine room," connecting tightly coupled components.
- Logs form the fabric visible to the rest of the plant: strategies, risk, P&L, monitoring, compliance.

Operational Considerations

Introducing queues alongside logs also brings some operational questions:

Monitoring and alerts. For each queue, you should track:

- Queue depth (number of pending messages).
- Age of the oldest message.
- Number of unacked messages.

Spikes in these metrics can indicate that workers are overloaded, misconfigured, or failing. On the hot order path, you should tie alerts on these metrics directly to trading controls; for example, temporarily throttling new orders if the internal queue between gateway and risk checks becomes backed up.

Failure handling. Decide how many times to retry a message and what to do with messages that keep failing:

- **Dead-letter queues** can hold problem messages for manual investigation, rather than being retried indefinitely.
- In trading, repeatedly failing messages may signal deeper issues: bad configuration, external service outages, or bugs in serialization or validation.

Consistency with the log. When using both queues and logs:

- Ensure that all externally observable events (orders, fills, risk state changes) are eventually written to the log, even if their immediate processing used queues.
- Be careful about ordering between queue-based actions and log-based events; for example, an event in the log should accurately reflect whether the corresponding queue-based action was accepted or rejected.

A disciplined approach is to treat the gateway or a small set of core services as the *source of truth* that bridges queues and logs. Those components own the precise sequence in which orders are accepted, risk-checked, forwarded, and recorded.

Message queues and distributed logs are complementary tools:

- Logs provide a durable, replayable, multi-consumer backbone for trading events.
- Queues provide low-latency, fine-grained task dispatch where each message is a piece of work to be done once and then forgotten.

For latency-critical order paths, queues—with explicit ack/nack semantics and carefully chosen delivery guarantees—let you tightly control task execution and failure behavior. For the broader plant, logs ensure that every significant event is visible, auditable, and replayable.

Designing an event-driven trading system is therefore not about choosing queues *or* logs, but about deciding:

- Which flows belong in the historical spine.
- Which flows are truly hot-path dispatch.
- How to connect the two so that every order, fill, and risk decision is both fast enough to trade and robust enough to be understood long after the fact.

In the next sections, we will see how schema management and back-pressure concerns cut across both queues and logs, and how disciplined design at those layers keeps your messaging backbone reliable as the system and the markets evolve.

2.5 Schema Management and Evolution

Up to this point we have treated messages as anonymous blobs riding on top of our logs and queues. We discussed how to route them, how to partition them, and how to move them at low latency. In practice, however, many trading outages and subtle P&L errors are not caused by the messaging infrastructure itself, but by the *shape* of the data being exchanged: fields that disappear, formats that change, or new flags that some services know how to interpret and others do not.

This section introduces *schema management* as a first-class discipline in an event-driven trading system. We will focus on how to design message schemas, how to version and evolve them, and how to coordinate changes so that producers and consumers can move independently without breaking live trading flows.

Why Schemas Matter in a Trading Plant

A *schema* is a formal description of the structure of a message:

- Which fields exist.
- What types they have (string, integer, decimal, enumeration, and so on).
- Which fields are required and which are optional.
- How nested structures, lists, or maps are arranged.

When you send messages between independent services—strategies, risk engines, gateways, monitoring, and reporting—you are effectively defining a contract. If that contract is implicit ("everyone just knows that the fourth field is the price, unless it is a special case"), then any change becomes dangerous.

Trading amplifies this risk:

- Many services consume the same topics: misinterpreting one field can corrupt risk and P&L across the plant.
- Changes must often be rolled out while markets are open.
- Regulations require that you explain and reconcile trades and risk: silent schema drift makes this hard.

Explicit schemas, and processes to manage them, make message formats:

- **Discoverable**: new services can find out what fields exist and what they mean.
- **Validated**: invalid messages are caught early instead of propagating.
- **Evolvable**: you can extend, deprecate, or refine fields without simultaneous rewrites of every client.

From Ad Hoc Payloads to Explicit Contracts

Many systems start informally: messages are JSON documents or delimited strings; the producer and consumer teams agree informally what fields exist. This works for prototypes but tends to fail at scale.

Common failure modes include:

- A producer changes a field name (for example, `qty` to `quantity`), breaking consumers that still expect the old name.
- A numeric field switches from integer basis points to decimal percentages, silently distorting risk calculations.
- A new field is added, but with no clear default; older consumers mishandle or ignore messages that rely on the new field.

To avoid this, mature plants adopt explicit schema systems (for example, Avro, Protocol Buffers, or similar). While the specific technology is less important than the discipline, explicit schemas typically provide:

- A machine-readable definition of each message type.
- Strong typing (integers vs. strings vs. decimals vs. enumerations).
- Options for default values, required vs. optional fields.
- Built-in rules for what counts as a compatible evolution.

Critically, these systems are typically supported by a *schema registry*: a central service that stores all schema versions, associates them with subjects or topics, and provides compatibility checks for new versions.

For our purposes, the takeaway is simple: messages in the backbone should be governed by explicit schemas that are known, versioned, and validated, not left as arbitrary blobs.

Producers, Consumers, and Schema Registries

A schema registry sits logically next to your messaging backbone. Producers and consumers interact with it when they start up or when they serialize/deserialize messages. The common pattern is:

- Each message type (for example, OrderSubmitted, OrderState, RiskSnapshot) has a subject name in the registry.
- The subject has one or more versions, each with a unique identifier.
- Producers and consumers fetch the schema by ID or by version when they encode or decode messages.

In practice, this yields several benefits:

- **Discovery**. A new consumer can discover, from the registry, what messages exist on a topic and how to interpret them.
- **Validation**. Producers can validate messages against the current schema before publishing, catching missing or ill-typed fields early.
- **Compatibility checks**. When you propose a new schema version, the registry can automatically check whether it remains compatible with existing versions under configured rules (explained below).

You can think of the registry as the "type system" for your event-driven plant. It does not replace documentation or human understanding, but it enforces a baseline of correctness and stability that ad hoc approaches struggle to achieve.

Compatibility Modes: Backward, Forward, and Full

Schema evolution is about change. To talk sensibly about change, we need to define what it means for a new schema to be *compatible* with an old one.

Three basic compatibility modes matter in trading systems:

- **Backward compatible**: New consumers can read data written by old producers. In practical terms: old messages conform to the new schema.
- **Forward compatible**: Old consumers can read data written by new producers. New messages conform to the old schema, perhaps by ignoring unknown fields.
- **Full compatible**: Both of the above: new consumers can read old data, and old consumers can read new data.

These modes translate into deployment guarantees:

- If you enforce **backward compatibility** per subject, you can safely upgrade consumers first. Old data in the log remains readable by the new code.
- If you enforce **forward compatibility**, you can safely upgrade producers first. New messages are still understandable by old consumers.
- If you enforce **full compatibility**, you get maximum deployment flexibility: you can upgrade producers and consumers in any order, at the cost of writing more conservative schema changes.

In a busy trading plant where you cannot always coordinate simultaneous rollouts of many services, full compatibility is attractive but can be restrictive. A common pragmatic pattern is:

- Use backward or full compatibility for critical topics on the trading spine (orders, fills, risk state), which are long-lived and heavily consumed.

- Allow more aggressive, possibly only-forward-compatible evolutions in internal analytics topics that are used by a smaller set of services.

What Changes Are Safe?

The schema technology and registry can help enforce compatibility, but only if you understand which changes are, in principle, safe.

Typical *backward-compatible* changes (new consumers, old data) include:

- Adding a new *optional* field with a sensible default.
- Adding new enumeration values if consumers treat unknown values carefully (for example, defaulting to a safe behavior).
- Widening a numeric type (for example, from 32-bit to 64-bit) if the on-wire representation supports it.

Changes that are usually *backward-incompatible* include:

- Removing a required field that existing messages depend on.
- Changing the meaning or unit of a field without changing its name or type.
- Changing field types in a way that makes old values invalid (for example, string to integer).

For forward compatibility (old consumers, new data), different rules apply. Old consumers must be able to:

- Safely ignore new optional fields they do not understand.
- Handle missing fields that they previously considered required, often by relying on defaults or fallback logic.

Full compatibility therefore tends to restrict you to additive changes (new optional fields, new enumeration members) or carefully orchestrated deprecations where:

- You first introduce new fields alongside old ones.
- Consumers are updated to read from the new fields while still accepting the old.
- Only when all consumers have moved can you remove or repurpose the old fields in a future major version.

The discipline may feel heavy at first, but it pays off in reduced risk of breaking running strategies when you deploy a schema change mid-session.

Versioning Patterns and Naming Conventions

To manage evolving schemas over time, you need conventions that make it clear which version of a message is in use and how it relates to others.

Some practical patterns include:

Subject naming in the registry. Use meaningful names that indicate the domain, not individual teams or services. For example:

- trading.OrderSubmitted
- trading.OrderState
- risk.ExposureSnapshot
- md.EquityQuote

Avoid baking service names into subjects (for example, oms1.OrderSubmitted); producers and consumers should see the same semantic concepts even as implementations change.

Schema versions as first-class citizens. Treat schema versions a bit like API versions:

- Maintain a numeric version in the registry (for example, 1, 2, 3) with clear release notes.

- Optionally include a schema version field in the message itself, especially if messages might be archived, transformed, or transported outside the usual registry-aware environment.

Topic-to-schema binding. Decide how topics and schemas relate:

- A simple approach is one dominant schema per topic, with version evolution over time.
- More advanced designs may allow multiple message types (with different schemas) on the same topic, distinguished by a type field or wrapper. This is more flexible but requires consumers to discriminate between types.

For trading spines, one-schema-per-topic is easier to reason about operationally: all messages on orders.state conform to the current OrderState schema, and schema evolution is tracked centrally.

Designing Schemas for Longevity

Even with good versioning mechanisms, some schema designs make evolution much easier than others. For trading systems, a few guidelines are particularly important.

Model domain concepts, not wire artifacts. Your schemas should reflect stable business concepts, not transient quirks of any single exchange or protocol. For example:

- Represent a price as a decimal or a price-plus-currency, not as "ticks of 1/32" just because one venue uses that unit.
- Represent side as an enumeration {BUY, SELL}, not as "B"/"S" just because a FIX tag does.

Adapters at the edge of your plant translate exchange-specific details into your domain schemas. This insulates the core of the system from protocol churn.

Use explicit, well-typed fields. Avoid overloading generic string or map fields with complex substructures. For example:

- Prefer limit_price, time_in_force, order_type as named fields over a single attributes map with arbitrary keys.
- Use enumerations for fields with a defined set of values, not free-form strings (for example, known order types, execution types, risk flags).

Explicit typing makes it easier for tools and registries to catch schema mistakes and for future readers to understand the intent.

Choose sensible defaults. When you add optional fields, define defaults that are:

- Safe (for example, "treat as most conservative risk setting if field is absent").
- Close to current behavior, so that older messages without the field are interpreted in a way consistent with legacy behavior.

Avoid excessive nesting and deep hierarchies. Deeply nested schemas are harder to evolve and reason about. Flatten where possible, especially for hot-path messages that are serialized/deserialized at high rates.

Rolling Out Schema Changes Safely

Even with compatible schemas, you must think about deployment choreography: the order in which you upgrade producers and consumers.

Consider adding a new optional field to the OrderSubmitted schema, such as a "client order classification" required by a new regulatory regime.

A safe rollout might look like this:

1. Extend the schema in the registry, enforcing backward compatibility (new consumers can still read old messages).
2. Update consumers that can make use of the new field. They will see it as unset for older messages.

3. Once consumers are deployed, upgrade producers to start populating the new field. Old consumers that are still running will simply ignore it, provided the evolution is forward-compatible.

More complex changes—such as splitting a field into two or changing units—may require multi-step evolutions:

1. Add new fields alongside old ones (for example, price_old_ticks and price_decimal).
2. Update consumers to prefer the new fields when present but still accept the old.
3. After a deprecation period, stop populating the old fields.
4. Only in a later major schema version, remove the old fields once you are sure no consumers depend on them.

This staggered approach is more work than a big-bang change, but it avoids synchronized downtime or fragile release trains: different services can update at their own pace.

Schema Discipline for Logs and Queues

The schema principles above apply both to distributed logs and to queues, but the emphasis is slightly different.

On logs. Logs retain history and enable replay. Schema discipline ensures that:

- Historical messages remain readable by newer tools and services.
- Replays for backtesting or risk recalculation do not fail because old data no longer matches current schemas.

For long-lived topics such as orders, fills, and risk snapshots, it is especially important to be conservative in schema changes and to avoid anything that would make historical data unintelligible.

On queues. Queues focus on transient work items that are usually not replayed for long periods. Still, schemas matter:

- For hot-path order and risk queues, schema errors can disrupt live trading even if messages are not stored long-term.
- For task queues (pricing, hedging), schema compatibility determines whether new versions of workers can safely coexist with old ones.

Because queues typically do not retain large histories, you may be able to roll out more aggressive schema changes by draining queues and performing synchronized upgrades. However, this should be the exception, not the default, especially in a 24-hour market environment.

Guardrails: Validation and Testing

Finally, schema management is not just a documentation exercise; it should be wired into your toolchain and operational practices.

Validation at the edges. Enforce schema validation where messages enter the backbone:

- Feed handlers validate market data messages before publishing them to the log.
- Order gateways validate incoming client orders against the OrderSubmitted schema before placing them on internal queues or topics.

Rejecting or quarantining malformed messages early prevents corrupt data from polluting downstream risk and P&L.

Compatibility checks in CI/CD. Integrate schema registry compatibility checks into your build and deployment pipelines:

- When a developer proposes a schema change, automated checks verify that it respects the configured compatibility mode (backward, forward, full).
- Builds fail if the change would break existing data or consumers, forcing a more careful evolution plan.

Replay-based tests. Use recorded event streams and schemas together:

- When changing schemas for critical topics, run test consumers against archived logs from past trading days.
- Verify that the new code can read and process historical messages without errors.

This kind of test is particularly powerful because it anchors your schema evolution in real-world data, not just synthetic samples.

In an event-driven trading system, the messaging and streaming backbone is only as reliable as the data contracts it carries. Schema management and evolution give you the tools to:

- Make message structures explicit and validate them.
- Version and evolve schemas in controlled, compatible ways.
- Allow producers and consumers to change independently without breaking trading flows.

By treating schemas as shared, versioned contracts—supported by a registry, disciplined compatibility modes, and careful deployment choreography—you turn your backbone into a stable platform on which many teams can build. Strategies can innovate, risk models can change, and regulatory fields can be added, all while the underlying flow of events remains coherent, auditable, and safe.

In the next section, we will examine another cross-cutting concern: backpressure and flow control. Just as schema management keeps the *shape* of your data sane as the system evolves, backpressure keeps the *rate* of your data under control as markets surge and your trading plant is pushed to its limits.

2.6 Backpressure and Flow Control

By now we have a picture of the messaging backbone as a powerful, flexible fabric: distributed logs for durable, replayable streams; queues for ultra-low-latency task dispatch; and well-designed schemas that keep data interpretable as systems evolve. All of this rests on one implicit assumption: that components can keep up with the flow of events.

Real markets constantly test that assumption. Message rates spike at the open, around macro announcements, during auctions, and when venues misbehave. In those moments, the backbone can be pushed far beyond its comfortable operating point. If you have not planned for this, queues fill up, latencies explode, and processes crash at the worst possible time.

This section focuses on *backpressure and flow control*: how to prevent fast producers and market bursts from overwhelming slower consumers, and how to design your plant so it degrades gracefully rather than collapsing.

Load, Capacity, and the Need for Backpressure

Every component in your trading plant—feed handlers, strategy engines, order gateways, risk services, analytics workers—has a finite processing capacity:

- A maximum rate of messages per second it can handle.
- A maximum rate of CPU-heavy operations (pricing, risk calculations).
- Limits on memory, file descriptors, network bandwidth, and thread counts.

Your messaging backbone itself has capacities:

- Per-partition write and read throughput.
- Maximum queue or topic depth before disk or memory fills.
- Limits on pending in-flight messages and connection counts.

Backpressure is the mechanism by which slower components communicate these limits to faster ones. Without backpressure, the system simply lets messages accumulate. The visible symptoms are:

- Growing queue depths.
- Increasing end-to-end latency (messages spend more time waiting in buffers).
- Eventually, dropped messages or process failures when resources are exhausted.

With backpressure, you aim for something subtler:

- When downstream cannot keep up, upstream slows down, drops or defers low-priority work, or temporarily limits new inputs.
- Critical flows (orders, risk) are preserved; less important flows (some analytics, logging, derived metrics) are trimmed during stress.

The goal is not to prevent overload—that is impossible in an open system connected to markets—but to control how the system behaves when overload occurs.

Where Backpressure Arises in a Trading Plant

It helps to visualize a few common hotspots:

Market data ingestion. At the open or during a news shock, exchanges may emit bursts of ticks far above the normal rate. Feed handlers must parse and normalize these messages, then publish them to the log. Strategies, order books, and analytics subscribe and try to keep up.

If any of these consumers fall behind, per-partition lags grow. Without backpressure, producers keep pushing ticks into topics, and the backlog grows until somewhere a buffer or disk limit is hit.

Order gateways and risk services. When many strategies fire at once (for example, reacting to the same event), the gateway may see a flood of order requests. Each request may require database lookups, risk checks, and external confirmations.

If the gateway or the risk engine cannot process requests as fast as they arrive, internal queues fill up. Orders wait longer and longer to be processed. Cancellations, which are often higher priority, may be delayed behind a wall of less urgent messages.

Analytics and reporting. Downstream systems, such as P&L explainers or intraday risk reporting, consume large volumes of events and may perform expensive computations. They often are not in the latency-critical loop, but if they fail under load they can:

- Stop producing risk snapshots, confusing traders and risk managers.
- Overload shared resources (databases, caches), indirectly affecting hot-path components.

These examples illustrate two patterns:

- Hot-path components (gateways, risk) where failure or slowdown directly affects trading decisions.
- Peripheral but important components (analytics, reporting) where failure mainly affects visibility and control.

Backpressure mechanisms and policies must reflect this difference.

Basic Flow-Control Mechanisms

At a mechanical level, flow control in messaging systems is implemented using a small number of primitives. Understanding them helps you choose which to use where.

Bounded Queues and Buffers

The simplest mechanism is to bound queue sizes:

- Each in-memory buffer or queue has a maximum capacity.
- When the buffer is full, attempts to add more messages either block or fail.

This naturally applies both within applications (for example, the queue between a network receiver thread and a worker pool) and in messaging brokers.

Two behaviors are typical when a bounded queue is full:

- **Blocking producers.** The producer call that enqueues the message blocks until space becomes available. This pushes backpressure upstream: the producer slows down or stops until downstream drains.
- **Dropping or rejecting messages.** The enqueue call fails, or the queue drops messages according to some policy (for example, drop oldest, drop newest, or drop low-priority messages).

Blocking is appropriate when:

- The upstream entity can safely slow down (for example, a strategy that should not send more orders until the gateway has caught up).
- Messages are critical and should not be dropped silently.

Dropping or rejecting is appropriate when:

- The queue carries non-critical data (such as some analytics) and it is better to lose detail than to stall the system.
- You have explicit, higher-level logic for how to degrade when overload occurs (for example, disable a class of analytics).

Credit-Based Protocols

In credit-based flow control, consumers *explicitly* advertise how much work they can handle:

- Each consumer maintains a "credit" count with the producer or broker.
- When a consumer is ready for more messages, it increases its credit (for example, "I can handle 50 more").

- The producer or broker only sends messages up to the credit limit.

This model is common in broker protocols and in some messaging libraries. It provides fine-grained control:

- Consumers can dynamically adapt their credit based on their own load (CPU usage, queue depth, external service latency).
- Producers do not have to guess downstream capacity; they rely on explicit signals.

In a trading plant, this might be applied between:

- An internal bus and a risk engine: the risk service advertises how many outstanding checks it can handle.
- A strategy engine and its internal worker pools: workers signal readiness so that the engine never floods them.

Pull-Based Consumption

Distributed logs naturally support a pull-based model:

- Consumers fetch batches of messages starting from their current offsets.
- If a consumer reads more slowly, it simply advances its offset more slowly.

In a pure pull model, the consumer completely controls its pace. However, because the log retains data independent of consumption, slow consumers do not propagate backpressure to producers by default. Producers can continue to append as fast as they like until the log's retention or storage limits are reached.

To turn pull-based consumption into effective backpressure, you combine it with:

- **Operational limits** on acceptable consumer lag (for example, risk consumers must not be more than N seconds behind).

- **Higher-level controls** that throttle producers or shed work when lag exceeds thresholds.

For example, if a risk engine's consumer group falls more than X seconds behind on the orders or fills topic, the system might automatically:

- Restrict certain types of trading strategies.
- Increase margins or reduce exposure limits.
- Alert operators to investigate.

Failure Modes Without Proper Flow Control

It is helpful to recognize common anti-patterns that arise in the absence of deliberate backpressure design.

Head-of-line blocking. Suppose you have a single queue or partition feeding several types of work, and one consumer is slow. If messages must be processed in order, a single long-running task can block all following tasks, even those that would be quick to handle.

In trading, this might look like:

- A risk engine processing a particularly large account snapshot while other small accounts' checks are queued behind it.
- A strategy handling a rare but expensive path that blocks ingestion of fast, simple signals.

Mitigations include:

- Separating flows into multiple queues or topics (for example, by account size or by task type).
- Using worker pools and task timeouts to prevent one slow item from blocking others.

Retry storms. When a downstream service slows or fails, upstream components may start retrying requests. If this is uncontrolled, retries can:

- Magnify load on the already-struggling service.
- Exhaust queues and connections.

For example, if a database used for risk reference data is slow, risk services may time out and retry, causing even more concurrent queries, making the problem worse.

Mitigations include:

- Exponential backoff and jitter in retries.
- Circuit breakers: temporarily stop sending new requests when a service is judged unhealthy.
- Graceful degradation: operate in a conservative mode with cached data instead of hammering the failing service.

Unbounded buffering. Without explicit limits, engineers may accidentally create unbounded in-memory queues: lists, mailboxes, or buffers that simply grow when overwhelmed.

Under normal load this seems fine. Under stress it leads to:

- Increased garbage collection and page faults.
- Eventual out-of-memory kills, often at unpredictable points.

The remedy is simple policy: *no unbounded queues* in hot-path components. Every buffer must have a maximum size and a defined behavior when the limit is hit.

Capacity-Aware Design: Measuring and Publishing Throughput

Good backpressure mechanics are useless if you do not know the capacities of your components. Capacity-aware design starts with measurement:

- For each service, measure input rate, processing rate, and average and tail latencies per endpoint or queue.
- Monitor queue depths, consumer lags, and memory usage.
- Track per-partition rates and lag in the distributed log.

These measurements should be:

- **Published** as metrics into your monitoring stack.
- **Alerted** on sensible thresholds (for example, risk processing lag exceeds N seconds).
- **Accessible** to other components that may need to react (for example, a strategy that adapts its behavior when the risk engine is under strain).

Over time, you can build a capacity profile for each service: "Under normal conditions, this risk worker can process 1,000 checks per second with sub-millisecond latency; under stress it begins to slow above 1,500 per second." These profiles inform:

- How many instances you deploy under different market regimes.
- Which backpressure thresholds you configure.
- How you prioritize different flows when the system is near its limits.

Graceful Degradation: Preserving the Core, Shedding the Fringe

When overload happens, you rarely want an all-or-nothing reaction. Instead, you design graceful degradation: the system intentionally reduces functionality or fidelity in lower-value areas to protect higher-value functions.

In a trading plant, prioritization is usually:

- Risk, orders, and gateway stability.
- Core strategy logic and P&L.
- Monitoring, alerts, and logging.
- Non-critical analytics and research feeds.

Examples of graceful degradation policies include:

- **Dropping low-value analytics.** If downstream analytics queues grow beyond a threshold, stop enqueuing new analytics tasks until the backlog drains.
- **Sampling market data.** For some non-critical consumers, process every Nth tick during bursts instead of every tick, while continuing to feed full data to strategies and risk.
- **Simplifying models.** Switch risk or pricing services to cheaper approximations under load, freeing CPU for order checks and essential calculations.
- **Tightening limits.** Automatically reduce position limits or leverage when certain system health metrics deteriorate, reducing the volume of new orders.

These policies should be:

- Explicitly designed and reviewed, not invented ad hoc during crises.
- Implemented in code, with clear triggers (metrics and thresholds).
- Tested in dry runs and simulations so you know how the plant behaves under stress.

Backpressure Across Logs and Queues

Backpressure works slightly differently in the two main backbone abstractions.

On message queues. Queues are naturally finite: you can set maximum lengths, timeouts, and unacked message limits. When these limits are hit, the system can:

- Block producers.
- Reject or drop new messages.
- Move problematic messages to dead-letter queues.

For the hot order path:

- Internal queues between the strategy and gateway should block the strategy when full, prompting it to slow or pause order generation.
- Queues feeding non-critical services (for example, certain reports) might prefer dropping or sampling rather than blocking.

On distributed logs. Logs do not naturally block producers based on consumer state; they are designed so producers can keep writing independently of consumption. Backpressure must therefore be imposed at a higher level:

- Set quotas or rate limits on producer write rates per topic or per client.
- Monitor consumer lag and implement policies when lag exceeds limits.
- Scale consumers horizontally when possible to catch up.

Moreover, within a log partition, slow consumers do *not* stop the partition from advancing; they simply fall further behind. This is acceptable for some workloads (for example, back-office analytics) but not for others (for example, real-time risk).

An effective strategy is to:

- Classify consumers by criticality.
- For critical consumers, treat large lag as a system-level incident: take corrective action such as throttling order intake or shedding sources of load.
- For non-critical consumers, allow them to lag or even skip ahead (for example, seek to more recent offsets) when they cannot keep up.

Testing Under Burst Loads

You cannot design robust backpressure mechanisms purely on paper. You must test how the system behaves under synthetic bursts.

Practical steps:

- Build tools that can generate realistic market data bursts and order streams, based on recorded days with high volatility.
- Run these against staging environments that mirror production capacities as closely as possible.
- Observe which components saturate first, where queue depth grows fastest, how latency curves behave, and whether degradation policies trigger as expected.

Focus on:

- End-to-end latency from market data tick to order decision and submission.
- Risk engine lag relative to the latest fills and positions.
- Behavior of monitoring and alert systems under their own increased load.

These tests often reveal unexpected bottlenecks: an overlooked shared database, an unbounded internal queue, or a logging subsystem that blocks when disks are slow. Adjusting the architecture and backpressure policies based on these findings is a key part of hardening a trading plant.

Visualizing the Effect of Backpressure

To make the impact of effective backpressure concrete, it helps to visualize how queue depth and latency behave during a market burst, comparing a naive system to one with well-designed flow control.

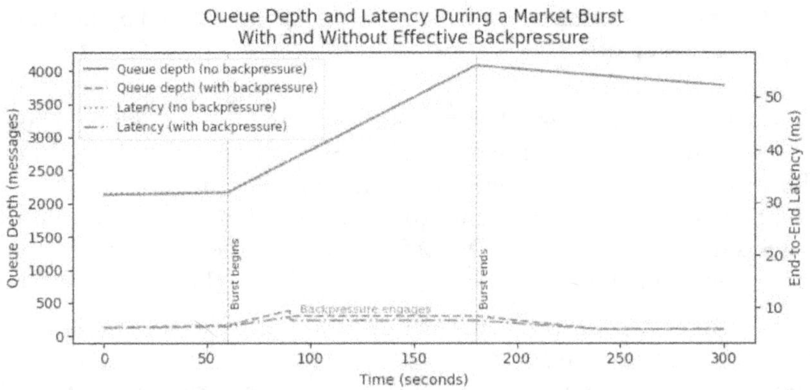

In this stylized chart, the system with no backpressure sees queue depth and latency continue to climb throughout the burst, with only partial recovery. The system with backpressure allows some buildup, then caps queue depth and latency by slowing producers or shedding work, and recovers more cleanly after the burst ends.

Bringing It Together

Backpressure and flow control are not isolated concerns; they connect back to all the topics covered in this chapter:

- Pub/sub and queueing patterns determine where faster producers meet slower consumers and how many copies of each message exist.
- Distributed log architecture dictates how consumer lag and retention interact, and where backpressure must be imposed outside the log.

- Partitioning and keys influence where hot spots and head-of-line blocking can arise.
- Queue semantics (ack/nack, visibility timeouts) shape how retries behave under overload.
- Schema management ensures that the data flowing under stress is at least structurally valid, so overload is not caused by cascades of parse errors.

Designing for capacity and backpressure is ultimately about being honest with yourself: no component, and no plant, has infinite throughput. Markets will find your weakest link. If you have thought about how each part of the system reacts when it is pushed beyond its limit—how it slows down, what it drops, what it preserves—then those inevitable stress events will be survivable and diagnosable, rather than chaotic.

In the broader context of event-driven trading, backpressure is what turns a fast system into a *reliably fast* system: one that remains predictable and safe even when the market is doing its best to knock it off balance.

Chapter 3

State, Consistency, and Stream Processing

When markets move in microseconds, your system's notion of "truth" is always a little bit out of date. The art of trading infrastructure is deciding exactly how stale you can tolerate that truth to be-and where you absolutely cannot compromise. In this chapter we move from theory to practice: we'll see how consistency models, transactions, sagas, stream processors, and state stores come together to maintain an authoritative book of record, power real-time risk checks, and keep user-facing views fast and correct enough for the edge you're trading for.

3.1 Consistency Models in Trading Systems

Up to this point we have treated the trading platform as an event-driven system: orders, fills, margin calls, and risk updates flow through a network of services. Those services keep state: order books, portfolios, limits, and many others. In this section we focus *how* that state is kept consistent in the face of concurrency, failures, and distribution across machines and regions.

Consistency is not a single on/off property. Instead, there is a spectrum of models that say what different readers are allowed to see, and in what order. A trading system typically uses several of these models at once: some components must behave as if all updates happen one-by-one in a global order, while others can tolerate slightly stale or reordered data.

Our goal is twofold:

- Build an intuitive vocabulary for consistency models.
- Map those models to concrete trading components, so you can decide what guarantees each component really needs.

Why Consistency Matters in Trading

Before naming models, it is useful to see the problem they solve.

Imagine three traders interacting with your system around the same time:

- Trader A submits a buy order.
- Trader B submits a sell order that matches Trader A.
- Trader C monitors positions and P&L on a dashboard.

These interactions touch many services:

- The *matching engine* updates the central order book and generates a trade.
- The *positions service* updates positions for both accounts.
- The *risk engine* recomputes exposures.
- The *reporting system* and *dashboard* display updated positions and P&L.

You cannot afford to have the matching engine and risk engine disagree about whether a trade exists. That would be a correctness and regulatory problem. On the other hand, it is acceptable if Trader C's dashboard lags by a second and briefly shows an outdated P&L, as long as it eventually catches up and never reports impossible combinations (for example, a negative quantity with a positive average price that could not have occurred).

This asymmetry is at the heart of consistency design in trading:

- Some invariants are *hard*: no double-spend, no negative cash beyond margin, no broken ordering in the central limit order book.
- Some views are *soft*: dashboards, analytics, and derived aggregates that can be slightly stale.

We will use this intuition as we walk through the main consistency models.

From ACID to BASE Thinking

A traditional relational database emphasizes ACID properties:

- **Atomicity** Each transaction is all or nothing.
- **Consistency** Each committed transaction preserves declared constraints.
- **Isolation** Concurrent transactions behave as if executed sequentially.
- **Durability** Once committed, data survives crashes.

In a single-node database, a strongly isolated transaction gives you a simple illusion: even though many clients are active, it looks as if one transaction runs after another in some global order.

As systems became distributed and high-volume, practitioners introduced a contrasting mindset called BASE:

- **Basically Available** The system aims to stay up even under partition or load.
- **Soft state** Data observed by one client may temporarily be out of date.
- **Eventual consistency** If no new updates occur, all replicas will converge.

Neither ACID nor BASE is "right" in general. In a trading platform, some subsystems lean ACID (for example, matching, ledger updates), while others lean BASE (dashboards, historical analytics). The art is to be explicit about where each style belongs.

Strong Consistency: Linearizability

The strongest common model is *linearizability*. Informally:

> Each operation appears to take effect at a single point in time, and all clients see the same global order of operations that respects real-time ordering.

Two aspects matter:

- **Single point in time:** Even if an update takes 5 milliseconds to execute, the system behaves as though it happened instantaneously at some moment in that interval.
- **Real-time respect:** If client X receives confirmation of its update before client Y submits a read, then Y's read will see X's update.

From the client's perspective, a linearizable system looks like a single, correct copy of the data.

In trading, linearizability is appropriate when:

- You maintain a *central limit order book* where the relative order of orders and trades must be unambiguous.

- You maintain an *account ledger* that cannot allow double-spending of cash or collateral.
- You commit *risk debits* (for example, margin reservations) that must not be applied twice or lost.

A typical example is a matching engine: it processes orders one-by-one in a strict sequence. Every participant, regulator, and post-trade system must agree on that sequence. The simplest way to achieve this is to funnel all matching for an instrument (or shard of instruments) through a single leader process that serializes operations.

The cost of linearizability is that it often requires a single leader or a consensus protocol (such as a replicated log with a leader) that limits scalability or adds latency, especially in geo-distributed setups. You do not want to pay that cost everywhere.

Sequential and Causal Consistency

Between "as strong as possible" and "eventual" there are intermediate models that are often sufficient for trading components that are important, but not as central as the order book.

Sequential Consistency

Sequential consistency relaxes real-time ordering but keeps a single global order:

> All operations appear in some single order that is consistent with the program order of each client, but this order does not necessarily reflect real-time.

Concretely, if trader X submits two updates A then B, every observer agrees that A happened before B. However, another trader's operation C might be placed between A and B in the global order, even if in real time C happened a bit later.

Many replicated databases and logs target something close to sequential consistency within a partition or a topic. For instance, if your positions service appends events to a partitioned log keyed by account ID, all events for that account appear in a single order. That order may not reflect the exact wall-clock times, but it is consistent across consumers.

For trading, this level of consistency is usually enough for:

- *Per-account position streams:* All updates to a single account's positions must be ordered consistently for correctness and reconciliation.
- *Per-instrument trade feeds:* All trades for one symbol must be ordered, but small deviations from real-time ordering are acceptable as long as the sequence is stable.

Causal Consistency

Causal consistency focuses on cause-and-effect relationships:

> If operation B may have been caused by operation A (because one client saw A and then issued B), then everyone must see A before B. Operations that are unrelated (concurrent) may be seen in different orders on different replicas.

In a trading context, causal consistency is helpful when:

- A risk engine issues a margin call because it saw a large price move.
- A follow-up action (for example, an automatic order to reduce exposure) is issued as a direct consequence of the margin call.

We want all observers to see the price move, then the margin call, then the reduction order, in that order. It is less important how those events interleave with unrelated actions in other instruments or accounts.

Causal consistency can be implemented cheaply using mechanisms such as session tokens, vector clocks, or simple dependency tracking in event flows.

Eventual Consistency and Session Guarantees

At the weak end of the spectrum lies *eventual consistency*:

> If no new updates are made, all replicas eventually converge to the same state.

Eventual consistency says little about what a client might see *during* convergence. Reads can be stale or even temporarily out-of-order, as long as the system stabilizes over time.

By itself, this is too vague for many trading components. To make eventual consistency usable, practitioners add *session guarantees* that constrain anomalies seen by a single user or process. The most common session guarantees are:

- **Read-your-writes:** After a client writes data, future reads in the same session will see that write.
- **Monotonic reads:** Once a client has seen a certain version of data, it will not see an older version later.
- **Monotonic writes:** Writes from a single client are applied in the order issued.
- **Writes-follow-reads:** Writes are based on at least as recent a state as was previously read.

For trading, eventual consistency with session guarantees is usually enough for:

- *Trader dashboards:* It is acceptable if a P&L chart lags by a few seconds, but you want monotonic reads so it does not jump backwards in time.
- *Historical analytics and reports:* Overnight risk reports or regulatory exports may be built from asynchronously replicated data, as long as they are internally consistent when finalized.

- *Cross-region portfolio views:* A trader in Region A and a risk officer in Region B may briefly see slightly different portfolio snapshots, as long as hard invariants (total exposure, margin breaches) are still enforced by more strongly consistent subsystems.

Mapping Models to Trading Components

We can now map these consistency models to a layered trading architecture. Think in terms of concentric circles:

- At the *core* are components where monetary or regulatory correctness is directly at stake.
- Around that core are *control and risk* components that must be accurate, but can sometimes tolerate narrowly scoped relaxations.
- On the outside are *views and analytics* where latency and scalability matter more than perfect freshness.

Core: Matching and Ledger

These components almost always require strong or linearizable behavior:

- **Order book / matching engine** Must serialize operations for each instrument (or shard). The matching engine is the authoritative source of truth for which orders are resting, which trades have occurred, and in what order.
- **Cash and collateral ledger** Must prevent double-spending and maintain invariant relationships such as cash balance plus collateral value minus margin equals equity. Concurrent debits and credits must be applied atomically and in a well-defined order.

From the system-design perspective, this often leads to:

- Single-leader services per symbol or account range.
- Replicated logs with strong consistency (for example, consensus protocols) for audit and replay.

Middle: Positions, Risk, and Limits

The next layer includes components that track derived state, usually fed by trades and market data:

- **Positions service** Computes net quantities, average prices, and realized/unrealized P&L per account and instrument.
- **Risk engine** Manages exposures, limits, and margin requirements.
- **Limits and controls** Enforce per-account and per-strategy constraints (for example, maximum order size, aggregate notional limits).

These components typically require:

- **At least** sequential consistency for each account or risk key: all updates for the same key are applied in a consistent order.
- Often causal relationships between price moves, exposure changes, and control actions.

However, they can often tolerate:

- Slight asynchrony between different accounts or between risk and positions, as long as hard checks (for example, block orders above a certain theoretical exposure) are enforced at the point of order acceptance.
- Different consistency choices per use case: for pre-trade risk, stronger; for overnight VaR analytics, more relaxed.

Outer Layer: Reporting, Dashboards, and Analytics

Finally, there are components where eventual consistency is the norm:

- **Trader and risk dashboards** Real-time-ish panels showing positions, P&L, and limits.
- **Analytics pipelines** Intraday and historical aggregations, factor analyses, latency statistics.
- **Regulatory and client reporting** Often built on end-of-day snapshots or replicated data warehouses.

These systems tend to be fed by event streams or replicated databases. They usually guarantee:

- Monotonic reads and read-your-writes for interactive users.
- Eventual convergence with the authoritative sources.

They intentionally avoid the strong coordination overhead of the core and middle layers so they can scale horizontally and withstand partial outages.

Layered Architecture Diagram

To make this mapping concrete, consider the layered architecture diagram. The diagram arranges trading components from bottom (core transactional layer) to top (views and analytics), annotated with the typical consistency model required at each layer.

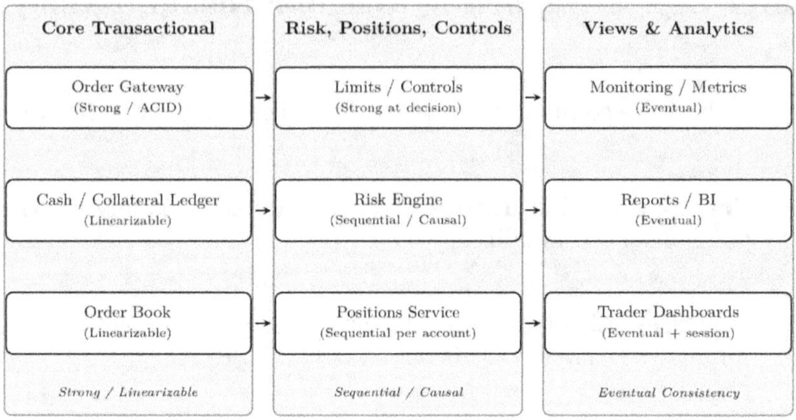

This diagram is not a fixed recipe; rather, it is a starting point for design discussions. For each component in your own architecture, you should ask:

- What invariants must never be violated, even transiently?
- Who consumes this data, and what anomalies can they tolerate?
- What latency and availability constraints do they have?

Once you answer these questions, you can place each component in the appropriate layer and choose the fitting consistency model.

Design Heuristics for Choosing Consistency

We conclude this section with concrete heuristics you can use when designing or reviewing a trading system.

Identify Hard Invariants First

Start from invariants whose violation would directly cause:

- Financial loss (for you or a client).

- Regulatory or contractual breaches.
- Irreconcilable data (for example, a ledger that cannot be made to balance).

Examples include:

- No client's net position in an instrument can exceed a hard limit without explicit authorization.
- Total debits and credits in a ledger must match across accounts and currencies.
- A trade reported to a venue must correspond to exactly one match in your order book.

For operations that maintain these invariants, prefer linearizable or strongly consistent designs, even if they cost more in latency or complexity.

Separate Authority from Views

Be explicit about which component is *authoritative* for a particular piece of data. For example:

- The order book is authoritative for live orders and trades.
- The ledger is authoritative for cash balances.
- The positions service is authoritative for intraday positions.

All other components should be treated as *views* derived from those authorities. Views can use weaker consistency, as long as discrepancies are bounded and understood. This mindset prevents you from accidentally building two "authoritative" but inconsistent sources.

Use Strong Consistency at Decision Boundaries

Many trading decisions happen at clear boundaries:

- Accepting or rejecting an order.
- Triggering a margin call or position liquidation.
- Sending a fill or confirmation to a client.

At these moments, a service must rely on state that is accurate enough to make a safe decision. Common patterns include:

- Using a strongly consistent local store for just the subset of data needed to evaluate a limit (for example, current exposure for that account).
- Combining weaker upstream feeds with conservative buffers or safety margins, so even slightly stale data does not lead to breaches.

In practice, you may use sequential or causal consistency internally, but wrap the final decision in a strongly consistent transaction.

Exploit Key-Based Isolation

Not all data needs global ordering. In many trading systems, critical invariants are scoped by key:

- Per account.
- Per instrument or symbol.
- Per strategy or risk bucket.

If you can express invariants in terms of such keys, you can often:

- Use strong or sequential consistency *within* a key (for example, all updates to one account's cash and positions).

- Allow weaker guarantees *across* keys (for example, between different accounts or instruments).

This leads naturally to partitioned logs and sharded services, where each shard provides strong semantics locally but does not coordinate with others on every operation.

Document Consistency in Service Contracts

Finally, do not leave consistency implicit. For every service interface, document:

- What consistency level it guarantees for reads and writes.
- How it behaves under failures and network partitions (for example, does it prefer availability with stale reads, or unavailability over inconsistency?).
- Any session guarantees it supports.

These details should be part of your service-level agreements (SLAs) and design documents. When architects and developers share a precise vocabulary, it becomes much easier to reason about cross-service workflows, especially as we move into the next sections on transactions, sagas, and stream processing.

Looking Ahead

In this section we built a conceptual map from abstract consistency models to concrete trading components. We saw that a realistic trading system is a patchwork of models: linearizable at the core, sequential and causal in the risk and positions layer, and eventual with session guarantees on the surface.

The next sections will dive into how to implement cross-service workflows that respect these consistency choices. We will see how transactions, sagas, and patterns like the outbox help you coordinate multistep changes, and how stateful stream processors maintain consistent derived state in real time.

3.2 Transactions, Sagas, and the Outbox Pattern

In the previous section we treated consistency as primarily a *read-side* concern: when different components look at state, what are they allowed to see, and in what order? We now turn to the *write side*.

Most interesting trading operations are not a single write. Placing an order may involve:

- Recording the order itself.
- Reserving margin.
- Updating intraday risk.
- Notifying a gateway to send the order to a venue.
- Emitting events for positions and downstream analytics.

These steps often span multiple services, databases, and message brokers. The central challenge is:

> How do we coordinate a multi-step operation across services so that the overall outcome is correct, even if any individual step or network hop fails?

We will start with classic distributed transactions, see why they are problematic in high-throughput trading, then introduce sagas as a more scalable alternative. Finally, we will show how the outbox pattern solves a specific but pervasive problem: dual writes when publishing events.

Single-Node Transactions: The Easy Case

On a single database server, life is simple. If all the state you care about lives in the same database, you can often rely on a single transaction:

- Begin transaction.

- Perform multiple inserts and updates.
- Commit or roll back.

The database provides atomicity and isolation. Either all changes become visible together, or none do. From the viewpoint of the trading workflow, you can think of "place order and reserve margin" as one indivisible step.

In early or small-scale systems, you may indeed implement the entire order lifecycle inside one monolithic database. But as volume grows and you decompose the system into services, this approach becomes fragile:

- The database becomes a performance and scaling bottleneck.
- Different parts of the system may require different technologies (for example, a document store for market data, a time-series store for metrics, a relational store for ledgers).
- Regulatory or organizational boundaries may force some data to be kept separate.

Once a workflow spans multiple databases or services, a single-node transaction is no longer enough.

Distributed Transactions and Two-Phase Commit

The natural extension is a *distributed transaction*. The idea is simple: coordinate a single logical transaction across multiple resources (databases, queues, etc.) so that either all commit or all roll back.

The classic algorithm for this is two-phase commit (2PC). Conceptually, 2PC involves:

- A *transaction coordinator* that manages the protocol.
- A set of *participants* (for example, the Orders database, the Accounts database, and a message queue).

The protocol runs in two phases:

- **Prepare phase**: The coordinator asks each participant, "Can you commit this transaction?" Each participant does all necessary checks and writes its changes to a log, but does not yet make them visible. Then it replies "yes" or "no."
- **Commit phase**: If all replies are "yes," the coordinator sends "commit" to everyone, and each participant makes its local changes durable and visible. If any reply is "no," the coordinator sends "roll back," and all participants undo their tentative changes.

From the application's point of view, 2PC recreates the illusion of a single transaction that spans all resources.

Why 2PC Struggles in Trading Systems

In practice, 2PC is rarely used at the core of modern trading architectures. There are several reasons:

Latency and Throughput

The prepare and commit phases add network round-trips and force all participants to coordinate on every transaction. When you need to process tens or hundreds of thousands of orders per second, this coordination overhead is costly.

Liveness Risk

If the coordinator fails at certain points, participants can remain in an uncertain state ("I have prepared but do not know whether to commit or roll back"). Recovering from such situations requires careful logging and recovery logic. In a time-sensitive trading environment, such uncertainty is dangerous.

Coupling and Evolution

2PC creates tight coupling between services. To join a distributed transaction, each service must implement the transaction protocol. Introducing a new service into a 2PC-protected workflow involves coordination across teams and technologies. This slows evolution and experimentation.

For these reasons, most high-throughput trading systems are built with *local transactions* only: each service uses its own database transaction, but there is no global, cross-service transaction. Instead, we coordinate multi-step workflows with messaging and compensating actions. This is the essence of sagas.

Sagas: Coordinating Local Transactions with Compensations

A *saga* is a sequence of local transactions, each in its own service, linked together by events. If one step fails, the saga runs compensating actions to undo or counterbalance earlier steps.

Represented abstractly, a saga might look like:

$$T_1, T_2, T_3, \ldots, T_n$$

where each T_i is a local transaction in some service. For each T_i there is a compensating transaction C_i that undoes its effect as best as possible.

There are two common styles:

- **Choreography**: Each service listens for relevant events and decides what to do next. There is no central orchestrator.
- **Orchestration**: A dedicated saga orchestrator service tells each participant what to do and listens for replies.

In trading, both styles appear, but orchestration often provides clearer control for critical flows like order placement.

A Concrete Saga: Order Placement

Let us work through an example of placing a client order with pre-trade risk checks. Suppose we have these services:

- **Order Service** (owns orders).
- **Risk Service** (manages exposure and limits).

- **Accounts Service** (manages cash and collateral).
- **Broker Gateway** (sends orders to external venues).

We want the overall behavior to be:

> Either the order is accepted with margin reserved and risk updated, or it is clearly rejected with no partial side effects.

However, we will not use a global transaction. Instead, each step is a local transaction plus events.

One possible orchestration could be:

- **Order Service:**
  - Begin local transaction.
  - Create an order in state "PendingRisk."
  - Commit.
  - Publish an *OrderCreated* event.
- **Risk Service:** On *OrderCreated*:
  - Begin local transaction.
  - Check current exposure and limits for the account and instrument.
  - If limits are exceeded, record a *RiskRejected* decision.
  - If within limits, record a *RiskApproved* decision and update exposure, possibly reserving headroom.
  - Commit.
  - Publish *RiskApproved* or *RiskRejected* event.
- **Accounts Service:** On *RiskApproved*:
  - Begin local transaction.
  - Reserve necessary margin in the account.
  - Commit.
  - Publish *MarginReserved* event.

- **Order Service:** On *RiskRejected* or *MarginReserved*:
  - Begin local transaction.
  - If *RiskRejected*, set order state to "Rejected."
  - If *MarginReserved*, set order state to "ReadyToSend."
  - Commit.
  - For "ReadyToSend," publish *OrderReady* event.
- **Broker Gateway:** On *OrderReady*:
  - Begin local transaction.
  - Enqueue the order for the external venue or send it immediately.
  - Commit.
  - Publish *OrderSent* or error events as appropriate.

Each step is protected by a local database transaction. The saga logic is encoded in the event flows and the state transitions.

Compensating Actions

What if something fails in the middle? Suppose the Accounts Service successfully reserves margin, but the order fails to send to the exchange due to a routing error. We do not want the account to be permanently over-reserved. A compensating action is needed.

In this saga, compensations may include:

- **Unreserve margin** if the order ultimately fails or is canceled before sending.
- **Release risk exposure** if the margin cannot be reserved or the order is rejected later.
- **Cancel pending order** if down-stream steps fail irrecoverably.

These compensations are triggered by events that indicate that the normal path cannot complete. They are not "true rollbacks" in the database sense, because external effects may already have happened (for example, a client saw an order in "PendingRisk"). Instead, they bring the overall business state back to a consistent and acceptable configuration.

Comparing Sagas to Distributed Transactions

It is helpful to summarize the trade-offs:

Atomicity

- 2PC aims for all-or-nothing atomicity across services.
- Sagas provide *business-level* atomicity through compensations. Some intermediate states are visible, but compensations converge them to a valid outcome.

Isolation

- 2PC, combined with strong isolation levels, can make concurrent workflows appear fully serialized.
- Sagas usually allow more interleaving; they rely on per-service isolation and careful design of invariants.

Availability and Scalability

- 2PC coordinates all participants on every transaction, which can harm throughput and availability.
- Sagas let each service commit independently and then coordinate via messages, which scales more easily and degrades more gracefully.

In a high-throughput trading platform, these scalability and availability advantages usually outweigh the convenience of global transactions, provided the saga logic is carefully designed.

Visualizing an Order Saga

To tie the ideas together, Figure shows a simplified sequence diagram of an order-placement saga. We focus on five lifelines:

- Order Service.
- Risk Service.
- Accounts Service.
- Outbox Relay (responsible for reliable event publication, discussed shortly).
- Broker Gateway.

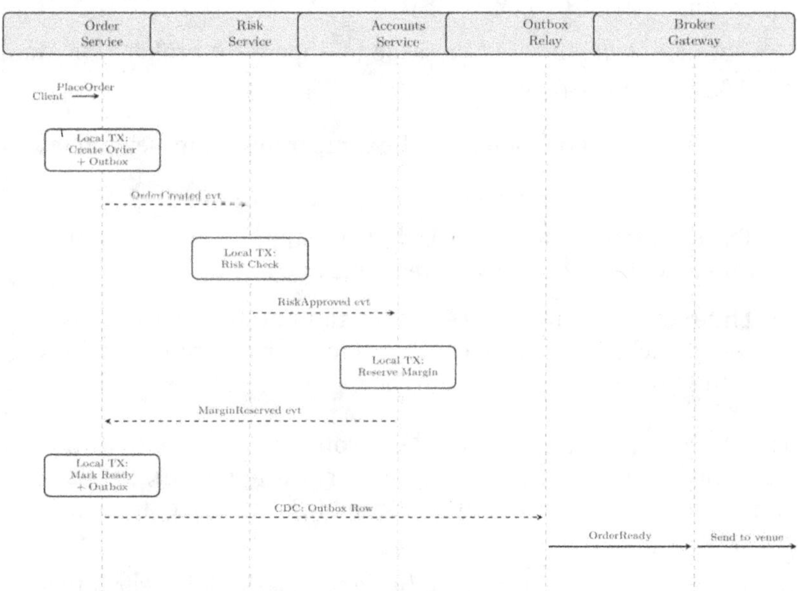

The diagram emphasizes three kinds of interactions:

- Solid arrows for direct messages or commands.

- Dashed arrows for saga events flowing between services.
- Local transaction boxes representing atomic updates within one service.

Next we will focus on a subtle but critical detail: how the Order Service safely combines updating its own state with publishing events such as *OrderCreated* and *OrderReady*. This is where the outbox pattern comes in.

The Dual-Write Problem

Suppose the Order Service, when it receives *PlaceOrder*, does the following:

- Write a new order row to its database.
- Send an *OrderCreated* message to a message broker (for example, Kafka or a queue).

If these two actions are not part of the same transaction, several failure modes appear:

- The database write succeeds, but sending the message fails. The order exists, but no downstream service is aware of it.
- The message send succeeds, but the database write fails or is rolled back. Downstream services react to an order that does not actually exist.

This is the classic *dual-write* problem: you are writing to two different systems (a database and a message broker) without transactional coordination. In a distributed trading system, this is unacceptable for core workflows.

One way to avoid dual writes is to bring the message broker into a distributed transaction (for example, 2PC across the database and the broker). As discussed earlier, this is often too heavy-weight. Instead, we can structure the system so that each service only needs a single local transaction, while events are reliably derived from that transaction. This is the motivation behind the outbox pattern.

The Outbox Pattern

The *outbox pattern* is based on a simple idea:

> Instead of writing both business data and messages to two different systems, write them to the same database in one local transaction. Then have a separate process reliably read from this "outbox" table and publish the messages to the broker.

Concretely, the Order Service maintains an *outbox table* in its own database. When it commits a business change that must be communicated, it also inserts a row into the outbox table within the same transaction. This guarantees:

- If the business change is committed, the outbox row exists.
- If the business change is rolled back, the outbox row does not exist.

A separate *Outbox Relay* process (which may run inside the same service or separately) periodically scans the outbox table for new rows, publishes corresponding messages to the broker, and marks the rows as sent.

Returning to our order placement example, when the Order Service:

- Creates an order in state "PendingRisk," it also writes an outbox row encoding an *OrderCreated* event.
- Later updates the order state to "ReadyToSend," it also writes an outbox row for an *OrderReady* event.

If the service crashes after committing the database transaction but before sending the message, the outbox row still exists. The Outbox Relay, when it resumes, can detect and send it. If the transaction is rolled back, there is no outbox row and hence no message.

Idempotent Outbox Processing

Outbox processing must be safe under retries and crashes. The Outbox Relay might:

- Send a message, then crash before marking the outbox row as "sent."
- Restart and resend the same message.

To handle this, the consumers of these messages (for example, the Risk Service, Accounts Service, or Broker Gateway) must be *idempotent*: processing the same message twice should have the same effect as processing it once.

Common techniques include:

- Assigning a unique identifier to each message and keeping a small "seen IDs" store to ignore duplicates.
- Designing state updates as upserts or conditional writes that do not double-apply the same logical change.

Idempotency is a broader topic that we revisit later in the chapter, but it is worth noting here because outbox processing relies on it.

Ordering Guarantees

In many trading workflows, the order of events matters. For example, consumers must not see *OrderReady* before *OrderCreated*. The outbox pattern must respect these relationships.

To preserve order, typical choices include:

- Using a monotonically increasing sequence or timestamp within the outbox table and processing rows in that order.
- Partitioning the outbox by key (for example, order ID or account ID) so that all events for a given key are processed in sequence.

- Using the broker's partitioning and ordering features (for example, key-based partitions in a distributed log) to ensure that consumers see messages in the correct order per key.

Importantly, you rarely need a single global order of all events across all keys. As discussed in the consistency section, per-key sequential consistency is usually enough.

Putting It All Together in a Trading Architecture

At this point we can sketch how these pieces fit into a typical event-driven trading system:

- Each domain service (Orders, Risk, Accounts, etc.) maintains its own database and uses local ACID transactions to update its state.
- When a state change needs to be communicated, the service writes an outbox row in the same transaction.
- Outbox Relays in each service publish events from the outbox to shared message streams or logs.
- Sagas are implemented by having services react to these events, perform local transactions, and emit new events as needed, including compensations on failure.
- Consumers of events are designed to be idempotent and to rely on per-key ordering guarantees provided by the broker and by the outbox processing order.

This architecture avoids global distributed transactions, yet still offers a disciplined way to reason about multi-step workflows. Each service has a clear consistency story:

- *Inside* the service: strong, transactional consistency over its own data and outbox.
- *Between* services: at-least-once event delivery with idempotent handlers and carefully designed sagas.

Design Guidelines for Sagas and Outboxes in Trading

To close the section, here are practical guidelines informed by real trading systems:

Keep Saga Steps Simple and Local

Each saga step should:

- Touch as few tables as possible within one service.
- Make a clear, meaningful state transition (for example, "PendingRisk" to "ReadyToSend").
- Emit exactly one outbox record per logical event type.

Complex, multi-purpose steps are harder to reason about, test, and compensate.

Design Compensations Up Front

Do not treat compensations as an afterthought. For each saga step, ask:

- If this step succeeds but a later step fails permanently, what must we do to restore a valid business state?
- Are there any side effects that cannot truly be undone (for example, an order already sent to an external venue)? If so, how do we manage and communicate that?

In trading, some effects cannot be reversed, only offset (for example, closing a position by sending an opposite trade). That offsetting logic should be part of the design.

Make Outbox Schemas Explicit and Versioned

Outbox records encode events that other teams and systems will consume. Treat the outbox schema as an explicit, versioned API:

- Use clear, stable field names and types.
- Include version markers to allow schema evolution.
- Provide documentation of each event type's meaning and guarantees (for example, ordering keys, idempotency behavior).

Monitor the Outbox and Saga Health

A neglected outbox or failing saga can silently create backlogs or inconsistent states. Important metrics include:

- Number and age of unsent outbox records.
- Saga instances "stuck" in intermediate states beyond an expected time window.
- Rate of compensations, which can signal upstream problems.

Operational visibility is as important as the design itself.

Align with Consistency Requirements

Finally, tie your saga and outbox designs back to the consistency models from the previous section:

- For core components that require strong consistency (for example, the ledger), keep sagas short and prefer local transactions that fully enforce invariants.
- For components that can tolerate eventual consistency (for example, dashboards), you can use longer sagas and more relaxed outbox processing, focusing on throughput.

- Use per-key ordering and idempotent handlers to approximate "effectively exactly once" behavior where it matters, even though the underlying infrastructure only offers at-least-once delivery.

With these patterns—local transactions, sagas, and the outbox—you now have a toolkit for coordinating complex trading workflows in a distributed, event-driven system. In the next section we will examine how to represent state itself as a stream of events through event sourcing and CQRS, building on the reliable processing foundation established here.

3.3 Event Sourcing and CQRS

In the previous sections we looked at two complementary questions:

- *What* consistency guarantees different trading components need.
- *How* to coordinate multi-step workflows across services using local transactions, sagas, and the outbox pattern.

We now turn to a deeper question about state itself:

> What should count as the *canonical* record of truth in an event-driven trading system: the current rows in databases, or the *events* that led to them?

Event sourcing answers this by putting events at the center. Instead of thinking "the position for account X is a row with quantity 10," we think "the position for account X is the result of folding over all the trades and adjustments that ever happened for that account." CQRS (Command Query Responsibility Segregation) then builds on this idea to separate how we *change* state from how we *query* it.

This section explains both ideas and shows how they can be used to build specialized read models in a trading platform: risk views, P&L curves, compliance alerts, and more.

From Current State to Event History

Most traditional systems are *state-centric.* For example, a positions table might have one row per account and instrument, with columns for quantity, average price, realized P&L, and so on. When a new trade arrives, a piece of logic:

- Reads the current row.
- Applies some arithmetic.
- Writes back the updated row.

The database only stores the latest snapshot. Earlier states are either lost or stored only in separate audit logs, often with a different structure and partial coverage.

In a trading system, this can be limiting:

- Risk models evolve. You may want to recompute yesterday's exposures under a new model.
- P&L questions often involve time: "What was my P&L at 10:15 after that particular spike?" A single row with the latest value cannot answer that.
- Debugging incidents almost always requires reconstructing *how* the system got to a certain state, not just *what* that state was.

Event sourcing takes the opposite view: the primary record is the *history of domain events*. The current state is a *derived* artifact.

What Is Event Sourcing?

Under event sourcing, each aggregate in your domain (for example, an account, an order, or a risk bucket) is represented as a sequence of immutable events that describe what happened over time. A few key points:

- **Events are facts, not commands.** They record something that has already occurred in the business domain: "OrderPlaced," "TradeExecuted," "MarginAdjusted."
- **Events are append-only.** Once an event is recorded, it is never changed or deleted (except under strict archival policies). Corrections are represented by new events, such as "TradeCorrected" or "AdjustmentPosted."
- **Current state is computed by replaying events.** To know the current position, you conceptually start from an empty state and apply each relevant event in order.

For example, for a single account and instrument, the event stream might look like:

- TradeExecuted (buy 100 @ $10).
- TradeExecuted (buy 50 @ $11).
- TradeExecuted (sell 30 @ $12).
- CorporateActionAdjusted (2-for-1 split).

From these events you can derive that the current quantity, average cost, and realized P&L have certain values, but the events themselves remain the canonical record.

Contrasting with CRUD

In a CRUD-style system (Create, Read, Update, Delete), the database row is the primary record, and events, if they exist at all, are secondary or derived. In event sourcing:

- *Create* is replaced by one or more initial events (for example, "AccountOpened").
- *Update* becomes one or more new events (for example, "MarginIncreased").

- *Delete* is rare and often replaced by a "Closed" or "Deactivated" event.

Reads may still hit a current-state view for performance, but that view is understood as a projection of the underlying events.

Why Event Sourcing Fits Trading

Trading is unusually well-suited to event sourcing because the domain is inherently eventful:

- Orders are placed, amended, and canceled.
- Trades are executed, corrected, and allocated.
- Prices change, limits are breached, collateral is posted.

Each of these is a natural event. Treating them as first-class citizens in your data model brings several benefits.

Auditability and Compliance

Regulators and clients frequently ask questions that are easiest to answer from an event history:

- "Show all the steps that led to this trade: original order, modifications, venue routing, partial fills."
- "What did the risk engine know at the time this order was approved?"

With event sourcing, the complete sequence is already there. You do not need to reconstruct it from partial logs and inferred changes to a row. This is particularly valuable for best-execution analysis, reconstruction of market abuse investigations, and internal audits.

Time-Travel Debugging

When something goes wrong, you rarely care only about the end result. You want to replicate how the system responded at each point in time. Since events are immutable and include timestamps and identifiers, you can:

- Rebuild state as of a specific time (for example, just before a risk breach).
- Replay events in a test environment under modified code to see if a bug has been fixed.

This "time travel" is nearly impossible if you only have final snapshots.

Recomputing Risk and P&L

Risk and P&L models change:

- You may change the way you bucket risk or weight factors.
- You may adjust how fees and costs are allocated.
- You may improve how you handle corporate actions or instrument-specific quirks.

With event sourcing, you can take the same stream of domain events and re-run it through a new model offline:

- Compute what P&L would have been using the new methodology.
- Compare with existing records.
- Backfill or correct reports if needed.

This preserves a clean separation between factual history ("what actually happened") and interpretation ("what your model said about it").

Designing Trading Events as a Canonical Log

To make event sourcing work well, event design must be deliberate. Consider a simplified trading domain:

- **Accounts** (clients, funds, internal books).
- **Orders** (intents to buy or sell).
- **Fills or trades** (executions against orders).
- **Adjustments** (fee postings, corporate actions, manual corrections).

For each, we define events that capture changes in business terms, not just low-level data operations.

Characteristics of Good Domain Events

Good domain events are:

- **Descriptive:** They describe *what* happened in domain language, such as "OrderPlaced," "TradeExecuted," or "MarginCallIssued."
- **Self-contained:** They include enough information for consumers to update their state without querying many other systems (for example, quantities, prices, identifiers).
- **Stable:** Their meaning should not change over time. You may add new fields or new event types, but avoid reinterpreting what an existing event represents.
- **Keyed:** They include identifiers (for example, account ID, order ID) that allow you to group events by aggregate for replay and partitioning.

A naive event that says "RowUpdated" with a blob of before/after data may technically reflect a change, but it is hard for downstream risk and P&L components to reason about. A richer event that clearly separates domain fields—quantity, price, side, instrument, account—makes projections easier and more robust.

Event Sourcing in the Context of Earlier Patterns

Event sourcing is easier to understand if you connect it back to sagas and the outbox pattern:

- Sagas already propagate domain events between services ("OrderCreated," "RiskApproved").
- The outbox pattern already creates an append-only log of outbound events in each service.

Event sourcing extends this idea:

- Instead of using events only for integration, you treat the event log as authoritative for the service's own state as well.
- Projections of this log into tables (for example, positions per account) become read models that can be rebuilt from scratch if necessary.

In practice, many teams adopt event sourcing gradually. They may start with outbox-based event publishing, then for certain domains—such as risk and P&L—elevate the event stream to canonical status.

CQRS: Separating Commands from Queries

Event sourcing changes how you think about *writes*. CQRS changes how you think about *reads*.

CQRS stands for Command Query Responsibility Segregation. The central idea is simple:

> Use different models for updating state (commands) and for reading state (queries), because they have different needs.

In a typical system:

- Commands are few but complex. For example, "place an order," "allocate fills," "liquidate a position." They enforce invariants and involve business rules.
- Queries are many but simple. For example, "show the top 10 positions," "plot last hour's P&L," "list all open margin calls."

With CQRS plus event sourcing:

- The *command side* processes commands, validates them, and appends domain events to the canonical event log.
- The *query side* subscribes to this log and maintains one or more specialized *read models* optimized for particular questions.

This lets you tailor read models to each use case without complicating the write side.

Building Specialized Read Models from an Event Stream

Once you accept that "truth" lives in the event log, you are free to build as many read models as you need. Each read model:

- Subscribes to the relevant event streams.
- Maintains its own local state (for example, a table or an in-memory cache) in a form optimized for queries.
- Can be rebuilt by replaying events if the schema or logic changes.

Let us look at three concrete read models in a trading system.

Intraday P&L Curves

Traders and risk managers care deeply about how P&L evolves over time, not just its latest value. An event-sourced P&L read model can:

- Consume events like "TradeExecuted," "FeeCharged," "CorporateActionApplied," and "FXRateUpdated."
- Maintain, for each account and instrument, a time series of P&L points (for example, every minute or at each event).
- Support queries like "plot P&L over the last session," "how much drawdown occurred after 14:00?" and "what fraction of P&L came from fees versus price moves?"

If the P&L methodology changes (for example, you refine your treatment of fees or overnight financing), you can:

- Take the historical event stream.
- Apply the new P&L logic offline.
- Rebuild the read model and compare with the old one.

Because events capture raw business facts (executions, fees, rates), you avoid hard-coding a particular modeling choice into the canonical record.

Risk Views and Limit Dashboards

Risk managers often need slices of exposure:

- By account.
- By instrument or asset class.
- By risk factor or scenario.

A risk read model can:

- Consume events such as "TradeExecuted," "PositionAdjusted," "LimitChanged," "RiskModelUpdated."
- Maintain rollups of notional, delta, vega, or other measures per risk bucket.

- Flag breaches and generate alerts when thresholds are crossed.

Again, the key advantage is decoupling:

- The command-side services simply record business events.
- The risk read model translates events into exposures according to the current risk model, which can evolve.

You can even maintain multiple risk read models in parallel—for example, one for the current production model and one for a candidate model—to compare their behavior.

Compliance and Surveillance Alerts

Compliance teams need to detect patterns of behavior: wash trading, spoofing, or violations of internal policies. A compliance read model can:

- Subscribe to a broad set of events: order placements, cancellations, trades, account attribute changes, reference data updates.
- Maintain state on recent activities per account, instrument, or strategy.
- Evaluate pattern-detection rules and raise alerts as new events arrive.

Because all logic is driven off the event stream, you can test new compliance rules by replaying past events and seeing what alerts would have been triggered, without interfering with production state.

Trade-offs and Practical Considerations

Event sourcing and CQRS are powerful, but not free. Before adopting them widely, consider the trade-offs.

Increased Write Complexity

Commands become more involved:

- Instead of "update a row," you must determine which event(s) correspond to the requested change.
- You must ensure the ordering of events per aggregate is correct.
- You must handle versioning and evolution of event schemas.

For very simple domains where history does not matter much, this extra complexity may not be justified.

Event Schema Evolution

Events, once emitted, are hard to change. Over time you may need to:

- Add new fields.
- Introduce new event types.
- Deprecate old fields or interpretations.

This requires discipline:

- Treat event schemas as part of your public contract between services and teams.
- Plan for backward compatibility: new consumers must be able to handle older events.

Eventually Consistent Read Models

Because read models are built asynchronously from the event stream, they are almost always *eventually consistent*:

- A freshly placed order may not appear immediately in a P&L dashboard.

- A recent trade may take a moment to reflect in a risk view.

For monitoring and analytics this is usually acceptable, but for *decision points* (for example, pre-trade risk checks) you may need stronger guarantees. A common pattern is:

- Use event-sourced read models for dashboards, analytics, and reporting.
- Use more direct, strongly consistent stores (perhaps also built from events but maintained with tighter SLAs) for real-time gating decisions.

Storage Growth

Events are append-only, so storage grows continuously. You will need:

- Retention policies (for example, keep full detail for N years, summarize beyond that).
- Archival mechanisms to move older events to cheaper storage.
- Strategies for partial replay (for example, starting from periodic snapshots to avoid replaying decades of data).

These are solvable problems, but they require forethought.

When Event Sourcing and CQRS Are Worth It

In a trading platform, event sourcing and CQRS are particularly compelling for domains where:

- **Auditability is critical:** orders, trades, margin, and risk.
- **Models change over time:** risk measures, P&L, compliance rules.
- **Multiple views are needed:** the same underlying facts feed portfolios, dashboards, reports, and analytics.

They may be less necessary for peripheral components:

- Static reference data with simple CRUD behavior.
- Internal configuration tables.
- One-off batch jobs with limited audit requirements.

A pragmatic approach is to start where the benefits are largest—often risk and P&L—and gradually expand as your team becomes comfortable with the patterns.

Event sourcing and CQRS bring a different mindset to state in event-driven trading systems:

- Events, not rows, are the primary record of what has happened.
- Current state is a projection of those events, not an independent source of truth.
- Commands and queries are separated so that each can be optimized for its role.
- Specialized read models—P&L curves, risk dashboards, compliance alerts—are built by consuming the canonical event stream.

These ideas build directly on the consistency and coordination techniques from earlier sections. Sagas and the outbox pattern give you reliable, ordered streams of domain events. Event sourcing and CQRS turn those streams into the backbone of your trading data architecture, enabling powerful analytics, better debuggability, and robust compliance, while keeping the core business facts simple and durable.

3.4 Stateful Stream Processing at Scale

In the previous sections we treated events mainly as records of change and as triggers for longer-running workflows. We saw how sagas coordinate local transactions and how event sourcing turns a log of domain events into a canonical history, from which we can build powerful read models.

We now move one step further: instead of occasionally replaying events in batches, we will keep *continuous computations* running over live streams of events. These computations maintain state in memory, react to each incoming event in milliseconds, and emit decisions or analytics in real time.

This is the domain of *stateful stream processing*. Our focus in this section is practical and trading-specific:

- What abstractions do modern streaming engines provide?
- How do keyed state and timers help us implement real-time risk checks, session logic, and aggregate analytics?
- How can we maintain strong correctness guarantees in the face of failures and out-of-order events?

From Batch to Streaming Thinking

Traditional analytics in trading often follow a batch pattern:

- Collect orders, trades, and prices over some period.
- Store them in a database or data warehouse.
- Periodically run jobs to compute P&L, risk measures, or reports.

This works well for end-of-day processes, but it is increasingly inadequate for:

- Real-time pre-trade and post-trade risk checks.
- Intraday liquidity monitoring.
- Live surveillance and anomaly detection (for example, runaway algos).
- Low-latency dashboards for traders and risk teams.

In these cases, you do not want to wait for a batch window. Instead, you want a standing computation that processes each event as it arrives:

> Every new order, trade, or price update is fed into a pipeline that maintains up-to-date state and emits decisions or metrics immediately.

Stream processing engines provide exactly this: a way to define computations over *unbounded streams* of events, with state and time-aware logic, running continuously on a cluster.

Core Abstractions: Streams, Operators, and Keyed State

At a high level, a streaming engine works with three core ideas:

- **Streams**: Ordered sequences of events (for example, orders, trades, quotes) flowing through the system.
- **Operators**: Processing steps that transform input streams into output streams (for example, filters, joins, aggregations).
- **Keyed state**: Per-key state attached to operators, indexed by a key such as account ID, symbol, or strategy ID.

Let us unpack *keyed state*, because it is central to scalable trading applications.

Keyed State: One State Machine per Account or Symbol

Imagine you want to track exposure per account in real time. For each account, you need to know:

- Current positions across instruments.
- Pending orders and their potential impact.

- Available headroom versus limits.

A naive design would maintain one big global map from account IDs to exposures in an in-memory object. This quickly becomes too large for a single machine and hard to shard manually.

Keyed state provides a structured alternative. You define:

- The input stream: for example, a unified stream of events that affect exposure (orders, trades, adjustments), each tagged with antexttt_account_id_.
- A key: account_id.
- An operator that maintains state per key: conceptually, one small state machine per account.

The streaming engine then:

- Partitions the stream by key across worker nodes (for example, by hashing account_id).
- Ensures that all events for the same key go to the same instance of the operator.
- Provides a local, persistent state store for that operator instance (for example, an embedded key-value store).

From your perspective, you can write logic as if you were maintaining a dedicated exposure calculator per account, all running in parallel on a cluster.

Timers and Windows: Making Time Explicit

Many trading questions involve time:

- "Has this strategy sent more than 100 orders in the last 10 seconds?"

- "What is the average fill price for this symbol over the last minute?"

- "If we do not receive a cancel confirmation by a certain time, escalate."

Streaming engines handle such logic with *timers* and *windows*.

- **Timers**: Allow an operator to schedule a callback for a specific time in the future. When the time is reached, the engine invokes the operator with access to its keyed state.

- **Windows**: Define bounded subsets of events based on time (for example, a fixed 5-second window) or event count (for example, after every 100 events).

Timers and windows, combined with keyed state, let you express rich temporal logic: "per account and per symbol, detect if more than N orders arrive within M seconds," or "per strategy session, compute rolling metrics and time out inactive sessions."

We will soon illustrate these with trading-specific patterns.

A High-Level Risk Pipeline

Before diving into examples, it is useful to visualize a typical stateful stream-processing pipeline in a trading system. Figure shows a simplified dataflow for real-time risk checks.

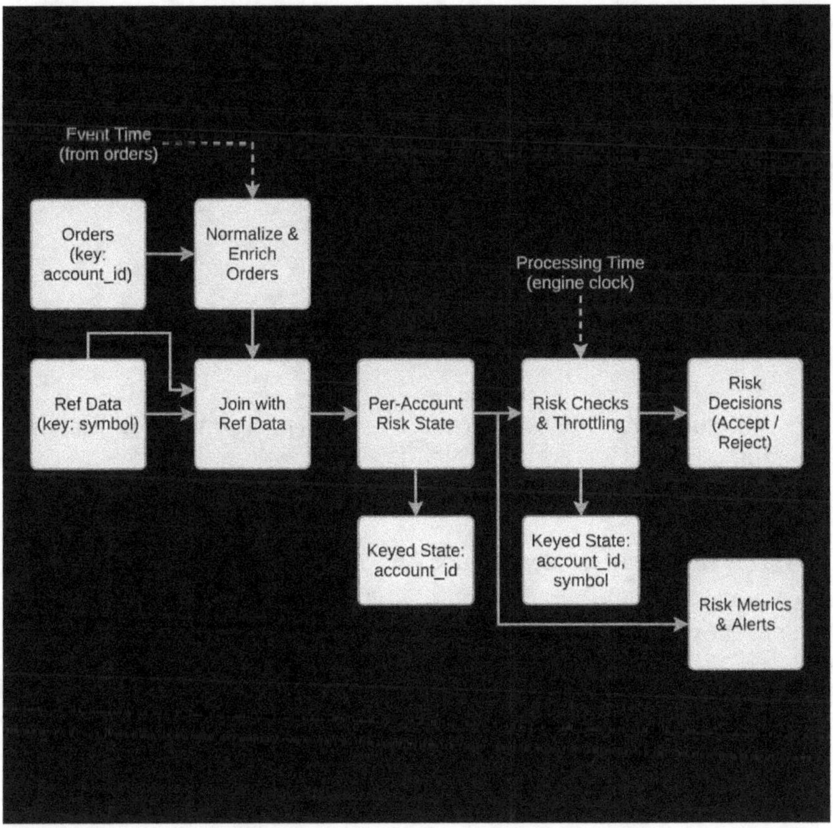

In this diagram:

- Orders and reference data are ingested as streams.
- Operators enrich orders with reference data, maintain per-account risk state, and enforce throttling and limits.
- Side-attached boxes represent keyed state stores-one keyed by account_id for risk, another by both account_id and symbol for throttling.
- The pipeline emits both real-time risk decisions (accept/reject) and aggregated analytics and alerts.

With this mental model in place, we now explore specific use cases.

Per-Order Pre-Trade Risk Checks

Pre-trade risk checks are often the first and most critical application of stateful streaming in trading.

The Basic Pattern

When an order arrives, you need to answer questions like:

- Will this order push the account over its position or notional limits?
- Is there enough margin or collateral for the potential exposure?
- Has this strategy already used its allocation for this period?

Each of these requires:

- Current state for the account (positions, exposures, margin).
- The incremental effect of the new order.
- A decision, ideally within a few milliseconds.

In a streaming engine, pre-trade risk checks fit naturally as an operator with keyed state:

- The input stream consists of "OrderProposed" events keyed by account_id.
- The operator's keyed state holds the current exposures per account and instrument.
- On each event, the operator:
  - Reads the state for that account.
  - Simulates the effect of accepting the order.

- Checks limits and rules.
- Emits an "OrderAccepted" or "OrderRejected" event.
- Updates the exposure state if the order is accepted.

Because state is partitioned by account, the operator scales horizontally: adding more accounts does not necessarily increase latency for any single one, as long as you add workers.

Joining with Reference Data

Pre-trade checks also depend on reference data:

- Contract specifications (for example, tick size, lot size).
- Risk weights by instrument or asset class.
- Real-time prices or margins.

Reference data often arrives as its own stream of updates. The streaming engine can join the orders stream with the reference-data stream, keyed by symbol, before performing the risk calculation. The joined operator maintains state for:

- The latest reference data per symbol.
- The latest risk parameters per instrument class.

This ensures that each risk decision uses the most recent known parameters, within the consistency and timing guarantees of the pipeline.

Session Logic and Throttling: Using Timers

Another common need is to detect abusive or malfunctioning behavior, such as:

- An algo sending too many messages in a short interval.

- A client starting and stopping activity in suspicious patterns.
- A gateway session becoming idle or unresponsive.

These are inherently time-based patterns. Timers make them straightforward to implement.

Rate Limits per Account or Strategy

Consider a requirement:

> Per account and symbol, do not allow more than 100 order submissions in any rolling 10-second window.

In a stateful stream processor:

- The input stream is order submissions, keyed by (account, symbol).
- The operator's keyed state, per key, includes:
  - A small log of timestamps for recent orders.
  - Possibly a pre-aggregated count over window buckets.
- Upon receiving an order, the operator:
  - Adds the current event's timestamp to the state.
  - Evicts timestamps older than 10 seconds.
  - Computes the number of orders in the remaining window.
  - Accepts or rejects based on the threshold.

To avoid scanning long histories, you may use windowing primitives provided by the engine, which maintain aggregates (counts, sums) over sliding or tumbling windows efficiently. Timers are used to trigger evictions and to update metrics even when no new orders arrive.

Detecting Idle or Broken Sessions

Suppose you want to detect when an order gateway session has gone unexpectedly silent:

> If no heartbeats or messages arrive from a session for 5 seconds, raise an alert and consider the session unhealthy.

This fits perfectly with per-session timers:

- The input stream consists of messages from clients or gateways, keyed by session ID.
- For each session, the operator's state holds:
  - The time of the last message received.
  - A scheduled timer for "last_message_time + 5 seconds."
- For each new message:
  - Update the last message time.
  - Cancel the old timer and set a new one 5 seconds ahead.
- When a timer fires:
  - Check whether a new message has arrived since the timer was set.
  - If not, emit a "SessionUnhealthy" event or alert.

All of this operates independently per session, leveraging keyed state and timers for scalability.

Aggregate Analytics: Rolling Risk and P&L Metrics

Beyond decisions, trading teams need aggregate analytics in near real time: rolling VaR estimates, sector exposures, or P&L breakdowns.

Per-Account Rolling Exposure

Exposure is often defined at multiple levels:

- Position and notional by instrument.
- Aggregation by sector, country, or asset class.
- Aggregation by strategy or desk.

A streaming risk-aggregation pipeline might:

- Consume events from the event-sourced position and trade logs.
- Maintain keyed state at several levels:
  - By (account, instrument) to track positions.
  - By (account, sector) to track sector exposures.
- Emit updated metrics whenever positions change or prices move.

Windows can then be applied to compute rolling metrics: for example, maximum drawdown in the last hour, or exposure changes over the last N minutes.

Intraday P&L in the Streaming World

Earlier we described P&L read models built by replaying events. A streaming engine turns that replay into a continuous process:

- The input stream is the canonical event log: trades, fees, FX rate updates, etc.
- A P&L operator, keyed by account (and perhaps by symbol), maintains:
  - Current positions and average costs.
  - Accrued fees and financing.
  - Current P&L and its decomposition.

- On each event, it updates P&L and emits new P&L snapshots to downstream dashboards or storage.

Because the P&L state is keyed, the engine can handle thousands of accounts in parallel. Exactness and recovery behavior will rely on robust checkpointing and exactly-once semantics, which we discuss later in the chapter.

Time Semantics: Event Time vs Processing Time

So far we have casually referred to "timestamps" and "windows," but in a distributed system there is an important distinction:

- **Processing time**: The time when an event is processed by the engine (that is, the wall-clock time on the machine doing the work).
- **Event time**: The time when the event actually occurred in the source system (for example, when a trade was executed).

In trading, network delays, market data bursts, and clock skew can cause large differences between event time and processing time. A burst at market open might be processed over several seconds; events may arrive out of order.

Why Event Time Matters

Consider a rate limit: "no more than 100 orders in any 10-second window." If you define the window in processing time, you might:

- Under-count if events are delayed (they fall into a later processing window than their true send time).
- Over-count if a burst of older buffered events and newer events are processed nearly together.

Using event time, the window is based on the timestamps embedded in the events themselves, which better reflects the behavior of the traders or algos. The challenge is that events can arrive late or out of order.

Watermarks and Lateness

Streaming engines address this with the concept of *watermarks*. Informally:

> A watermark is a marker that says, "the engine believes that all events with event-time up to T have now arrived, except possibly for a known bound on lateness."

You configure a maximum allowed lateness (for example, 2 seconds). The engine then:

- Computes windows based primarily on event time.
- Waits to close a window until the watermark passes the end of the window.
- Optionally handles late events by updating prior results or dropping them according to your policy.

In trading applications:

- For risk decisions, you often prefer conservative rules that treat uncertain or late data cautiously (for example, assume worst-case exposure).
- For analytics, you can accept slightly delayed "final" numbers in exchange for greater accuracy with late events.

Designing time semantics is therefore both a technical and business decision.

Correctness: Exactly-Once Processing in Streaming Pipelines

Streaming engines advertise various processing guarantees:

- **At-most-once**: Events may be lost but never processed twice.

- **At-least-once**: Events are never lost, but may be processed more than once.
- **Exactly-once**: Each event affects state and outputs as if processed exactly once.

In a real trading system that spans brokers, logs, and databases, truly global exactly-once semantics are hard to achieve. However, within a streaming pipeline, we can often get very close.

Coordinating State and Output

The key challenge is similar to the dual-write problem: when an operator processes an event, it:

- Updates its internal keyed state.
- Produces output events (for example, risk decisions, metrics).

If the engine crashes after updating state but before outputting the event, or vice versa, you can end up with inconsistencies. To avoid this, modern engines:

- Periodically take consistent checkpoints of both state and the positions in input streams.
- Optionally use transactional writes or idempotent protocols to update external sinks (for example, Kafka topics, databases).

On recovery, the engine:

- Restores state from the latest checkpoint.
- Resumes reading input streams from the corresponding positions.
- Reapplies events if necessary, relying on idempotency to avoid double-counting in external sinks.

We discuss checkpointing and state stores in more detail in the next section; here the takeaway is that:

> You can design streaming risk and analytics pipelines so that, even under failures, state and outputs correspond to some consistent prefix of the input streams, without missing or double-applying events within that prefix.

Integrating Streaming with the Broader Architecture

Stateful streaming is not a separate world; it must integrate with the event-driven architecture we developed earlier.

Inputs from Canonical Event Logs

Event-sourced services (orders, trades, accounts) typically write their events to a log or messaging system. Streaming pipelines should:

- Consume these canonical events, rather than scraping databases directly.
- Use well-defined schemas and keys (account, symbol, strategy) that align with how state is partitioned and invariants are expressed.

This produces a clean layering:

- Command side: services validate commands, update their own state, and emit events via outbox patterns.
- Streaming side: consumes those events and maintains derived, real-time state for risk, P&L, and analytics.

Outputs as Events and Views

Streaming outputs should also be events whenever possible:

- "OrderRejectedByPreTradeRisk."
- "RiskLimitBreached."
- "StrategyAnomalyDetected."

These events can feed other services and dashboards, and can themselves be event-sourced and audited. Additionally, the streaming engine may maintain materialized views (for example, in key-value stores) for fast reads by APIs and dashboards.

Design Guidelines for Stateful Streaming in Trading

To conclude, here are some practical guidelines when designing streaming pipelines for trading applications:

- **Express invariants in terms of keys.** If you can express risk and limit rules per account, per symbol, or per strategy, keyed state lets you enforce them efficiently and in parallel.
- **Use event time for behavior, processing time for operations.** Base rate limits and behavioral analytics on event time; use processing time timers for operational tasks like health checks and backpressure handling.
- **Keep operators focused.** Each operator should do one conceptual job: join reference data, maintain risk state, detect anomalies, or aggregate metrics. This makes correctness reasoning and scaling easier.
- **Design for recovery.** Assume nodes will fail. Choose checkpoint intervals, state backends, and idempotent sinks so that a restarted pipeline quickly recovers without corrupting risk state.
- **Separate decision-critical and analytic paths.** For some workflows (for example, order acceptance), you may need tighter SLAs and stronger guarantees than for analytics. Consider distinct pipelines or operator branches with different performance and recovery tuning.

Stateful stream processing brings together the ideas developed earlier in the chapter: consistency models, sagas, event sourcing, and outbox-based logging. When used carefully, it allows you to implement real-time risk checks, session logic, and aggregate analytics at scale, while maintaining the correctness and auditability that trading systems demand.

3.5 Snapshotting, Checkpointing, and State Stores

In the previous section we treated stateful stream processing as if state simply lived "inside" operators: keyed exposure maps, rolling windows, and P&L accumulators that are updated as events flow by. That picture is useful for understanding logic, but incomplete from an operational perspective.

Real trading pipelines run continuously for days or weeks. Machines fail, processes are restarted for upgrades, and workloads burst during market events. If state only exists in process memory, a single node failure could wipe out your view of exposures or P&L, forcing you to replay huge histories and risking inconsistent decisions during recovery.

This section explains how modern streaming engines persist and recover large in-memory state efficiently. We will:

- Distinguish types of state and storage backends.
- Explain checkpointing and snapshotting, and how they interact with input streams.
- Explore trade-offs between write amplification, recovery time, and operational complexity.
- Ground everything in trading examples: per-account exposure operators, risk model backfills, and safe upgrades.

Local Operator State vs External State Stores

A stateful streaming application maintains state at two broad levels:

- **Local operator state** Data structures directly managed by the streaming engine on each worker: keyed exposure maps, window buffers, session information.
- **External state stores** Databases or key-value stores outside the engine: risk databases, audit logs, materialized views exposed via APIs.

Local Operator State

Local operator state is what you conceptually write when you say:

> "For each account, maintain its current exposure as events arrive."

In an implementation, the engine might store this in an embedded key-value store (similar to RocksDB) on each worker node. The engine controls:

- How state is partitioned across nodes (for example, by hash of account_id).
- How state is serialized, compacted, and backed up.
- How to restore it after failures.

This state is optimized for tight integration with the streaming runtime: very low-latency reads and writes, co-located with the processing thread, and efficient spill to disk when it grows beyond memory.

External State Stores

External state stores are separate systems with their own replication and durability guarantees, such as:

- A relational database holding intraday risk snapshots.
- A distributed cache feeding dashboards.

- A time-series store used for historical analytics.

Streaming pipelines often write derived results to these stores so that other services and humans can query them. However, relying on external stores alone for *internal* pipeline state would impose high latency and load, and make consistent recovery harder.

Modern designs therefore treat local operator state as the primary working set for streaming logic, and use external stores mainly for exported views. The challenge is to make local state durable and recoverable without sacrificing performance.

The Core Problem: Consistent, Efficient Durability

Durability for streaming state has two requirements:

1. **Consistency across operators and inputs:** After a failure, restored state must match some prefix of the input streams. You must not "forget" to process some events or process them twice in a way that corrupts your state.
2. **Operational efficiency:** Persisting state must not slow down normal processing too much, and recovery must be fast enough to meet your SLAs.

These are addressed by two closely related mechanisms:

- **Checkpointing** Periodic, coordinated snapshots of operator state *plus* the positions in each input stream.
- **Snapshotting** The actual act of persisting the contents of state (for example, copying or incrementally updating a backup image).

In practice, people often use "checkpoint" to mean the full consistent savepoint of the system at a particular logical time, and "snapshot" to mean the stored image of state for an operator or task. We will follow that convention.

Checkpointing: Capturing a Consistent View

Consider a risk pipeline that consumes trade events from a log and maintains per-account exposures. When a checkpoint is taken, we want to record:

- For each operator instance: its current local state (exposures, timers, window buffers).
- For each input partition: the offset or sequence number of the last event that has been fully processed.

A *coordinator* (part of the streaming engine) orchestrates the checkpoint:

1. It injects a special "checkpoint barrier" into each input stream at a chosen logical point.
2. As events flow, these barriers travel through the operators alongside normal data.
3. When an operator receives barriers on all its input channels for a given checkpoint, it:
    - Temporarily pauses emitting results for that checkpoint ID.
    - Writes out a snapshot of its local state as of that moment.
    - Reports completion to the coordinator.
4. Once all operators have reported completion, the checkpoint is considered successful.

The key idea is that barriers slice the flowing streams into segments. All events before the barrier are considered part of the "past" for that checkpoint; all events after are "future." Because barriers are aligned across operators, the checkpoint captures a consistent global view.

If a failure happens later, the engine can:

- Restore each operator's state from its latest snapshot.

- Restart consuming input streams from the corresponding recorded offsets.

From the pipeline's perspective, it is as if it had been paused at the checkpoint and then resumed.

Snapshotting: How State Is Persisted

Checkpointing defines *when* and *what* to save. Snapshotting concerns *how* to write state to durable storage.

There are two broad strategies:

- **Full snapshots** Copy the entire state of each operator at every checkpoint.
- **Incremental snapshots** Only record changes since the last snapshot, leveraging the state backend's internal logs or compaction mechanics.

Full Snapshots

Full snapshots are simple conceptually:

- At each checkpoint, the engine reads all keys and values from the local state stores and writes them to a durable store (for example, object storage or a replicated file system).
- Each checkpoint has a self-contained copy of the state.

The downside is obvious: for large state (for example, hundreds of millions of keys for per-account exposures), copying everything frequently is expensive in I/O and network bandwidth. This leads to:

- Longer checkpoint times.
- Potential backpressure or pauses in processing.
- Larger storage consumption.

For small or moderate state, full snapshots can still be fine and are attractive due to their simplicity. But for large trading systems, incremental techniques are usually needed.

Incremental Snapshots

Incremental snapshots exploit the fact that state changes gradually:

- Most keys do not change between successive checkpoints.
- Even for active keys, only a small part of the data may change.

State backends like RocksDB already maintain write-ahead logs (WALs) and sorted tables (SSTables) to support durability and compaction. Streaming engines can integrate with these mechanisms:

- When a checkpoint is taken, they mark which files and log segments belong to the state as of that point.
- New updates go to new files and logs, which will be included in later checkpoints.

This means that:

- A checkpoint only needs to record a set of references to existing state files, plus any small metadata.
- Large immutable files are shared across checkpoints.

As a result, incremental snapshots dramatically reduce write amplification and enable frequent checkpoints even for very large state, which in turn improves recovery time.

State Backends: Embedded vs Remote

Underlying snapshotting and checkpointing is a choice of *state backend*. Two major patterns are:

- **Embedded key-value store** The engine links in a key-value library (such as RocksDB-like storage) that writes to local disks on each worker.
- **Remote state store** The engine interacts with an external storage system over the network for reads and writes (for example, a replicated database, a distributed key-value service, or a specialized state backend).

Embedded Key-Value Stores

With an embedded store:

- Reads and writes happen on the same machine as the operator, usually via local disk and memory.
- Latency is low and predictable.
- State can be sharded and rebalanced automatically by the engine.

Checkpointing typically works by copying or referencing the on-disk files of the embedded store to a durable shared storage. Recovery involves:

- Downloading the relevant files for each operator.
- Reconstructing the local store to the checkpointed version.

This pattern tends to give the best performance for high-throughput trading pipelines, especially when state is tightly coupled to streaming logic (for example, per-account exposure and throttling state).

Remote State Stores

In some environments, you may want to centralize state in an external system:

- To share it with other applications.

- To leverage an existing HA database cluster.
- To simplify operational management of disks and backups.

In this case, each operator issues network calls to the remote store for reads and writes. Advantages include:

- Simpler recovery: remote store already replicates and persists data.
- Potential for direct querying of state by other services.

However, there are significant trade-offs:

- Higher latency per state access, which can add up for per-event operations.
- Increased load on the remote database during market bursts.
- Harder to achieve consistent checkpoints that align stream positions and database contents, unless the remote store is tightly integrated.

In many trading systems, embedded state backends are preferred for performance-critical streaming logic, with remote stores used for exported, queryable views.

Balancing Checkpoint Frequency and Overhead

Checkpointing involves work: serializing state and coordinating barriers. Choosing how often to checkpoint is a central tuning decision. There is a clear trade-off:

- **Frequent checkpoints:** Less processing lost on failure (smaller reprocessing window), faster recovery to up-to-date state, but higher CPU and I/O overhead during normal operation.

- **Infrequent checkpoints:** Lower overhead during normal operation, but slower recovery and more events to replay after a failure.

In a trading context, the acceptable recovery time is constrained by:

- Market conditions (for example, a failure during a volatile period is more critical than overnight).
- Regulatory or internal requirements for availability of risk controls.

A practical approach is:

- Use incremental snapshots to keep per-checkpoint overhead low.
- Set a moderate checkpoint interval (for example, tens of seconds) for steady-state operation.
- Optionally trigger ad-hoc checkpoints before planned maintenance or high-risk periods (for example, before a central risk component upgrade).

Failure and Recovery Scenarios

To understand how all of this works in practice, consider a concrete trading example: a per-account exposure operator, running in a cluster, that feeds pre-trade risk checks.

Single-Node Failure

Suppose one worker node fails unexpectedly:

1. The engine detects the failure via heartbeats or resource manager signals.
2. It determines which partitions of input streams and which shards of state were hosted on that node.

3. It assigns those responsibilities to other nodes in the cluster.

4. On each new node:

   - It loads the latest snapshot of the operator's state shard from durable storage.
   - It resumes consuming the associated input partitions from the recorded offsets of the same checkpoint.

During the recovery period, new orders for affected accounts may be temporarily routed to backup risk checks, throttled, or rejected based on conservative rules, depending on your design. Once state is restored, full functionality resumes.

If checkpoints are frequent and state is large but incrementally snapshotted, this entire sequence can complete in seconds.

Cluster-Wide Restart or Upgrade

Consider a planned upgrade where you need to restart the entire streaming application:

1. You trigger a "savepoint" or final checkpoint and wait for it to complete.

2. All operator state and input offsets are persisted.

3. You stop the current job and deploy the new version of the code.

4. You start the job from the saved checkpoint.

If state schema and logic are compatible (or if you have migration tools), this allows a near-seamless upgrade with predictable recovery to a well-defined point. For a trading risk pipeline, this is crucial: you cannot afford to rebuild exposures from scratch every time you release a new version.

Backfilling a Risk Model

Sometimes you want to recompute risk with a new model using historical data. Checkpointing and snapshotting can help here too:

- You start a separate streaming job that reads historical event logs from a chosen point.
- It maintains its own state (for example, exposures under the new model), with checkpoints for resilience.
- Once caught up to real time, you can promote this job to production, potentially using its latest checkpoint as a handover point.

This avoids reprocessing from "day zero" and lets you iteratively refine models.

Designing State Schemas for Efficient Compaction and Migration

State is not just values; it has structure. The way you model state affects:

- How easily it can be compacted and snapshotted.
- How you add or remove fields over time.
- How you partition and rebalance load.

Some guidelines:

- **Prefer narrow, per-key records.** For example, store exposure per (account, instrument) as individual keys, rather than a single huge blob per account. This localizes updates and improves incremental snapshot efficiency.
- **Use stable keys.** Keys should be durable identifiers like account IDs or strategy IDs, not opaque hashes of mutable attributes.

- **Version your state.** Include version markers in stored values so that newer code can interpret older state and, if necessary, migrate it during recovery or maintenance windows.
- **Align partitioning with invariants.** If risk limits are per account, partition state by account so that all relevant information is local to one operator instance, simplifying both processing and checkpointing.

Thoughtful state design pays off when you need to compact logs, reclaim storage, or adjust partitioning to handle changing load patterns.

Operational Considerations and Trade-offs

Finally, snapshotting and checkpointing must be understood in the broader operational context of a trading firm.

Storage and Networking Costs

Durable snapshots typically live on shared storage: network-attached disks, distributed file systems, or object stores. You should:

- Estimate the growth of snapshot data based on state size and checkpoint frequency.
- Implement retention policies (for example, keep recent N checkpoints, plus periodic archival checkpoints).
- Monitor network usage to ensure that snapshot traffic does not interfere with latency-sensitive market connectivity.

Testing Recovery Paths

It is not enough to configure checkpointing; you must test recovery:

- Periodically simulate node failures and full restarts in non-production and, carefully, in controlled production windows.

- Verify that restored pipelines produce consistent results and that risk state remains correct.
- Test version upgrades using savepoints to ensure that state schema changes are handled gracefully.

In high-stakes systems, recovery drills are as important as disaster recovery plans in traditional IT.

Separation of Concerns

Finally, remember the separation between:

- **Streaming engine responsibilities:** Coordinating checkpoints, storing snapshots, recovering state and input positions.
- **Application responsibilities:** Designing state schemas, ensuring idempotent outputs, choosing acceptable recovery windows for business logic.

A well-designed architecture will keep these concerns clear: the engine provides reliable mechanics; you, as an application designer, decide what correctness and availability mean in your trading context.

Stateful stream processing gives trading systems powerful real-time capabilities, but it also introduces the challenge of managing large, dynamic state over long-running computations. Snapshotting, checkpointing, and state stores address this by:

- Treating local operator state as first-class, with embedded backends for performance.
- Coordinating periodic, consistent checkpoints across operators and input streams.
- Using full or incremental snapshots to persist state efficiently.
- Enabling fast, predictable recovery from failures and safe upgrades.

By carefully balancing checkpoint frequency, state backend choice, and state schema design, you can keep your real-time risk, P&L, and surveillance pipelines both fast and resilient. In the final section of this chapter, we will connect these mechanisms back to end-to-end delivery semantics and idempotency, showing how to approximate "exactly-once" behavior across the entire trading stack.

3.6 Delivery Semantics and Idempotency

So far in this chapter we have treated state and consistency largely from the perspective of *where* data lives and *how* it is updated: consistency models, sagas, event sourcing, and streaming with checkpoints. In this final section we look at a subtler but equally important layer: what happens when messages themselves are lost, duplicated, or reordered on their way between components.

No matter how carefully you design your databases and stream processors, you still rely on message brokers, queues, HTTP calls, or logs to carry commands and events. These transports come with different *delivery semantics*. If you ignore those semantics, your nicely designed state models can still be corrupted by duplicate commands or missing events.

Our goal is to connect:

- The guarantees offered by messaging systems: at-most-once, at-least-once, and exactly-once delivery.
- Application-level techniques: idempotent handlers, deduplication, idempotency keys, and sequence numbers.

Together, these allow you to approximate *end-to-end exactly-once behavior* where it really matters (for example, ledgers, risk decrements) while accepting looser guarantees for non-critical analytics.

Transport-Level Delivery Semantics

Messaging systems and stream processors typically describe their delivery behavior using three labels.

At-Most-Once

"At-most-once" means:

> A given message may be processed zero or one times, but never more than once.

This is usually the default behavior of simple UDP-like protocols or naive "fire-and-forget" queues:

- The sender sends a message.
- The system makes a best effort to deliver it.
- If something fails before the consumer processes it, the message is lost.

At-most-once is rarely acceptable for core trading workflows:

- A lost order or trade event could mean unhedged exposure or incomplete reporting.
- A lost risk update could leave limits stale.

It can be adequate for low-importance telemetry (for example, debug logs or metrics where approximate counts are fine), but not for state-changing business flows.

At-Least-Once

"At-least-once" means:

> A given message will be processed one or more times. It will not be silently lost, but may be delivered and processed more than once.

Most reliable queues and distributed logs provide this guarantee by default:

- Messages are persisted on the broker before acknowledgment.
- Consumers acknowledge messages after processing.
- If a consumer fails before acknowledging, the broker redelivers the message.

This eliminates silent loss but introduces duplicates. In a trading context:

- An at-least-once stream of trade events might send the same fill twice.
- An at-least-once order command may cause the same order to be submitted multiple times if the consumer is not careful.

If your handlers are naive—simply "add quantity," "debit cash," or "insert row"—duplicates can create serious errors: double-counted positions, over-debited accounts, or duplicate venue orders.

Exactly-Once

"Exactly-once" is the ideal:

> Each message affects the system's state and outputs as if it were processed exactly once, with no loss and no duplicates.

Some streaming systems advertise "exactly-once processing" within their own boundaries, typically by combining:

- Durable input logs.
- Stateful processing with transactional checkpoints.
- Transactional or idempotent writes to sinks.

However, when you step back to the full trading architecture-multiple services, databases, brokers, and external venues-true global exactly-once is usually unattainable:

- External systems (exchanges, custodians) rarely participate in your transactions.
- Different teams may use different technologies with different guarantees.
- Network partitions and partial failures make some error cases fundamentally ambiguous.

This is why it is essential to complement transport-level guarantees with *application-level* techniques.

Why At-Least-Once Needs Idempotency

Given the choice between losing messages and risking duplicates, at-least-once is usually the right base for trading:

- You would rather see a trade twice than not see it at all.
- You would rather receive a margin call twice than miss it entirely.

But you cannot leave it there. You must make your handlers *idempotent*.

An operation is idempotent if performing it multiple times with the same input has the same effect as performing it once. For example:

- Setting a field to a value (for example, "mark order status as FILLED") is naturally idempotent.
- Incrementing a balance or inserting a new row is *not* naturally idempotent; repeating it would double the effect.

The rest of this section is about building idempotent behavior on top of at-least-once infrastructure, so that duplicate messages do not cause financial or logical errors.

Idempotency Keys on Commands

One of the simplest and most powerful tools is the *idempotency key.*

Concept

When a client sends a command that may be retried-such as "place order" or "cancel order"-it generates a unique idempotency key (for example, a UUID or a client-generated sequence number) and includes it with the request.

The receiving service then:

- Stores the key and the outcome the first time it processes the command.
- On subsequent commands with the same key:
  - Returns the original outcome (success or error) without re-executing the business logic.
  - Does not apply any additional side effects.

From the client's perspective, it can freely retry the command until it receives a definitive response, without worrying about creating duplicates.

Order Placement Example

For order placement:

- The client generates client_order_id, which acts as an idempotency key.
- The Order Service:
  - Checks whether an order with this client_order_id already exists.
  - If not, validates and creates a new order, marking it as associated with that key.
  - If yes, returns the existing order's state.

If the client times out and retries, the second request is recognized as a duplicate, and no second order is created.

Deduplication Stores and Message IDs

Idempotency keys are most obvious on client-facing commands, but the same idea applies inside the system. Whenever a service consumes messages from a broker, it can maintain a *deduplication store* keyed by message ID.

Basic Pattern

Each message carries a unique identifier-either assigned by the producer or derived from stable business keys. The consumer:

- Before applying the business logic, checks a small persistence (for example, a local key-value store or database table) to see if this message ID has been processed.
- If not, it:
  - Executes the handler.
  - Records the message ID as processed, often within the same local transaction as the state update.
- If yes, it skips the handler, treating this as a benign duplicate.

The deduplication store only needs to retain recent IDs (for example, a few hours or days, depending on the maximum redelivery window) and can be garbage-collected over time.

Trading Example: Fills and Positions

Imagine a Position Service that updates positions based on a stream of "FillExecuted" events from the matching engine. The underlying broker offers at-least-once delivery, so a fill may be delivered twice.

Naively, the handler would:

- Add the fill quantity to the position.
- Recompute average price and P&L.

If a fill is duplicated, this doubles the position. Instead, by using a deduplication store keyed by fill_id:

- The first time a given fill_id is seen, the position is updated and the ID is recorded.
- On subsequent deliveries with the same fill_id, the handler sees the ID in the dedup store and skips the update.

This turns an at-least-once fill stream into effectively exactly-once updates to positions.

Natural-Key Idempotency: Upserts and Conditional Writes

Sometimes the state itself contains a natural key that can be used to enforce idempotency without a separate deduplication store.

Upserts by Business Key

Instead of inserting a new row blindly, you can:

- Upsert a record keyed by a stable business identifier such as trade_id or client_order_id.
- Use conditional writes (for example, "insert if not exists," "update only if current version is X").

This ensures that:

- The first time a key is seen, a new record is created.
- Subsequent attempts with the same key either update the same record consistently or are rejected as duplicates.

For example, a ledger might maintain a row per transaction ID, so replaying or redelivering a transaction does not create additional ledger entries.

Stateful Stream Processing Context

In the streaming world, natural-key idempotency often appears as:

- Keying the stream by a business identifier.

- Designing keyed state so that updates are always merges into that key rather than additive append-only operations.

As long as events for the same key have stable semantics, duplicates can be suppressed or merged correctly.

Sequence Numbers and Ordered Streams

Idempotency handles duplicates, but you often also care about *order*. For example:

- Order modifications and cancellations must be applied in the correct sequence.
- Account balance adjustments might arrive out of order due to network delays.

Sequence numbers add a simple form of causality:

- Each event for a given key (for example, an order or account) carries a monotonically increasing sequence number.
- Consumers track the highest sequence number they have processed per key.
- If an event arrives with a sequence number less than or equal to that, it is either a duplicate or stale and can be ignored.

This mechanism does two things:

- Provides a built-in deduplication key (sequence number).
- Prevents older updates from overwriting newer state ("last write wins" becomes "highest sequence wins").

In a matching engine, for example, each cancel/replace might be assigned a sequence number by the gateway or client session; the engine applies only strictly increasing sequences, discarding repeats or regressions.

Combining Techniques: Toward Effectively Exactly Once

In isolation, each tool-idempotency keys, deduplication stores, natural-key idempotency, sequence numbers-addresses part of the problem. In practice, you combine them to approach exactly-once behavior across multiple hops.

Example: Order to Trade to Position

Consider the path:

$$\text{Client} \rightarrow \text{Order Service} \rightarrow \text{Broker} \rightarrow \text{Matching Engine} \rightarrow \text{Trade Log} \rightarrow \text{Position Service.}$$

You might apply:

- **Client to Order Service:** Idempotency key on "place order" commands (for example, client_order_id), so client retries do not create duplicate internal orders.
- **Order Service to Broker:** Outbox pattern and a deduplication-aware gateway to ensure each logical order is sent once, even if internal events are retried.
- **Matching Engine to Trade Log:** Strong consistency and unique trade_id per match.
- **Trade Log to Position Service:** At-least-once delivery combined with a deduplication store keyed by trade_id, turning duplicated trade messages into idempotent position updates.

Viewed end-to-end, the business effect is: each client order either results in exactly one corresponding change in positions or is cleanly rejected, despite possible retries and redeliveries at each step.

Risk Decrements and Ledger Updates

For risk and ledger flows you might further enforce:

- A unique transaction ID for each ledger entry.

- A requirement that any adjustment or reversal refers explicitly to the transaction(s) it amends.
- Idempotent posting logic: posting the same transaction twice is a no-op after the first time, because the transaction ID is already present.

This design turns at-least-once message delivery into effectively exactly-once ledger semantics.

Interaction with Checkpointing and Stream Processing

In stateful stream processors, we saw that checkpointing and exactly-once processing can coordinate operator state and outputs. Idempotency techniques complement this in two ways:

- **Within the engine:** If the engine replays some events from a checkpoint, your operators must handle this replay as intended (for example, reproducing the same output or avoiding double side effects on external systems).
- **At the edges:** When the engine writes to external sinks (databases, other services), those sinks must be ready to receive duplicate or retried writes and treat them idempotently.

For example, a streaming P&L pipeline might:

- Maintain P&L state internally with exactly-once semantics.
- Emit periodic "PnLSnapshot" events with monotonically increasing sequence numbers.
- A downstream dashboard store upserts snapshots keyed by (account, sequence), ignoring duplicates.

If a checkpoint and replay cause some snapshots to be emitted twice, the dashboard state remains correct.

Where to Aim for Strong Guarantees (and Where Not To)

Not every flow in a trading system deserves the full treatment. Trying to make everything effectively exactly-once can be overkill and may introduce unnecessary complexity and latency.

Critical Paths

Aim for strong, end-to-end guarantees on:

- Ledger updates: cash, collateral, and securities balances.
- Risk debits and limit decrements that gate trading decisions.
- Regulatory and compliance logs that must be complete and auditable.
- Trade and position feeds that serve as legal or contractual records.

In these domains, duplicated or missing effects can directly cause losses or regulatory breaches. Invest in idempotency keys, deduplication, sequence numbers, and careful design of state updates.

Non-Critical Analytics

You can accept looser guarantees for:

- Monitoring metrics and telemetry counters.
- Exploratory analytics and dashboards not used for decisions.
- High-level performance statistics where a small margin of error is tolerable.

Here, at-most-once or simple at-least-once delivery may suffice, and you can keep handlers simple.

Documentation and Contracts

Finally, the effectiveness of these techniques depends on clear contracts between teams and services. For each API or stream, document:

- The delivery expectations: at-most-once, at-least-once, or stronger within a particular scope.
- The idempotency contract: whether consumers can safely retry, which fields form the idempotency key, and how duplicates are handled.
- Ordering guarantees: per-key or global, and how out-of-order messages should be treated.

This documentation should be as explicit as SLAs for latency and uptime. Developers should know, for example, that "FillExecuted events are delivered at-least-once, keyed by `trade_id`, and consumers must treat `trade_id` as a unique idempotency key."

Delivery semantics and idempotency are the glue that binds together the stateful, event-driven architecture described throughout this chapter:

- Messaging systems and stream processors inevitably operate in at-most-once or at-least-once regimes; global exactly-once is unrealistic across the entire stack.
- Application-level patterns-idempotency keys, deduplication stores, natural-key idempotency, and sequence numbers-allow you to tame duplicates and out-of-order messages.
- By combining these patterns with sagas, event sourcing, and stream-processing checkpoints, you can achieve *effectively exactly-once* outcomes where they matter most, while keeping the rest of the system lighter and more flexible.

Armed with this toolbox, you can now reason systematically about reliability in trading systems: not as a vague hope that "the queue will deliver messages," but as a set of concrete, layered guarantees from transport up through business logic and into the ledgers and risk books that ultimately matter.

Chapter 4

Time, Ordering, and Reliability Guarantees

In live markets, every microsecond has a story, and your system must tell it in exactly the right order-even when the network lies, clocks disagree, and machines disappear. This chapter shows how professional trading stacks impose structure on time, enforce ordering, and engineer reliability so that P&L and regulatory truth remain intact despite latency spikes, out-of-order data, and partial outages.

4.1 Event vs Processing Time Semantics

Trading systems live in time. Orders, quotes, fills, and risk checks are all events that unfold on extremely fine time scales, and yet every layer of your architecture sees these events through a slightly different clock. If you do not name and manage these different notions of time explicitly, your system will slowly drift away from reality: volumes will not add up, latency measurements will be misleading, and P&L attribution will be hard to defend.

In this section we separate three timelines that every event-driven trading system must juggle:

- *Event time*: when something actually happened in the market or business domain.
- *Ingestion time*: when your system first observed and accepted the event.
- *Processing time*: when a particular component or job handled the event.

We then show how to build aggregations (for example, VWAP, order-book imbalance, and hit ratios) that remain logically correct even when the infrastructure around them is noisy: packets are delayed, messages are retried, and streams are replayed.

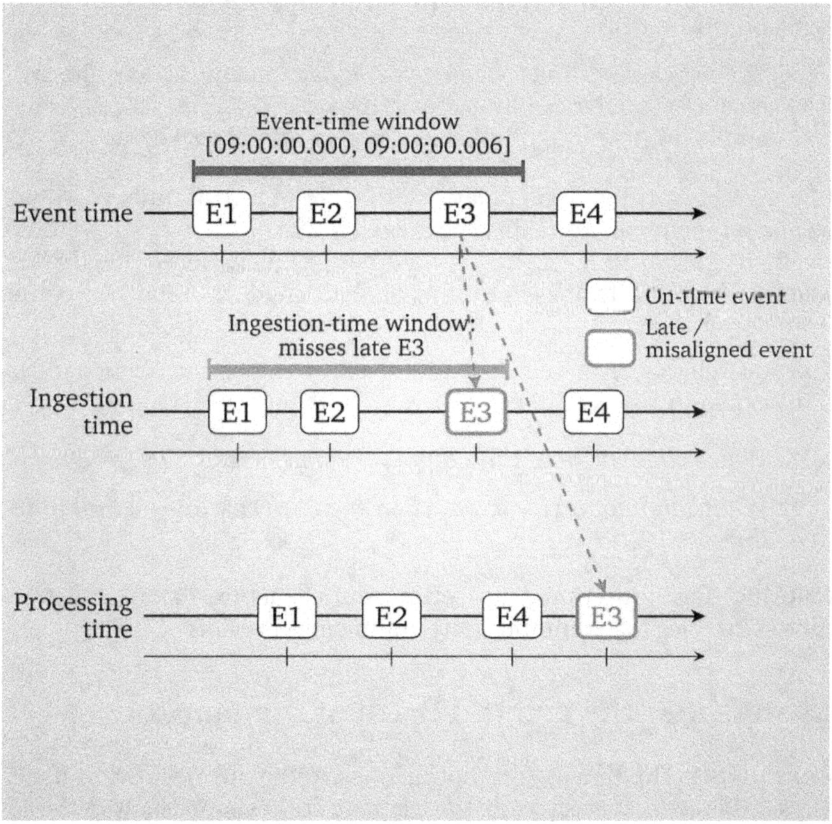

Three timelines for every event

Consider a simple example: you place a buy order for 10,000 shares of a stock at 09:00:00.003 according to the exchange clock. The exchange matches you at 09:00:00.006. Eventually, your trading system sees the fill, updates positions, and feeds that fill into analytics such as VWAP and realized P&L.

This single fill has at least three important timestamps:

- The *event time* of the fill: the exchange match time, 09:00:00.006.
- The *ingestion time*: when a gateway process in your infrastructure received and accepted the fill message, for example 09:00:00.008.
- The *processing time*: when a particular consumer—say, the risk engine or analytics job—actually processed the message, for example 09:00:00.050 if the system was briefly backed up.

In a perfect world with no delay or jitter, these three numbers would be almost identical. In reality, particularly during market stress, they can drift apart by milliseconds, sometimes by much more. That drift is exactly where subtle bugs in trading analytics and risk reporting come from.

To work reliably, every aggregation or metric must answer two questions explicitly:

1. *Which timeline does this computation use?*
2. *What behavior do we want when events arrive late on that timeline?*

Ignoring these questions and letting infrastructure defaults dictate time semantics is a common source of incorrect results.

Event time: the ground truth of the market

Event time is the timestamp that belongs to the business event itself. For market data, it is typically the exchange timestamp that the venue attaches to each trade or quote. For orders and fills in your own system, it may be the timestamp assigned at the moment the order is created, matched, or cancelled, according to a trusted clock.

Event time answers questions like:

- What was the true best bid and offer at 09:30:00.000?
- How many shares traded between 09:30:00 and 09:30:01?
- What was my VWAP over the first five minutes of the open?

These are questions about what actually happened in the market, not what your systems happened to observe at some later time. For that reason, whenever accuracy matters—measurement, backtesting, P&L attribution, compliance—you almost always want to anchor your logic to event time.

This has an important consequence: your system must treat event timestamps as first-class data, not as incidental fields. They should be:

- Captured as close to the source as possible using well-synchronized clocks.
- Preserved end-to-end through the messaging and storage layers.
- Used consistently when defining windows and aggregations.

If event timestamps are missing, unreliable, or overwritten by later components, the rest of the design cannot reliably reconstruct what happened.

Ingestion time: when data enters your system

Ingestion time is the moment a record crosses a boundary into your control: when a feed handler accepts a packet, a message broker appends a record to a topic, or a REST gateway successfully parses and validates an incoming request.

Ingestion time has two main uses:

1. **Operational monitoring.** You may want to know whether a market data source has gone quiet. If you see no new records ingested for a symbol in 500 milliseconds, that might be an alert, regardless of event time.

2. **Fallback ordering when event time is missing or broken.** Some sources do not provide reliable timestamps, or provide them only at coarse granularity. In those cases, ingestion time can be a pragmatic approximation to maintain ordering and windowing.

In a streaming platform, ingestion time is often the default notion of time. For example, many message brokers assign an internal timestamp when a message is appended to a partition. If you create a "last 5 seconds" aggregation without thinking about time semantics, you often get an ingestion-time window by default.

This is convenient but dangerous in trading. If network delays grow during market stress, the ingestion stream no longer reflects what is currently happening in the market; it reflects what the network was able to deliver recently. If you treat that as event time, your view of the world becomes skewed exactly when you care most about accuracy.

Processing time: when work actually happens

Processing time is the local clock at each consumer or component. It tells you when a particular piece of code ran. Processing time is mainly useful for:

- Measuring *latency*: how long after event time or ingestion time did processing occur?

- Scheduling background tasks: for example, a nightly reconciliation job runs at 02:00 processing time.

- Operational behavior under backpressure: a slower component will see processing times that lag behind ingestion times as it consumes a backlog.

Processing time is usually the easiest time to access: it is just "now" from the perspective of the code. But it is also the least stable for reasoning about the market. If a consumer falls behind, its notion of "the last one second of messages" will gradually slide further away from real-world recent events, and closer to a small historical window of backlog.

Therefore, processing time is typically reserved for operational and performance metrics, not for financial logic or market-facing analytics.

How skew and jitter corrupt naive metrics

To see the impact of choosing the wrong time semantics, consider a simple VWAP computation. You want the volume-weighted average price of all trades in the first minute after the open, from 09:30:00.000 to 09:30:59.999, according to the exchange clock.

If you define your one-minute window using event time, any trade whose event timestamp falls inside that interval contributes to VWAP, regardless of when your system sees it. A trade that is delayed by a network hiccup but still carries an event time of 09:30:00.100 will still be included eventually. The VWAP converges to the correct value as delayed trades arrive.

If instead you implement the VWAP over "the last 60 seconds of processing time," you get a moving approximate VWAP that depends on how smoothly messages flow through the network and through your consumers. Under calm conditions, this may be close to the true event-time VWAP. Under stress, it can diverge badly. A burst of delayed trades might land in the processing-time window even though they belong to an earlier market interval, pushing the VWAP away from the price at which liquidity actually traded during that minute.

The same pattern appears across many metrics:

- **Order-book imbalance.** If quote updates for the bid side are systematically delayed compared to the ask side, a processing-time snapshot of the book may consistently underestimate bid depth relative to ask depth, leading to a biased imbalance signal.
- **Hit and fill ratios.** When counting how many child orders were filled within a certain time after being sent, you must correlate

events by event time (or at least by a shared, trusted clock) rather than by when each component happened to process its own messages.

- **Risk exposure.** If you aggregate positions or Greeks in near real time using processing time windows, delayed fills can cause temporary inconsistencies between your reported risk and your true market exposure.

Skew (systematic delay in one part of the pipeline) and jitter (random variation in delay) are facts of life in distributed systems. The only robust way to defend financial correctness against them is to anchor key computations to event time and treat ingestion and processing time as secondary views.

Defining windows with explicit time semantics

Streaming systems often talk about windows: fixed intervals or regions over which you aggregate data. For trading analytics, the three most common forms are:

- **Tumbling windows:** fixed, non-overlapping intervals, such as "per 1 second" or "per 1 minute" summaries.
- **Sliding windows:** moving intervals that advance by a step smaller than their length, such as a 10-second window advanced every second.
- **Session windows:** intervals that expand as long as new events keep arriving, and close after a period of inactivity (for example, per-trader "bursts" of activity).

For each window, you must decide:

1. Which timeline defines the window boundaries.
2. How strictly you enforce that events belong to exactly one window or may update windows after the fact.

In trading systems:

- *Accuracy-critical analytics* (VWAP, volume by interval, short-term volatility) should use **event-time windows**. The boundaries are defined in terms of exchange or domain time. Late events update or correct earlier windows.
- *Operational dashboards* (ingestion throughput, feed health) commonly use **ingestion-time windows**. They tell you what your infrastructure has seen recently.
- *Component performance monitoring* (consumer lag, processing latency) use **processing-time windows**. They reflect how the component behaves over its local wall clock.

What matters is not only choosing the appropriate time, but also documenting it. Two graphs both labelled "per-second trade volume" can tell very different stories depending on whether they are event-time or ingestion-time metrics. For internal and regulatory investigations, you must be able to say which you are looking at.

Practical examples of late and replayed data

Real trading environments routinely generate late or out-of-order events. Three common sources are worth examining.

Late-arriving market data packets.

Under normal conditions, exchange market data flows smoothly. During volatile periods, link congestion or intermediate routers can cause bursts of delay. For a handful of milliseconds, you might not receive certain symbols' updates, and then they arrive in a clump.

In an event-time design, those delayed updates still slot into the correct windows once they arrive. Your "per-second" volume for 09:31:05 may be updated slightly later when the delayed fills land, but the final value is accurate. Operationally, you may also maintain an ingestion-time metric that shows a gap during the delay, which is a separate concern.

Replayed drop-copy streams.

Drop-copy feeds (for example, from an exchange or broker) often need to be replayed from a certain point after a failure or disconnect. When you replay, you are deliberately delivering historical events into a live system. If your aggregations are defined over processing time, replayed messages will contaminate “live” windows. If they are defined over event time, the replayed messages simply repair any gaps in the historical windows to which they belong.

In practice, you may choose to:

- Treat replay processing as a separate mode or environment, so that operational dashboards and alerts know they are catching up rather than seeing new activity.
- Allow event-time windows to be updated during and after replay, then mark them as complete once the replay is finished and watermarks (discussed later in the chapter) have advanced.

Delayed risk acknowledgements.

A risk engine may consume orders and market data, run risk checks, and emit acknowledgements or rejections. If that risk engine is momentarily overloaded, acknowledgements can be delayed relative to orders and fills. If you compute a “time to risk decision” metric in processing time based on when acknowledgements are produced, you will see artificial spikes whenever the engine backlogs.

Instead, measure the elapsed time between the event time (or ingestion time) of the triggering order and the event time of the acknowledgement as assigned by a trusted clock close to the risk engine. This separates true risk-check latency from transient queueing delays further downstream in analytics consumers.

Design patterns for handling time semantics

Putting these ideas into practice in a trading system involves a few repeatable patterns.

Carry event timestamps as first-class columns.

Every event type—orders, fills, quotes, risk decisions, P&L events—should include:

- A clear event-time field with semantics defined in the schema (for example, “exchange match time” or “order creation time”).

- Ingestion-time and/or broker-time fields where applicable.

Avoid overwriting these timestamps in downstream components. If a component must add its own processing-time view, add a new field rather than reuse the event-time field.

Tag metrics with their time semantics.

In documentation, dashboards, and configuration, make the time basis explicit. For example:

- vwap_1s_event_time
- md_ingestion_rate_per_source
- consumer_lag_vs_event_time

This naming discipline reduces confusion and makes it easier to debug disagreements between systems.

Use ingestion-time fallbacks under defined failure modes.

Sometimes, event timestamps are missing or clearly wrong (for example, an upstream bug sets them all to zero). In such cases, you may temporarily fall back to ingestion time to keep the pipeline moving.

If you do this, treat it as an explicit, degraded mode:

- Raise an alert that event-time correctness is compromised for affected streams.
- Mark downstream outputs (for example, files or database tables) with metadata indicating that they were computed under ingestion-time assumptions.
- Plan for later correction once valid event timestamps are available, perhaps via replay.

Separate correctness from freshness.

Traders often want "the most up-to-date number" and are tempted to accept processing-time approximations for speed. The better design is usually to provide:

- A fast, approximate processing-time metric clearly labeled as such, and
- A slightly lagged but event-time-correct metric that is authoritative for reporting, P&L, and risk.

By separating these, you let users benefit from fast feedback while keeping a solid ground truth for anything that must stand up to scrutiny.

Event-driven trading systems cannot get away with a single notion of time. Event time describes what truly happened in the market or business process. Ingestion time captures when your infrastructure first saw each event. Processing time reflects when individual components handled that event. Skew and jitter between these timelines are unavoidable, especially during market stress.

To keep analytics, P&L, and risk reporting reliable, you must:

- Anchor financial and market-facing calculations to event time.
- Reserve ingestion and processing time for operational and performance monitoring, and for well-defined fallback modes.
- Define windows and aggregations with explicit time semantics, and document those choices throughout the system.

With these foundations in place, you can then address more advanced topics such as watermarks and out-of-order handling, which we will explore next. They build directly on the distinction between event time and processing time introduced here, turning it into a systematic strategy for managing late and reordered data in production.

4.2 Ordering Guarantees and Reordering Buffers

In the previous section we separated the different notions of time in an event-driven trading system and saw how skew and jitter can silently corrupt metrics if we are careless. Time, however, is only part of the story. Even if every event carried a perfect event-time timestamp, your system would still need to reason about the *order* in which those events are delivered and processed.

Trading is full of order-dependent logic:

- An order must be *created* before it can be *acknowledged*, *partially filled*, or *cancelled*.
- A margin call must be evaluated after the position update that triggered it, not before.
- A reconciliation process expects that a "final" end-of-day position comes after all intraday trades have been seen.

When events arrive out of order, or are duplicated, naive consumers can easily end up in impossible states: a cancel with no prior order, a negative position for an account that never traded, or a risk engine that undoes the wrong trade because it mis-identified the latest one.

This section explains:

- What ordering properties the underlying messaging infrastructure can and cannot promise.
- How to design your own per-key ordering guarantees on top of those primitives.
- How to use reordering buffers to tolerate modest out-of-order delivery while still presenting a clean, strictly ordered stream to business logic.
- How to remain robust when partitions and consumers are rebalanced, restarted, or rescaled.

What ordering really means in practice

Before discussing infrastructure, it helps to be precise about what we mean by "ordering."

At the business level, we usually care about *per-entity* order: the sequence of events for one order, one instrument, one account, or one portfolio. For example, you may want to ensure that:

- For a given order ID, all status updates are processed in the same order in which the exchange produced them.
- For a given account, trades and cash flows are applied in the order they actually occurred, so that balances never go negative erroneously.

This is different from a *global order* of all events in the system. Global order would mean you could take every trade, order, balance update, and risk decision, sort them into a single exact sequence, and know that every consumer sees that exact sequence. That is rarely achievable, and almost never needed, in distributed trading architectures.

The important lesson is:

> Aim for per-key ordering for the entities that matter, not for global ordering across the entire system.

The "key" is the field (or combination of fields) that defines what "belongs together" from an ordering perspective: often an order ID, instrument ID, account ID, or strategy ID.

Ordering guarantees from common messaging systems

Modern messaging and streaming platforms (for example, log-based brokers) typically offer a specific and limited set of ordering guarantees. In broad terms, you can usually rely on the following:

Per-partition ordering. Within a single partition or shard, messages are appended in a well-defined sequence. A consumer that reads from that partition will see them in that same sequence, as long as it does not explicitly seek or jump around.

However:

- There is *no* guarantee about the relative order of messages in different partitions.
- If you have two events for the same logical entity and they land in different partitions, the infrastructure cannot preserve their order for you.

At-least-once delivery. To achieve durability and fault tolerance, many systems choose at-least-once delivery: a message may be delivered more than once (for example, after a consumer restart or rebalancing), but the broker promises not to lose it.

This implies:

- You must tolerate duplicates; order-dependent logic cannot assume each message is unique.
- A duplicated message may appear "late" relative to other events, even if originally it was earlier.

No global ordering across topics or partitions. Even if you use a single topic for all your trading events, once you have multiple partitions for scalability, there is no single global sequence that all consumers agree on. The platform may deliver messages from partition 0 and partition 1 interleaved in different ways to different consumers.

This is often surprising to teams that come from single-threaded or single-queue backgrounds. Distributed logs provide high throughput and fault tolerance, but the price is that ordering is only strong *within* each partition.

Choosing keys so partitions work *for* you

Given that per-partition ordering is what the infrastructure can support efficiently, your design goal is to align your per-key ordering needs with partition boundaries.

Conceptually, you want:

- All events that must be consistently ordered with respect to one another to share the same key when they are published.
- The broker to route all events with the same key to the same partition.

Common patterns include:

- **Order-centric keying:** Use the order ID as the key for all order lifecycle events (new, replace, cancel, fill, rejection). This ensures that the full lifecycle for one order flows through a single partition and is delivered in order to any consumer.

- **Account-centric keying:** Use the account or book ID as the key for all position, margin, and cash events. This ensures that the balance and risk state for one account are updated in a consistent sequence.
- **Instrument-centric keying:** Use the instrument ID or symbol as the key for market data and trading analytics when your computations are per-instrument (for example, order-book construction).

You cannot satisfy every desirable ordering property simultaneously. For example, you might like both "all events for a given order" and "all events for a given account" to share a partition. That will not scale. You must prioritize:

- Which entities need strong, real-time per-key ordering (for example, per-order lifecycle).
- Which entities can live with softer guarantees, recomputed views, or separate reconciliation processes (for example, end-of-day account summaries).

Once you choose a keying scheme for a topic, treat it as part of the contract. Changing it later can affect partitioning, consumer scaling, and ordering behavior.

Why consumers still see out-of-order events

Even when you key correctly and rely on per-partition ordering, real consumers still see out-of-order events at the business level. Common causes include:

- **Multiple sources for the same entity.** An order may be updated by both an internal OMS and an external exchange drop-copy. Their messages may arrive in different streams or topics and be merged later.

- **Retries and duplicates.** If a consumer crashes and restarts, it may re-read some messages. If producers or upstream gateways retry send operations, duplicates can enter the log.
- **Backfills and replays.** Historical data or corrections may be replayed into the same topics that carry live data, interleaving old and new events.

From the consumer's perspective, this means:

- Even if the broker delivers messages in partition order, the *logical sequence* of business events (for one key) may have gaps, repeats, or reversals.
- Your stateful logic—order books, positions, risk states—must therefore be tolerant of seeing "older" events after "newer" events, and of seeing the same event more than once.

This is where reordering buffers come in.

Per-key reordering buffers: the basic idea

A reordering buffer is a small, per-key data structure that:

- Accepts events as they arrive (possibly out of order).
- Uses some notion of sequence (event time, sequence number, or logical version) to determine their correct ordering.
- Holds onto events for a limited window to allow late arrivals to be placed correctly.
- Emits a clean, strictly ordered stream of events for that key to the downstream business logic.

You can think of it as a "shock absorber" between the messy real world and the core state machine that implements your trading logic.

To build such a buffer, you need:

1. A way to *identify the key* for each event (for example, order ID).

2. A way to *compare* two events for the same key and decide which should logically come first (for example, sequence number, exchange event time, or a monotonic version counter).
3. Policies for:
   - How long you are willing to wait for a potentially missing earlier event.
   - What to do when you detect a gap that does not fill.
   - How to handle duplicates and conflicting events.

Bounding the buffer: time-based and size-based limits

In theory, you could buffer events indefinitely until every possible earlier event arrives. In practice, you must limit how far you are willing to reorder. Otherwise, a single missing message could stall progress for a key forever.

Common strategies include:

Time-based bounds. For each key, you keep a window of events ordered by their sequence attribute, but you only wait a certain amount of real time for gaps to fill. For example:

- If event 5 arrives and event 4 is missing, you wait up to, say, 50 milliseconds.
- If event 4 still has not arrived after that, you proceed with 5 (perhaps marking that you skipped 4), or emit an error or alert.

Time-based bounds are useful when:

- You have empirical data about typical network jitter and out-of-order behavior.
- You cannot afford unbounded delays for downstream consumers.

Size-based bounds. Alternatively, you limit the number of buffered events per key. For example:

- You allow up to 10 un-emitted events per order ID.
- If adding the 11th would exceed the limit and earlier gaps have not filled, you decide on a resolution strategy (skip, log, or drop the key into a "needs manual attention" stream).

Often a hybrid approach is best: a time bound to avoid long stalls, and a size bound to prevent unbounded memory usage if a key becomes pathological.

Handling sequence gaps and duplicates

Let us look at two specific problems that reordering buffers must handle gracefully.

Sequence gaps. Suppose for a given order ID you expect messages with sequence numbers 1, 2, 3, 4, ... You see:

$$1, 2, 5, 6, 3, 4, 7, \ldots$$

Here the infrastructure preserved per-partition order, but some components delivered 5 and 6 before 3 and 4. A reordering buffer for this key would:

1. Accept 1 and 2, emit them immediately.
2. Accept 5 and 6, notice that 3 and 4 are missing, and buffer 5 and 6 rather than emitting them.
3. When 3 and 4 arrive (within the configured window), insert them into the buffer in the correct place and then emit 3, 4, 5, 6 in order.

If 3 and 4 never arrive within the time or size bounds, you need a policy. For example:

- Emit 5 and 6 anyway, but log that events 3 and 4 were missing, and perhaps mark the order as "incomplete history."
- Or move this key's events to a side channel for investigation and stop driving business logic from it until reconciled.

The right choice depends on whether your use case is latency-sensitive (for example, real-time trading decisions) or accuracy-critical (for example, official client reporting). Often, the trading path accepts approximation with logging, while the reporting path requires exactness and may tolerate delay.

Duplicates. Now suppose the consumer restarts and re-processes some events. For the same order ID you might see:

$$1, 2, 3, 3, 4, 5, 5, 5, 6, \ldots$$

Without defenses, your business logic might:

- Apply the same partial fill multiple times, inflating the executed quantity.
- Transition state backwards and forwards between "accepted" and "rejected" as it sees repeated status messages.

A reordering buffer (or more generally, idempotent state machine) should:

- Detect that an event with sequence number 3 has already been processed for this key.
- Either drop the duplicate silently or treat it as a no-op update.

This requires the buffer (or downstream state) to remember the highest sequence number processed per key, and sometimes to retain a small history of recent events in case updates are not perfectly idempotent.

Resynchronizing state after restarts

In real deployments, consumers crash and restart. When they do, they often:

- Rewind slightly in the log, replaying some messages.
- Start with empty in-memory buffers and caches.

To remain order-aware and correct across restarts, consider the following patterns:

Persisted offsets plus checkpoints. In addition to storing the broker offset (for example, "I have processed up to message N in partition P"), you maintain a compact checkpoint of your per-key state at regular intervals. On restart:

- You restore the latest checkpoint.
- You resume consuming from the corresponding offset.
- Any re-read messages are treated idempotently because the state machine and buffers know which sequence numbers or versions have already been applied.

Self-healing via authoritative sources. For some entities (for example, positions), you may have an external authoritative source (for example, the back office or prime broker). After a restart, instead of trying to perfectly reconstruct state from replayed events, you:

- Query the authoritative source for the current state.
- Use events primarily to stay up to date between such reconciliations.

In this pattern, reordering buffers still matter for short-term correctness, but long-term drift is bounded by periodic reconciliation.

Partition rebalancing and key migration

Messaging platforms distribute partitions across consumer instances for scalability. When instances join or leave a consumer group, partitions are reassigned: this is rebalancing.

Rebalancing affects ordering in two ways:

- A given partition (and therefore a set of keys) may now be processed by a different consumer instance.

- In-flight events that were buffered but not yet emitted at the time of reassignment must be handled carefully to avoid loss or duplication.

To remain robust during rebalancing:

Tie reordering buffers to partitions, not instances. Conceptually, the "truth" for a key lives in:

- The log partition that carries its events.
- The last committed offset for that partition.

A consumer instance is just a temporary holder of the buffer and state. When a partition moves, its new owner:

- Starts from the last committed offset.
- Rebuilds any necessary buffers from the events it reads, respecting sequence numbers and idempotency.

Use cooperative or graceful rebalancing when possible. Some systems allow a consumer to:

- Finish processing in-flight messages.
- Flush its per-key buffers and commit offsets cleanly.

before it relinquishes a partition. This reduces the amount of replay and reordering the new owner must handle.

Avoid mixing key spaces across partitions. If you maintain a cache that merges events for a key across multiple topics or partitions, ensure that each such merged view has clear rules about which source is authoritative and how updates are reconciled. The simpler the mapping "key $\rightarrow$ partition $\rightarrow$ consumer," the easier it is to reason about rebalancing.

Designing idempotent, order-aware processors

Reordering buffers are only half of the solution. The processors that consume from these buffers must also be designed to tolerate retries and partial failures without corrupting state.

Key design practices include:

- **Explicit state machines.** Model the lifecycle of key entities (orders, accounts, trades) as explicit states and allowed transitions. Reject or flag transitions that are impossible even after accounting for out-of-order delivery (for example, a fill before a new order).

- **Idempotent updates.** Define updates in terms of target states rather than increments when possible. For example, "position becomes 1,000 shares long" rather than "add 100 shares." This makes duplicates harmless.

- **Monotonic identifiers.** Use fields such as sequence numbers, event times, or version counters to decide whether a new event is "newer" than what you already have. Ignore or treat as corrections any events that are older.

- **Side channels for anomalies.** When an event violates ordering assumptions (for example, arrives too late to be safely applied), route it to a separate stream or log for investigation rather than forcing it into the main state.

Ordering in event-driven trading systems is not a binary property you either have or do not have. Infrastructure provides specific guarantees: per-partition order and at-least-once delivery, but no global ordering and no free protection from duplicates. Your job is to:

- Choose keys (order ID, account, instrument, strategy) so that the per-key order you care about aligns with partitions.

- Recognize that out-of-order and duplicate events will still occur due to multiple sources, retries, and replays.

- Use per-key reordering buffers with bounded time and size to smooth over modest out-of-order delivery.

- Design idempotent, order-aware processors and state machines that tolerate retries, restarts, and partition rebalancing without corrupting positions, risk states, or client reports.

With time semantics from the previous section and ordering guarantees from this one, we now have the building blocks needed to reason about late and out-of-order events more systematically. The next section introduces watermarks and allowed lateness as formal tools to manage the trade-off between freshness and completeness in real-time trading metrics and alerts.

4.3 Watermarks and Out-of-Order Handling

By now we have two ingredients in place. First, we learned that serious trading analytics should be anchored to *event time*, not to ingestion or processing time. Second, we saw that the infrastructure cannot guarantee perfectly ordered delivery, even per key, and that consumers must be prepared to buffer and reorder a little.

If we put these together, a natural question appears:

> If events can arrive late and out of order, how do we ever decide that a given event-time window is "complete enough" to publish a result?

For example, suppose you want a per-symbol, per-second volume and VWAP metric. You define the one-second windows using event time, as you should. But a trade with event time 10:00:01.500 might physically arrive at 10:00:02.200 because of network congestion. How long should you wait before deciding that the 10:00:01 window is complete? One millisecond? Ten? A full second? What if an entire micro-burst of trades for that symbol is delayed by 200 milliseconds under stress?

Watermarks and *allowed lateness* are the standard tools to manage this trade-off between **freshness** (publishing numbers quickly) and **completeness** (making sure you do not silently miss late events that belong to past windows). In this section we will:

- Define watermarks intuitively and show how they interact with event-time windows.

- Explain instrumental concepts like allowed lateness and window corrections.
- Work through trading examples such as late drop-copy fills and backfilled market data.
- Discuss practical strategies for configuring watermarks and monitoring lateness in production.

What is a watermark?

A *watermark* is the system's evolving guess about how far it has progressed along the event-time axis. More precisely:

> A watermark at event time T says: "I believe I have seen *all* (or almost all) events whose event time is earlier than T. Any additional earlier events are rare enough that I can treat them as exceptional."

Notice that a watermark is not a hard guarantee. It is a promise made under uncertainty, based on:

- How late events typically arrive from each source.
- What delays your network, brokers, and consumers usually introduce.
- Any explicit progress signals your data sources emit.

This is why we call it the system's *best guess*. In practice, watermarks are implemented as moving thresholds:

- As you ingest more data, your watermark advances forward.
- As you observe late events, you may slow down watermark advancement or adjust your heuristics.

Once the watermark moves past the end of a window (for example, beyond 10:00:01.000 for the 10:00:00–10:00:01 window), you are allowed to *close* that window and emit final results for it, with the understanding that any further events from before that event time will be treated as late.

Watermarks and window closing

To see how this works, imagine a per-symbol, per-second volume aggregation:

- Windows are defined in event time: [10:00:00.000, 10:00:00.999], [10:00:01.000, 10:00:01.999], and so on.
- Trades arrive with their event timestamps, sometimes out of order.
- The system maintains per-window accumulators for each symbol.

Without watermarks, you would never know when to stop accepting events for the 10:00:00 window. You could, in theory, see a trade with event time 10:00:00.500 hours later because of some replay or backfill. You need a rule that says, "for real-time metrics, we are willing to stop updating the 10:00:00 window after some point."

With watermarks, the rule becomes:

> Close and publish the 10:00:00 window once the watermark is at or beyond, say, 10:00:01.000.

At this moment, you assume you have seen all trades that happened before 10:00:01.000, and that the 10:00:00 window is now complete for real-time purposes.

Where do watermarks come from?

There are two main approaches to constructing watermarks in practice.

Heuristic (observed) watermarks.

In this approach, watermarks are derived purely from the events you have seen so far. A simple version is:

- Track the maximum event time observed across all events from a given source or pipeline.

- Define the watermark as "maximum event time seen minus a safety margin."

For example, if the latest event time observed from an exchange feed is 10:00:02.500, and you know from experience that 99% of events arrive within 100 milliseconds of their true event time, you might set the watermark to 10:00:02.400. That way, windows ending before 10:00:02.400 are closed, while windows that might still receive late events remain open.

Heuristic watermarks are easy to implement and work well when lateness patterns are fairly stable. Their downside is that they can be misled by extreme outliers (for example, an event with an incorrectly set event time far in the future) and do not distinguish between sources with different delay distributions.

Source-driven (explicit) watermarks.

Some sources can emit explicit signals about their progress. For example:

- A gateway might periodically insert a "checkpoint" message stating, "I have sent you all trades up to event time 10:00:01.000 for this symbol."
- A batch job might send a final "end-of-segment" message after replaying all events for a historical period.

These explicit signals are much stronger than heuristics because they reflect knowledge from the source about its own completeness. You can treat them as authoritative for that source's contribution.

In many trading systems, you combine both:

- Use explicit watermarks where available (for example, from proprietary gateways you control).
- Fall back to heuristic watermarks for third-party feeds or legacy systems that cannot emit explicit progress.

Allowed lateness: forgiving but bounded

Even with carefully tuned watermarks, some events will occasionally arrive after the watermark has passed their event time. These are *late events*. How you handle them is a policy choice that directly reflects a business trade-off.

Two extreme positions are:

- **Zero tolerance**: once the watermark has passed, any earlier event is discarded or sent to a side channel. Real-time metrics are never revised.
- **Full tolerance**: late events are always incorporated, and historical windows are updated forever. Real-time metrics may keep changing long after you first published them.

Trading systems often choose a middle ground called *allowed lateness*. The idea is:

> Even after a window is first closed, we will continue to accept and correct that window for late events up to some additional delay. After that, the window becomes final.

Concretely, suppose:

- The window [10:00:00, 10:00:01) is initially closed and published when the watermark reaches 10:00:01.000.
- You set an allowed lateness of 500 milliseconds.

Then:

- Between watermark times 10:00:01.000 and 10:00:01.500, any new trade with event time in [10:00:00, 10:00:01) is still accepted into the window and triggers an updated result.
- Once the watermark advances beyond 10:00:01.500, that window is considered permanently closed. Any further event with timestamp in [10:00:00, 10:00:01) is rejected as "too late" for real-time processing, and handled separately.

Allowed lateness thus gives you a two-stage lifecycle for each window:

- **Open stage**: Still collecting events, no results published.
- **Correction stage**: Initial results published, but further corrections allowed within a grace period.
- **Final stage**: Window frozen, further late data handled out-of-band.

This approach strikes a balance:

- Traders see up-to-date numbers quickly, with the understanding that small revisions may follow within a short interval.
- P&L attribution and regulatory reports can rely on final, stable numbers once the allowed-lateness window has passed.

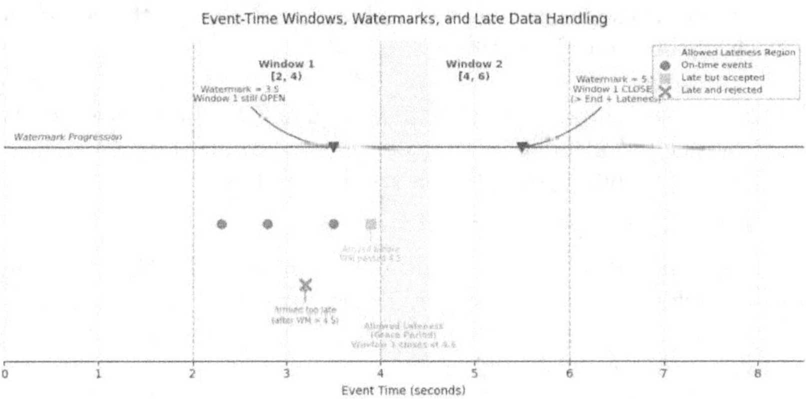

Freshness vs completeness: trading examples

Let us see how these ideas play out in typical trading workflows.

Per-symbol volume and short-term volatility.

Suppose you compute a rolling 1-second volume and volatility metric per symbol for:

- Feed health monitoring.
- Detecting quote-stuffing or sudden bursts of activity.

These signals are mainly *operational* and *tactical*. Traders and support staff want to know almost immediately if a symbol's activity is spiking or if a data feed has gone quiet.

In this context:

- You prioritize **freshness**. You might accept watermarks that trail only, say, 50–100 milliseconds behind the maximum event time seen.
- You allow limited lateness, perhaps another 50–100 milliseconds, to catch a typical tail of slightly delayed events.
- Events that arrive much later (for example, more than 200 milliseconds late) are treated as anomalies. They may be logged or fed into separate diagnostics but do not change the real-time chart the trader is watching.

The result is a dashboard that responds quickly to the market, at the cost of occasionally undercounting slightly late trades in past windows. For operational monitoring, this is usually acceptable.

Drop-copy fills feeding real-time risk.

Now consider a drop-copy feed of executions for your firm, coming from an exchange or prime broker. These fills feed into:

- Your real-time risk engine.
- Strategy-level P&L and exposure dashboards.

Here the trade-off is sharper:

- Risk needs as accurate a picture as possible of current positions and P&L.
- Traders also want timely information; a multi-second lag is uncomfortable.

A common pattern is:

- Use slightly **more conservative watermarks** than for pure market-data analytics, perhaps trailing event time by 200–500 milliseconds instead of 50–100.
- Allow a longer allowed-lateness window, for example one or two seconds, during which corrections to P&L are acceptable.
- Beyond that, treat additional arrivals as late corrections that may feed into reconciliation processes rather than real-time risk displays.

In quiet markets, this may feel overly cautious; in stressed conditions, it is often the difference between having a stable, defensible risk view and constantly shifting numbers that nobody trusts.

Historical backfills and live processing.

Sometimes you need to replay historical data into the same pipeline that is also handling live events. For example:

- You discover a gap in data for a symbol between 09:35 and 09:36.
- You obtain missing trades from the exchange and inject them into the system later in the day.

From the perspective of event time, these backfilled events are extremely late: hours or days. If you fed them into your real-time pipeline without care, they would violate every watermark and allowed-lateness assumption you made.

Typical strategies include:

- Separating backfill and live streams logically, even if they share some infrastructure.
- Configuring the backfill path with very different watermark policies (or none at all), letting it recompute historical windows offline or in a sandboxed environment.
- Once the historical corrections are applied, replacing or annotating the stored results that downstream systems use for reporting.

The key is not to let extreme late data intended for repair pollute your routine real-time metrics. Watermarks and allowed lateness should reflect your expectations for *normal* streaming behavior, not rare administrative operations.

Implementation patterns for watermarks

There are several ways to implement watermarks across a distributed trading system. The right choice depends on how centralized or decentralized your streaming architecture is.

Per-source watermarks.

Each source (for example, each exchange feed handler or gateway) maintains its own watermark based on what it has seen and emitted. Downstream components then:

- Track the watermark for each upstream source.
- Combine them to form a *global* watermark, often as the minimum of all source watermarks.

The intuition is:

> You cannot consider a window complete until *all* relevant sources believe they are past that window in event time.

For example, per-symbol volume might depend on:

- Trades from the primary venue.
- Trades from dark pools.
- Internal crossing or internalization fills.

You may choose to compute a separate watermark for each of these, and then use the minimum as the effective watermark for that instrument.

Per-partition watermarks.

If you are using a partitioned log (such as a topic with multiple partitions), you can track a watermark for each partition based on the events consumed from that partition. A consumer that aggregates across partitions then:

- Maintains a watermark per partition.
- Defines its effective watermark as the minimum across the partitions it depends on.

This mirrors the per-source case but aligns with infrastructure boundaries rather than business sources. It is useful when partitions are already organized by key (for example, symbol) and each partition can advance semi-independently.

Central vs distributed watermark management.

In some systems, a central service computes and publishes global watermarks. In others, each consumer or job computes its own watermarks based on the data it sees.

Central management can simplify reasoning—everyone agrees on the same notion of progress—but at the cost of an extra moving piece. Distributed management is more flexible but requires careful documentation and monitoring; different jobs may make slightly different tradeoffs.

Whatever you choose, the goal is to make watermarks:

- **Visible**: expose current watermarks in metrics and logs.
- **Configurable**: allow tuning per source, instrument, or use case.
- **Testable**: simulate late arrivals in non-production environments to see how watermarks behave.

Observability: measuring lateness in the wild

Because watermarks are based on assumptions about lateness, you need to continuously validate those assumptions. Helpful practices include:

Lateness histograms.

For each source and for key pipelines, measure:

- The distribution of (ingestion time – event time).
- The tail behavior: 95th, 99th, 99.9th percentile latencies.

Plotting these over time tells you:

- Whether your chosen safety margins still cover typical delays.
- Whether certain venues or instruments behave differently (for example, illiquid products that batch their reports).

Watermark lag metrics.

Expose metrics such as:

- watermark_lag_ms: the difference between "now" (processing time) and the current watermark.
- max_event_time_seen vs watermark_time.

If the watermark frequently lags much more than expected behind the maximum event time or behind processing time, you may be overly conservative. If it runs too close and you see many late rejections, you may be too aggressive.

Late-event counters.

Count how many events are:

- Accepted into open windows.
- Accepted into correction windows (within allowed lateness).
- Rejected as too late.

High or climbing rejection rates mean your watermarks and allowed-lateness settings are out of sync with real conditions and need adjustment.

Surfacing corrections to users and systems

When you accept late-but-within-lateness events and update previous windows, you are effectively emitting *corrections*. Downstream users and systems need to understand that numbers can change.

Practical patterns include:

- **Versioned outputs.** Attach a version or sequence number to each window's published result. If a later correction arrives, emit a new version. Consumers that care about stability can decide whether to always take the latest version or to lock in a particular version after some time.
- **Correction streams.** Instead of overwriting earlier outputs in place, emit delta updates or "correction events" that specify how a previous aggregate changed. This helps audit trails and allows downstream stores to apply changes incrementally.
- **User interface cues.** For trader dashboards, visually indicate that certain metrics are "provisional" and may be revised within a short interval. Once the allowed lateness has passed, switch them to a "final" label.

The important point is psychological as much as technical: if users expect numbers to change slightly during a correction window, they are not surprised by small adjustments. If they believe every number is instantly final, even tiny corrections can erode trust.

Out-of-order and late events are an unavoidable reality in event-driven trading systems. Watermarks and allowed lateness give you a principled way to live with that reality:

- Watermarks capture your best estimate of how far along the event-time axis your system has progressed, letting you decide when to close windows.
- Allowed lateness defines a grace period during which windows can still accept corrections from late-arriving events, after which results become final.

- Different trading use cases—from feed monitoring to risk to historical backfills—prefer different points along the freshness-completeness trade-off and therefore need different watermark and lateness configurations.
- Observability around lateness and watermark behavior is essential; your assumptions must be continuously validated against real production data.

With event-time semantics, ordering guarantees, reordering buffers, and watermarks, you now have a toolkit for building streaming analytics that are both timely and defensible. The next step is to ensure that the timestamps underlying all of this logic are themselves accurate and trustworthy, which brings us to clock synchronization and regulatory time requirements.

4.4 Clock Synchronization and Regulatory Accuracy

In the previous sections we treated timestamps as if they were objective facts: each event had an event time, and our job was to respect that time when building windows, watermarks, and ordering guarantees. In real systems, however, timestamps are created by clocks, and clocks are imperfect physical devices. If you are not careful, your "ground truth" event times will be inconsistent across machines, data centers, and venues.

For a trading firm, this is not a minor technical nuisance. It affects:

- **Competitive edge**: microsecond differences in perceived latency can change routing and arbitrage decisions.
- **Internal forensics**: when something goes wrong, you must be able to reconstruct what happened in the correct order.
- **Regulatory compliance**: regimes such as MiFID II and others impose strict limits on timestamp error and require firms to keep detailed, accurate audit trails.

In this section we focus on how to synchronize clocks and timestamp events in a way that supports the time- and ordering-sensitive machinery we have built so far, and satisfies regulatory expectations.

Why clock accuracy matters in trading

To see why clock accuracy is so important, imagine the following simple situation:

- Your trading engine sends an order to Venue A at what it believes is 10:00:00.000.
- Venue A timestamps the receipt of the order at 10:00:00.050 according to its own clock.
- A few microseconds later, your engine sends a similar order to Venue B, which timestamps it at 09:59:59.980.

If your internal clocks are skewed relative to the venues (and to each other), you may infer that:

- Venue B is faster than it really is, because your local send time appears later than their receive time.
- Venue A is slower or more congested than it really is.

On this distorted picture you might base routing decisions, performance analysis, or even compliance reports about best execution. In extreme cases, poor clock discipline can make it appear that you violated rules (for example, trading after a halt) when you did not, or vice versa.

From a technical perspective, inaccurate or inconsistent clocks show up in many places:

- **Latency measurements** between components or to venues.
- **Cross-feed comparisons** between different market data sources.

- **Replay and backtesting**, where you try to align events from multiple logs into a single timeline.
- **Regulatory audit trails**, which expect that timestamps from different systems can be meaningfully compared.

The rest of this section is about engineering your time infrastructure so that, for your purposes, “10:00:00.000” means the same thing everywhere that matters.

Layers of time: from reference clocks to applications

The time story in a trading firm has several layers. It is helpful to visualize it as a hierarchy:

- At the top, an external or internal **reference clock** (for example, GPS-disciplined atomic clocks, GNSS receivers, or time services from telecom providers).
- In the middle, one or more **time distribution systems**, such as NTP (Network Time Protocol) and PTP (Precision Time Protocol), that propagate time from the reference to your data centers.
- At the bottom, **local consumers of time**: operating systems, network interface cards (NICs), middleware, trading applications, and logging systems.

Your goal is not to perfectly align every clock on every device in the firm—that is impossible—but to:

- Keep all relevant clocks within a known, monitored error bound relative to a chosen reference.
- Use the most accurate clock available when assigning timestamps to critical events.
- Record enough context to understand the accuracy of each timestamp later.

NTP: a baseline for coarse synchronization

NTP is the traditional workhorse protocol for synchronizing computer clocks over IP networks. It works by exchanging timestamped messages between clients and servers and estimating:

- The round-trip delay between them.
- The offset (difference) between their clocks.

NTP is relatively easy to deploy and sufficient for many IT systems. On a well-behaved network, NTP can often keep machines within a few milliseconds (and sometimes tens or hundreds of microseconds) of each other.

In trading, NTP is useful, but has clear limitations:

- **Variable network delay**: NTP runs over general-purpose networks where latency and asymmetry (different delays in each direction) are not tightly controlled. This makes fine-grained accuracy difficult.
- **Software timestamping**: Timestamps for NTP packets are usually taken in software, after traversing the OS networking stack, adding jitter.
- **Regulatory margins**: Some regulatory regimes permit millisecond-level timestamp error for certain activities, but high-frequency or high-volume trading strategies often need microsecond-level precision to reason soundly about latency and sequencing.

For non-latency-critical systems (for example, back-office applications, reporting databases, some risk aggregation layers), NTP is often entirely adequate. For trading gateways and low-latency analytics, it is usually only the starting point.

PTP: precision time in the data center

For higher precision, many trading firms deploy PTP (IEEE 1588 Precision Time Protocol). PTP is designed for environments where time synchronization at the microsecond—or even sub-microsecond—level is required.

Key ideas in PTP include:

- **Grandmaster clocks**: Designated master devices that have a high-quality time source (such as GPS) and serve as the root of the time hierarchy.
- **Boundary and transparent clocks**: Network switches and routers that participate in time distribution, compensating for their own internal delays and passing more accurate timing information to downstream devices.
- **Hardware timestamping**: NICs and switches that capture timestamps at the moment a packet enters or leaves the physical interface, dramatically reducing jitter compared to software timestamping.

In a well-designed PTP deployment, you can often keep servers within tens of nanoseconds to a few microseconds of the grandmaster. The exact accuracy depends on:

- The quality of the hardware.
- Network topology and load.
- Environmental factors such as temperature (which affect oscillators).

For trading use cases such as:

- High-frequency order gateways.
- Co-located market data handlers.
- Latency-sensitive analytics and internal routing.

PTP-backed hardware timestamping is often the only realistic way to produce timestamps that you can treat as "good enough" ground truth.

Hardware timestamping: getting close to the wire

Recall from earlier sections that we distinguish between event time, ingestion time, and processing time. When market packets arrive from an exchange, or orders leave your gateway, the *earliest* trustworthy point to capture their time is as close as possible to the network wire.

Hardware timestamping achieves this by:

- Letting the NIC or switch insert a timestamp into packet metadata at the moment the first bit of the frame is received or transmitted.
- Using PTP-synchronized clocks inside the NIC and network devices so those timestamps are consistent with the rest of the system.

Compared to relying on application-level timestamps (for example, taking the time after a packet has moved through the kernel and user-space stack), hardware timestamps:

- Eliminate much of the jitter caused by variable queueing and processing delays.
- Provide a more stable basis for latency measurements and event time assignment.

In many architectures, you will see multiple timestamp fields associated with a single event:

- **Exchange timestamp**: When the venue says the trade or quote occurred, according to its clock.
- **NIC receive timestamp**: When the packet carrying that message hit your network hardware.
- **Application receive timestamp**: When your process decoded it.

For market data, you may treat the exchange timestamp as the "true" event time, using your own NIC and application timestamps for latency analysis. For orders you originate, your own hardware send timestamp (and your synchronized clock) define the event time from your side.

Clock drift, skew, and leap seconds

Even with NTP or PTP, clocks are not perfect. Understanding their failure modes helps you design safe systems.

Drift.

Each clock (oscillator) tends to run slightly fast or slow compared to the reference. This deviation is *drift*. Time synchronization protocols correct drift periodically, but between corrections, the local clock may move away from the reference.

For example:

- A server's clock drifts by 1 microsecond per second relative to the grandmaster.
- If it is not corrected for 10 seconds, it may be off by about 10 microseconds.

The more often you resynchronize, and the better your hardware, the smaller this drift becomes.

Skew and step corrections.

When a synchronization client discovers that its local clock is off by some amount, it can:

- **Slew** the clock: gradually speed it up or slow it down so it converges to the correct time without jumping.
- **Step** the clock: jump directly forward or backward to the correct time.

Slewing is gentler and avoids time "going backwards" (which can cause serious bugs in time-based logic), but it takes longer to correct large errors. Stepping is faster but must be done carefully and usually only during controlled periods (for example, during startup, or in components that do not drive real-time decisions).

For trading engines and timestamping services, it is common to:

- Allow slewing for small corrections within specified bounds.
- Trigger alerts or even failover if the required correction exceeds a safe threshold, rather than stepping in place.

Leap seconds and time standards.

Coordinated Universal Time (UTC) occasionally inserts leap seconds to keep clock time aligned with Earth's rotation. This means that a specific minute (for example, 23:59 UTC on a given day) might have 61 seconds.

Leap seconds can cause subtle issues:

- Some systems smear leap seconds over a longer period, gradually adjusting clock speed.
- Others apply a hard step, repeating or skipping a second.

You do not need to become a timekeeping expert, but you *do* need a documented firm-wide policy:

- How are leap seconds handled by your reference clocks and distribution systems?
- How should trading and risk systems interpret timestamps around leap seconds?

Regulators and auditors are unlikely to accept "we did not think about leap seconds" as an excuse for misaligned logs.

Regulatory expectations for timestamp accuracy

Regulatory regimes differ in their exact numbers and wording, but they generally expect that:

- You timestamp key events (order receipt, order transmission, execution, cancellation, system decisions) at a sufficiently fine granularity.
- Your timestamps are accurately synchronized to an external time standard (usually UTC) within a specified maximum error.
- You can demonstrate and document how clocks are synchronized and monitored.
- You retain logs and evidence for a defined period, so that regulators can reconstruct events.

A typical structure of requirements includes:

- **Maximum timestamp error**: For example, important systems must be synchronized to UTC within a certain number of microseconds or milliseconds, depending on activity type.
- **Granularity**: Timestamps must be recorded to a certain resolution (for example, one millisecond or one microsecond).
- **Traceability**: Firms must document their time sources and synchronization mechanisms and keep records of clock offsets and failures.

From a system design perspective, this implies:

- Your clock infrastructure (NTP, PTP, hardware) must be engineered to consistently beat the regulatory maximum error margin, with headroom.
- You must monitor and record offsets and synchronization quality for relevant machines, not just configure them once and assume everything is fine.
- You must propagate timestamps through your event-driven pipelines in ways that preserve their meaning and precision.

Propagating and labeling timestamps end-to-end

Earlier in the chapter we stressed carrying event timestamps as first-class data. With synchronization in mind, we can refine that advice:

- Distinguish clearly between *exchange timestamps*, *local timestamps* (for example, NIC receive time), and any derived *event time* fields your system uses.
- For each timestamp, record (at least implicitly) the time source and approximate accuracy.

Examples of good practice include:

- For incoming market data:
  - Preserve the original exchange timestamp field.
  - Add fields such as local_recv_time_ptp, which is the NIC or host time on receipt.
- For outbound orders:
  - Timestamp the moment an order leaves your system at the NIC, using PTP-synchronized hardware.
  - If the venue echoes back your order with its own timestamp, retain both and track the difference.
- For internal events (risk decisions, strategy signals):
  - Use the local PTP-synchronized time as the event time.
  - Include system identifiers so you can later correlate offsets if needed.

Downstream, when you join data from multiple sources:

- Prefer exchange or venue timestamps for market sequencing questions ("which trade happened first?").
- Use local timestamps to analyse path latency ("how long between us sending and the venue acknowledging?").

Being explicit about which clock each timestamp came from avoids subtle bugs such as comparing a PTP-synchronized timestamp from one server with an NTP-only timestamp from another and treating them as equivalent.

Monitoring synchronization quality in production

A synchronization setup is only as good as its monitoring. You should treat time as a critical shared resource, just like network connectivity or power. Practical monitoring includes:

Offset dashboards.

For each PTP or NTP client:

- Track the measured offset from its upstream server or grandmaster.
- Record these offsets over time and expose them via metrics dashboards.

Alarm when:

- The offset exceeds a configured threshold (well below any regulatory maximum).
- The offset variance (jitter) grows unusually large.

Grandmaster health and failover.

If you rely on one or more PTP grandmasters:

- Monitor their lock to the external time source (for example, GPS signal quality).
- Define clear failover behavior if a grandmaster degrades: which backup takes over, and how clients detect and adapt.
- Log transitions between grandmasters; those times may matter in later investigations.

Synthetic probes and round-trip tests.

In addition to relying on protocol-level metrics, you can:

- Periodically send synthetic messages between key components and measure apparent one-way and round-trip delays using their local clocks.
- Compare those with expectations; large unexplained asymmetries may reveal synchronization problems.

Integration with event pipelines.

Finally, integrate time health with your event-driven monitoring:

- If a machine's clock drifts beyond safe bounds, consider pausing or isolating trading on that machine.
- Flag events from unsynchronized systems in logs and analytics so they are not silently mixed with high-quality timestamps.

Safe fallbacks and failure modes

No time infrastructure is perfect. You must decide in advance how trading systems behave when time quality degrades. Examples of policies include:

Graceful degradation.

If a trading node's clock offset exceeds a soft threshold but remains within a hard limit:

- Continue trading, but:
  - Annotate all events from that node as having degraded time accuracy.
  - Possibly restrict activities that depend heavily on precise latency measurement.

Automatic isolation or shutdown.

If the offset exceeds a hard threshold, or if a grandmaster fails and no reliable backup is available:

- Automatically remove affected nodes from trading clusters or consumer groups.
- Trigger alerts and, if necessary, firm-wide kill switches as discussed later in the chapter.

Fallback to coarser sources.

In some cases, a PTP infrastructure may fail but NTP remains available. You might:

- Temporarily accept lower accuracy for non-latency-critical activities (for example, high-level risk dashboards).
- Suspend activities that require tight microsecond-level guarantees until PTP is restored.

The important point is to design and document these behaviors in advance, not improvise during an incident.

Bringing it all together

Clock synchronization underpins everything we have discussed in this chapter:

- **Event vs processing time**: Without accurate clocks, even well-designed event-time semantics lose their meaning across components.
- **Ordering guarantees and reordering**: When combining streams from different machines or venues, synchronized clocks make it possible to reason about the order in which things truly happened.
- **Watermarks and lateness**: Watermarks rely on credible event timestamps; if those drift, your freshness-completeness trade-offs may be based on false assumptions.

From a practical viewpoint, building a robust time infrastructure for a trading firm involves:

- Choosing appropriate technologies (NTP vs PTP vs hardware timestamping) for each tier.
- Designing a time distribution hierarchy (reference clocks, grandmasters, boundary clocks) that matches your data center topology.
- Ensuring that critical timestamping happens close to the wire, using synchronized hardware where possible.
- Propagating timestamps and their meaning through your event-driven architecture without dilution.
- Monitoring offset, jitter, and failures continuously, with clear thresholds and playbooks.
- Aligning all of this with regulatory requirements and being able to demonstrate your discipline to auditors.

If you treat time as a first-class system, on par with networking and storage, you give your trading platform a stable temporal foundation. The reliability and interpretability of your queues, state, and processing then follow much more naturally.

4.5 Retry Strategies, Backoff, and DLQs

Up to this point, the chapter has focused on correctness under normal, if noisy, conditions: clocks may drift, events may arrive out of order, and windows must trade off freshness against completeness. In production, however, your trading system also has to survive more direct problems: services go down, exchanges throttle you, databases return errors, and messages turn out to be malformed or semantically invalid.

In an event-driven architecture, these problems surface as *failed message deliveries* or *failed message processings*. If you handle these failures naively—by immediately retrying every error in a tight loop—you can:

- Overload shared components (brokers, databases, gateways) at the worst possible moment.

- Amplify small glitches into widespread outages.
- Corrupt positions and risk state if retries are not idempotent.

This section explains how to design retry strategies, backoff policies, and dead-letter handling so that transient failures heal automatically, while persistent problems are isolated and investigated without endangering the rest of the system.

Transient vs persistent failures

The first conceptual step is to distinguish between two broad classes of failure:

- **Transient failures**: Problems that are likely to resolve themselves if you wait and try again.
- **Persistent failures**: Problems that cannot be fixed by retrying; they require a code or configuration change, or manual intervention.

Examples of transient failures include:

- Brief network glitches or timeouts when calling an external venue gateway.
- Temporary throttling or "try again later" responses from an exchange during a burst of traffic.
- Short-lived overload in an internal risk engine or pricing service.

If you wait a short period and then retry, the call will probably succeed.

Examples of persistent failures include:

- A malformed FIX message from a client that violates the protocol.
- A new field in an upstream message that your schema cannot parse.

- A business rule violation, such as an order that exceeds the maximum allowed size or a trade that would breach risk limits.

No amount of retrying will make these messages valid. They are "poison" for your processing pipeline unless they are corrected or handled by a different path.

The core design principle is:

> *Retry transient failures automatically with care; route persistent failures to separate handling paths as early as possible.*

Retry strategies, backoff, and dead-letter queues are the tools that embody this principle.

Why naive retries are dangerous

It is tempting to implement error handling like this:

> If a call fails, retry immediately, and keep trying until it works.

In a single-threaded, toy system this might appear to work most of the time. In a real trading environment, it is dangerous for several reasons:

- **Retry storms**: If a shared dependency (for example, a risk service) becomes slow or temporarily unavailable, dozens or hundreds of callers may all start retrying aggressively at once. Instead of giving the service time to recover, they flood it with more requests, deepening the outage.
- **Resource exhaustion**: Each retry consumes CPU, memory, connection slots, and queue capacity. If you retry without bounds, you risk exhausting these resources for all clients, not just the ones that are failing.
- **Unbounded latency**: For a given message or order, endless retries can mean you never declare failure. From a trading perspective, it may be better to give a clear, quick failure ("we could

not place this order") than to leave the client hanging for minutes while you quietly retry.

To address these issues, you need two controls:

- **How to retry**: spacing retries out over time, with some randomness, rather than hammering the dependency.
- **How much to retry**: limiting the total number of attempts or total time spent before declaring failure and moving the message to a dead-letter path.

Exponential backoff and jitter

A widely used pattern for safe retrying is *exponential backoff* with *jitter*.

Exponential backoff.

With exponential backoff, the delay before each retry attempt grows, often doubling each time up to a maximum. Intuitively:

- A first retry happens quickly, on the assumption that the failure might have been a brief glitch.
- If the error persists, the system waits longer and longer between attempts, giving the failing component more time to recover and reducing load on it.

For example, you might try after 50 milliseconds, then 100, then 200, 400, 800, and so on, up to some cap (for example, 5 seconds between attempts).

Jitter.

If many clients follow the same exponential backoff schedule, they can still synchronize: all of them fail at the same time, wait the same 100 milliseconds, then all retry at once, and so on. This produces load spikes precisely when the failing service is most fragile.

Jitter means adding a small random variation to each delay so that retries for different clients and messages are spread out over time. For instance, instead of waiting exactly 200 milliseconds, one client waits 180 ms, another 230 ms, and so on. This smoothing reduces the risk of aligned "thundering herd" behavior.

Tailoring backoff to trading workflows.

In trading, you must balance backoff against latency expectations:

- For **client-facing order entry**, you may accept only a small number of fast retries (for example, within a few hundred milliseconds total) before signalling failure and perhaps suggesting the client resubmit or route elsewhere.
- For **background processes** such as enrichment, analytics, or non-critical notifications, you can afford longer backoff sequences and more aggressive retry budgets, since user-facing SLAs are looser.

The key is to align retry behavior with the business importance and time sensitivity of the operation.

Retry budgets and failure policies

A *retry budget* defines the maximum effort you are willing to spend trying to process a message before you admit defeat and move it aside. Budgets can be defined in terms of:

- **Maximum attempts**: for example, "no more than 5 tries per message."
- **Maximum elapsed time**: for example, "no more than 2 seconds of waiting across all retries."
- **Combination of both**: for example, "up to 5 attempts, but not longer than 1 second total."

Once the budget is exhausted, the system must make a deliberate choice:

- Drop the message and log an error (usually not acceptable for trading events).

- Block the pipeline, effectively halting processing of subsequent messages (dangerous in a shared system).
- Route the message to a *dead-letter queue* (DLQ) for separate handling.

In event-driven trading systems, DLQs are usually the right answer for important but persistently failing messages. They let the main flow continue while preserving failing events for analysis and potential repair.

Per-message vs batch retries

When you design retries in a streaming context, it is important to distinguish between:

- **Per-message retries**: handling each event independently according to its own retry policy.
- **Batch or offset-based retries**: re-processing a whole batch of messages or re-seeking to an earlier offset in a log.

Per-message retries are straightforward conceptually: if processing event X fails transiently, you wait and retry X. However, if you are consuming from a log that enforces ordering, you must decide whether:

- You are allowed to *skip* X temporarily, continue with later messages, and come back to X later, or
- You must fully process X before moving on to messages that come after it in the log.

In trading, strict in-order processing is often required per key (e.g., order ID or account), but not necessarily across unrelated keys. Design choices include:

- Offloading the problematic message X to a side topic so the main consumer can advance, while a specialized worker deals with X separately.

- Using a per-key processing model, where the failure of one key (one order) does not block other keys, because they are processed in separate streams or tasks.

Batch or offset-based retries (for example, "rewind to this offset and reprocess everything from there") are sometimes used to recover from systemic problems such as a bad deployment. They are powerful but dangerous if your processing is not idempotent, since the same events will be applied again. For that reason, batch replays are often confined to controlled recovery procedures rather than everyday retry logic.

Idempotency: making retries safe

Retries only work safely if re-processing the same message does not corrupt state. This is the essence of *idempotency*: applying the same operation multiple times has the same effect as applying it once.

For trading events, idempotent design includes:

- **Using unique identifiers**: each order, fill, and cash movement should have stable identifiers (for example, order ID + exchange ID + fill ID) so you can detect duplicates.
- **State transitions with guards**: when you receive an order status update, you update state only if the new status is logically later than the current one. Duplicate or out-of-order updates become no-ops rather than rewinding state.
- **Absolute updates instead of increments**: where possible, define events as "set position to X" rather than "add Y to position," so that duplicates do not double-count.

With idempotent processors, you can afford to be more aggressive in retrying operations: if a request is issued twice because of a timeout or restarted consumer, the downstream effect remains correct.

Dead-letter queues: handling poison messages

A *dead-letter queue* (DLQ) is a dedicated destination for messages that cannot be processed successfully despite retries. Instead of blocking the main stream or silently discarding problematic events, you:

- Capture the offending message.
- Annotate it with metadata about the failure.
- Route it to a DLQ topic or store.

From there, human operators or specialized tools can:

- Inspect what went wrong (for example, a malformed field, unknown instrument, or business rule violation).
- Decide on a corrective action (for example, fix and replay, compensate, or discard with explanation).

What to store in a DLQ.

For each dead-lettered message, you should retain at least:

- The **original payload**, exactly as received.
- Identifiers such as **message key**, **partition**, **offset**, and any **source IDs**.
- The **error reason**: exception message, error codes, stack traces (if applicable), and which component failed.
- The **retry history**: how many attempts were made, at what times, with what backoff.
- Correlation IDs linking the message to client orders, accounts, or strategies, so you can assess business impact.

This information is crucial both for debugging and for explaining to clients or regulators what happened.

DLQ workflows.

A DLQ is not a dumping ground to forget about. You need a clear, repeatable workflow:

- **Alerting**: generate alerts when DLQ volumes exceed expected baselines or when certain severity thresholds are reached (for example, risk events in DLQ).
- **Triage**: classify DLQ entries into categories such as client error, internal bug, configuration issue, or external dependency failure.
- **Remediation**: for fixable problems, correct the data (for example, patch a malformed field) and replay the message into the normal stream, or generate compensating events if replay is not safe.
- **Governance**: document which DLQ issues led to code or configuration changes and close the feedback loop.

A well-run DLQ process turns failures into learning opportunities and strengthens the system over time.

Examples from trading workflows

To make these ideas more concrete, consider a few common failure scenarios.

Risk check failing due to configuration drift.

Imagine an order validator that calls a risk engine to ensure an order is within limits. For certain accounts, the risk engine starts returning "unknown account" because of a configuration drift between two systems.

From the validator's perspective:

- Retrying will not help; this is a persistent failure until configuration is fixed.
- If you treat it as transient and keep retrying, orders will be delayed indefinitely, annoying or harming clients.

A better design:

- Detect the "unknown account" error as a *persistent* failure type.

- Immediately route the order event to a DLQ for investigation, with metadata indicating the account and the error.
- Return a clear rejection message to the client, indicating that the account configuration needs attention.

Exchange gateway returning transient throttling errors.

Now consider a gateway that sends orders to an exchange. Under heavy load, the exchange responds with temporary throttling errors: "too many requests, try again later."

Here:

- The error is transient; retrying after a short delay may succeed.
- Immediate, frequent retries from many clients could worsen the exchange's congestion.

A sound strategy:

- Recognize throttling codes as transient errors.
- Apply exponential backoff with jitter for retries, perhaps with a modest retry budget (for example, a few attempts over a couple of hundred milliseconds).
- Coordinate with higher-level rate limiters and circuit breakers (discussed later in the chapter) to reduce total traffic to the exchange when throttling persists.

Malformed FIX messages from a client.

Suppose a client sends in a burst of FIX messages that violate your schema (for example, missing required fields or using invalid enumerations). Every attempt to parse these messages fails.

The right approach:

- Classify parse errors as persistent failures.
- Avoid retrying parsing of the same exact message more than once; instead, send the raw message to a DLQ with full context.

- Notify client support and the client's technical contacts with details so they can correct their system.

Here, retries inside the pipeline add no value; the fix must happen at the client.

Interaction with time and ordering semantics

Retry and DLQ design must coexist with the time and ordering semantics introduced earlier in the chapter.

Preserving event time.

When a message is retried or delayed:

- Its *event time* should remain the same; you do not change when the underlying business event occurred.
- Its *processing time* changes, sometimes significantly.

This means that:

- Retries can cause events to appear late from the perspective of watermarks and allowed lateness.
- Windows and aggregations that rely on event time must be prepared to receive corrected or delayed updates due to internal retries, not just network skew.

Maintaining per-key ordering.

Retries must also respect any per-key ordering guarantees you have established:

- If an earlier event for an order is still outstanding due to retries, you cannot safely process later events that depend on it, unless you can guarantee idempotent correction later.
- Reordering buffers help absorb some delay, but beyond their tolerance, retries may force you to choose between blocking the key or moving problematic messages to DLQ.

In practice, combining per-key ordering with retries suggests per-key queues or task executors, so that one misbehaving order does not stall unrelated orders, while still preserving order for that specific key.

Retries, backoff, and dead-letter queues are the reliability counterparts to the time and ordering mechanisms discussed earlier in this chapter. Together they ensure that:

- Transient failures are handled automatically and gracefully, without overloading shared infrastructure.
- Persistent or poison messages are isolated quickly and captured for investigation, rather than blocking pipelines or being silently lost.
- Idempotent, order-aware processors can tolerate duplicates and replays introduced by retries.
- Event-time semantics and watermarks remain meaningful even when internal processing delays and retries introduce additional lateness.

A thoughtful design here turns failures from catastrophic surprises into manageable, well-understood events in the life of your trading system. In the next section, we will look at higher-level protective mechanisms—circuit breakers, rate limits, and kill switches—that complement retries by controlling when and how you place load on fragile dependencies in the first place.

4.6 Circuit Breakers, Rate Limits, and Kill Switches

In the previous section we focused on making individual message failures safe through retries, backoff, and dead-letter queues. Those mechanisms are local: they answer the question, "What do I do when processing *this* event fails?" In a live trading system, you also need mechanisms that act at a higher level and ask a different question:

What should the system do when a *dependency* is unhealthy, or when the overall flow of orders and events itself becomes dangerous?

This is the domain of circuit breakers, rate limits, and kill switches. Together they form a protection stack that lets you:

- Fail fast instead of hammering a sick downstream system.
- Shed load in a controlled way when capacity is constrained.
- Halt or sharply reduce trading when conditions cross a hard safety boundary.

In trading, these mechanisms are not optional. They are the difference between a noisy but contained incident and a runaway event that produces large unintended positions, severe P&L swings, or regulatory trouble.

Why local retries are not enough

Retries with backoff address the case where an individual request to a dependency fails. They assume the dependency is *mostly healthy*: occasional glitches, a short warm-up phase, light transient throttling. When a dependency is genuinely unhealthy—crashing repeatedly, returning errors for most calls, or operating far below normal capacity—retries alone can do more harm than good.

Without higher-level controls you may see:

- **Self-inflicted denial of service**: after a venue gateway slows down, all trading engines keep retrying in parallel, effectively DDoS-ing the gateway further.
- **Backlogs everywhere**: queues build up in front of failing services; latency soars even for operations that could have been failed fast.
- **Unbounded risk exposure**: despite signs that risk or hedging services are misbehaving, strategies keep sending new orders because nothing is stopping them.

Circuit breakers and rate limiters address these systemic aspects. Kill switches define deliberate, high-impact responses when risk is no longer acceptable.

Circuit breakers: failing fast on unhealthy dependencies

A *circuit breaker* is a component that monitors the outcome of calls to a dependency—such as an exchange gateway, pricing service, or risk engine—and changes its behavior based on recent error patterns.

The analogy is electrical:

- In the **closed** state, calls flow normally.
- If failures or timeouts become too frequent, the breaker **opens**, and new calls are rejected immediately rather than forwarded.
- After a cooling-off period, the breaker enters a **half-open** state, allowing a small number of test calls to see if the dependency has recovered.

If the tests succeed, the breaker closes again; if they fail, it reopens and the cycle repeats.

The key idea is to protect both sides:

- **The dependency** is protected from being overwhelmed by a flood of doomed calls.
- **The callers** are protected from waiting on slow or failing operations; they get quick, predictable errors.

Choosing trip conditions.

A circuit breaker needs a policy for when to open. Typical conditions include:

- Error rate over a sliding window exceeds a threshold, for example, more than 50% of the last 100 calls failed or timed out.

- Average latency over a window exceeds an upper bound, indicating the service is overloaded.
- A specific pattern of errors appears, such as repeated "service unavailable" or throttling responses from a venue.

These thresholds should reflect:

- The normal operating profile of the dependency: what constitutes "unusual" failure or latency.
- The tolerance of your trading logic for delayed or failed responses.

You want to avoid both extremes:

- A breaker that trips too eagerly, interrupting normal trading on minor glitches.
- A breaker that almost never trips, allowing severe degradation to propagate unchecked.

Open and half-open behavior.

Once open, the breaker should:

- Immediately fail new requests with a clear error indicating the dependency is unavailable.
- Optionally, offer a cheap fallback (for example, using stale prices or a simplified pre-computed risk limit) if business rules permit.

After a configured *cool-down* time, the breaker moves to half-open:

- Only a small number of requests are allowed through as probes.
- Their results determine whether to close (if they succeed) or reopen (if they fail).

In trading, you may differentiate traffic during half-open:

- Prefer sending low-risk or synthetic test requests first.
- Delay or restrict real client orders until the dependency proves healthy again.

Rate limiters: controlling how much you send

While circuit breakers react to observed failures, *rate limiters* proactively cap how much traffic a system will generate or accept. They protect:

- Downstream services from overload (e.g., order gateways, risk engines, databases).
- Upstream clients from self-harm (e.g., runaway strategies flooding the market).

Rate limiting is about answering, in advance of trouble:

> How many of *this kind* of request per second (or per minute) are we willing to send or process?

Dimensions of limiting.

In trading systems, common axes for rate limiting include:

- **Per client or session**: maximum order rate for a particular client, API key, or connection.
- **Per instrument or venue**: maximum quote or order rate to a specific symbol or exchange, reflecting venue rules or capacity.
- **Per strategy or desk**: maximum aggregate activity for a trading strategy, to protect against bugs or runaway logic.
- **Global limits**: firm-wide caps on total order messages per unit time.

Each axis gives you a lever to contain damage in one dimension without shutting down everything else.

Prioritization under load.

Rate limiting becomes especially powerful when combined with *prioritization*. Not all traffic is equally important. During stress, you may want to:

- Always allow order cancels and risk checks to pass, even if you are limiting new order submissions.
- Throttle optional analytics, enrichment, or non-critical notifications first.

A simple way to view this is as a hierarchy:

- **Safety-critical traffic**: cancels, risk limit enforcement, kill-switch actions.
- **Core trading traffic**: new and modify orders essential to current strategies.
- **Ancillary traffic**: analytics, logs, optional enrichments, non-critical reports.

When capacity is strained, you progressively shed load from the bottom of this hierarchy upward, keeping the safety and core functions as intact as possible.

Coordinating rate limits and circuit breakers

Circuit breakers and rate limiters are most effective when they work together.

A typical interaction pattern:

- A service begins to degrade; error rates rise.
- The circuit breaker detects the trend and eventually opens, protecting both sides.

- As the breaker nears its thresholds (before opening), rate limiters may already start cutting back traffic to the dependency to give it a chance to recover.

This suggests a layered design:

- **Local rate limiting** at each caller to avoid flooding a dependency and to enforce per-client or per-strategy caps.
- **Shared or central rate limiting** close to the dependency, coordinating aggregate traffic from all callers.
- **Circuit breakers** on each consuming component, tuned to the behavior and importance of the specific dependency.

In a trading system, you might, for example:

- Apply client-level rate limits at the edge (FIX gateways, APIs).
- Apply venue-level limits near the exchange adapters.
- Use circuit breakers on each adapter as a last line of defense against persistent issues with that venue.

Kill switches: deliberate, scoped shutdowns

Circuit breakers and rate limiters manage interactions with dependencies and load. A *kill switch* is different: it is a deliberate mechanism to stop or dramatically reduce trading activity based on risk, compliance, or operational signals.

In other words, a kill switch answers the question:

> If something has gone badly wrong—either in the markets or in our own systems—how do we stop, and how do we stop *cleanly*?

Kill switches come in various scopes:

- **Per-strategy**: halt one algorithm or model while others continue.
- **Per-client or per-desk**: halt trading for a particular client, desk, or book.
- **Per-venue**: stop trading on a specific exchange.
- **Firm-wide**: stop or drastically curtail all new risk-taking activity.

In all cases, a kill switch is only as good as its operational clarity: everyone must know what it does, how to invoke it, and what to expect afterwards.

Conditions that trigger kill switches

Kill switches may be triggered *manually* by traders or risk managers, or *automatically* by systems. Common triggers include:

Runaway order rates or error rates.

Indicators such as:

- An algorithm sending far more orders per second than expected.
- A spike in rejects or cancellations that suggests a feedback loop or bug.

In such cases, a per-strategy or per-client kill switch can stop further orders while allowing the rest of the platform to continue operating.

Risk limit breaches.

If aggregate exposure, P&L drawdown, or margin usage crosses predefined firm-level or desk-level limits, automatic triggers can:

- Freeze new position-increasing orders.
- Allow only risk-reducing actions (for example, liquidations or hedges).

- Escalate alerts to human decision-makers.

Systemic infrastructure failures.

If critical components such as:

- The central risk engine.
- The primary price or reference data feed.
- The clock synchronization infrastructure.

fail or fall outside safe bounds, firm-wide or venue-specific kill switches may be required. Continuing to trade blindly without risk, price, or time integrity is rarely justifiable.

Designing predictable kill-switch behavior

A kill switch should not be an improvised "big red button" bolted on at the end of the design. Its behavior must be well-defined and rehearsed.

Important design elements include:

Scope and impact.

For each kill switch, document:

- **What it affects**: strategies, accounts, venues, products.
- **What it does**: stop all new orders; allow cancels only; allow position-reducing trades; etc.
- **Where it is enforced**: at order entry gateways, internal routers, or strategy engines themselves.

Ambiguity here leads to confusion when you most need clarity.

State transitions.

Define what happens when a kill switch toggles:

- How quickly does the change propagate through the system?

- What happens to in-flight orders and messages?
- Are pending asynchronous operations (for example, queued orders) flushed, cancelled, or allowed to complete?

Ideally, switching off should be as close to atomic as practical for the chosen scope.

Auditability and authorization.

Kill switches have major business and regulatory implications. Systems should:

- Require appropriate authorization to activate or deactivate a kill switch (for example, dual approval, role-based control).
- Log every activation and deactivation with precise timestamps, actors, and reasons.
- Provide clear audit trails so you can demonstrate governance after an incident.

Human factors and interfaces.

Interfaces to kill switches—GUIs, command-line tools, APIs—must be designed for use under stress:

- Labels should be unambiguous (e.g., "Halt new orders for Strategy X; allow cancels" rather than "Disable X?").
- Feedback should confirm which scope is now active.
- Mis-clicks should be minimized, perhaps via confirmations or two-step actions for high-impact switches.

Combining the protection layers in a trading flow

To see how these pieces fit together, consider a simplified path for an order generated by a strategy:

- The strategy proposes an order.

- A per-strategy or per-client rate limiter checks order rate against configured limits.
- A kill-switch check verifies that the strategy, client, venue, and firm are allowed to trade in the requested direction and size.
- The order is enriched, risk-checked, and routed. Circuit breakers on the risk engine or enrichment services may short-circuit calls if those components are unhealthy.
- The exchange adapter receives the outbound order. Venue-level rate limits and circuit breakers protect the adapter and the venue from overload or misbehavior.
- Responses (acknowledgements, fills, rejects) come back and are processed, again subject to kill-switch and circuit-breaker logic where appropriate.

If any layer signals trouble:

- Local retries and backoff may address small transient issues.
- Circuit breakers prevent repeatedly hitting a failing service.
- Rate limiters prevent runaway traffic.
- Kill switches provide a final, explicit halt when wider risk calls for it.

The aim is not to eliminate all incidents—that is impossible—but to ensure that when things go wrong, they fail in contained, understandable ways.

Testing and rehearsing protective mechanisms

Protection mechanisms that are never exercised in anger can decay or behave differently than expected. You should treat circuit breakers, rate limits, and kill switches as active parts of your system and:

Unit and integration tests.

Test:

- Circuit-breaker transitions under simulated error patterns.
- Rate-limiter behavior at and beyond configured thresholds.
- Kill-switch propagation and the resulting behavior of strategies and gateways.

Game days and simulations.

Run periodic exercises where:

- A dependency is artificially slowed or made to fail; observe whether circuit breakers and rate limiters behave as designed.
- A kill switch is activated for a strategy or desk in a test environment; verify that only the intended scope is affected and that unwinding positions proceeds as planned.

Post-incident reviews.

After real incidents:

- Analyze whether breakers tripped at the right time, whether rate limits were appropriate, and whether kill switches were used or should have been used.
- Adjust thresholds, scopes, and procedures based on what you learn.

Retries and DLQs help your trading system survive individual message or call failures. Circuit breakers, rate limits, and kill switches extend that resilience to systemic and extreme situations:

- Circuit breakers detect repeated failures or slowness in dependencies and fail fast instead of compounding the problem.
- Rate limiters cap and prioritize traffic to keep critical services within safe capacity, especially under stress.
- Kill switches provide deliberate, scoped shutdown mechanisms that can halt or sharply reduce trading when risk, compliance, or infrastructure conditions demand it.

When they are thoughtfully designed, monitored, and rehearsed, these mechanisms ensure that your event-driven trading system does not blindly push forward into unsafe territory. Instead, it can recognize trouble, shed load, and—when necessary—stop, giving humans space to understand what is happening and to decide on the next move.

4.7 High Availability and Disaster Recovery

Up to now this chapter has focused on the reliability of *individual events*: getting timestamps right, preserving order, handling late data, and surviving processing failures with retries and kill switches. In this section we zoom out. Instead of asking, "What happens to this message if a component fails?", we ask:

> How does the *whole trading system* behave when machines fail, networks partition, or an entire data center becomes unavailable?

Designing for these scenarios is the domain of *High Availability* (HA) and *Disaster Recovery* (DR). HA is about operating smoothly through routine, local failures—servers going down, processes crashing, rolling upgrades. DR is about rare but severe events—loss of a primary site, prolonged cloud-region outage, or major data corruption—and how you recover your business.

A good mental model is:

- HA keeps you trading when "small things" break, ideally with no visible impact to users.
- DR gets you trading again, with acceptable data loss, when "big things" break.

Both must be designed consciously and tied to business objectives, not just left to infrastructure defaults.

Defining availability goals in business terms

Before drawing any architecture diagrams, you need crisp statements of what level of availability is expected and what kinds of failures you are designing for. Two related questions help:

- For each function (order entry, risk, market data, reporting), how much downtime per year is acceptable? Under what kinds of degradation?
- In a disaster, how quickly must we be able to trade again, and how much data can we afford to lose?

This is where two standard metrics come in:

Recovery Time Objective (RTO).

RTO is the maximum acceptable time to restore a function after a failure or disaster. For example:

- Real-time order entry for major markets: RTO of a few minutes or less.
- End-of-day reporting: RTO of several hours may be acceptable.

Recovery Point Objective (RPO).

RPO is the maximum acceptable amount of data loss, measured as time from the last consistent point. For example:

- Positions and executions: RPO of a few seconds—losing more than a few seconds of trade history is usually unacceptable.
- Some analytics or logs: RPO of minutes or even hours may be fine.

These targets should be driven by trading, risk, and compliance stakeholders. The technology design then flows from them. Without RTO and RPO, architecture discussions become hand-wavy and you either overspend on infrastructure or accept more risk than everyone realizes.

High availability: staying up through routine failures

HA is about designing the system so that routine failures do not disrupt trading. Common failure modes include:

- A single server crashes or loses power.
- A process dies due to a bug.
- A network link between two racks goes down.
- You deploy a new version and need to restart services.

To tolerate these, HA designs typically rely on:

- Redundant instances (no single point of failure).
- Automated failover mechanisms.
- Careful separation of stateful and stateless components.

Stateless vs stateful services

The first design question is: which parts of your trading system can be *stateless*, and which are inherently *stateful*?

Stateless services.

A stateless service does not keep critical durable state in memory between requests. If it goes down, another instance can take over immediately as long as it can reach the same backing stores and message streams. Examples include:

- API gateways and FIX gateways (if they do not hold positions in memory).
- Simple enrichers that join messages with reference data from shared stores.
- Many analytics consumers that treat the streamed data or a central store as the source of truth.

HA for stateless services is relatively straightforward:

- Run multiple instances behind a load balancer or in a consumer group.
- Monitor health and automatically replace failed instances.
- Deploy updates in a rolling fashion, taking instances in and out of rotation one by one.

Stateful services.

Stateful services maintain important, mutable state that cannot be recomputed quickly from elsewhere—for example:

- Position and risk state keyed by account or book.
- Order books in an internal matching engine.
- Durable logs and databases that hold trades and orders.

Stateful components are harder to make highly available because:

- You cannot simply spin up a fresh instance and continue; that instance needs the latest state.
- Multiple active instances must coordinate to avoid inconsistent or conflicting updates.

Common HA patterns for stateful services include leader-follower replication, quorum-based clusters, and shared log designs. The messaging and log architectures discussed earlier in the book are part of this picture: replicated partitions and consumer groups give you HA at the event-stream level, but you still need to propagate that to trading-specific state.

Active-active vs active-passive

When you have replicated services or sites, you must decide how they share the work.

Active-active.

In an active-active setup, multiple instances (or sites) are all serving traffic simultaneously. Advantages:

- Better use of hardware resources; capacity is not sitting idle.
- Failover can be very fast: if one node or site fails, the others are already warm and taking load.

Challenges:

- You need to keep state consistent across active instances, often via distributed consensus or shared logs.
- You must handle partitioning: what if the link between active sites is lost but each is still up? Which one is authoritative?

Trading examples of active-active include:

- Two co-located gateways at the same exchange POP, both sending and receiving orders.
- Multiple stateless API endpoints in the same region, behind a load balancer.

Active-passive.

In an active-passive setup, one instance or site handles all live traffic (primary), while another is on standby (secondary). The passive side:

- Replicates state from the primary.
- Is periodically tested but does not serve live trades until a failover.

Advantages:

- Simpler consistency model: only one active writer; secondaries replicate and are promoted if needed.

- Clear notion of authority: the primary is the source of truth.

Drawbacks:

- Higher hardware cost per unit of live capacity; passive resources are underutilized.
- Failover may take longer while the secondary promotes itself, warms caches, and is switched to by clients.

For many trading firms, a hybrid is common: active-active within a site for stateless components, active-passive between sites for stateful data stores, depending on RTO/RPO needs.

Aligning HA with the messaging layer

Event-driven trading systems often rely on partitioned, replicated logs (for example, topics with multiple partitions and replicas). Your HA design should align with the behavior of this messaging layer:

- **Partition replication** gives you durability and availability for the event stream itself. If one broker node fails, leaders for partitions can move to replicas.
- **Consumer groups** provide HA for consumers: if one consumer instance dies, another in the group can be assigned its partitions and resume from the last committed offsets.

To make full use of this:

- Ensure critical consumers (like risk, positions, and order-routing services) are deployed as redundant instances in appropriately configured consumer groups.
- Design consumers to be idempotent and able to rebuild in-memory state from the stream after a restart or failover, as discussed earlier in the chapter.

- Monitor consumer lag and rebalance events; a stuck consumer should not silently hold partitions while other instances idle.

This tight coupling between messaging HA and application HA is one of the main benefits of event-driven architectures: you get built-in replay and failover primitives that stateful services can leverage.

Disaster recovery: preparing for the worst

Disaster Recovery planning assumes that an entire site or region can become unavailable or unreliable for an extended period. Causes include:

- Data center power incidents or fires.
- Network failures isolating a region.
- Cloud provider outages.
- Major data corruption or operator errors (for example, accidental deletion of critical data).

The DR question is: given a disaster, how do we:

- Protect client assets and positions.
- Resume critical trading functions within the agreed RTO.
- Do so with at most the agreed RPO of data loss.

Multi-region strategies

DR for a trading firm often involves multiple physical sites or cloud regions. Typical patterns include:

Primary + warm standby.

One region is primary for trading. A second region hosts:

- Replicated copies of critical databases and logs.

- Pre-deployed versions of key services, running at lower capacity or even idle.

In a disaster:

- You promote the standby to primary, reroute order and market data connectivity, and resume trading.
- RPO is determined by how frequently data is replicated from primary to standby and how replication latency behaves under load.

This model suits firms that want DR capability but are not ready to run full multi-region active-active trading.

Active-active multi-region.

In more advanced setups, multiple regions trade live concurrently, with:

- Regional connectivity to local exchanges.
- Cross-region replication of positions, orders, and risk data.

Advantages:

- Very low RTO for regional disasters: surviving regions are already trading.
- Potential performance benefits from proximity to local markets.

Challenges:

- Complex global consistency: reconciling positions, risk, and client limits across regions with non-zero replication latency.
- Complex failure semantics: if replication between regions breaks but each region is otherwise healthy, do you allow both to continue taking risk independently?

The design must reflect business decisions about how much temporary divergence is acceptable and how it will be reconciled.

RTO/RPO trade-offs in concrete terms

To make RTO and RPO meaningful, translate them into trading examples.

RPO of 5 seconds vs 5 minutes.

If your position store has an RPO of 5 minutes, a regional disaster could mean:

- The DR site's latest known positions are up to 5 minutes out of date.
- You must either:
  - Reconstruct missing trades from exchange and broker drop-copies before resuming trading, or
  - Accept that you will trade temporarily with incomplete position knowledge and compensate later.

For many strategies, 5 minutes of missing trades is unacceptable; it risks breaching capital or exposure limits without realizing it. An RPO of a few seconds (using synchronous or near-synchronous replication) is much safer but more technically demanding and potentially more expensive.

RTO of 30 seconds vs 30 minutes.

If you commit to an RTO of 30 seconds for client order entry, then:

- Failover between sites must be automated, not manual.
- Connectivity to key venues must be pre-configured and tested at the DR site.
- Operational runbooks must be simple and drilled; there is no time for ad-hoc decisions.

If instead the business accepts that, in a true disaster, it is acceptable to pause trading for 30 minutes while you assess and bring up DR, you can use simpler architectures and more manual steps. The cost is the lost opportunity (and possibly reputational impact) of being offline.

Data replication and consistency

Achieving your RPO is mainly a question of how you replicate data between HA and DR sites. Common mechanisms include:

- **Synchronous replication**: writes are only considered committed when they are durable in both primary and secondary. This minimizes RPO (approaches zero) but increases write latency and couples site availability.
- **Asynchronous replication**: writes are committed at the primary and shipped to the secondary later. This avoids cross-site latency on the critical path but allows some data loss if the primary is destroyed before the secondary catches up.

You do not need the same replication mode for all data:

- Positions, trades, and cash balances might warrant near-synchronous or very frequent replication.
- Large historical quote archives or low-value logs might be replicated less aggressively.

Design choices here must consider network characteristics, storage technology, and failure modes (for example, what happens if the primary hangs but is not fully gone).

Operational practices: runbooks and game days

An HA/DR design on paper is only half the story. The other half is operational discipline.

Runbooks.

Runbooks are step-by-step procedures for common failure and disaster scenarios. They should cover:

- How to detect and declare a disaster (versus a local incident).
- Who has authority to trigger DR failover.

- What exact steps are taken to:
  - Promote the DR site (or another region) to primary.
  - Reroute market data and order flow.
  - Communicate with clients, venues, and regulators.
- How to later fail back to the original primary when it is safe.

These documents must be maintained and accessible. In a crisis, nobody wants to hunt for an outdated PDF.

Game days (disaster simulations).

Regularly simulate failures in non-production environments, and occasionally in production under controlled conditions, to test:

- That automatic failover mechanisms behave as expected.
- That teams know how to follow runbooks under time pressure.
- That no hidden single points of failure exist (for example, an overlooked configuration store that is not replicated).

Game days often reveal subtle dependencies and gaps that are invisible in design diagrams.

Ownership, governance, and cost trade-offs

HA and DR are not purely technical decisions; they involve organizational and financial trade-offs.

Ownership.

Someone must own:

- The HA/DR architecture and its evolution.
- The runbooks and game-day schedule.
- The relationship with business stakeholders around RTO/RPO expectations.

Without clear ownership, priorities drift and the system may not be ready when needed.

Cost vs risk.

Higher availability and lower RTO/RPO targets almost always cost more, in:

- Extra hardware and licenses for standby sites.
- More complex replication and coordination logic.
- Increased operational effort and testing.

These costs should be made explicit and weighed against:

- The potential financial loss and reputational damage of prolonged outages or data loss.
- Regulatory and contractual obligations to clients.

In some cases, the right choice is to accept higher RTO/RPO for non-critical functions, focusing resources on the truly time- and safety-critical components of the trading stack.

Bringing it all together

High Availability and Disaster Recovery round out the reliability picture painted in this chapter:

- Time and ordering semantics ensure that, when the system is running, you interpret events consistently.
- Watermarks and late-data handling keep real-time analytics trustworthy under jitter.
- Retries, circuit breakers, rate limits, and kill switches manage local and systemic failures in dependencies.
- HA and DR ensure that the platform as a whole can continue to operate—or recover quickly—even when individual machines, services, or entire sites fail.

Designing event-driven trading systems with queues and state is not just about performance; it is about building a platform whose behavior remains understandable and controllable under stress. Clear availability goals, carefully chosen architectures, and disciplined operations are the tools that make that possible.

Chapter 5

Performance and Low-Latency Engineering

In event-driven trading, speed is not a single trick but an ecosystem of tight engineering decisions-from how packets land on a NIC queue to how objects are laid out in memory. This chapter dissects the entire tick-to-trade path, showing how to turn a conventional event-driven system into a carefully profiled, deterministic engine that keeps its latency promises even when markets go nonlinear.

5.1 Networking and OS Fundamentals

In the previous chapters we treated "the network" as a black box that delivers market data events into your engine and carries orders back to the exchange. For event-driven trading at microsecond scales, that mental model is no longer sufficient. Each packet takes a very specific journey through hardware and software layers before your strategy code ever sees it, and each step can add latency, jitter, and queueing that you must understand and control.

In this section we build a concrete, end-to-end picture of a single market data packet: from the exchange's network interface, across the wire, into your network interface card (NIC), through the operating system's networking stack, into your process, and finally onto the CPU core running your strategy. We will name the important components along this path and explain how they behave under load. Later sections will show how to tune and re-architect these pieces; here we focus on understanding where time is spent and why that time is variable.

The Tick's Journey: From Wire to User Space

When a new quote or trade update is published by an exchange, this event is eventually encoded into one or more Ethernet frames and transmitted over the physical link to your server. From your strategy's point of view this may feel instantaneous, but in reality the packet passes through a sequence of queues and handlers. Thinking explicitly in terms of this journey is the foundation of performance work:

- **Exchange NIC** serializes the packet onto the wire.
- **Network fabric** (switches, fiber, copper) transmits the packet to your rack.
- **Your NIC** receives the bits, verifies them, places them into a receive queue in memory, and signals the CPU.
- **Kernel network stack** processes the packet: protocol parsing (Ethernet, IP, UDP or TCP), routing decisions, socket dispatch, and buffering.
- **OS scheduler** decides which CPU core and which thread runs next to handle the data.
- **User-space trading process** finally reads the packet from a socket or shared buffer, decodes the market data message, and feeds it into your internal event pipeline.

Each stage has at least two important characteristics:

- A **baseline latency**: the time this stage takes when the system is nearly idle.
- A **queueing behavior**: how the latency grows when bursts of packets arrive faster than they can be processed.

Once you begin measuring nanoseconds and microseconds, seemingly minor buffering decisions—in the NIC, in the kernel, or in your own process—become visible as shifts and "fat tails" in your latency distribution. The rest of this section will walk through this path more slowly, layer by layer.

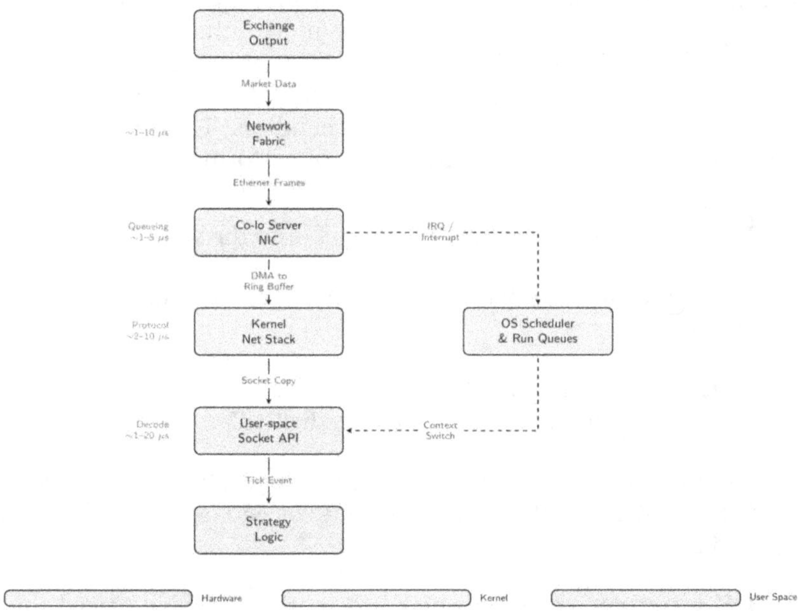

Hardware: Wire, Switches, and the NIC

On-the-wire latency. At the very left of the path is pure physics: the time it takes to serialize the packet and propagate it over the link. This includes:

- **Serialization delay**: how long it takes to "push" all bits of the frame into the wire. For typical Ethernet speeds this is tens to hundreds of nanoseconds for market data sized packets.
- **Propagation delay**: the time the electromagnetic signal needs to travel through fiber or copper. Over a few hundred meters, this is again on the order of microseconds or less.
- **Switching delay**: if the packet goes through one or more switches, each switch must at least inspect the header and forward the frame. Modern switches add very little jitter when they are not congested, but they can queue packets when bursts exceed the output port's capacity.

For co-located trading, these physical delays are usually a small, stable component of total latency. You cannot change the speed of light, but you *can* influence how much buffering happens in switches by negotiating private or less-contended connections and by understanding your peak traffic relative to link capacity.

NIC receive behavior and queues. The network interface card in your server is the first part of the chain that you directly control. When a frame arrives:

- The NIC's **physical layer** decodes the analog signal into bits.
- The NIC checks Ethernet and IP headers, discards corrupted frames, and usually performs some offloads (such as checksumming).
- The payload is written via **DMA** (direct memory access) into preallocated receive buffers in main memory.
- The NIC writes a descriptor into one of its **receive queues** (RX queues) pointing to the buffer.
- The NIC signals the CPU, typically using an **interrupt**, to say "there is new data in RX queue number k".

Two places where latency and jitter appear here:

- **RX queue depth and contention.** Each NIC RX queue is effectively a ring buffer of descriptors. If bursts of packets arrive faster than the driver and CPU can drain this ring, the NIC queues them, increasing one-way latency. If the ring overflows, packets are dropped.
- **Interrupt moderation.** To avoid overwhelming the CPU with one interrupt per packet, NICs often group several packets and raise a single interrupt. This reduces CPU load but intentionally adds delay: the NIC waits a short time to see "if more packets arrive" before signaling. The configuration of this moderation is a major tuning knob we will revisit.

At this hardware level, your main mental model should be: *the NIC has a limited number of RX queues, each is a finite ring buffer, and both moderation and ring occupancy determine when a given packet is handed to the CPU.*

Kernel Network Stack: From RX Queue to Socket

Once the NIC has indicated that a receive queue contains new packets, the operating system's kernel network stack takes over. While implementations differ by OS and version, the essential steps for a typical Linux-based trading server are:

Interrupt handling and softirqs. When the NIC triggers an interrupt:

- The CPU stops executing whatever it was doing and jumps into a small **interrupt handler**. This handler belongs to the NIC driver.
- The handler usually does *minimal* work: it acknowledges the interrupt, notes which RX queue has data, and schedules a software interrupt (a "softirq") to perform the heavier processing outside the hard IRQ context.
- The softirq then runs in the context of a kernel thread on some CPU core, draining the RX ring: it walks the list of descriptors,

processes each packet, and passes it into the generic networking code for protocol handling.

Two important latency effects appear here:

- **Interrupt-to-softirq delay.** The softirq does not necessarily run immediately. If the core is handling other interrupts or is temporarily disabled for critical sections, there can be short, variable delays before the RX ring is serviced.
- **Softirq backlog.** If bursts of packets arrive, the softirq may process many packets in a batch. Earlier packets in the batch experience less softirq-induced delay than later packets, even though they arrived at the NIC at nearly the same time. This creates intra-burst jitter.

Protocol parsing and socket dispatch. Once in the generic network stack, each packet is:

- Parsed through the layered protocols: Ethernet, IP, and then either UDP or TCP.
- Validated (checksums, header lengths, sequence numbers for TCP).
- Matched to a **socket**, using criteria such as local port, remote address, and protocol.
- Enqueued into a per-socket **receive buffer**, usually a queue of packet fragments or reassembled messages.

Here, think of multiple levels of queues:

- The NIC RX ring, where fully received packets wait for the kernel to pick them up.
- The kernel's per-socket receive queue, where packets targeting your process wait for the application to read them.

Under heavy load, both levels can back up. If your process is not draining its socket fast enough, the kernel receive buffer grows and may eventually reach limits, causing drops or backpressure at higher protocol layers. Even before that, larger socket buffers imply more data to scan and manage, which slightly increases per-packet processing time and can stretch out tails.

TCP versus UDP in trading. For market data, many venues use UDP multicast or unicast; for order entry they typically use TCP or a higher-level protocol on top of TCP.

At microsecond scales, the trade-offs look different than they do in conventional application development:

- **UDP** is simple: each datagram is independent, there are no retransmissions, and the kernel does not maintain per-connection state for flow control. This means lower per-packet overhead and no *head-of-line blocking*: a lost or delayed packet does not directly stall later packets. However, your application must handle loss and out-of-order delivery, which can itself add complexity and latency in recovery paths.
- **TCP** provides reliability and ordering. The kernel maintains a sequence number space, retransmits lost packets, and presents your process with a clean, in-order byte stream. The flip side is that *one* delayed or lost packet can stall the entire stream: this is head-of-line blocking. Under microbursts, TCP's congestion and buffering behavior in the kernel can introduce extra jitter compared to a carefully designed UDP feed.

For low-latency trading, the key is not that one protocol is universally better, but that you understand how each protocol's semantics translate into buffering, CPU work, and failure modes in the kernel.

OS Scheduling, Cores, and NUMA

By the time a packet has been placed into your socket's receive queue, the kernel has already spent several microseconds on your behalf. Before your code runs, there is another gate: the operating system scheduler.

Run queues and context switches. The scheduler maintains a **run queue** for each CPU core: a list of threads that are ready to execute. When a thread blocks on I/O (for example, waiting in a recv call), the kernel marks it as sleeping and removes it from the run queue. When data arrives on its socket:

- The kernel wakes the thread, placing it back into a run queue.
- At the next scheduling decision, the scheduler chooses a thread from the run queue to run on the core.
- When your thread is chosen, the CPU performs a **context switch**: it saves the state of the currently running thread and loads the state (registers, program counter) of your thread.

Context switches are not free. They:

- Take time themselves—thousands of CPU cycles.
- Disrupt the CPU's caches: instruction and data cached for the previous thread may no longer be relevant for your trading code, so your first memory accesses after a context switch can be slower.

Under low load, a dedicated trading thread that mostly stays runnable and has a core to itself will see relatively few context switches and therefore a tight latency distribution. Under contention—for example, if other daemons or batch jobs share the same cores—your thread may sometimes be delayed in the run queue by several scheduling quanta, pushing some packets far into the tail.

NUMA and cross-socket penalties. Modern servers used in co-location are typically multi-socket with a non-uniform memory access (NUMA) architecture. In simple terms:

- Each CPU socket has its own local memory controllers and DIMMs.
- Memory attached to one socket is still accessible from cores on another socket, but with higher latency and sometimes lower bandwidth.

- NICs are physically attached to a particular socket's PCIe root complex, making their DMA transfers naturally local to that NUMA node.

If your trading thread runs on a core on the *other* socket from the NIC, each read of newly arrived packet data may require a cross-socket memory access. These remote accesses add tens of nanoseconds each and interact with caches in subtle ways. More importantly, if the kernel's interrupt handling or softirq processing runs on a core on one socket and your application runs on another, the NIC's receive buffers may repeatedly bounce between sockets, increasing both latency and cache contention.

The mental model to cultivate is: *for lowest and most predictable latency, keep related work and data on the same NUMA node.* That means aligning NIC RX queues, kernel handlers, and your application threads to cores within the same socket when possible.

User-Space: From Socket to Strategy

Once your thread is scheduled and running, it calls into the OS to receive data, decodes the message, and feeds it into your own event-driven architecture.

System call overhead and copying. A typical user-space receive path for UDP might look like:

- Application thread calls into the kernel (a system call) to check for data on its socket.
- The kernel copies or maps data from the kernel's receive buffer into user-space buffers.
- The thread returns from the system call and begins decoding the payload.

Every system call has a fixed overhead to transition between user space and kernel space, perform validation, and return. On modern hardware this cost is small but not negligible at sub-10-microsecond targets.

In addition, any copying between kernel and user buffers consumes memory bandwidth and pollutes caches.

Later chapters will explore alternatives such as memory-mapped I/O, user-space network stacks, and batching reads to amortize fixed costs. For now, the important idea is that *even before you start parsing messages, you may already have spent several microseconds in the kernel and in system call overhead.*

Application-level queues and parsing. Inside your process, it is common to introduce further queues:

- A thread dedicated to reading from the socket and pushing market data into a ring buffer.
- One or more threads responsible for decoding and applying updates to your order book.
- A strategy thread that consumes normalized events (best bid/ask, trades, derived signals) and makes trading decisions.

These queues are useful for structuring the system and for parallelism, but they introduce yet another dimension of queueing latency and jitter. During bursts, upstream queues can fill faster than downstream stages can drain them, extending end-to-end tick-to-trade times. Even with lock-free structures, cache contention and backpressure can affect distribution tails.

On top of this, message parsing itself has a cost. Verbose encodings with variable-length fields and complex checksums can take significantly longer to decode than compact binary formats designed for the hot path. At moderate loads this cost may be invisible; under sustained bursty load it shows up as additional microseconds in p99 and beyond.

Latency, Jitter, and Queueing in the Microsecond Regime

With the whole path in view, we can now connect the components to the latency metrics you actually monitor.

Baseline latency budget. Imagine an ideally tuned, lightly loaded system:

- Wire and switching add a small, stable one-way delay.
- The NIC places packets into RX buffers with negligible queuing.
- Kernel interrupt handling and softirq processing run quickly on isolated cores.
- Your trading thread is already running on the right core when data becomes available.
- Socket receive and parsing cost only a few microseconds.

Summing these contributions produces a *baseline latency*—perhaps a few microseconds from wire to decision. Tight engineering can push this down, but more importantly, it ensures that the *variance* around this baseline is small.

Sources of jitter. Jitter is the variation around that baseline. In the context of our packet journey, common sources are:

- **NIC interrupt moderation:** a packet arriving just before an interrupt is raised experiences little additional delay; one arriving just after a batch cut-off may wait for the next moderation window.
- **RX ring backlog:** if bursts briefly exceed the processing rate, some packets sit in the ring longer than others.
- **Softirq scheduling:** if the kernel's networking softirq is briefly delayed by other activity, all pending packets incur extra waiting time.
- **Run queue contention:** if your trading thread must wait behind other runnable threads, context switch timing adds variability.
- **Cache state and NUMA:** depending on which core happens to run your thread and whether data is already in that core's cache, the same code path can take slightly different times.
- **Application queues:** if downstream stages have temporary backlogs, events pile up and some experience much higher end-to-end latencies.

The hallmark of these mechanisms is that they affect mostly the *tails* of the latency distribution. Median latency might not change much, but p99, p99.9, and beyond can stretch dramatically.

Queueing effects and burst handling. Markets are inherently bursty: a macro headline or opening auction can create sudden spikes in message rates. When arrival rates exceed processing capacity at any stage for any period of time, queues grow.

You should think of each component we have described (NIC RX ring, kernel socket buffer, application ring buffers, scheduler run queue) as a queue with:

- A **service rate**: how many packets or messages per second it can handle.
- A **buffer size**: how many items it can hold when temporarily overloaded.

If the arrival rate briefly rises above the service rate, the queue absorbs the difference. Latency increases linearly with the number of items in the queue: the n-th item in the backlog must wait for the n items in front of it. If the overload persists long enough to fill the buffer, items are dropped, and other mechanisms (recovery, retransmission) kick in, adding even more variability.

At microsecond scales, even small queues with tens or hundreds of entries can add several microseconds of delay when full. Because bursts often involve correlated events across symbols, the impact on your P&L can be outsized: exactly when the market is most interesting, your system is most likely to be stressed.

What to Care About as a Low-Latency Practitioner

The purpose of this section is not to turn you into a device driver engineer, but to give you a clear map of the territory. When you look at a latency histogram for your strategy, you should be able to hypothesize which parts of the path are contributing to features such as:

- A persistent floor: likely the sum of physical transmission, NIC DMA, kernel parsing, and minimal user-space work.

- Occasional "shoulders" around certain microsecond values: often associated with interrupt moderation intervals, fixed timer ticks, or batch-processing behavior in the stack.
- Long tails under bursty load: almost always the result of queueing somewhere in the pipeline, from RX rings to application-level buffers.

In the next section, we will take this conceptual map and translate it into concrete tuning actions: aligning NIC queues with CPU cores, adjusting interrupt coalescing, choosing between kernel and user-space networking, and configuring the OS to minimize unnecessary context switches and cross-socket traffic. With that foundation, your event-driven trading system can turn from a best-effort consumer of market data into a predictable, instrumented engine where each microsecond has a known home.

5.2 Kernel and NIC Tuning Techniques

In the previous section we treated the network and operating system as a chain of queues and handlers from wire to user space. You now have a mental picture of NIC receive rings, interrupts, softirqs, socket buffers, run queues, and NUMA nodes, and how each can add latency and jitter.

This section turns that picture into a tuning playbook. The goal is not to memorize every kernel option, but to learn *how to think* about tuning: identify where packets wait, where the CPU wastes effort, and how to reshape that pipeline so that market data flows predictably to your strategy.

We proceed from hardware outward: starting at the NIC, then moving through interrupts and kernel networking options, and finally to choices about bypassing the kernel stack entirely. At each step, we will connect concrete settings to their effect on three things that matter most for event-driven trading:

- **Context switches:** how often the CPU has to stop what it is doing and switch to something else.

- **Cache locality:** whether the data and code you need are already "warm" in the core's caches.
- **Queueing behavior:** how bursts are absorbed (or not) at each stage.

Principles Before Knobs

Before touching configuration files, it is important to internalize a few principles. These will guide every tuning choice you make:

- **Specialize cores.** Do not let all CPUs do all jobs. Instead, assign specific cores to specific roles: NIC receive, user-space market data, strategy logic, housekeeping tasks. Specialization reduces unnecessary context switches and improves cache reuse.
- **Keep related work on the same NUMA node.** Packets arriving on a NIC attached to socket 0 should be processed by cores on socket 0, and user-space threads handling that data should also live on socket 0. This minimizes slow cross-socket memory traffic.
- **Prefer predictable over optimal-looking averages.** Settings that shave a microsecond from median latency but occasionally add tens of microseconds of jitter are usually a bad trade for trading systems.
- **Measure one change at a time.** The stack has many interacting parts. Change a single parameter, observe the impact under a controlled load, then move on. Blindly applying "low-latency recipes" is a good way to get surprising tails.

With that mindset, we can now walk through the main tuning layers.

Shaping the NIC: Queues, Rings, and Moderation

Your NIC is your first line of defense against unpredictable latency. It converts bursts on the wire into work items for the CPU. Three groups of settings matter most in practice: how queues map to cores, how big the rings are, and how interrupts are coalesced.

Mapping NIC Queues to Cores

Modern NICs expose multiple receive queues. Each queue can be steered to a particular CPU core, and the hardware can choose which queue a given packet goes to, often based on hash functions over IP addresses and ports.

For a trading engine, the design goal is:

> Packets for a given feed or connection should land in a dedicated RX queue, whose interrupt is handled on a specific core that also runs the corresponding user-space thread.

This direct mapping has several benefits:

- **Fewer context switches.** The same core that handles the NIC interrupt can immediately wake and run the user-space thread, without bouncing across cores.
- **Better cache locality.** The core's caches hold recent packet data and code paths for both kernel and user handlers.
- **Less cross-core contention.** Other cores are not constantly interrupted to deal with market data they do not ultimately process.

In practice, you configure:

- **Number of RX queues.** Enough to separate major flows (e.g., one for each high-volume market data feed and one or more for order entry), but not so many that you dilute per-queue traffic and make tuning harder.
- **Receive-side steering** rules so that specific feeds map to specific queues.
- **Interrupt affinity** so that each queue's interrupt is bound to the desired core on the correct NUMA node.

Conceptually, imagine each RX queue as a private mailbox for a single core. You want the packets that will be consumed by core 3 to go directly into core 3's mailbox, not into a shared mailbox that any core happens to check.

Ring Sizes: Big Enough, But Not Buffers-for-Everything

Each NIC queue is backed by a ring buffer of receive descriptors. A common temptation is to "solve" loss by making these rings extremely large, so that even massive bursts fit without overflow. This is usually counterproductive for low latency.

Ring size decisions involve a trade-off:

- **Larger rings** can absorb bigger bursts before dropping packets, but they also allow the system to *fall behind more* before noticing. A heavily backlogged ring means some packets spend microseconds or tens of microseconds waiting in the NIC before the kernel even sees them.
- **Smaller rings** force timely processing and make backlogs visible quickly, helping you detect that your system is overloaded. However, if sized too small relative to peak bursts and softirq service rate, they can overflow and cause loss.

For a trading plant, a good mental model is:

> Size rings to comfortably handle the *largest expected short burst* at your target message rate, but not to hide sustained overload.

Concretely, that often means rings in the hundreds or low thousands of entries, not tens of thousands. You confirm this with targeted load tests: replay peak historical bursts and watch for ring overflows and latency blowouts.

Interrupt Moderation: Trading CPU Load for Jitter

By default, NICs may raise one interrupt per several packets or per a fixed time window. This is called interrupt moderation or coalescing. It smooths CPU usage by batching work but introduces exactly the kind of timing noise you are trying to avoid.

You can think of moderation as a gate at the end of the RX ring that opens periodically:

- If the timer or packet-count threshold is short, gates open frequently. Packets do not wait long, but the kernel must handle more interrupts.
- If the thresholds are long, gates open less often and let through bigger batches. CPU efficiency improves, but packets that arrive just after a gate closes may sit for the entire moderation interval before being serviced.

For ultra-low-latency feeds:

- You typically **reduce** or **disable** interrupt moderation on the queues carrying the most time-sensitive data.
- You may keep more aggressive moderation on queues that carry less critical traffic (for example, admin connections or lower-priority feeds).

The right setting depends on your core budget. Disabling moderation entirely means more interrupts per second, which can be acceptable if you have dedicated cores and carefully limited workload on them. Again, measurement is your friend: observe how median and tail latency shift as you tighten moderation, and watch CPU utilization and context-switch rates on the affected cores.

Aligning the Kernel: IRQ Affinity, RPS/RFS, and Busy Polling

Once packets leave the NIC, the kernel drivers and network stack determine which cores do the work and how.

IRQ Affinity: Keeping Work on the Right Cores

Every hardware interrupt is associated with one or more cores that are allowed to handle it. If you leave this to defaults, the kernel may spread NIC interrupts across many cores in an attempt to balance load. This is terrible for cache locality and predictability in a trading context.

You instead want to:

- **Bind NIC interrupts** for latency-sensitive queues to specific cores on the NIC's NUMA node.
- **Reserve those cores** so that general-purpose tasks and background daemons do not run there.
- **Co-locate user threads** for the associated connections on the same cores or, at least, on sibling cores that share caches.

With this setup, when a packet arrives:

- The NIC raises an interrupt to the designated core.
- That core runs the RX handler and softirq, placing data into the socket buffer.
- The same core then schedules and runs the user thread that consumes the data.

The entire journey from RX ring to strategy now happens without cross-core hops, dramatically improving determinism.

Receive Packet Steering (RPS/RFS): Use With Care

Many kernels offer features like Receive Packet Steering (RPS) and Receive Flow Steering (RFS). These spread or steer processing of incoming packets across cores in software, beyond what the NIC hardware does.

In a general-purpose server, this helps:

- Distribute network processing load across many cores.
- Align flows with the cores where consuming threads run.

For a carefully pinned trading engine, however, RPS/RFS can be counterproductive:

- They introduce additional queuing and handoff points inside the kernel.

- They can move processing away from the core that took the interrupt, undermining the locality you worked to create.
- Their internal queues can become bottlenecks in their own right when message rates spike.

As a rule of thumb:

> Disable RPS/RFS on latency-critical paths once you have explicit NIC and thread affinity in place.

There are exceptions. For example, if you must run many strategy instances on a shared host and cannot dedicate cores, allowing RFS to steer flows to the cores where sockets are read may help. But in tightly controlled co-lo setups, simplicity and direct mapping typically win.

Busy Polling: Spinning Instead of Waiting

Ordinarily, the kernel waits for an interrupt to be raised before running the receive path. An alternative is *busy polling*, where a thread repeatedly checks the NIC or socket for new packets without blocking, consuming CPU even when there is no work.

Busy polling is like standing at your front door watching for the mail carrier, instead of going about your day and waiting for the doorbell. It trades higher baseline CPU usage for:

- **Lower wake-up latency.** When a packet arrives, there is no need to deliver an interrupt and wake a sleeping thread; a polling loop running on a core can see and handle it almost immediately.
- **Fewer context switches.** The core remains in the polling loop and application code, reducing scheduler activity.

For low-latency feeds, busy polling can be useful if:

- You can afford to dedicate one or more cores to the task.
- Message rates are high enough that those cores are rarely idle anyway.

You must be disciplined about where you enable it. Applying busy polling broadly will starve other tasks and can raise system-wide latencies.

Taming the Scheduler: CPU Isolation and Run Queues

Even with NIC and kernel tuning, the OS scheduler can undermine your hard work if it freely moves threads across cores or time-slices trading threads alongside noisy neighbors.

Isolating Cores for Trading

Most modern operating systems allow you to *isolate* certain cores from the general scheduler. The idea is simple:

- You mark several cores (for example, two on each NUMA node) as reserved.
- System daemons, background jobs, and the default run queues avoid these cores.
- You explicitly pin your latency-sensitive threads and NIC interrupts to the isolated cores.

In effect, you create a small "real-time island" inside a general-purpose server. On this island:

- There is little or no run queue contention: the trading thread is the only runnable task most of the time.
- Context switches are rare and, when they occur, mostly due to your own design (for example, between I/O and compute threads).
- Cache contents remain dominated by your code paths and data structures, not by random background activity.

Outside this island, the rest of the system continues working as normal, handling logging, monitoring, disk I/O, and so on.

Pinning Threads and Respecting NUMA

Isolating cores is not enough; you must also ensure that your processes and threads actually run where you intend.

Practical steps include:

- **Pin market data threads** to the cores serving the associated NIC RX queues.
- **Pin strategy threads** either to the same cores (for maximum locality) or to a small set of nearby cores that share caches with the NIC cores.
- **Bind memory allocations** for hot data structures (order books, risk state) to the appropriate NUMA node so that most accesses are local.

This alignment reduces cross-socket traffic. Without it, the kernel may schedule a thread on a core that has to access data freshly DMA'd into memory attached to another socket, adding hidden tens of nanoseconds repeatedly.

When to Bypass the Kernel: DPDK and Friends

So far we have assumed you use the operating system's standard network stack. For many trading strategies, a well-tuned kernel can reach sub-10-microsecond wire-to-user latencies with acceptable jitter. For the most demanding applications, or for extremely high message rates, teams sometimes bypass the kernel stack altogether.

User-Space Networking: Direct NIC Access

Frameworks such as DPDK provide:

- Direct user-space access to NIC queues via polling, often using huge pages and special drivers.
- Tight control over how packets are received and transmitted, including custom ring buffers and processing loops.

- Minimal involvement of the general-purpose kernel network stack.

Architecturally, you can imagine moving the RX softirq and much of the socket handling into your process. Your code talks almost directly to the NIC.

The benefits are:

- **Lower and more stable latency** at very high packet rates.
- **Reduced jitter** from avoiding kernel scheduling decisions, RPS queues, and generic protocol handling you do not need.
- **Fine-grained control** over batching, prefetching, and CPU affinity.

The costs include:

- **Complexity.** You are now responsible for many things the kernel used to handle: resource management, error handling, and sometimes even your own TCP or sequencing logic.
- **Portability and maintainability.** Code tightly coupled to a specific NIC and user-space stack can be harder to port and to support.
- **Integration.** You may still need regular sockets for some parts of the system, which means running a hybrid setup.

User-space networking is therefore a tool for teams that have already extracted most of the benefit from kernel tuning and still need more. It is often used for pure market data ingestion and immediate strategy triggers, while order entry and less latency-sensitive functions continue to use normal sockets.

Modern Kernel Alternatives: Efficient I/O with io_uring

Between the traditional socket API and full user-space stacks sits a middle ground: mechanisms that make kernel-based I/O more efficient. One such mechanism is *io_uring*.

You can think of io_uring as:

A way for user space to submit many I/O operations to the kernel in batches and to receive their completions via shared memory, reducing system call overhead and enabling efficient polling.

For network I/O, this can:

- Reduce the number of context switches needed to perform frequent small reads.
- Allow you to combine multiple socket operations into a single interaction with the kernel.
- Provide a polling mode that keeps cores busy with I/O work when data is available and avoids excessive wake-up latency.

While io_uring does not eliminate the kernel network stack, it helps you extract more performance from it without stepping entirely outside the OS.

From Settings to Process: A Tuning Workflow

It is easy to get lost in individual knobs. To avoid that, it helps to impose a simple, repeatable workflow for kernel and NIC tuning:

- **Clarify your target.** Decide what matters: is your goal to get median latency below a certain number, or to shrink p99 and p99.9 under bursty load? The answer affects which trade-offs (for example, busy polling versus CPU savings) are acceptable.
- **Establish a baseline.** Measure your current end-to-end latencies and per-stage timings under a realistic replay of market data. Capture CPU utilization, context-switch counts, interrupt rates, and queue occupancies.
- **Stabilize the environment.** Isolate a few cores, reduce background noise, and align NIC queues and thread affinities without changing anything else. Re-measure.

- **Tune NIC behavior.** Adjust RX ring sizes and interrupt moderation on the critical queues. Use tools and counters to observe drops and backlog during synthetic bursts. Aim for minimal but sufficient buffering.
- **Simplify kernel processing.** Set IRQ affinities explicitly. Disable RPS/RFS if they are not needed. Consider enabling busy polling on the most critical paths if you have the core budget.
- **Iterate cautiously.** Make one change at a time, re-run the same workload, and compare latency distributions. Keep notes: successful tuning is as much about disciplined experimentation as it is about technical insight.
- **Decide on advanced options.** Only after exhausting kernel-level improvements should you evaluate whether user-space networking or io_uring are warranted for your use case.

The guiding idea is that low-latency performance is an *engineering process*, not a one-time configuration dump. By starting from a clear mental model—packets moving through queues, handlers, and cores—you can reason about why a particular change should help and verify that it actually does.

In the next sections we will turn to other major contributors to latency and jitter: memory management, garbage collection, batching, and concurrency. The techniques you have just learned for reasoning about NICs and kernels will carry forward: in all cases, you are looking for unnecessary waiting, avoidable work, and lost locality along the tick-to-trade path.

5.3 Memory Management and GC Tuning

In the first two sections of this chapter we treated latency as a question of getting packets quickly from the wire to your strategy thread. We focused on NICs, interrupts, the kernel, and CPU scheduling. In many trading shops that is where the performance effort stops.

However, once those foundations are in place, a different class of problems emerges. You may find that your median tick-to-trade time looks excellent, but your p99 and p99.9 are surprisingly large, especially during volatile periods. Profiling shows no obvious bottleneck in network or CPU scheduling. Instead, the long pauses occur inside your process, at moments when the system decides to allocate or reorganize memory.

This section is about that "invisible" layer: how memory is allocated, laid out, and reclaimed, and how these mechanisms can quietly dominate tail latency in event-driven trading systems. We will focus on three themes:

- How general-purpose allocators and garbage collectors behave under bursty loads.
- How poor data layout and sharing multiplies cache misses and contention.
- How to engineer around these issues using pre-allocation, pooling, and NUMA-aware placement.

The aim is not to turn you into a garbage collector implementer, but to give you a practical mental model of where memory-related delays come from and how to contain them.

Why Memory Matters After You Fix the Network

Once your network, kernel, and scheduling paths are tuned, the cost of getting a packet into your process may be only a few microseconds. At that point, every step inside your application becomes relatively more important. Two patterns are particularly dangerous:

- **Allocations on the hot path.** Code that creates short-lived objects every time a tick arrives or an order is updated. For example, allocating new message wrapper objects, temporary collections, or string buffers.
- **Irregular data access.** Data structures that are scattered all over the heap, forcing the CPU to fetch from many different memory locations for each tick.

These patterns hurt you in two ways:

- They increase *average* CPU work per event, reducing throughput headroom.
- They trigger *periodic pauses* when the allocator or garbage collector has to clean up, which stretch your latency tails.

In low-latency trading you are not only optimizing for speed, you are optimizing for predictability. Memory behavior is one of the biggest sources of unpredictability.

A Gentle Mental Model of Heaps and Allocators

Regardless of language, most trading systems use a *heap*: a large region of memory from which variable-sized blocks are handed out to satisfy allocations.

At a high level, the allocator:

- Keeps track of which parts of the heap are free and which are in use.
- On each allocation request, finds a suitably sized free chunk, marks it in use, and returns a pointer.
- On deallocation, marks the chunk as free again, possibly merging it with neighboring free chunks.

Over time, as you allocate and free different-sized objects, the heap can become *fragmented*: free space is broken into many small pieces scattered throughout the heap. Even if the total free space is large, there may be no single chunk large enough for a new allocation without further work.

To manage this, allocators often:

- Maintain per-thread or per-core caches to avoid contention on global data structures.

- Group allocations by size classes to simplify reuse.
- Occasionally perform more expensive operations, such as searching larger lists, consolidating free blocks, or even asking the operating system for more pages of memory.

Most allocations are therefore fast, but a small fraction can be much slower. From a latency perspective, those occasional slow allocations are problematic: they tend to occur at times of pressure, when many events are flowing and your code is allocating more aggressively.

Garbage Collection: Convenience With a Price

Many trading stacks are built in languages with automatic memory management: Java, C#, or other managed runtimes. These provide a garbage collector (GC) that periodically scans the heap for objects that are no longer reachable and reclaims their memory.

While GC frees developers from manual memory management, it introduces two latency risks:

- **Stop-the-world pauses.** At certain points, the runtime temporarily stops all application threads (or at least those touching memory) so the GC can safely update references and reclaim memory. These pauses can last from microseconds to many milliseconds, depending on heap size, allocation rate, and GC algorithm.
- **Concurrent overhead and surprise slowdowns.** Modern GCs often run concurrently with the application to reduce pause times. But they still need special moments of coordination, and concurrent marking and sweeping can consume CPU and memory bandwidth, subtly slowing down your code.

GC algorithms are sophisticated, but for our purposes we can simplify their behavior into a few patterns:

- **Generational heaps.** Most objects die young. The heap is divided into young and old regions. Collections of the young generation are frequent and usually fast; collections of the old generation are rarer but more expensive.

- **Trigger conditions.** GC runs when allocation has filled certain regions of the heap or when internal heuristics suggest it is needed. During bursts of message traffic (and therefore bursts of allocations), you are more likely to hit these conditions.
- **Compaction.** To reduce fragmentation, some collectors move live objects together, leaving larger contiguous free spaces. This compaction takes time and often requires stop-the-world phases.

In a trading engine that allocates per-tick objects, you end up with:

- Continuous background allocation as ticks stream in.
- Frequent young-generation GCs, which are often short but non-zero pauses.
- Occasional old-generation or full-heap GCs, which are longer and more disruptive, appearing as spikes in tail latency.

You will recognize these in production as *latency cliffs*: everything seems fine until a sudden, out-of-the-blue multi-millisecond pause that coincides with a GC log entry.

Memory Layout and the CPU Cache

Even without GC, memory layout can quietly erode performance. Modern CPUs rely heavily on caches: small, fast memory close to the core that holds copies of recently accessed data. Accessing cached data is much faster than fetching it from main memory.

Your data structures determine how effective these caches are:

- If related fields are stored contiguously in memory, a single cache line fetch brings in several useful values at once.
- If related fields are scattered across the heap, each field may require a separate cache line, causing multiple memory accesses per event.

Two contrasting styles illustrate this:

- **Array of structures.** You store an array where each element is a full object: price, quantity, timestamp, and so on, together. This is intuitive but can be suboptimal if you often only need a subset of fields.
- **Structure of arrays.** You store separate arrays for prices, quantities, and timestamps, each tightly packed. This can be friendlier to caches and vectorized operations when you process many elements in the same way.

For a book of thousands of levels or a history of recent trades, these design choices can mean the difference between a few cache hits and a cascade of cache misses for each tick.

In the context of NUMA, layout also has a location dimension: if your hot data structures are allocated on the wrong NUMA node, every access may be slightly slower, and remote memory traffic may contend with other cores. Over millions of events, these small penalties accumulate into visible latency.

Engineering Around GC and Allocation

Having recognized the dangers, we now turn to mitigation techniques. The overarching strategy is:

> Move as much memory work as possible *off the hot path* and replace dynamic allocation with predictable reuse.

Pre-allocation of Critical Structures

Certain data structures are clearly bounded by design: order books for known symbols, risk limit tables, per-session state machines. For these, you can:

- Allocate all necessary storage at startup, when latency does not matter.

- Use fixed-size arrays or tables, indexable by instrument ID, venue, or connection.
- Avoid creating and destroying objects in response to every tick; instead, update already-allocated entries.

For example, instead of constructing a new "order book level" object every time you see a price level, you allocate a fixed set of levels per instrument and simply update quantities and timestamps. You trade some memory for a large reduction in allocation and GC pressure.

Object Pools and Reuse

Not all objects can be completely pre-allocated, but many follow predictable patterns: message wrappers, temporary buffers, or small records. For these, object pools can be effective.

An object pool is a stash of already-allocated objects that can be:

- Checked out when needed, instead of allocating a new one.
- Reset to a clean state and returned when no longer used.

From a latency point of view:

- Most object uses become simple pointer swaps and field resets, which are fast and cache-friendly.
- The total pool size is bounded, so allocation spikes are limited to pool growth, which you can drive to zero in steady state by sizing the pool appropriately.

Well-designed pools are often per-thread or per-core to avoid contention. They must be implemented carefully to avoid subtle bugs (for example, returning an object to the pool while still in use), but when done right they dramatically reduce GC activity.

Slimming Down Object Graphs

GC cost is correlated with how much live data must be scanned and how complex the object graph is. You can lighten this load by:

- Avoiding deep chains of small objects in hot structures. Flatten nested objects where possible.
- Preferring primitive fields and compact arrays over boxes and collections for frequently accessed data.
- Limiting the scope of references: once a message is processed, drop references to it promptly so the GC can easily see it as garbage.

The mental model here is: each extra pointer the GC has to follow is another potential memory access. Flattening the graph reduces the amount of memory the collector must touch, lowering both pause times and concurrent GC overhead.

NUMA-aware Allocation

As discussed earlier, non-uniform memory access means that not all memory is equally close to all cores. To avoid cross-socket penalties:

- Place per-core or per-thread data structures (such as pools and ring buffers) on the same NUMA node as the cores that use them.
- Keep communication between sockets explicit and limited to higher-level events rather than having book or risk data ping-pong between nodes.

In practice, this often means:

- Initializing and allocating data on the target core, so that the OS naturally places it on the local node.
- Using runtime or OS options to bind processes and their memory areas to specific nodes.

NUMA awareness works together with pre-allocation and pooling: by giving each core its own local pool and state, you reduce both allocator contention and remote memory traffic.

GC Tuning Strategies in Managed Runtimes

If you are using a managed language, you can go beyond structuring your code to also configure the GC itself.

Choosing the Right GC Mode

Most runtimes offer different GC modes or collectors, such as:

- **Throughput-optimized collectors,** which aim to maximize overall work done but may tolerate longer pauses.
- **Low-pause or real-time collectors,** which try to cap individual pause durations, possibly at the cost of more background CPU usage.
- **Concurrent collectors,** which run much of their work alongside your application threads.

For trading systems, the typical preference is:

- Avoid pure throughput-oriented collectors that allow rare, very long pauses.
- Favor low-pause or concurrent collectors that produce shorter, more frequent pauses, and tune them to suit your latency SLOs.

The right choice is workload-dependent and should be made based on measurement, not vendor marketing. Look specifically at how the GC mode changes your tail latencies under market bursts.

Sizing the Heap

Heap size affects GC behavior in two directions:

- **Too small,** and you trigger collections frequently, adding many small pauses and GC overhead.
- **Too large,** and each full or old-generation collection has more memory to scan, increasing the worst-case pause time.

The sweet spot depends on your allocation rate and object lifetime patterns. A good tuning process is:

- Start with a moderate heap size based on peak live data requirements plus a safety margin.
- Run realistic load tests and record GC logs, focusing on pause durations and frequency.
- Gradually adjust heap sizes and generation ratios, aiming for pauses that are short enough and infrequent enough to meet your latency goals.

Remember: the goal is *predictable* behavior. A configuration that modestly increases average GC CPU time but removes very long pauses is often desirable.

Controlling Allocation Patterns

Most GCs are optimized for many short-lived objects. You can work with them rather than against them:

- Ensure that truly short-lived objects (for example, temporary parsing buffers) do not accidentally become referenced from long-lived structures, which would promote them into older generations and increase full-GC costs.
- Batch allocations where possible: parsing and constructing several related objects together can improve locality and may allow the GC to treat them efficiently.
- Avoid allocating in the innermost loops when an alternative design using pre-allocated buffers or reusable containers is feasible.

These steps reduce pressure on the young generation and delay or shrink old-generation collections.

Visualizing the Impact: Latency Distributions

The effect of good memory engineering is most visible in latency distributions. Two systems can have similar medians but radically different tails depending on how they allocate and reclaim memory.

After you have implemented pre-allocation, pooling, and GC tuning, you should expect to see:

- Modest improvement in median and p90 latencies.
- Dramatic collapse of p99 and p99.9 latencies, especially under sustained or bursty loads.

The following figure illustrates this contrast by comparing two trading loops: one that allocates heavily and relies on default GC settings, and one that uses pre-allocated structures and pools with a tuned collector.

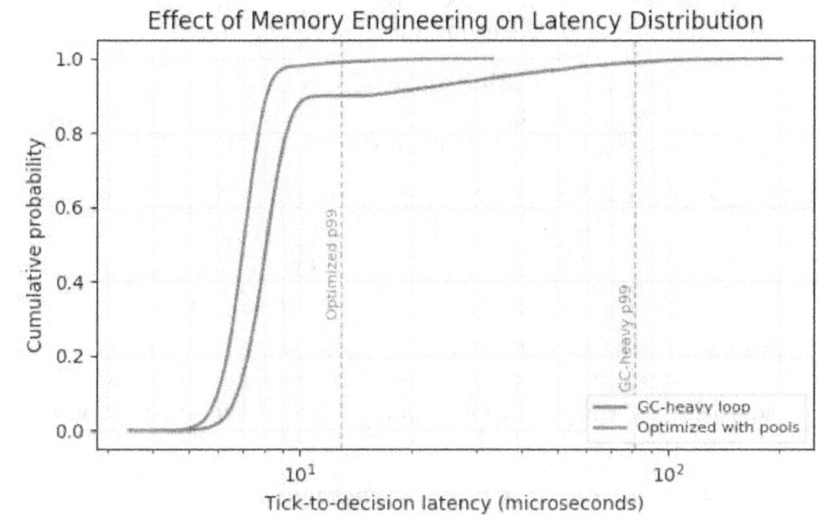

This kind of plot is a powerful motivator when prioritizing engineering work. It makes clear that the main benefit of memory-aware design is not shaving a microsecond off the median; it is eliminating rare, but costly, excursions into multi-millisecond delays.

A Practical Tuning Workflow

As with NIC and kernel tuning, memory and GC tuning is an iterative process rather than a one-time configuration. A practical workflow looks like this:

- **Instrument and observe.** Enable GC logging or equivalent metrics. Capture per-tick latencies along with when GC events occur. Look for correlations between pauses and latency spikes.
- **Find hot allocations.** Use profilers or allocation sampling tools to identify where in your code allocations are happening on the hot path. Rank call sites by allocation volume and frequency.
- **Eliminate or move allocations.** For the top offenders, redesign data structures to pre-allocate, reuse, or simplify. Move unavoidable large allocations to startup or off the critical path (for example, into background initialization steps).
- **Introduce pools judiciously.** For recurring allocations that cannot be eliminated, add well-scoped pools. Prefer per-thread or per-core pools to avoid introducing lock contention.
- **Tune the GC.** Once allocation patterns have been improved, adjust GC mode and heap sizing to target your desired balance between pause time and overhead. Validate changes with controlled load tests.
- **Validate under real bursts.** Replay historical high-volatility intervals and monitor both latency distributions and GC behavior. Ensure that rare, large pauses have been significantly reduced.
- **Document invariants.** Record assumptions, such as "no allocations in this function" or "this pool must never grow beyond N objects." Add checks in test environments to catch regressions when code evolves.

The key mindset is the same as for network and kernel tuning: every source of variability can and should be traced to a specific mechanism. Memory allocation and garbage collection are not mysterious forces of nature; they are engineered systems whose behavior you can shape with appropriate design and tuning.

In the next section we will build on this foundation by looking at batching, vectorization, and serialization. Many of the same themes will reappear: organizing data to favor caches, choosing encodings that avoid unnecessary work, and being explicit about where you pay fixed costs so that your event-driven trading system remains responsive even when the market is anything but calm.

5.4 Batching, Vectorization, and Serialization

In the previous sections we focused on moving a single tick through the system as quickly and predictably as possible. We tuned NICs and kernels, reduced context switches, and brought memory allocation under control. In this section we turn to a complementary question:

> Given a fixed amount of hardware and a latency budget, how can we do *more useful work* per microsecond without destroying our tails?

The answer lies in three related ideas:

- **Batching**: handling small groups of messages at once to amortize fixed costs.
- **Vectorization**: structuring data and computation so that the CPU can operate on many items in parallel using a single instruction.
- **Serialization choices**: using compact binary formats and zero-copy schemes to avoid wasting cycles turning bytes into objects and back.

Done well, these techniques increase throughput and often improve stability. Done poorly, they introduce additional queues and processing spikes that show up as latency jitter precisely when markets are busiest. The aim of this section is to show you where the sweet spots are and how to reason about them.

Fixed Costs Along the Tick-to-Trade Path

Every tick that enters your system pays a series of *fixed* costs that are largely independent of how much actual "trading logic" you run:

- A system call or user-space poll to check for new data.
- A cache miss or two to bring socket buffers and book state into the CPU.
- Function call overhead to dispatch the message to the right handler.
- Network stack and encoding overhead to construct any outbound messages.

If you process ticks one at a time, each tick bears the full cost of these steps. If you can safely process small groups of ticks together, that group can share many of the fixed costs:

- One system call to read several messages.
- One cache line fetch that contains multiple quotes or orders.
- One pass through a risk check function evaluating several candidate orders at once.

This is the core intuition behind batching and vectorization: *pay the overhead once, use it multiple times.*

The challenge is that financial markets are time-sensitive. You cannot arbitrarily delay a decision for the sake of rounding up a bigger batch. There is a trade-off between throughput (how many messages you handle per second) and latency (how long any given message waits before being acted upon). We will explore this trade-off, then connect it to data layout and serialization choices.

Batching: From Single Messages to Micro-batches

It is helpful to think of batching as a spectrum rather than an on/off switch. At one extreme, you process each tick as soon as it arrives. At the other, you aggregate thousands of ticks and operate on them like an offline analytics job. Trading systems usually live somewhere in between: they use *micro-batches*.

Sources of Natural Batching

Even if you never explicitly design for it, your system already performs some batching:

- The NIC and kernel may deliver several packets per interrupt or per softirq run.
- Socket reads often return more than one message at a time if multiple packets are queued.
- Your strategy might receive many independent events with the same timestamp during an auction or after a news release.

One goal of performance engineering is to *align** your application-level batching with these natural batch boundaries, so you neither leave efficiency on the table nor introduce additional artificial queues.

For example, if your socket read frequently returns 8 messages at a time, you can often decode and apply them as a group while still maintaining acceptable per-message latency, instead of dispatching each one through a separate call stack and risk check.

Where Batching Helps Most

Batching tends to pay off in three main areas:

I/O and system calls. Making a system call has a fixed entry and exit overhead. Reading or writing multiple messages per call significantly reduces per-message overhead. Similarly, when sending orders, grouping several into a single outbound packet (if allowed by the protocol and exchange) can cut down header and checksum work.

Cache behavior. Market data often has locality: many consecutive quotes refer to the same symbol or a small set of symbols. Reading and updating several book levels for the same instrument while they are already in cache is far cheaper than repeatedly loading and evicting the same data for one update at a time.

Risk and pricing computations. Some operations, such as checking portfolio risk limits or recalculating a derived signal, can be applied to several candidate trades or quotes at once. Instead of recomputing the same invariants repeatedly for individual ticks, you compute them across a small batch.

Latency Trade-offs and Batch Size Selection

Every batch introduces at least a small delay:

- The first message in the batch waits while the system accumulates the rest of the batch.
- The last message in the batch benefits most from batching (because it arrives just before processing starts) but has less opportunity to amortize fixed costs.

The key is to choose a batch size (or time window) small enough that this waiting time is negligible relative to your latency budget, yet large enough to meaningfully amortize overhead.

In practice, you rarely fix a single static batch size. Instead you:

- Set a small maximum time window (for example, a few microseconds or tens of microseconds, depending on your strategy) within which to accumulate messages.
- Process immediately if you reach a certain count (for example, 8–16 messages) before the time window expires.
- Fall back to single-message processing when traffic is very light.

This adaptive approach lets you capture batching benefits during bursts without imposing unnecessary delays during quiet periods.

Vectorization: Doing Many Operations at Once

Batching creates opportunities for *vectorization*: applying the same operation to multiple data items in parallel. Modern CPUs can operate on vectors of numbers with a single instruction using SIMD (Single Instruction, Multiple Data) units.

While you do not need to know SIMD intrinsics to benefit, you do need to organize your data so that compilers and libraries can use vector instructions effectively.

Data Layout for Vectorization

Recall the contrast between:

- **Array of structures (AoS)**: each object (for example, a quote) contains all its fields, and you store an array of these objects.
- **Structure of arrays (SoA)**: you maintain separate arrays for each field (prices, quantities, timestamps), indexed consistently.

Vectorization works best when you perform the same operation on a long, contiguous sequence of values. For example:

- Revaluing a set of positions using new prices.
- Applying the same risk check threshold to a batch of candidate orders.
- Computing aggregate quantities across multiple levels of the book.

In these cases, a SoA layout is attractive: the array of prices or quantities is a contiguous block of memory. The CPU can load several values into a vector register and execute the operation in one instruction. The compiler may be able to automatically generate such vectorized code when loops are simple and data is contiguous.

In contrast, with an AoS layout where each object is scattered across the heap, the CPU must chase pointers, and each field access may require a separate cache line. Vectorization becomes much harder.

Practical Uses in Trading Systems

There are several practical areas in a trading engine where vectorization naturally fits:

Signal computation. Momentum indicators, moving averages, volatility estimates, and other time-series transforms are often computed across arrays of past values. Expressing these computations as operations on arrays rather than on linked lists of objects helps both the compiler and specialized numerical libraries.

Portfolio- and book-level risk checks. When validating multiple potential trades or quotes against portfolio limits, you can group instrument-level exposures and apply the same arithmetic to arrays of values. This avoids recomputing scalar operations for each proposal.

Aggregation and statistics. Computing sums, maximums, or counts across sets of venues, instruments, or orders can be done more efficiently on arrays.

The common pattern is: *move from object-by-object thinking to column- or array-based thinking* for the parts of your system that process many similar items.

Serialization: Turning Bytes Into Objects and Back

So far we have considered what happens once data is in memory. We now turn to the cost of getting it there and back out again: serialization and deserialization.

Trading systems must interact with multiple external protocols: exchange-native binary formats, FIX, proprietary feeds, and internal messages between components. The way you represent these messages greatly affects latency.

The Cost of Verbose Formats

Human-friendly formats such as JSON and XML are convenient for development and debugging. They are, however, extremely inefficient on the hot path:

- Field names are repeated in every message.
- Numbers must be parsed from text into binary, which is surprisingly expensive.

- Messages have variable lengths and complex nesting, which complicates parsing.

Even structured binary formats like generic protocol buffers can introduce overhead:

- Field tags and lengths add parsing work for every field, even when the schema is known and fixed.
- Variable-length integer encodings require branching logic, which hurts branch prediction.
- Allocating separate objects for each nested message can trigger GC and fragment the heap.

For back-office workflows and low-frequency tasks, these costs are acceptable. On a tick-triggered trading path that must respond within microseconds, they are often unacceptable.

Flat Binary Layouts for the Hot Path

On the hot path, you ideally want messages to be:

- **Fixed-width where possible.** Fields such as prices, quantities, and IDs should have fixed binary sizes, so you can compute offsets into a message with simple arithmetic.
- **Contiguous.** All fields needed for a decision should reside in a single, compact buffer, preferably in the order they are used.
- **Aligned.** Aligning multi-byte fields to natural boundaries (for example, 4 or 8 bytes) can improve load/store efficiency on some architectures.

This leads to designs where:

- Message types have predefined, static layouts that both sender and receiver agree on.

- The receiver can treat an incoming byte array as a "view" onto a message by casting or slicing, without copying.
- Parsing beyond simple bounds checking is minimal: you read fields directly at known offsets.

Many exchange protocols already follow this principle. Internally, you can apply the same idea to messages passed between components of your trading system.

Zero-Copy Designs

The most extreme optimization is to avoid copying data altogether. A *zero-copy* design aims to:

- Leave market data in the buffers where the NIC or kernel placed it.
- Interpret those buffers directly as message structures.
- Pass references or indices around within your process instead of creating new objects or copying payloads.

For example, a market data ingestion thread might:

- Receive a batch of packets into a ring of pre-allocated buffers.
- For each packet, identify its message type and write a small descriptor into a shared ring buffer (for instance, buffer index plus offset).
- A strategy thread reads these descriptors and accesses the original packet buffer directly to extract only the fields needed.

This design minimizes:

- Memory bandwidth usage (no redundant copies).
- GC pressure (no short-lived message objects).

- Cache pollution (you touch only the parts of the message you actually need).

Zero-copy is not free: you must manage buffer lifetimes carefully to ensure that a buffer is not reused or freed while some component still references it. But with disciplined design, it is a powerful way to keep both latency and jitter low in high-throughput scenarios.

Combining Batching, Vectorization, and Serialization Choices

These techniques are mutually reinforcing:

- Batching gives you groups of similar messages to process together.
- Vectorization lets you apply the same operation across these groups efficiently, especially when data is laid out in arrays.
- Compact, fixed-layout binary encodings make it easy to parse batches quickly and feed them into vectorized kernels without intermediate object allocations.

A well-engineered tick-to-trade pipeline might therefore look like this:

1. A NIC or user-space networking stack delivers micro-batches of packets into a ring of pre-allocated buffers.
2. A parser thread walks each buffer, identifies messages using fixed headers, and writes lightweight descriptors into a per-strategy queue, avoiding allocations and copies.
3. Strategy threads pull descriptors in small batches, load the required fields into arrays (or treat them as such), and invoke vectorized computations for risk checks and signal updates.
4. Outbound orders are constructed using fixed-layout templates, with only a few fields filled in per order, possibly batched together for transmission.

Throughout, you minimize per-message fixed costs and the number of times data moves between memory locations.

Visualizing the Trade-offs

To make these ideas concrete, it helps to visualize two aspects:

1. How throughput and latency change as you vary micro-batch size.
2. How different serialization choices affect per-message processing time.

The following figure presents both views. The first plot shows a typical pattern: as batch size grows from 1 to a modest number, throughput climbs quickly while latency initially rises slowly—this is the "sweet spot." Beyond a certain point, additional batching provides diminishing benefits and starts to degrade latency more steeply.

The second plot compares the approximate per-message processing time for three encodings on the hot path: JSON, a generic binary protocol like protobuf, and a custom zero-copy binary format.

These sketches are illustrative rather than prescriptive. Your exact curves will depend on hardware, strategy, code, and load patterns. The point is that the relationships are *shape-stable*: there is almost always a region where modest batching and efficient binary formats deliver a large throughput gain for a small latency cost, and a region beyond which further batching and abstraction layers cause latency to explode.

A Measurement-Driven Design Mindset

The overarching lesson of this section is not that "bigger batches are better" or that "text formats are bad." Rather, it is that:

- Every design choice—batch size, data layout, encoding—implicitly shapes your latency and throughput curves.

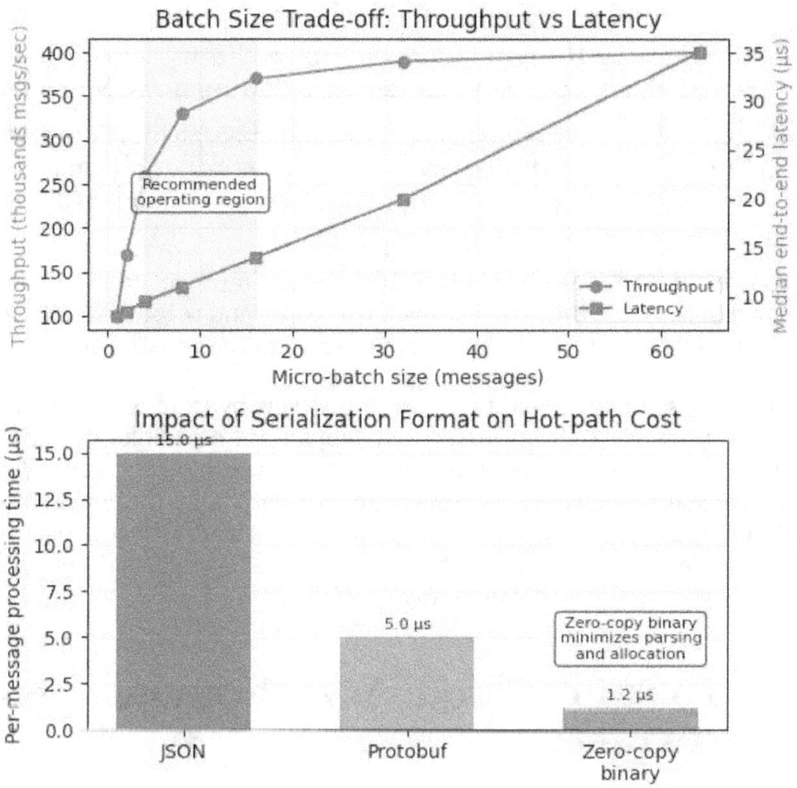

- You can often trade a small amount of additional per-message waiting for a large improvement in stability and capacity, but only up to a point.
- The right choices depend on your strategy's sensitivity to delay, the volatility regime you trade in, and your hardware.

Therefore, approach batching, vectorization, and serialization as you did NIC and GC tuning:

1. **Form a hypothesis.** For example, that processing up to 8 messages per batch will improve throughput significantly without vi-

olating your latency budget.

2. **Change one thing.** Introduce micro-batches in a specific stage, or switch a specific hot-path message flow from JSON to a flat binary format.
3. **Measure the full distribution.** Look at p50, p90, p99, and p99.9 latencies under realistic bursty loads, and monitor CPU usage.
4. **Decide and document.** If the change improves tails without unacceptable trade-offs elsewhere, keep it and record the reasoning so that future maintainers understand the constraints.

In the next section we will build on these ideas by examining concurrency structures—ring buffers, event loops, and actor-like designs—that let multiple cores cooperate without undermining the gains you have just achieved. There, as here, the goal is the same: maintain a disciplined, queue-aware architecture that extracts as much work as possible from each microsecond while keeping latency tails well-behaved when markets are most demanding.

5.5 Lock-Free and Asynchronous Concurrency

In the previous sections we concentrated on making a *single* tick as fast and predictable as possible: we shortened its path through the network stack, removed avoidable allocations, and used batching and compact encodings to do more work per microsecond. In a live trading system, however, many ticks are in flight at once, and multiple cores must cooperate to ingest data, update state, run strategies, and send orders.

How these cores coordinate has a profound impact on latency, jitter, and failure modes under stress. A concurrency design that looks fine at low message rates can fall apart when markets spike, turning into a tangle of threads waiting on locks, fighting over shared data structures, and producing highly irregular response times.

This section introduces a set of concurrency patterns that are well-suited to event-driven trading:

- **Ring buffers** for high-throughput, low-overhead message passing between threads.
- **Event loops** that let a single core handle a sequence of events without lock contention.
- **Actor-like message passing** where each core "owns" a shard of state and coordination happens via messages, not shared locks.

The goal is not to chase clever lock-free tricks for their own sake, but to build architectures that *remain deterministic and debuggable* even when message rates surge.

Why Traditional Concurrency Breaks Under Spikes

Most general-purpose server applications are built on a simple model:

- Many threads share access to key data structures (for example, order books, risk limits, caches).
- Mutual exclusion locks (mutexes) and condition variables are used to protect shared data and signal state changes.
- The operating system scheduler decides when to run each thread, often on a best-effort basis.

This model is easy to program against in small systems, but it has several pathological behaviors when message rates are high and latency budgets are tight.

Lock Contention and Convoying

When multiple threads frequently try to acquire the same lock:

- Some threads are forced to wait while another holds the lock.
- Even when the critical section is short, the *serialization* of access can create queues at the lock.

- If the thread holding the lock is descheduled (for example, preempted by the OS), all other threads needing that lock are blocked until it gets CPU time again.

This creates a phenomenon called *lock convoying*: a whole convoy of threads lines up behind a lock, and their progress is synchronized to the scheduling of the lock holder. The result is bursty, unpredictable processing of events—the opposite of what you want in trading.

Heisenbugs and Priority Inversion

With complex lock hierarchies:

- It is easy to introduce subtle deadlocks that only appear under certain timing conditions.
- You can get *priority inversion*, where a low-priority thread holds a lock needed by a high-priority one, effectively inverting their priorities.
- Debugging becomes harder because behavior now depends sensitively on the scheduler's interleaving of threads.

These problems may only surface during exactly the conditions you care about most: volatile markets, high news volume, auctions, or exchange restarts.

Design Principle: Divide State, Pass Messages

In contrast, low-latency event-driven systems aim to:

- **Partition state** so that each core or thread owns a well-defined subset (for example, a set of symbols, a particular exchange session, or a stage of the pipeline).
- **Communicate via messages** passed through queues or ring buffers instead of shared mutable variables.

- **Keep hot paths single-threaded** with respect to the state they manipulate, so locks are unnecessary and execution is easier to reason about.

This approach draws inspiration from actor systems and from the design of high-performance network stacks and databases. The trading engine becomes a network of small, mostly independent components that send each other events.

Before we explore specific patterns, it is useful to visualize how a lock-based design differs from a message-passing one.

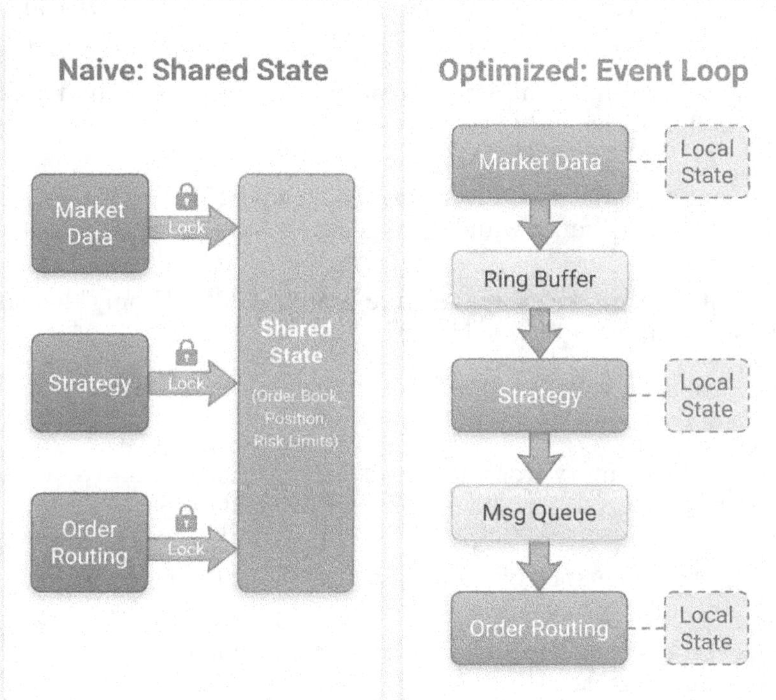

On the left, all threads converge on a single shared state protected by locks. On the right, each thread owns its own state and communicates through queues, eliminating shared locks from the hot path.

Ring Buffers: Simple, Fast Message Channels

A *ring buffer* (or circular buffer) is one of the simplest and most powerful tools for lock-free communication. It is essentially a fixed-size array used as a queue:

- A **producer** writes messages into the array in order, advancing a write index.
- A **consumer** reads messages in the same order, advancing a read index.
- When the end of the array is reached, indices wrap around to the beginning, hence "ring."

In the common single-producer, single-consumer (SPSC) case, you can implement a ring buffer without any locks:

- Only the producer updates the write index, and only the consumer updates the read index.
- Each side reads the other's index to check whether the buffer is empty or full.
- Careful memory ordering (provided by language primitives or the CPU) ensures that data is visible in the right order.

From a trading perspective, ring buffers are ideal for:

- Passing normalized market data events from an I/O thread to a strategy thread.
- Feeding orders from a strategy thread to an order-routing thread.
- Transferring work items between stages of a pipeline where each stage is assigned to a dedicated core.

Because the buffer is pre-allocated, there are no allocations on the hot path. Because it is fixed-size, you have an explicit bound on how much work can be queued between stages. Under overload, the ring will eventually fill, which you can treat as a backpressure signal.

Behavior Under Load

Ring buffers respond gracefully to bursts:

- Short bursts temporarily increase the number of occupied slots; the consumer catches up as soon as the arrival rate drops below processing capacity.
- Tail latency increases roughly in proportion to how full the buffer becomes; you can observe and measure this and decide when to shed load or degrade gracefully.

This is very different from lock-based designs where contention can lead to complex, scheduler-dependent delays. With ring buffers, the queuing behavior is explicit and localized.

Event Loops: One Core, Many Events

A second key pattern is the *event loop*: a dedicated thread that repeatedly pulls events from one or more queues and processes them in sequence. Rather than having many threads compete to handle events, you give one thread per core clear ownership over a stream of work.

How Event Loops Help

Event loops bring several advantages:

- **No shared locks on owned state.** Since a single loop owns the data it manipulates (for example, a set of order books), it can operate on them without taking locks.

- **Predictable control flow.** Events are processed in a well-defined order, usually the order they arrive in each input queue, making reasoning about state transitions easier.
- **Efficient batching.** The loop can naturally process small batches of incoming messages on each iteration, benefiting from the batching and vectorization techniques discussed earlier.

For instance, a strategy event loop might:

1. Read up to N market data events from its input ring buffer.
2. Apply them to the in-memory order books it owns.
3. Recompute signals and risk metrics as needed.
4. Emit zero or more order intent messages to an outbound queue.

This entire sequence happens on a single core, with no shared locks. Other cores performing different roles (for example, order routing or P&L aggregation) operate on their own event loops and state.

Multiple Loops and Sharding

To scale beyond what one core can handle, you deploy multiple event loops, each responsible for a subset of the workload:

- **By symbol.** For example, one loop handles instruments starting with A–M, another N–Z.
- **By venue or session.** One loop per exchange or per order gateway.
- **By function.** Separate loops for market data normalization, strategy evaluation, and order routing.

Sharding reduces the need for cross-core synchronization. When coordination is necessary (for example, cross-instrument risk checks), you can introduce higher-level messages between loops rather than exposing raw shared state.

Actor-like Message Passing: Cores as Independent Agents

The event loop pattern extends naturally into an *actor-like* architecture. In an actor model:

- Each actor has its own mailbox (queue) and encapsulated state.
- Actors communicate only by sending messages to each other's mailboxes.
- Each actor processes messages sequentially, in a loop.

You do not need a full actor framework to benefit from this style. The essential idea is to think of each thread or core as an independent agent with:

- A **clearly defined responsibility** (for example, "maintain order books for instruments X–Y" or "handle all communication with exchange Z").
- A **well-defined interface** consisting of message types it accepts and emits.
- **No external access** to its internal data; other components must send messages to request actions or information.

Under this discipline:

- Traditional shared-memory races are largely eliminated. Two actors do not accidentally update the same data concurrently; they must coordinate via messages.
- Backpressure and overload become visible as growing message queues, which you can monitor.
- Testing and simulation become easier: you can feed recorded message streams into an actor and verify its behavior in isolation.

In a trading engine, this might mean:

- A set of *market data actors*, each owning a subset of symbols and normalizing raw feed messages into a common format.
- A set of *strategy actors*, each implementing a particular strategy and reacting to normalized events.
- One or more *order session actors*, responsible for maintaining connections to exchanges and translating strategy intents into protocol-specific orders.

Messages flow along well-defined paths, often implemented with ring buffers or message queues. The architecture looks more like a messaging system than a tangle of threads holding locks.

Lock-Free Does Not Mean Risk-Free

Lock-free and asynchronous patterns are powerful, but they are not magic. A few cautions are in order.

Atomic Operations and Memory Ordering

Lock-free data structures rely on atomic operations and precise memory ordering to work correctly. While libraries or language constructs hide some of the complexity, you should:

- Prefer **well-reviewed, off-the-shelf** ring buffer and queue implementations where possible.
- Keep your own use of atomics simple and localized, and document invariants clearly.
- Avoid overly clever lock-free algorithms that are hard to reason about under weak memory models.

Your goal is not to win a concurrency design contest; it is to build a system that other engineers can understand and maintain without fear.

Backpressure and Queue Management

Queues can also be a source of latency if mismanaged:

- If producers outpace consumers for too long, queues fill, leading to unbounded increases in tail latency.
- Multiple queues in series can mask where bottlenecks are; packets may sit in several small queues en route to the strategy.

Design your message paths so that:

- Queue sizes are **bounded** and chosen based on realistic burst analysis.
- Overload handling policies are explicit: dropping low-priority messages, switching strategies to safer modes, or slowing intake when queues approach capacity.
- Monitoring exposes queue depths in real time so you can see where pressure builds during live trading.

Ordering and Idempotency

Message passing introduces questions of ordering and duplication:

- If multiple producers send to a consumer, you must be explicit about the order in which messages are processed.
- Some messages may be retried or replayed, especially in failure recovery scenarios.

To handle this cleanly:

- Include sequence numbers or timestamps in messages where exact ordering matters.
- Aim for **idempotent** handlers where possible: processing the same message twice has no harmful side effects.
- Document which order guarantees each queue or subsystem provides.

Putting It Together: A Lock-Free Trading Pipeline

Let us bring these ideas together in a concrete, if simplified, architecture for a co-located trading engine:

1. **NIC and kernel.** As earlier sections described, NIC RX queues are pinned to specific cores, and kernel processing is streamlined.
2. **Market data threads.** On each relevant core, a market data thread runs an event loop that:
   - Reads packets from a user-space or kernel socket interface.
   - Parses them into normalized events using zero-copy or minimal-copy techniques.
   - Writes event descriptors into one or more SPSC ring buffers feeding strategy threads.
3. **Strategy threads.** Each strategy thread owns:
   - A subset of instruments or venues.
   - An in-memory order book and any derived signals or state for its universe.
   - An input ring buffer from its associated market data source(s).
   - An output ring buffer leading to an order session thread.

   It runs an event loop that:

   - Batches incoming events from its ring buffer.
   - Updates its local books and signals.
   - Emits order intents as messages to the order session.
4. **Order session threads.** One or more threads handle communication with exchanges:
   - They own session state, sequence numbers, and resend logic.
   - They receive order intent messages from strategy threads via queues.

- They format and send orders, handling acknowledgments and rejections, again as messages.

5. **Auxiliary actors.** Separate event loops manage slower, less latency-critical concerns: P&L calculation, logging, persistence, and monitoring. These may use different batching and buffering strategies appropriate to their needs.

Throughout this pipeline:

- Each thread or actor owns its state and does not expose it directly to others.
- Communication paths are explicit and measurable: each ring buffer or queue can be monitored for depth and throughput.
- There are few or no locks on hot paths; most synchronization is implicit in message ordering.

Under market spikes, this design tends to *bend rather than break*: queues grow in predictable places, latencies increase smoothly rather than erratically, and you have clear levers for shedding load or throttling components.

A Practical Adoption Path

Transitioning from an ad-hoc, lock-heavy design to a message-passing, event-driven one does not have to be all-or-nothing. A sensible path is:

1. **Identify hot locks.** Use profiling to find locks that cause the most contention or waiting under load, especially in market data and strategy paths.
2. **Refactor around a ring buffer.** For a critical lock, ask: can we instead serialize access through a single owner thread and feed it work via a ring buffer?
3. **Encapsulate state.** Move the data protected by that lock into a component or actor owned by one thread. Replace direct access with message-based requests and updates.

4. **Iterate and expand.** Once one part of the system is converted, work outward: convert other shared-state regions into actors and connect them with queues.
5. **Instrument and validate.** At each step, measure how contention, tail latency, and behavior under synthetic bursts change.

As with all the performance work in this chapter, the guiding mindset is consistency and observability. Lock-free and asynchronous concurrency are not goals in themselves, but means to the end of an event-driven trading system whose behavior you can predict and trust even when markets are chaotic.

In the next and final section of this chapter we will close the loop by focusing on load and latency profiling: how to build realistic workloads, measure not just averages but full distributions, and use those measurements to drive iterative improvements across the entire tick-to-trade pipeline.

5.6 Load and Latency Profiling

By this point in the chapter we have accumulated a substantial toolbox: NIC and kernel tuning, memory and GC discipline, batching and vectorization, lock-free queues, and actor-like concurrency. All of these techniques promise lower latency and tighter tails, but none of them matter if you cannot *measure* their impact and relate it to realistic market conditions.

This final section is about turning performance engineering into a disciplined, repeatable process. We will cover three questions:

- How do you generate *realistic workloads* that stress your system the way real markets do?
- How do you *measure latency* in a way that reveals tail behavior and hidden queueing, not just reassuring averages?
- How do you run an *iterative optimization loop*: form hypotheses, collect evidence, change one thing at a time, and converge on a robust tick-to-trade pipeline?

The emphasis will be on practical methods that you can apply even in complex, distributed trading architectures.

What "Realistic Load" Means in Trading

In many software domains, load testing means generating a steady stream of requests at a target rate. Markets do not behave like that. They are bursty, correlated, and regime-dependent. A trading system that looks perfect under a smooth synthetic load can still misbehave during a volatile open or a macro announcement.

To build useful load tests, you must first understand the shape of real workloads.

Burstiness and Correlation

Real market data and order flow tend to exhibit:

- **Short, intense bursts**: volumes spike around the open, close, auctions, and news events.
- **Cross-symbol correlation**: many related instruments move together, causing simultaneous updates and opportunities.
- **Protocol-specific patterns**: some venues deliver data in frames or snapshots that cluster many updates, others in continuous tick streams.

Your load tests should therefore capture:

- **Peak message rates** over short windows (for example, 1 ms, 10 ms, 1 s), not just daily averages.
- **Joint activity** across instruments and venues you actually trade.
- **Message size and content distributions**, since parsing and GC behavior depend on payloads.

Sources of Realistic Load

There are three primary sources you can use to construct such workloads:

Historical market data. Most venues and data vendors offer full-depth replay feeds or raw capture files. You can:

- Extract representative intervals: volatile opens, quiet mid-days, stress events.
- Replay them into your system at original timing, or at scaled-up rates to test headroom.

This is the gold standard: it preserves the real-time structure of messages.

Recorded production traces. In some setups, you can log the raw packets or normalized events that actually passed through your production plant. Replaying these traces:

- Captures not only exchange behavior but also idiosyncrasies of your connectivity (gaps, retransmissions, throttling).
- Allows you to reproduce specific incidents, such as overflow events or unexpected latency spikes.

Synthetic generators. Where you lack data, you can build synthetic generators that mimic observed patterns. For example:

- Poisson-like arrivals with occasional heavy-tailed bursts.
- Correlated updates across symbol clusters.
- Randomized payloads consistent with protocol schemas.

Synthetic generators are especially useful when you want to probe extreme scenarios beyond what has happened historically, or when you are still designing a system and do not yet have real feeds wired up.

Defining the Measurement Targets

Before wiring up timers everywhere, you must decide what you want to measure. At a minimum, a trading system should track:

- **End-to-end tick-to-decision latency**: from arrival of market data at your boundary to the moment a trading decision is made.
- **End-to-end decision-to-wire latency**: from a decision to send an order to the moment it is on the wire towards the exchange.
- **Per-stage latencies**: time spent in each major component (market data normalization, strategy logic, risk checks, order routing).

You can then decompose spikes in overall latency into contributions from specific stages.

Placing Timestamps Carefully

To measure meaningfully, timestamps should be:

- **Taken as close to the boundary as possible**. For inputs, this means on receipt from the kernel or user-space networking stack, not after multiple internal queues. For outputs, timestamp just before sending into the kernel or NIC.
- **Monotonic and high-resolution**. Use clocks that do not jump backward or forward with system time adjustments and that have microsecond or better granularity.
- **Consistently applied**. The same logical event should have a unique identifier (for example, a sequence number) whose timestamps you can compare across stages.

In a multi-process or multi-machine setup, clock synchronization is an extra concern. For this chapter we assume you are primarily profiling within a single host; distributed timing issues are addressed elsewhere in the book.

Percentiles, Not Just Averages

Average latency is almost meaningless for trading. What matters is:

- **Median (p50)**: the "typical" case.
- **High percentiles** like p95 and p99: how often you get slow responses.
- **Extreme tails** like p99.9: rare events that may coincide with the most lucrative or dangerous market conditions.

Your measurement system should therefore maintain:

- **Histograms or approximate quantile summaries** (such as streaming quantile estimators) for each latency metric.
- **Separate views by workload segment**: for example, latencies during the first 5 minutes of trading versus midday; during normal operation versus when GC fired; per instrument or venue.

Well-designed dashboards will show these percentiles over time, with annotations for noteworthy system events.

Detecting Hidden Queueing and Multi-modal Behavior

One of the key motivations for modeling your system as a series of queues is that latency distributions often become *multi-modal*: you see multiple distinct "humps" or plateaus, each corresponding to a different path or state.

Recognizing Queue-induced Patterns

Some typical signatures:

- **A sharp floor with a long smooth tail**. The floor represents your best-case path; the tail suggests growing queues or occasional slow paths (for example, cache cold misses, GC pauses).

- **Double peaks**. One peak may represent messages that sailed through when queues were empty; the other, messages that arrived during a burst and sat in one or more queues before being processed.
- **Stair-step percentile curves**. As you move from p90 to p99 to p99.9, you see plateaus corresponding to typical queue depths: for instance, 1, 2, or 4 messages ahead of you.

By correlating these patterns with internal metrics (queue depths, CPU utilization, GC logs, interrupt rates), you can hypothesize where messages are waiting.

Per-stage Latency and Tracing

To go beyond guesswork, you can:

- Assign each tick or order a **trace ID** that accompanies it through the system.
- At each major component, record a timestamp and perhaps a small amount of context (queue length on entry, CPU ID).
- Later reconstruct the path and stage-wise latencies for sampled events.

A simple form of this is enough to answer questions like:

- "When p99 tick-to-decision latency doubled during this test, did the extra time accumulate in market data normalization, strategy logic, or order routing?"
- "Do slow ticks usually see long waits in the NIC RX ring, kernel socket buffers, application rings, or risk engine?"

More sophisticated setups use distributed tracing tools, but even lightweight, custom logging can yield large insights.

Tools for Profiling Under Load

With realistic workloads and metrics in place, you can bring in specialized tools to pinpoint CPU and memory hotspots.

CPU Profiling and Flame Graphs

CPU profilers and flame graphs help answer: *Where is time actually going?* Under load, you can:

- Attach a sampling profiler to your trading process to collect stacks at regular intervals.
- Visualize the results as a flame graph, where wide stacks indicate functions consuming more CPU time.

Flame graphs are especially powerful when:

- You compare **before and after** a tuning change (for example, introducing pooling or changing a data layout).
- You run them **under different load regimes**: quiet mid-session versus volatile open, to see which paths light up.

However, remember that CPU time and latency are not identical. A function may consume little total CPU but introduce large latencies if it is invoked rarely but with long pauses (for example, GC collections). Profiling must be interpreted alongside latency measurements.

Hardware Performance Counters

Modern CPUs expose counters for:

- Cache misses at different levels (L1, L2, L3).
- Branch mispredictions.
- Instructions retired, cycles stalled, and more.

By sampling these counters while your system runs a load test, you can:

- Confirm that data layout improvements actually reduced cache misses in critical loops.
- Detect when a tuning choice (for example, more aggressive batching) inadvertently increased branch mispredictions or cache thrash.

These counters help connect high-level design decisions—such as moving to a structure-of-arrays layout—to low-level hardware effects.

GC and Memory Profiling

For managed runtimes, you should:

- Enable GC logging with timestamps and pause durations.
- Track allocation rates over time, ideally broken down by code path.
- Correlate GC events with latency spikes, queue buildups, and CPU utilization.

Many runtime environments also provide tools to profile heap contents, identify large object graphs, and pinpoint allocation hotspots. Use these as part of your continuous profiling, not just when a crisis occurs.

An Iterative Optimization Workflow

Armed with data, you can now run a disciplined optimization cycle. A simple but effective workflow is:

- **Baseline.** Choose a representative workload (for example, replay of a volatile open) and run your system with current settings. Capture:

  - End-to-end latency distributions (p50 to p99.9).
  - Per-stage latencies for key components.
  - CPU, memory, GC, and queue depth metrics.

- **Identify the worst pain.** Decide whether you care most about:
  - Bringing down median latency (p50).
  - Shrinking tails (p99, p99.9).
  - Increasing maximum sustainable throughput before tails explode.

  Use your measurements to locate the biggest contributor. For example: p99 latencies are dominated by time spent in order routing; GC pauses are rare but extremely long; NIC RX rings are occasionally near full.

- **Form a hypothesis.** Propose a specific change and why it should help. For instance:
  - "Pin the market data thread and its NIC RX queue to the same core to reduce cross-socket traffic."
  - "Introduce pre-allocation and pooling in the book update path to reduce GC-triggered pauses."
  - "Replace JSON-based internal messages between components X and Y with a flat binary encoding."

- **Make one change.** Modify only that aspect of the system. Keep everything else—configuration, code version, workload—constant.

- **Re-run and compare.** Execute the same workload and:
  - Plot new latency distributions alongside the baseline.
  - Compare CPU and memory metrics.
  - Confirm that any observed improvement matches your hypothesis (for example, GC pauses shrank, not just moved around).

- **Decide and document.** If the change is beneficial, keep it and document:

- The reasoning behind it.
- The metrics before and after.
- Any trade-offs (for example, higher CPU on dedicated cores).

If not, revert and record why it did not work; this history is valuable for future engineers.

- **Repeat.** Performance optimization is rarely finished. As strategies evolve, venues change, and hardware is upgraded, revisit your profiling and tuning.

This methodical approach supports a culture where changes are justified by data, not folklore.

Visualizing Improvement Over Time

It is motivating and informative to visualize how your latency profile changes as you apply successive optimizations. A useful visualization combines:

- A **percentile latency curve** (for example, plotting latency against percentile from p50 to p99.99).
- An **annotated timeline** of optimization steps, showing when each change was introduced and how the curve shifted.

The following figure sketches such a visualization. For simplicity, we present one curve per "version" of the system, each representing the latency distribution after a major tuning step.

Reading this kind of plot, you can see:

- The baseline curve has an acceptable median but very heavy tails.
- NIC and kernel tuning mainly reduce p90–p99 and trim some of the extreme tail.
- GC and memory layout work further compress the tail, especially beyond p99.

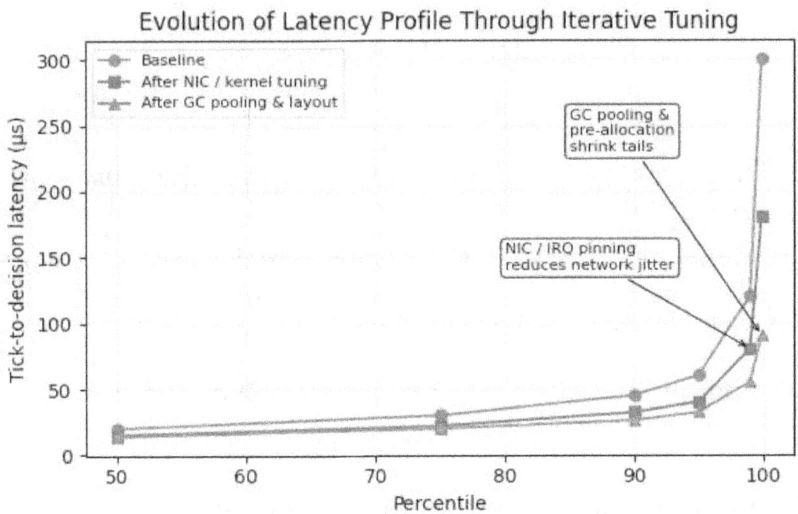

Over time, adding new curves for each significant change gives you a visual history of your system's maturation.

Closing the Loop

Performance and low-latency engineering in trading is not a one-off project. It is an ongoing discipline that intersects with every design decision you make: protocol choices, data structures, thread layout, even what you choose to log.

This chapter has walked from the outside in:

- From the network and operating system, where packets and threads first meet.
- Through memory management and data layout, where you either amplify or dampen jitter.
- Into the concurrency architecture, where you decide whether cores cooperate via locks or messages.

- And finally to the feedback loop of load and latency profiling, which ties all of these layers together.

The unifying themes are:

- Think in terms of **queues and flows**, not just functions and classes.
- Care deeply about **tails and burst behavior**, not just averages.
- Use **measurement and iteration**, not folklore, to guide tuning choices.

Armed with this mindset and the tools described here, you can build event-driven trading systems that are not only fast on paper, but reliably responsive when it matters most: in the seconds when markets are moving, liquidity is thin, and every microsecond can change the outcome.

Chapter 6

Core Trading System Components

Every profitable trading idea eventually collides with reality: noisy exchange feeds, brittle gateways, partial fills, and risk checks that must fire in microseconds without ever blinking. This chapter walks through the core components that keep a modern trading system honest-market data, order and execution management, risk, safety controls, and reconciliation-and shows how events flow between them when markets are fast, messy, and unforgiving.

6.1 Market Data Ingestion and Normalization

In an event-driven trading system, the market data pipeline is the front door through which the outside world enters your stack. Every strategy decision, every risk check, and every PnL calculation ultimately depends on the quality of this pipeline. Its job is conceptually simple but practically demanding: accept raw exchange feeds, keep sessions alive, decode a variety of protocols, reconstruct limit order books, and then emit a clean, consistent stream of venue-agnostic events that the rest of the system can trust. In this section we unpack that pipeline stage by stage, focusing on how to design for correctness, low latency, and resilience to bad or missing data.

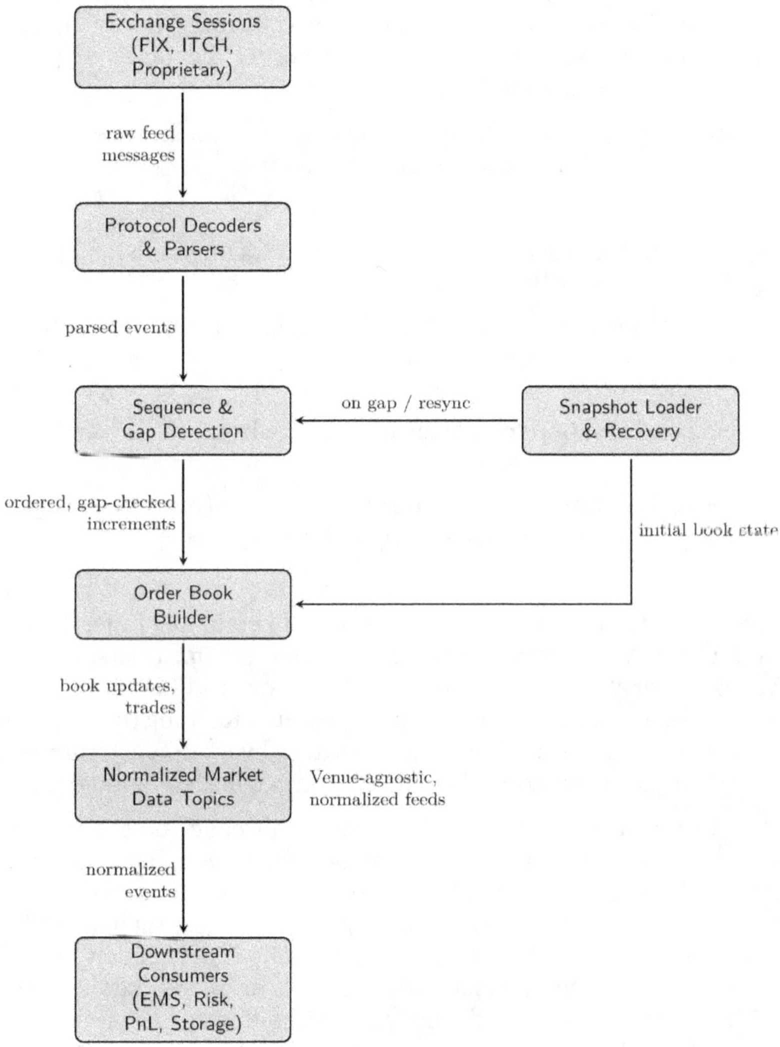

From Exchange Sessions to Internal Events

At the very edge of the system are the exchange sessions: long-lived connections to venues that speak protocol dialects such as FIX for market data, ITCH/OUCH-style depth feeds, or venue-specific binary formats. Although the protocols differ, all share a few core ideas: there is a session-level notion of connection (logon, logout), a way to detect liveness (heartbeats), and a mechanism to order messages (sequence numbers or sequence-like fields).

Session management. Session management is the first responsibility of the pipeline. For each connection you must:

- Establish the session (authentication or logon handshake).
- Track sequence numbers from the venue and your own outgoing counters where applicable.
- Send and respond to heartbeats to prove liveness.
- Detect disconnects and decide how to recover (reconnect, request replay, or fail over to a backup line).

It is useful to think of each session as a small state machine: *Disconnected*, *Connecting*, *Logged On*, *Suspect*, and so on. Transitions are driven by timers (heartbeat missed), network events (TCP disconnect), and protocol messages (logon accepted, logout). Keeping this state machine correct and observable is vital, because every downstream component depends on whether the data stream is believed to be complete.

Hot path versus control path. Even at this edge you should separate hot-path traffic from slower control information. Hot-path messages are those that directly affect trading decisions on every tick: order book updates and trades. Control-path messages, such as trading status, symbol definitions, or reference data, change much less frequently. Handling them in separate channels or queues allows you to optimize for low latency on the hot path without losing the richness of control information.

Decoding Diverse Protocols

Once you can reliably receive messages, the next step is decoding. Each exchange protocol defines a message layout: field types, lengths, and semantics. Your decoders translate this into a compact internal representation that can be processed quickly by later stages.

Designing protocol handlers. A good mental model is a layer cake:

- **Framing layer:** identifies message boundaries in the raw byte stream.
- **Parsing layer:** turns bytes into typed fields: integers, flags, strings.
- **Semantic layer:** interprets the meaning: "add order at price 100," "best bid changed," "trading status halted," and so forth.

Each layer should be as simple as possible. The framing and parsing layers should avoid complex logic and allocate as little as possible; they are on the fastest part of the critical path. The semantic layer is where you map venue-specific codes into internal enums and decide which internal event type to emit for each incoming message.

Internal event representation. Downstream, you want to stop caring whether an update came from ITCH, FIX, or a proprietary feed. That means defining a neutral internal schema for market data events, for example:

- *BookUpdate*: side, price, quantity, action (add, modify, delete), and an internal symbol identifier.
- *Trade*: price, quantity, aggressor side if known, and trade identifier.
- *StatusChange*: trading status (open, halted, auction), reason, and effective time.

The decoders' job is then to map each raw message into one or more of these internal events. This is where you hide protocol quirks and normalize differences in field naming, scaling (e.g., prices in ticks versus prices in absolute units), and symbol representation.

Sequence Numbers and Gap Detection

Market data feeds are designed to be processed in order. Almost all venues include either explicit sequence numbers or an implied ordering. Your pipeline must enforce this ordering and detect gaps, because a missed message will otherwise silently corrupt your reconstructed order book.

Why gaps are dangerous. Imagine a simple feed where messages 101, 102, 103 describe three consecutive changes to the best bid. If you never see message 102, you will happily apply 101 and 103 and believe you are synchronized, but your book will in fact be wrong in a way that can persist until the next full refresh. For trading systems that rely on precise depth, this can cause mispricing, incorrect risk calculations, and poor execution decisions.

Gap detection logic. For each session and stream you maintain the "next expected" sequence number. When a new message arrives:

- If its sequence equals the expected one, accept it and increment the expected sequence.
- If it is greater than expected, you have a gap: one or more messages were missed.
- If it is less than expected, it is a duplicate or replay; you discard or handle it specially, depending on the protocol.

Handling gaps raises a design decision: what should happen to downstream consumers during the gap? There are three common strategies:

- **Block and recover:** stop emitting further updates for the affected symbols until you are back in sync, to avoid propagating inconsistent views.
- **Degrade and flag:** continue emitting updates but mark the stream as "suspect" so that risk engines or strategies can choose to be more conservative or even ignore that venue.
- **Fail over:** if you have redundant feeds (e.g., a primary multicast plus a secondary unicast), switch to a backup source.

In all cases, you must record the gap and the decisions you made; this is important for both debugging and regulatory investigations.

Snapshots and Incremental Recovery

Gaps are inevitable: networks drop packets, sessions disconnect. To recover, exchanges typically offer one or both of two mechanisms:

- **Incremental replay:** the venue resends messages from a specified sequence number onward.
- **Snapshots:** a separate channel exposes periodic "full state" images of the order book at a point in time.

A resilient pipeline integrates these tools into an automatic resynchronization process.

Snapshot-then-incremental approach. A common recovery pattern works as follows:

- Detect a gap in the incremental stream.
- Request or read the latest full snapshot for the affected instrument or channel.
- Identify the snapshot's sequence number or timestamp.
- Replay incremental messages from just after the snapshot's point up to "now."
- Once caught up, resume processing fresh incremental updates as usual.

During this process, the order book builder (described below) can reset its state from the snapshot and then apply the incremental messages as if they had just arrived. The key is to ensure you do not apply any incremental messages twice or skip any; careful bookkeeping of sequence ranges is essential.

Cold start and fast warm-up. At system start-of-day, you often have the option to begin directly from snapshots. Rather than replaying millions of overnight incremental updates, you can:

- Load an end-of-day or start-of-day snapshot for each active symbol.
- Apply a small tail of incremental updates to catch up to the current market.

This reduces startup time and allows your strategies to become active faster, while still preserving a correct book state.

Building and Maintaining Limit Order Books

With ordered, gap-checked updates available, the next step is to maintain a limit order book: the structured representation of all resting buy and sell interest at each price level. Downstream components rarely want raw add/modify/delete messages; they want to know the current best bid and ask, the full depth, and how these change over time.

Per-venue semantics. Different venues expose depth in different ways:

- Some provide full depth: every visible order is included.
- Others give only aggregated depth at each price level.
- Some report changes as "deltas" (e.g., "add 100 at price 10"), others report absolute levels ("total quantity at price 10 is now 500").
- Certain derivatives venues include "implied" liquidity, where combinations of instruments create additional effective orders.

The order book builder must understand these nuances. For each venue you configure a set of rules describing how to interpret its messages and how to apply them to the internal book structure.

Book data structures. Conceptually, a limit order book is composed of two ordered collections:

- A set of bid price levels, sorted from highest to lowest price.
- A set of ask price levels, sorted from lowest to highest price.

At each price level you track total displayed quantity, and in some cases, per-order details (e.g., number of orders, time priority). In practice, implementations use arrays, trees, or specialized containers to represent this structure efficiently. For understanding the pipeline, it is enough to remember that the book builder maintains a mutable state that is updated for each *BookUpdate* event and periodically emitted as snapshots or deltas to consumers.

Handling partial updates. Many feeds do not update the entire book on each message; they only change a few price levels. There are two common patterns:

- *Level-by-level updates:* Each message explicitly names a price level and the new total size or a change in size.
- *Top-of-book updates:* Only the best bid and ask are updated; depth beyond the top may be absent or less reliable.

The book builder must carefully apply these partial updates while leaving other levels unchanged. If a level's size becomes zero, that level is removed. Changes must be processed in the exact order they occur, which is why the earlier sequence and gap handling is so critical.

Symbol mapping and identity. Exchanges identify instruments in their own ways: numeric tokens, long text codes, or composite identifiers. Within your system, you should map these into stable internal identifiers, often simple integers. The mapping is typically established from reference data feeds or configuration files and loaded before the market opens. The book builder and all downstream consumers then operate on the internal identifiers, which avoids ambiguity and simplifies joins between market data, orders, and positions.

Normalization Across Venues

Once you can build per-venue order books, the next design goal is to normalize the information. A multi-venue trading system wants to compare apples to apples: best bid/ask across venues, depth metrics that mean the same thing wherever they are measured, and consistent event types.

Venue-agnostic events. Normalization is largely about defining a stable contract for downstream consumers. Rather than exposing internal details of each book builder, you choose a set of event types and fields that capture what strategies and risk components actually need, such as:

- **Top-of-book events**: symbol, venue, best bid price and size, best ask price and size, and timestamp.
- **Depth events**: symbol, venue, side, a list of price levels with price and size, possibly up to a configured depth.
- **Trade events**: symbol, venue, trade price, quantity, aggressor side, and trade timestamp.
- **Status events**: symbol or venue-level status (e.g., trading halt, auction), plus reason code.

Each venue's internal representation feeds into this schema. The mapping may involve unit normalization (e.g., converting prices and quantities to consistent decimal scales), tick size handling, or local-market conventions.

Time and ordering. Normalized events carry timestamps and, where possible, sequence information. There are subtle choices here:

- You may attach both the exchange's own timestamp and the time the message was observed at your gateway.
- For internal ordering across symbols or venues, you might use a monotonically increasing internal sequence as events pass through the normalization stage.

Downstream systems can then choose which notion of time to rely on: exchange time for economic ordering, or internal time for causality within your infrastructure.

Topic design for event distribution. In an event-driven architecture, normalized events are typically published to messaging or streaming topics. Designing these topics is part of normalization. Common patterns include:

- One topic per venue and asset class (e.g., "Equities Venue A Depth").
- One topic per symbol group (e.g., an index constituent set).
- One unified topic with routing keys or partitions per symbol.

The right choice depends on your scale and the expected consumers. What matters is that each topic has a clear contract: what event types it carries, what the ordering guarantees are, and what consumers should expect in the face of gaps or replays.

Reliability, Backpressure, and Resynchronization

So far we have implicitly assumed that everything runs smoothly. In reality, real-time feeds are messy. Exchanges misbehave, network paths suffer bursts and pauses, and consumers can fall behind. A robust market data pipeline includes explicit mechanisms to handle these stresses without losing correctness.

Detecting and handling backlog. Each stage in the pipeline—session receivers, decoders, gap detectors, book builders, and publishers—has a finite capacity. When messages arrive faster than a stage can process them, queues build up. This is backpressure. If it goes unchecked, queues can overflow and drop data or introduce unacceptable latency.

There are several complementary strategies:

- **Monitoring**: Track queue lengths, processing times, and end-to-end latency per symbol and per venue.
- **Load shedding**: In extreme cases, you might intentionally drop less-critical events (for example, deep-book levels) while preserving top-of-book and trades.
- **Scaling**: If your architecture allows, add processing capacity to the most heavily loaded stages.

The design should make these choices explicit and auditable; implicit, silent data loss is the enemy of reliable trading.

Failing fast versus buffering. When downstream consumers cannot keep up, you face a choice:

- Buffer more and increase latency, hoping that the burst subsides.
- Fail fast by cutting off new consumption or marking the consumer as unhealthy.

For trading decisions that depend on fresh data, a bounded latency increase is acceptable, but beyond a certain point stale data is worse than no data. Many firms therefore set explicit latency budgets and, if breached, will have the affected strategy stand down or switch to a safer mode until the pipeline recovers.

Resynchronization under failure. When something does go wrong—a software bug, a failed process, or a corrupted state in the book builder—you need deterministic ways to restore consistency. This often involves:

- Dropping current in-memory state for affected symbols or venues.
- Reloading state from a recent snapshot.
- Replaying a segment of historical events from a durable log or from the venue's replay service.

Because your pipeline is built around events, these resynchronization operations can use the same code paths as live processing: snapshots plus replayed events are indistinguishable from "real" messages once they enter the book builder. This reduces the likelihood of subtle inconsistencies between normal and recovery modes.

Observability and Operational Discipline

Finally, a resilient pipeline is not only about data structures and protocols; it is also about how operators observe and control the system during live trading.

Key metrics. You should be able to answer, in real time:

- Are we in sync with each venue? If not, which symbols or channels are affected?
- What is the current end-to-end latency from exchange to normalized event for a given symbol?
- Where are queues building up? Which stage is the bottleneck?
- How often are gaps occurring, and how long do recoveries take?

Dashboards that surface these metrics, with clear alarms when thresholds are breached, are essential tools for both day-to-day operations and crisis management.

Audit trails. For future analysis—whether after an incident or during regulatory reviews—you need a reliable record of what the pipeline saw and did. This includes:

- Logs of session state transitions and gap events.
- Records of snapshot loads and replay ranges.
- Checksums or sequence markers written into normalized event streams to prove integrity.

This audit trail closes the loop: you can reconstruct not only the state of the order books at any point in time, but also the path the data took and the decisions the pipeline made when conditions were imperfect.

6.2 Order Management System

In the previous section we focused on market data: how raw exchange feeds are transformed into a clean, gap-free stream of events describing the external world. The Order Management System (OMS) plays the complementary internal role. If the market data pipeline is the eye of the trading system, the OMS is its memory and nervous system for orders. It is the authoritative record of every order you submit, every change you request, and every acknowledgment or fill you receive from the market.

This section treats the OMS as a lifecycle state machine driven by events. We will emphasize three core ideas:

- Every order has a well-defined progression of states.
- State changes are driven by events that must be processed *idempotently* so that retries and duplicates do not corrupt the record.
- The ground truth is a durable log of these events, from which you can always reconstruct OMS state by replay.

By the end, you should see the OMS less as a "database of orders" and more as a carefully designed event-processing system with strong guarantees about consistency, auditability, and recoverability.

Core Responsibilities of the OMS

Although different firms draw boundaries slightly differently, a robust OMS usually has the following responsibilities:

- **Accept intent**: take in order instructions from clients, internal strategies, or higher-level systems such as a portfolio optimizer.
- **Validate and normalize**: ensure that each requested order is well-formed, within allowed parameters, and represented in a canonical internal format.
- **Assign identity**: generate stable internal identifiers for orders so that every subsequent event can be unambiguously tied to the correct order.
- **Manage lifecycle**: record and enforce the order state machine as the order is routed, worked, filled, modified, or canceled.
- **Persist history**: append all order-related events to a durable log that serves as the system of record.
- **Serve queries**: answer questions such as "What is the current state of order X?" or "What are all working orders for account Y in symbol Z?"

Crucially, the OMS is *not* responsible for everything that happens to an order. It typically does *not* implement low-level exchange session logic or detailed routing algorithms; those belong in the Execution Management System (EMS) and gateway layers. The OMS instead focuses on the business meaning of order changes and on maintaining a coherent history across the entire trading stack.

Orders as Lifecycle State Machines

A helpful way to understand the OMS is to think of each order as a small state machine. At any point in time, an order is in exactly one lifecycle state, and events trigger transitions between these states. This is analogous to how we treated exchange sessions in the market data pipeline, but here the subject is the order itself rather than a network connection.

Typical Order States

Exact naming differs across firms and asset classes, but most OMS designs use a set of states similar to the following:

- **New**: the order has just been accepted by the OMS and has not yet been routed.
- **Working**: the order, or at least some child representation of it, is active in the market.
- **Partially Filled**: one or more fills have occurred, but some remaining quantity is still working.
- **Filled**: the entire order quantity has been executed.
- **Rejected**: the order has been rejected, either by internal checks or by an external venue, and will not be worked.
- **Canceled**: the order has been canceled and is no longer active.
- **Error or Terminal Failure**: the order has reached a state where further automated processing is not possible without intervention (for example, an irreconcilable mismatch between internal and exchange states).

Some firms distinguish further between a *Pending New* state (before external acknowledgment), *Pending Cancel* (cancellation requested but not yet confirmed), and so forth. The key is that the OMS maintains a consistent internal vocabulary, even though each venue may use its own status codes.

Events that Drive Transitions

States change only when events occur. These events can originate from:

- **Clients or strategies**: new order requests, modification requests (change price or quantity), and cancel requests.
- **The EMS and gateways**: routing decisions (which venue to use), confirmations that an order has been sent or canceled at the venue level.
- **Exchanges**: acknowledgments, rejections, fills, partial fills, cancel confirmations, or cancel rejects.

The OMS translates each incoming event into a transition in the state machine for the relevant order. For example, a successful "new order acknowledgment" from an exchange might move the order from *New* to *Working*. A "full fill" event might move it from *Partially Filled* to *Filled*. A "reject" might move it from *New* to *Rejected*.

Right after we specify the OMS's responsibilities, it is helpful to visualize this lifecycle concretely.

Diagrammatic representation:

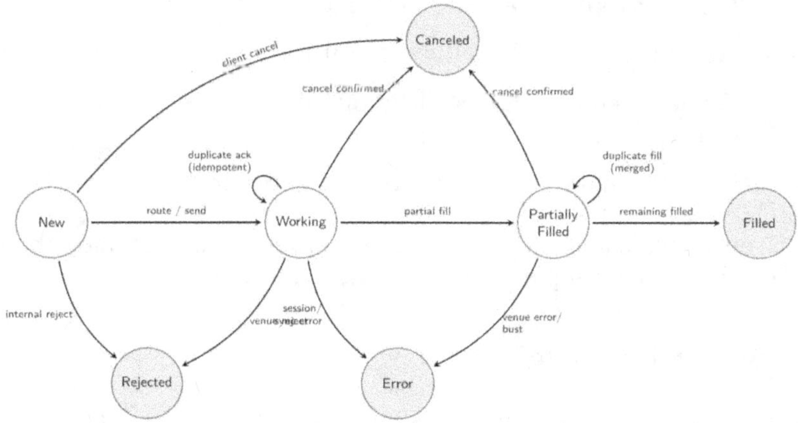

This diagram is intentionally simplified, but it captures the essence: arrows correspond to events from clients, the EMS, or exchanges, and some arrows (labeled as duplicates) represent idempotent processing where the OMS intentionally does *not* change state.

Event-Sourced Design: The OMS as a Log of Facts

So far, we have described the OMS in terms of state machines. In implementation, this perspective is complemented by an *event-sourced* view: rather than storing only the latest state of an order, the OMS stores every event that ever happened to that order in an append-only log.

Events as Immutable Facts

Every meaningful change related to an order is represented as an immutable record:

- "Client A submitted a New Order for 10,000 shares of XYZ at 10:00:01."
- "That order was accepted by internal risk at 10:00:01.500."

- "The EMS routed the order to Venue B at 10:00:01.800."
- "Venue B acknowledged the order at 10:00:02."
- "Venue B reported a partial fill of 2,000 shares at price 100 at 10:00:02.200."
- "Client A requested a cancellation at 10:00:05."

Each such fact is appended to a durable, ordered log. Together, these events define the complete history of the order.

Reconstructing State by Replay

From these events you can reconstruct the current state of any order by replaying them in order and applying the state machine rules. For example:

- Start from an initial state (*New* after creation).
- Read each subsequent event and update the order state accordingly.
- After processing all events, the final state tells you whether the order is still working, fully filled, canceled, and so on.

This is exactly analogous to how the market data pipeline reconstructs the order book by applying a stream of book updates. The difference is that the OMS's stream is private and under your control, and the objects being reconstructed are order lifecycles rather than price levels.

This design has several advantages:

- **Auditability**: you can explain, step by step, how an order reached its final state.
- **Time travel**: you can answer questions such as "What was the state of this order at 14:32:00?" by replaying events up to that point.
- **Rebuild and recovery**: if a database or cache is lost or corrupted, you can rebuild state from the log rather than relying solely on backups.

Idempotent Event Processing

In a perfect world, every event would be delivered exactly once, in order, and never retried. In real distributed systems, you have to assume the opposite: messages can be delayed, duplicated, or even reordered. Idempotent processing is the discipline of designing your OMS so that processing the same event more than once does not change the outcome beyond the first application.

Why Duplicates Occur

Duplicates arise for several reasons:

- A client or strategy retries a request because it did not receive a timely acknowledgment and cannot be sure whether the request was processed.
- A messaging system delivers the same message twice under failure conditions.
- An exchange retransmits an acknowledgment or fill message when it suspects a communication issue.

Without careful design, such duplicates can create "phantom" orders, double-counted fills, or contradictory states.

Techniques for Idempotency

A few practical techniques make idempotent processing manageable:

Stable identifiers for requests. When a client submits a new order or a cancel request, it should include a unique identifier that the OMS echoes back in all related acknowledgments. If the client retries, it uses the same identifier. The OMS then:

- Recognizes that the second request refers to the same logical intent.
- Either acknowledges that the request was already processed or safely applies it once if it had not yet been.

Event keys for exchange messages. Exchange-side events such as fills often carry their own identifiers: execution IDs, trade IDs, or composite keys. The OMS maintains, for each order, a set of known execution IDs. When a fill event arrives:

- If its execution ID is new, the OMS applies it (updates filled quantity, PnL, and so on) and records the ID.
- If the execution ID is already known, the OMS treats the event as a duplicate and ignores or logs it without changing state.

Idempotent transitions. Some events correspond to transitions that are naturally idempotent. For example, a cancel confirmation that arrives twice should not move the order from *Canceled* to some other state. Instead, the OMS sees that the order is already canceled and treats the second confirmation as a harmless repetition.

Designing the state machine with these cases in mind—and explicitly coding transitions that treat duplicates as no-ops—is essential for robustness.

Durable Logs as the System of Record

In event-sourced OMS design, the durable log is more than just a byproduct; it *is* the authoritative data store. The log may be implemented using a distributed log system, a carefully designed database table, or a combination of both. The critical properties are:

- **Append-only**: events are added to the end of the log and never mutated in place.
- **Ordered**: within each partition or stream, events are strictly ordered.
- **Durable**: once acknowledged, events survive process crashes, machine failures, and restarts.

Serving Real-Time State from Logs

While the log is the system of record, you rarely want to query it directly for every real-time operation. Instead, the OMS typically maintains one or more *materialized views* derived from the log:

- In-memory maps from order ID to current state and key fields.
- Indexes by symbol, account, or strategy, listing all working orders.
- Summary statistics such as total working quantity per symbol and account.

These views are continuously updated as new events are processed. If a view is lost (for example, due to a process restart), it can be reconstructed by replaying the log from a checkpoint, just as the market data order book can be rebuilt from snapshots plus incremental updates.

Snapshots and Checkpoints

Replaying an entire log from the very beginning of time would eventually become too slow. To avoid this, the OMS periodically takes *snapshots* of its state:

- A snapshot captures the full state of all active orders and relevant indexes at a particular log position.
- To recover, the OMS loads the most recent snapshot and then replays only the events that occurred after that snapshot.

This snapshot-plus-log approach is similar in spirit to how you maintain limit order books with snapshots and incremental updates. In both cases, the underlying principle is the same: long-lived state is derived from a shorter, manageable slice of the event history.

Boundaries with EMS, Risk, and Gateways

To keep the system comprehensible and maintainable, it is important to be clear about what belongs inside the OMS and what should be handled by other components.

OMS vs. EMS

The OMS focuses on:

- Recording the business-level state of parent and child orders.
- Ensuring consistency and recoverability.
- Providing a stable API to clients and higher-level systems.

The EMS, by contrast, focuses on:

- Choosing venues and execution algorithms.
- Slicing large parent orders into many child orders across venues and time.
- Reacting to market data and fills with routing decisions.

The OMS should know that a parent order has spawned child orders and track the aggregate state (for example, total filled quantity across all children). However, the detailed logic of how those children are placed and managed at the exchange levels belongs in the EMS.

OMS vs. Risk Engine

The risk and limits engine, which we will discuss in the next section, uses OMS events as one of its inputs. It applies credit limits, position caps, and other checks to decide whether a new order or modification is allowed.

The OMS and risk engine interact closely but have distinct responsibilities:

- The OMS records that a risk check was performed and its result (approved, blocked, overridden).
- The risk engine contains the limit logic and relevant risk state.

This separation mirrors the split between market data ingestion and trading strategies: one component maintains clean, authoritative state, while another makes dynamic decisions based on that state.

Operational Considerations and Query Patterns

Beyond core correctness, an OMS must support the everyday needs of traders, risk managers, and operations staff.

Common Query Patterns

The system must respond efficiently to questions such as:

- "Show me all working orders for account A in symbol XYZ."
- "For this strategy, what orders have been rejected in the last hour?"
- "What is the status and fill history of order ID 12345?"

Supporting these queries implies maintaining suitable indexes and summary views. These can be built on top of the same event log, but their design must be considered up front rather than left as an afterthought.

Audit and Compliance

Regulators and internal audit teams often require detailed explanations of trading behavior: why certain orders were placed, how they were routed, why particular fills occurred, and what decisions were made in response to venues or risk constraints.

Because the OMS is event-sourced, it is naturally well-suited to these tasks:

- The full event history for an order provides a complete narrative.
- Timestamps and identifiers tie OMS events to external records such as exchange drop copies and clearing reports.
- If necessary, you can reconstruct historical OMS views as of a specific time to compare with contemporaneous logs from other systems.

The Order Management System is the core ledger of trading intent inside an event-driven trading stack. It treats each order as a lifecycle state machine, driven by events from clients, the EMS, and exchanges. By processing these events idempotently, appending them to a durable log, and maintaining materialized views for real-time use, the OMS achieves three crucial goals: it provides a single source of truth about orders, it can always reconstruct its state by replay, and it offers a rich, auditable history of trading activity.

Just as the market data pipeline transforms noisy external feeds into a clean representation of the market, the OMS transforms noisy, failure-prone messaging around orders into a coherent, reliable internal record. The next section builds on this foundation by examining the risk and limits engine, which consumes both market data and OMS events to control the firm's exposure in real time.

6.3 Risk and Limits Engine

In the previous sections we established two crucial sources of truth for a trading system: the market data pipeline, which maintains a clean view of external prices and depth, and the Order Management System (OMS), which maintains a durable, replayable history of trading intent. The risk and limits engine sits directly between these two worlds. Its job is to take the aggressive ideas coming from strategies and the OMS, combine them with the reality of current and potential exposures, and decide—for every order and amendment—whether the firm is willing to take on that additional risk.

In this section we will treat the risk engine as an inline, event-driven component on the order flow hot path. We will explain:

- The main categories of risk controls: credit, position, concentration, price, and velocity limits.
- How these controls must operate inline, with latency budgets at least as strict as the trading logic itself.
- The state the risk engine needs to maintain and how it derives that state from OMS and market data events.
- What it means to *fail closed*: blocking or throttling risk-taking when state is uncertain or performance degrades.
- How configuration, overrides, and audit trails are managed so that risk decisions are deterministic and replayable.

The aim is to show that a well-designed risk engine is not just a set of ad hoc checks, but a carefully structured stateful component with clear contracts, just like the OMS and market data pipeline.

Inline Risk on the Hot Path

When a new order or modification request arrives at your system, there is a critical sequence of questions that must be answered before it leaves the firm and hits an exchange:

1. Does this client or internal strategy have sufficient *credit* to take on the potential exposure?
2. Does this order keep positions within allowed *size* and *concentration* limits?
3. Is the requested price reasonable, or does it look like a *fat finger* error?
4. Is the system sending and canceling orders at a pace that remains within allowed *velocity* and venue rate limits?

These checks cannot be deferred. They must execute inline on the hot path, synchronously with the handling of the order request, and they must produce a clear outcome: allow, block, or sometimes allow with specific tagging or throttling. This is what differentiates pre-trade risk from slower back-office risk: the engine must make a decision within microseconds to milliseconds, not minutes.

To do this safely and quickly, the risk engine maintains its own internal state, derives inputs from the OMS and market data, and is wired so that every outbound order and amendment passes through its decision logic.

Core Categories of Risk Controls

Although firms implement many nuanced checks, most risk engines share a set of fundamental control categories.

Credit and Notional Limits

Credit limits restrict how much total exposure a client, strategy, or legal entity can take on. They can be expressed in different ways:

- Maximum gross notional: the sum of absolute values of open positions (price times quantity).
- Maximum net exposure: the net long or short exposure across instruments.
- Per-venue or per-product limits: caps on exposure to specific exchanges or asset classes.

When a new order arrives, the risk engine estimates the *incremental notional* that the order could add if fully filled. It then compares the resulting total against configured limits. If the order would breach a limit, the engine blocks or potentially scales the order (if such behavior is allowed and configured).

Credit limits are often hierarchical: a firm-level limit, broken down into desk-level, account-level, and strategy-level limits. The risk engine must keep track of the aggregate exposure at each level and enforce all of them simultaneously.

Position and Concentration Limits

Even if total credit across the portfolio looks acceptable, you rarely want a single instrument or small set of instruments to dominate exposure. *Position limits* constrain how large any single symbol position can become, while *concentration limits* restrict the share of total exposure that any symbol or sector can represent.

For example:

- A desk might have a limit of 1 million shares long or short in a single stock.
- A strategy might not be allowed to hold more than 20% of its total notional exposure in one sector.

The risk engine uses current positions (from PnL and position engines) plus in-flight working orders to estimate where positions could land if all orders filled. Then, each new order is tested against these projected positions before being approved.

Price Bands and Fat-Finger Checks

A small typo in a price field can be catastrophic. To mitigate this, most systems implement:

- **Static bands**: absolute minimum and maximum allowed prices for a symbol, sometimes based on historical or regulatory limits.
- **Dynamic bands**: price ranges relative to current market prices, such as "no more than 5% away from last trade or mid-quote."

The risk engine uses live market data to evaluate whether an order's limit price is suspiciously far from the current market. If so, the order can be rejected outright, or forced to be reviewed, tagged, or capped at safer levels.

Size and Velocity Limits

Size limits constrain individual orders: maximum quantity per order, maximum notional per order, or maximum leverage on a single trade.

Velocity limits constrain the rate at which orders and cancels are sent:

- Maximum number of new orders per second per account or symbol.

- Maximum number of cancels or modifications per second.
- Ratios such as cancel-to-fill or message-to-trade ratios.

These checks are not just about client behavior; they also protect against runaway algorithms or feedback loops between strategies and market conditions. The risk engine maintains counters over short rolling windows and blocks or slows down activity when thresholds are reached.

Risk State: Fast but Correct

To apply all these checks inline, the risk engine must maintain internal state that reflects, as closely as possible, the firm's current exposure. This state is necessarily approximate at microsecond time scales, because fills arrive asynchronously, venues may bust or correct trades, and network delays are unavoidable. A key design challenge is to be *fast but correct enough* for safe decision-making.

Pre-Aggregated Exposure

Instead of recomputing exposures from scratch for every check, the risk engine typically maintains pre-aggregated metrics such as:

- Per-account, per-symbol working quantity (sum of open order quantities, adjusted for direction).
- Filled quantity and realized exposure per symbol.
- Notional exposure by account, desk, and firm.

These aggregates are updated incrementally as events arrive from the OMS and gateways:

- When an order is accepted and sent, working exposure increases.
- When fills occur, working exposure decreases and filled exposure/positions adjust.
- When orders are canceled or expire, working exposure reduces accordingly.

By using these maintained aggregates, pre-trade checks can execute in constant or small-bounded time per order, instead of scanning large lists of orders or positions.

Consuming OMS and Market Data Events

The risk engine is an event consumer. From the OMS it receives:

- Order creation, modification, and cancellation intents.
- State transitions for orders (e.g., from working to filled, or rejected).
- Confirmed cancellations and venue rejects.

From market data it receives:

- Prices needed for notional calculations and price bands.
- Trading halts or status changes that may affect which symbols or venues are eligible for trading.

By treating these inputs as event streams, the risk engine maintains a coherent picture of exposure that can be reconstructed, audited, and—importantly—reacted to in real time.

Fail-Closed Philosophy

No matter how carefully you design the system, there will be moments when the risk engine cannot be certain of the current exposure. Examples include:

- A network partition prevents it from seeing the latest fills.
- A process restart has forced it to reload state from a snapshot, and it has not yet fully caught up with the latest OMS events.
- Internal performance degradation means that state updates lag behind incoming orders.

In these situations, a choice must be made: continue approving new risk-taking based on stale or incomplete information, or block (or at least drastically limit) new activity until confidence is restored.

A *fail-closed* philosophy means choosing safety over availability. Concretely, it implies:

- If position or exposure data are incomplete or suspect, block new orders or restrict them to closing-only (reducing existing positions but not opening new ones).
- If latency of risk checks exceeds defined thresholds, throttle or reject traffic until the engine can again keep up.
- If the risk engine loses its internal state and cannot reload it reliably, force a global or scoped trading halt until resynchronization is complete.

This can be painful in the short term, especially during volatile markets when opportunities are plentiful. However, from a survival and regulatory standpoint, trading without reliable risk controls is unacceptable. Designing the system around an explicit fail-closed stance sets expectations for both technology and business stakeholders.

Inline Wiring: Where Risk Sits in the Flow

To understand how risk interacts with other components, it helps to mentally trace the path of an order:

1. A strategy or client sends a new order request to the OMS.
2. The OMS performs syntactic and basic semantic validation (e.g., fields present, symbol known) and assigns a stable order identifier.
3. Before the OMS (or EMS) routes the order to any venue, it forwards the request to the risk engine for evaluation.
4. The risk engine evaluates the order against current limits and state:

- If approved, the OMS records the approval event in its log and proceeds to routing and execution via the EMS.
- If blocked, the OMS records the rejection, notifies the client or strategy, and the order goes no further.

5. As fills and cancel confirmations arrive from exchanges via the EMS and gateways, they are recorded in the OMS and also sent to the risk engine to update exposure state.

This positioning ensures that:

- No order can leave the firm without passing through risk checks.
- Every event that changes exposure eventually feeds back into the risk engine, enabling consistent view updates.

It is tempting to embed risk checks directly in the OMS or EMS. While minor checks sometimes live in those layers for practical reasons, the conceptual separation of "state of orders" (OMS) and "state of risk" (risk engine) is valuable. It makes it easier to reason about, test, and evolve each component independently.

Dealing with In-Flight Orders and Uncertainty

A subtle challenge in pre-trade risk is handling *in-flight* orders: those that have been sent to exchanges but are not yet fully reflected in fills or cancellations. The risk engine must avoid both undercounting and double counting.

Working vs. Filled Exposure

A useful approach is to distinguish:

- *Working exposure*: quantity that is still active in the market and could be filled.
- *Filled exposure*: quantity already executed and incorporated into positions.

When a new order is approved and sent, its quantity increases working exposure. When fills arrive, some working exposure is converted into filled exposure. When an order is canceled and the cancellation is confirmed, working exposure decreases.

For the purpose of pre-trade checks, both working and filled exposure matter. Working exposure tells you the *maximum additional* risk you might take on if everything fills suddenly. Filled exposure tells you the *current* position. The risk engine typically uses a conservative combination of the two, often assuming that all working orders could fill.

Conservative Assumptions under Delay

There will be small windows of time where exchange acknowledgments and fills are still in flight, especially during fast markets. A conservative risk engine biases toward safety by:

- Assuming cancel requests may fail until confirmed, so working exposure remains high until explicit confirmation arrives.
- Treating fills as effective as soon as the OMS has recorded them, even if some downstream systems have not yet updated.
- Imposing temporary throttles when acknowledgments are slow, indicating that something may be wrong with external connectivity or internal processing.

These conservative rules ensure that temporary informational gaps do not open a back door for excessive exposure.

Configuration, Overrides, and Auditability

Risk engines are not static. Limits change as clients are onboarded or re-assessed, markets open and close, and supervisors make tactical decisions in response to events. Managing this variability without undermining determinism and auditability is a major design concern.

Versioned Configuration and Limits

Limits and rules should be treated as data, not hard-coded logic. Good practice includes:

- Storing limit configurations in versioned, immutable records (for example, “Limit set version 17” for a given day).
- Applying configuration changes via explicit events that are themselves logged, with timestamps and author information.
- Ensuring that risk decisions can always be associated with the exact configuration version in effect at that time.

This makes it possible, later on, to explain why a particular order was allowed or blocked, based on the rules and limits in force at that moment.

Overrides with Strong Audit Trails

Occasionally, human supervisors may need to override automated limits—for example, to allow a one-off larger order for a trusted client, or to temporarily relax a band during a controlled test. If overrides are allowed at all, they must be carefully constrained and fully recorded:

- Each override is an explicit event, tied to a specific scope (client, symbol, time window) and authorized user.
- Overrides have clear expiration conditions and are automatically removed when expired.
- Every order that relied on an override is tagged accordingly, so it can be identified in reports.

This approach recognizes the reality of human judgment in trading while preserving the transparency and replayability of automated risk decisions.

Pre-Trade vs. Post-Trade Risk

The focus here has been on *pre-trade* risk: checks that decide whether to allow a new order to enter the market. There is also an important *post-trade* dimension:

- Monitoring positions and PnL as fills accumulate, including stress tests and scenario analyses.

- Detecting breaches of intraday or overnight limits and triggering responses, such as reducing risk or halting new trading.
- Reconciling front-office exposures with clearing and custodial records.

While post-trade risk often operates at slightly slower time scales (seconds to minutes rather than microseconds), the same event-driven mindset applies. Post-trade engines consume the same streams of OMS events, fills, and market data, but may apply more complex calculations that are too heavy for the inline hot path. Their outputs can, in turn, adjust or tighten pre-trade limits dynamically, closing the feedback loop.

Alerts, Monitoring, and Operator Interaction

Because the risk engine stands at the gateway between trading intent and the market, its health and behavior must be extremely visible to operators.

Real-Time Alerts

Useful alerts include:

- Impending limit breaches: when utilization reaches a high percentage (say 80–90%) of a configured limit.
- Sudden spikes in message velocity or cancel-to-fill ratios.
- Transitions into degraded or fail-closed modes (for example, due to lagging state updates).

Early warning allows humans to intervene, adjust limits if appropriate, or investigate potential algorithmic issues before hard stops are triggered.

Operator Dashboards

Dashboards should expose, in an intuitive way:

- Current utilization of key limits by account, desk, and firm.

- Status indicators for risk engine health, including latency and data freshness.
- Recent blocked orders, with reasons and related limit information.

These tools transform risk from a "black box" that sometimes says no, into a transparent partner that provides actionable information.

The risk and limits engine converts raw trading intent into controlled exposure. Sitting inline on the hot path, it applies credit, position, concentration, price, size, and velocity checks to every order and amendment before they leave the firm. To do this effectively, it maintains fast-but-correct state derived from OMS and market data events, and it adheres to a fail-closed philosophy under uncertainty or performance degradation.

By treating limits as data, recording every risk decision and override in a durable log, and designing for deterministic, replayable behavior, the risk engine becomes a first-class component of the event-driven trading architecture—on par with the market data pipeline and OMS. In the next section, we will build on this foundation and examine the Execution Management System, which must respect both OMS state and risk decisions while routing orders efficiently across venues.

6.4 Execution Management System

Up to this point we have built the foundations of an event-driven trading stack. The market data pipeline gives us a clean, synchronized view of prices and order books. The Order Management System (OMS) records the full lifecycle of trading intent as an event-sourced state machine. The risk and limits engine sits inline on the hot path, deciding which orders are safe to release into the market.

The Execution Management System (EMS) is the next layer. If the OMS is the ledger of *what* we intend to trade, the EMS is the orchestrator of *how* and *where* that intent is executed. It takes validated, risk-approved orders and turns them into concrete interactions with exchanges and other liquidity venues. In doing so, it manages multiple exchange sessions, monitors their health, runs execution algorithms, and enforces safety mechanisms such as cancel-on-disconnect.

This section views the EMS as a real-time routing brain that is deeply aware of market data, OMS state, and risk decisions, but does not duplicate their responsibilities. Instead, it coordinates them, ensuring that every order is executed according to strategy while remaining within the system's safety and reliability constraints.

The EMS in the Overall Architecture

Conceptually, the EMS sits between two worlds:

- Upstream: OMS and risk engine, which present orders that are authorized in terms of business logic and exposure.

- Downstream: exchange gateways and sessions, which are responsible for speaking venue-specific protocols and dealing with low-level connectivity.

The EMS receives orders from the OMS, chooses venues and execution strategies, decomposes orders when needed, directs them through the appropriate gateways, and reacts to fills and market events by adjusting its behavior.

Right after this conceptual introduction, it is helpful to visualize the EMS in context.

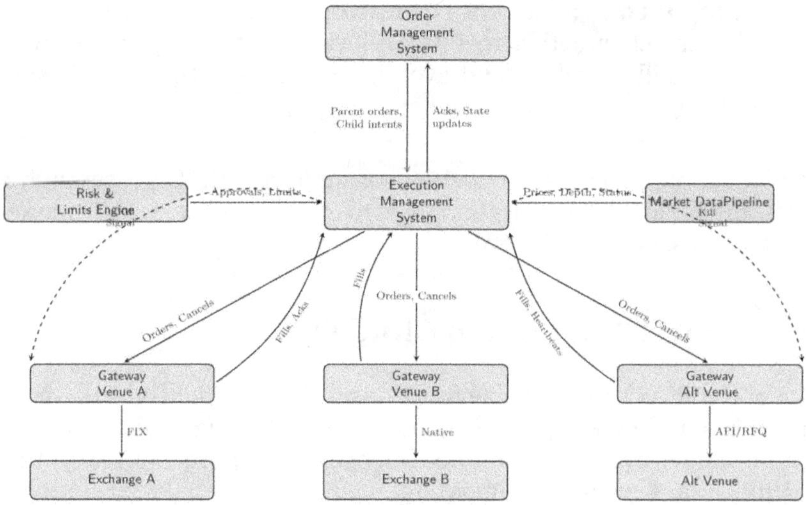

This hub-and-spoke view emphasizes that the EMS is not just a thin pass-through. It has several distinct responsibilities, which we will now unpack systematically.

Primary Roles of the EMS

A well-designed EMS typically fulfills four main roles:

- **Routing**: choosing the venue or venues where each order, or part of each order, should be executed.
- **Execution algorithms**: implementing tactics such as time-weighted average price (TWAP), volume-weighted average price (VWAP), liquidity seeking, or custom strategies that govern how and when to place child orders.
- **Session management and health**: monitoring multiple sessions per venue, managing heartbeats and sequence numbers, and respecting venue-specific rules about throttling and disconnects.

- **Safeguards and coordination**: integrating cancel-on-disconnect, reacting to session-level rejects, cooperating with global kill switches, and avoiding conflicts with the OMS and risk engine.

All of these happen in an event-driven fashion: the EMS is essentially a set of stateful event handlers that react to incoming orders, fills, market data updates, and session events.

From Parent Orders to Child Orders

One of the EMS's most visible functions is taking a *parent* order from the OMS and breaking it into smaller, concrete *child* orders that are sent to venues over time. This decomposition supports both execution quality and operational control.

Parent vs. Child Orders

A parent order represents the overall trading objective, such as:

- "Buy 500,000 shares of XYZ between 10:00 and 11:00."
- "Sell 1,000 futures contracts across two exchanges at best effort."

Executing this as a single large order may cause market impact or reveal your intentions. The EMS therefore creates many smaller child orders, possibly across multiple venues and times, to achieve the parent's goal.

Importantly:

- The OMS tracks the parent's lifecycle and its aggregate fills.
- The EMS owns the logic of how many child orders exist, where they go, and how they are staggered in time and price.

Routing and Venue Selection

Routing is where the EMS transforms high-level intent into specific actions. Decisions may be based on:

- **Available liquidity**: depth in order books, historical fill rates, and hidden liquidity indications.
- **Latency and reliability**: round-trip times to venues, recent reject rates, and current session health.
- **Costs and rebates**: differences in fees, rebates, and other economic factors across venues.
- **Regulatory or client constraints**: rules about where certain instruments or clients may trade.

At the implementation level, routing often takes the form of policies or algorithms that, for each new slice of a parent order, decide:

- Which venue or combination of venues to target.
- What order type to use (limit, market, peg, midpoint, and so on).
- What initial price and size to choose.

The EMS must maintain state about each parent order's progress (filled quantity, remaining quantity, time left in the schedule) to make these choices coherently.

Execution Algorithms as Stateful Event Handlers

Execution algorithms are central to the EMS. They encode the behavior you want over the life of a parent order. Conceptually, each algorithm is a small state machine that reacts to events:

- **Order events**: parent order created, modified, or canceled by the OMS.
- **Fill events**: child orders filled or partially filled at venues.
- **Market data events**: price and volume changes, spread widening or narrowing, trading halts.
- **Risk feedback**: risk engine tightening limits or switching the account to closing-only mode.

Simple Scheduled Algorithms

Consider a TWAP algorithm. Its high-level logic might be:

- Divide the total parent quantity into equal slices across the target time window.
- On each time tick, place a child order for the next slice at a price consistent with current market conditions and risk constraints.
- Adjust future slices based on fills achieved so far (e.g., if you are behind schedule, place slightly larger slices).

The algorithm maintains state such as:

- Total target quantity and time window.
- Quantity already filled and quantity currently working in the market.
- Schedule of remaining slices and the next scheduled send time.

Fills and market data events cause the algorithm to recalculate this state and decide whether to place, modify, or cancel child orders.

More Adaptive Tactics

More sophisticated algorithms may:

- Increase aggressiveness when spreads are tight and liquidity is abundant.
- Back off when volatility spikes or when the risk engine reports tightening constraints.
- Opportunistically "take" liquidity when favorable prices appear, even if ahead of schedule, while maintaining an overall trajectory.

Despite this complexity, the core idea remains: algorithms are stateful event processors, and the EMS provides the infrastructure for their state and event streams. This includes:

- Access to normalized market data events.
- Callbacks on fills and order acknowledgments.
- Timers and scheduling primitives.
- A clear interface to issue child order actions that the EMS routes through gateways.

Managing Exchange Sessions and Health

Underneath the EMS are multiple sessions to each venue, often via separate gateway processes. The EMS must treat these sessions as distinct resources, each with:

- Its own connection state (logged in, disconnected, recovering).
- Its own throttling and rate limits.
- Its own error modes and restart behaviors.

Session State as a First-Class Input

In earlier sections we treated exchange sessions in the market data pipeline as state machines with heartbeats and sequence numbers. The same concept applies to order-entry sessions under the EMS. For each session, the EMS needs to know:

- Is the session currently live and able to accept new orders?
- Are heartbeats arriving and being responded to within expected intervals?
- Have there been recent protocol-level rejects or sequence errors?

This state feeds directly into routing decisions. For example:

- If a session is declared *suspect*, algorithms may temporarily avoid routing new child orders via that session.

- If a session is *disconnected* or in recovery, the EMS may cancel or reroute working orders if supported by venue rules and internal policy.

Heartbeats, Liveness, and Jitter

The EMS often delegates low-level heartbeat handling to gateways, but it must interpret the results. Venue-specific behavior matters:

- Some venues send explicit heartbeats that must be echoed.
- Others rely on regular message flow as implicit liveness.
- Timeouts and disconnect semantics can vary.

In practice, the EMS consumes normalized "session status" events from gateways. These events represent transitions such as "heartbeat missed," "logon successful," "disconnect detected," or "sequence mismatch." The EMS then updates its internal view of session health and may:

- Pause routing to a degraded session.
- Trigger cancel-on-disconnect procedures.
- Alert operators and, in extreme cases, engage kill switches.

Cancel-on-Disconnect and Other Safeguards

A critical safeguard provided or coordinated by the EMS is *cancel-on-disconnect* (CoD). The idea is simple: if the connection between the firm and a venue is lost or becomes unreliable, you do not want orphaned working orders lingering in the market without your visibility or control.

Mechanics of Cancel-on-Disconnect

Depending on the venue, CoD can be implemented in several ways:

- **Venue-side configuration**: you register that if a particular session disconnects, the venue should automatically cancel all working orders associated with that session.

- **Gateway-side behavior**: upon detecting a disconnection or serious protocol error, the gateway sends cancel messages for all known working orders before or during reconnect.
- **EMS-driven policy**: the EMS, upon receiving a session-failed event, marks all child orders on that session as suspect and either assumes they are canceled (if venue-side CoD is guaranteed) or initiates explicit cross-checks and cancel attempts.

In all cases, the EMS must coordinate closely with the OMS and risk engine:

- The OMS's view of each order's state must be updated as cancellations are confirmed or inferred.
- The risk engine must adjust working exposure accordingly, removing orders that are no longer truly active.

Interaction with Kill Switches

Global and scoped kill switches (discussed in a later section) often use the EMS as a key enforcement point. When a kill signal is issued:

- The EMS stops accepting new parent orders from the OMS or, at least, stops transforming them into child orders.
- It sends cancel instructions for all working child orders across affected venues and sessions.
- It confirms, via session status and acknowledgments, that orders have indeed been canceled, escalating if not.

Because the EMS has a unified view of all active child orders and their venues, it is a natural place to implement or orchestrate these safety controls.

Clear Boundaries: EMS vs. OMS and Risk

To keep complexity manageable, the EMS must not reimplement the core responsibilities of the OMS or risk engine, even though it uses their outputs heavily.

What the EMS Should Not Do

Specifically, the EMS should *not*:

- Become a second system of record for order lifecycles. The OMS remains the authoritative ledger of order state.
- Maintain its own independent risk limits or position accounting outside of agreed areas (such as local counters for velocity management). All substantive exposure decisions should flow through the risk engine.
- Implement low-level exchange protocol details beyond what is necessary for coordination. Gateway processes or specialized libraries are usually better suited for that.

When these boundaries blur, you risk subtle inconsistencies: an order might appear canceled to the EMS but still active in the OMS, or risk might see different working quantities than the EMS believes are in flight.

What the EMS *Should* Know

At the same time, the EMS must be very aware of:

- OMS order IDs and states, so that parent-child relationships and final outcomes are correctly tied back to the system of record.
- Risk approvals and current limit regimes, so that algorithms do not schedule child orders that would be blocked downstream.
- Market data, especially around prices, spreads, and trading halts, so that routing and execution tactics respect the real-time environment.

The design goal is a clear layering: OMS for order history and intent, risk for exposure decisions, EMS for routing and execution tactics, gateways for protocol and connectivity.

Operational Observability and Debugging

Because the EMS is at the center of execution, it must be highly observable. When things go wrong—missed fills, unexpected routing choices, latency spikes—you need to be able to answer "why?"

Key Metrics and Logs

Useful EMS metrics include:

- Per-venue and per-session order send rates and fill rates.
- Latency from OMS parent order creation to first child order placement, and from child send to venue acknowledgment.
- Distribution of execution prices versus benchmarks (e.g., mid-quote, VWAP) for each algorithm.
- Session health indicators: heartbeat delays, reconnect counts, reject rates.

Logs should record key events in the EMS's decision-making:

- Why a particular venue or algorithm was chosen for a parent order.
- How a parent order was sliced over time and across venues.
- How the EMS reacted to session failures or risk engine signals.

This event trail, especially when tied back to the OMS log and market data, makes it possible to reconstruct execution behavior for both internal reviews and client reporting.

The Execution Management System is the orchestrator that brings together market data, order intent, and risk constraints to produce concrete execution in the market. It accepts parent orders from the OMS, runs routing and execution algorithms that generate child orders, manages multiple exchange sessions and their health, and enforces safety mechanisms such as cancel-on-disconnect and kill switch propagation.

Crucially, the EMS is an event-driven, stateful component in its own right. It is not simply a conduit; it is a set of carefully designed state machines and schedulers that react to orders, fills, market data, and session events. By keeping its responsibilities clearly separated from, yet tightly integrated with, the OMS and risk engine, the EMS helps ensure that trading is both effective and controlled, even under stress and partial failures.

In the next section we will follow the consequences of execution into the PnL and position engines, where fills, fees, and corporate actions are turned into a coherent view of financial outcomes and exposures over time.

6.5 PnL, Position, and State Reconciliation

The previous sections described how orders are created and tracked (OMS), how they are constrained (risk engine), and how they are executed in the market (EMS). All of that activity ultimately matters because it changes two things that everyone in a trading firm cares about: positions and profit-and-loss (PnL). If the firm cannot say with confidence what it owns and what those holdings are worth, then pre-trade limits, execution quality, and even regulatory compliance become shaky.

This section treats PnL and position as *derived* state in an event-driven system. Rather than being primary databases maintained by ad hoc nightly jobs, they are views built by continuously streaming and reconciling events from trades, fees, and corporate actions. We will:

- Clarify what we mean by positions and by realized and unrealized PnL in an implementation-friendly way.
- Show how to maintain real-time positions and PnL as events arrive from the OMS, EMS, and market data pipeline.
- Examine why front-office views often diverge from back-office records and how to design reconciliation loops.
- Explain snapshotting and "time travel" for PnL and exposure: reconstructing the state at any past point in the trading day.

- Discuss reporting and operational practices that make PnL and position engines first-class, reliable components.

Throughout, the emphasis is on streaming and reconciliation, not on intricate pricing formulas. The goal is faithful bookkeeping in a noisy, distributed environment.

Positions and PnL as Derived Views

In an event-driven architecture, the canonical inputs for PnL and position are:

- **Execution events**: fills and busts coming from venues via the EMS and recorded in the OMS.
- **Allocation events**: how trades are allocated across client accounts, internal books, or strategies.
- **Fee and cost events**: commissions, exchange fees, financing charges, borrow costs, and rebates.
- **Market data events**: prices used to value positions and compute unrealized PnL.
- **Corporate action events**: splits, dividends, symbol changes, and similar adjustments.

Each of these is an event in a durable log somewhere in your system. PnL and positions are not new primary truths; they are the result of processing these events through well-defined rules.

This has two important consequences:

1. You can rebuild PnL and positions if something goes wrong, provided you still have the underlying events.
2. Discrepancies between different views (front office vs. back office, for example) can be investigated by comparing the events and rules that each view applied.

Core Concepts: Positions, Realized and Unrealized PnL

Before tackling the streaming mechanics, it is useful to agree on working definitions.

Positions

A *position* describes how much of a given instrument an account, strategy, or legal entity currently holds, including directional sign and any relevant attributes (long/short, settlement currency, etc.). At a very basic level:

- Starting from zero, each buy fill increases the position; each sell fill decreases it (or vice versa for short-first markets).
- Positions can be tracked at multiple aggregation levels: per order, per account, per desk, per firm.

Conceptually, positions are counters built by integrating execution events over time.

Realized vs. Unrealized PnL

PnL reflects value changes associated with trading and holding positions. Practitioners usually split it into:

- **Realized PnL**: profit or loss from completed trades, where the economic risk has been closed out (for example, buying and then later selling the same number of shares).
- **Unrealized PnL**: current gain or loss on open positions, based on current market prices compared to some reference (such as average cost or prior close).

From an implementation standpoint, the exact formulas and accounting conventions (FIFO, LIFO, average cost, local GAAP vs. IFRS, etc.) vary. What matters for the engine is that these rules are:

- Clearly specified.
- Applied deterministically to the same stream of events.
- Versioned over time when policies change.

With that in place, the job becomes processing events consistently rather than arguing about accounting philosophy inside the engine.

Streaming Positions and PnL in Real Time

The simplest mental model for a PnL and position engine is a long-lived process that subscribes to several event streams:

- Trade fills and busts from the OMS/EMS.
- Allocation adjustments from order and booking systems.
- Fee and cost events from brokers and internal fee models.
- Price updates (marks) from the market data pipeline.

Each time an event arrives, the engine updates its internal state for the affected accounts and instruments, and potentially emits new PnL and position events to downstream subscribers (dashboards, risk reports, etc.).

Processing Fills and Busts

Execution events are the backbone of PnL and position updates. For each fill event, the engine typically:

- Adjusts the position quantity and notional for the relevant account and symbol.
- Updates realized PnL according to the chosen accounting method.
- Records the trade in a trade ledger for potential later adjustments.

Busted or corrected trades are handled as compensating events:

- A bust may be represented as a negative fill that reverses the position and PnL impact of the original.
- A correction may be represented as a cancel-plus-rebook: reversing the original and applying the corrected trade.

Because the PnL engine is event-driven, it naturally supports this style of compensating actions: it applies the events in order and the state transitions follow.

Incorporating Fees and Costs

Trades are not free. To correctly reflect economic performance, the engine must also process events representing:

- Broker commissions and exchange fees.
- Taxes or levies per trade or per notional.
- Financing and borrow costs for margin and shorts.
- Internal transfer pricing or desk-level charges.

These may be modeled as separate PnL components (for example, "Trading PnL" vs. "Fees" vs. "Financing") but they arrive as events just like fills, often from different systems or with some delay.

A robust design reads these fee events as they become available and applies them to the relevant accounts and positions, even if that means updating PnL for trades executed earlier in the day. This is another reason why PnL must be re-computable and time-aware, not just a running total in a spreadsheet.

Marking to Market

Real-time unrealized PnL requires current prices (marks). The PnL engine typically subscribes to:

- End-of-day official prices for formal reporting.
- Intraday market prices (mid, bid, ask, last, or model prices) for live risk and PnL monitoring.

When a new price arrives for a symbol, the engine recalculates unrealized PnL for all positions in that symbol. Because a single price affects many accounts and strategies, efficient data structures and aggregation strategies are important, but the logical pattern remains: a price event arrives, and PnL state is updated.

Again, time matters: the engine should be able to distinguish between the state at 10:00 and the state after a price jump at 10:01, even if both are later recomputed from logs.

Sources of Divergence and Reconciliation Needs

Even with perfect streaming, front-office and back-office views of PnL and positions will not always match exactly. Understanding and designing for these divergences is central to reliable reconciliation.

Typical sources of difference include:

- **Timing differences**: front-office PnL may update on execution reports from the venue, while back-office PnL may wait for clearing or settlement confirmations.
- **Late or missing events**: some fills, busts, or fees may arrive late or be temporarily missing due to system delays or outages.
- **Different pricing conventions**: internal systems may use intraday marks, while accounting systems use end-of-day official prices.
- **Corporate actions**: splits and dividends may be processed in different ways or at different times across systems.

Because of these factors, the goal is not to eliminate all small discrepancies instantly, but to:

1. Make discrepancies visible and explainable.
2. Have structured processes to bring views back into alignment.

Designing Reconciliation Loops

Reconciliation is the systematic comparison of two or more sources of truth and the resolution of any significant differences. In an event-driven PnL and position system, reconciliation itself is an event-driven process.

Front-Office vs. Back-Office Views

A common pattern is dual-bookkeeping:

- **Front-office view**: maintained by trading infrastructure (OMS, PnL engine) using venue execution reports and internal pricing models. It is optimized for speed and intraday decision-making.
- **Back-office (official) view**: maintained by middle/back office systems using clearing and settlement data, reference data, and accounting policies. It is optimized for accuracy and compliance, often at end-of-day or T+1 granularity.

The reconciliation loop between these two may be:

- **Automated comparison**: after end-of-day, positions and PnL per account and symbol are compared across views.
- **Tolerance thresholds**: small differences (for example, due to rounding or timing) may be tolerated temporarily, while larger ones are flagged as *breaks*.
- **Break investigation workflow**: operations staff investigate breaks, identify root causes (missing trades, mis-booked corporate actions, incorrect fees), and generate adjustment events where appropriate.

Once an adjustment is agreed upon, it is applied via explicit events (for example, a manual trade correction or journal entry), not silent database edits. The front-office engine ingests these as part of its event stream, ensuring that future replays produce consistent results.

Reconciliation with External Records

Beyond internal systems, firms must reconcile with:

- Clearing brokers and central counterparties, which provide official trade and position records.
- Custodians, which report holdings of securities and cash balances.
- Prime brokers and lenders, which track borrow and financing positions.

These external reports are often delivered as files or messages. The reconciliation process parses them into structured events, compares them against internal derived views, and flags discrepancies. This is similar in shape to front-vs.-back reconciliation, but often at coarser time scales.

The key architectural idea is the same: even reconciliation inputs and adjustments are treated as event streams that can be logged, replayed, and audited, rather than as opaque manual interventions.

Snapshotting and Time-Travel for PnL and Positions

Just as the OMS and market data pipeline use snapshots and incremental logs to manage long-lived state, the PnL and position engine benefits from the same pattern.

Why Time Travel Matters

Risk managers, regulators, and sometimes clients often ask questions like:

- "What was our net exposure to sector X at 14:32:00 on this trading day?"

- "What was the PnL of strategy Y at the time we triggered a risk limit breach?"
- "How did our positions and PnL evolve during a specific market event?"

Answering these questions reliably requires the ability to reconstruct historical states, not just report the latest values. Because positions and PnL are derived from event logs, you can do this by replaying events up to a chosen cutoff point.

Snapshots for Fast Recovery

Full replay from the beginning of trading history would quickly become impractical. Instead, the PnL engine uses periodic snapshots:

- Each snapshot records the full state of positions and PnL for all accounts at a specific point in time, along with the log offset or sequence number corresponding to the last processed event.
- To recover or time-travel to a later point, you load the most recent snapshot before that time and then replay events from the snapshot's offset up to the target time.

This is directly analogous to replaying order book updates on top of a book snapshot. The pattern—*snapshot plus log*—is a recurring one in event-driven trading systems.

Making PnL and Position Engines First-Class Citizens

In many legacy architectures, PnL and position calculations are implemented as end-of-day batch jobs or as fragile spreadsheets. In an event-driven architecture, they must be treated as core, always-on services with clear responsibilities and interfaces.

Interfaces and Contracts

The PnL and position engine should clearly define:

- The event types it consumes (fills, corrections, fees, marks, corporate actions, adjustments).
- The event types it emits (position updates, PnL updates, reconciliation findings).
- The guarantees it provides (for example, ordering per account, consistency under replay, latency bounds for intraday updates).

Other components—risk, reporting, dashboards—should rely on these outputs, not reimplement their own private PnL calculations. This reduces duplication and inconsistency.

Monitoring and SLAs

Because decisions are made on top of PnL and position data, their freshness and correctness must be monitored:

- Metrics should track ingestion lag (how far behind real time the engine is), event processing throughput, and reconciliation break counts.
- Service-level agreements (SLAs) should specify acceptable latencies for intraday updates and acceptable windows for resolving reconciliations.
- Alerts should fire when data becomes stale (for example, prices not updated for certain symbols) or when breaks cross tolerance thresholds.

In this framing, PnL and position services are peers of OMS, risk, and EMS in importance, not downstream consumers that can be neglected.

Example Flow: From Trade to Reconciled PnL

To tie the ideas together, consider the journey of a single trade:

1. A strategy submits an order; the OMS records it, risk approves it, the EMS routes it, and a venue executes part of it.
2. The venue's execution report arrives via the gateway and EMS; the OMS appends a fill event to its log.
3. The PnL and position engine consumes this fill event:
    - Updates the position for the symbol and account.
    - Updates realized PnL according to the configured method.
    - Emits a position/PnL update event, which dashboards display.
4. Shortly afterward, a fee event arrives from the broker system for that trade; the engine:
    - Reduces PnL by the fee amount.
    - Tags PnL components so that fees are visible separately from trading gains or losses.
5. At end-of-day, the back-office system loads trade and position reports from the clearer and custodian, computes its official PnL, and compares them to the front-office view.
6. A small discrepancy in one account is found due to a late trade correction; an adjustment event is created and fed back into both systems, eliminating the break.

Throughout this flow, no one edits positions or PnL in place by hand. Instead, the state evolves through events, and reconciliation is an explicit closed loop rather than an afterthought.

PnL and position are not static tables to be patched by nightly scripts; they are dynamic, event-driven views over streams of trades, fees, prices, and corporate actions. By treating them this way, a trading firm gains:

- Real-time visibility into exposures and performance.
- The ability to reconstruct historical states for analysis and compliance.
- Structured reconciliation processes that explain and resolve discrepancies across systems and external records.

Architecturally, the PnL and position engine mirrors the design of the market data pipeline and OMS: it consumes events from durable logs, maintains state incrementally, uses snapshots for fast recovery, and provides well-defined outputs for other components. This consistency of design makes the overall trading system more understandable, testable, and robust.

In the next section, we will shift from steady-state calculations to emergency controls, examining kill switches and safety mechanisms that can rapidly halt or unwind trading while preserving the integrity of all this carefully maintained state.

6.6 Kill Switches and Safety Controls

We now have all the machinery needed to trade at scale: clean market data, an event-sourced Order Management System, a rigorous risk engine, and an Execution Management System that routes and manages orders across venues. These components are powerful, but they are not infallible. Strategies can misbehave, markets can gap violently, infrastructure can degrade in subtle ways, and external parties (exchanges, regulators) can demand an immediate halt.

Kill switches and safety controls are the last line of defense. Their mission is simple but unforgiving: when activated, they must rapidly drive the system to a safe, well-defined state—freezing or unwinding trading activity—without corrupting state or leaving the firm in a half-killed limbo.

In this section we will:

- Classify kill mechanisms by *scope* (what they affect) and *trigger* (how they are activated).

- Describe what "safe state" means in practice and how it differs from merely "not sending new orders."
- Show how kill signals propagate through the OMS, risk engine, EMS, and gateways.
- Emphasize the importance of monotonic, one-way kill logic that cannot be silently overridden.
- Discuss observability, testing, and drills, so these controls work under real stress and not just on paper.

Scope and Triggers of Kill Mechanisms

Not all crises are firm-wide catastrophes; many are local. A robust design acknowledges this by offering multiple scopes and triggers for safety controls.

Scopes: From Local to Global

Typical kill scopes include:

- **Per-order or per-algorithm**: stop one misbehaving strategy or cancel a problematic parent order while leaving others running.
- **Per-account or per-book**: freeze trading for a client, fund, or desk that has hit a risk boundary or is under investigation.
- **Per-venue**: halt activity on a single exchange or broker link that is misbehaving (for example, sending incorrect fills or exhibiting extreme latency).
- **Firm-wide**: immediately stop all new trading and aggressively cancel working orders across all venues and strategies.

Each scope corresponds to a different blast radius. Local controls are useful for day-to-day incidents; global controls are reserved for existential threats or external mandates.

Triggers: Manual, Automated, and External

Triggers fall into three broad categories:

- **Manual**: a human operator or supervisor presses a "panic button" in a control dashboard, or issues a command through a secure console. Manual triggers are essential when judgment and context are required.
- **Rule-based automation**: the system automatically activates a kill based on measurable conditions, such as hitting a firm-level loss limit, detecting runaway order rates, or observing major inconsistencies in positions or PnL.
- **External mandates**: an exchange, regulator, or client may require immediate cessation of trading in certain instruments or accounts (for example, during a market-wide circuit breaker or a corporate event).

Whatever the source, the trigger must ultimately be represented as a well-defined internal event: "Kill scope X activated by Y at time T for reason R." This event then drives a deterministic sequence of actions.

What It Means to Reach a Safe State

It is tempting to think of a kill switch as "stop sending new orders." In practice, that is not sufficient. A safe state typically involves three coordinated behaviors:

1. **Freeze new risk**: block or heavily constrain any new order that would increase exposure in the affected scope.
2. **Cancel or reduce working exposure**: for affected scopes, send cancels for open child orders and, if appropriate, consider controlled unwinds of existing positions.
3. **Preserve integrity and observability**: ensure that OMS state, risk state, PnL, and logs remain consistent and that humans can see what is happening.

The exact combination depends on the nature of the kill:

- A per-strategy kill might allow existing positions to be held but blocks new orders and cancels all working child orders belonging to that strategy.

- A firm-wide kill might block all new orders, cancel all working orders everywhere, and possibly restrict any subsequent activity to closing-only until the incident is resolved.

The key is that "safe state" must be explicitly defined for each scope and encoded into the system, not left to improvised human judgment during a crisis.

Layered Kill Architecture and Propagation

Because the trading system is layered (risk, OMS, EMS, gateways), kill logic must be layered as well. A kill event should propagate from a higher-level controller into each layer in a clear, one-way fashion.

After introducing the notion of scopes and triggers, it is useful to visualize these layers and their interactions.

Diagrammatic representation:

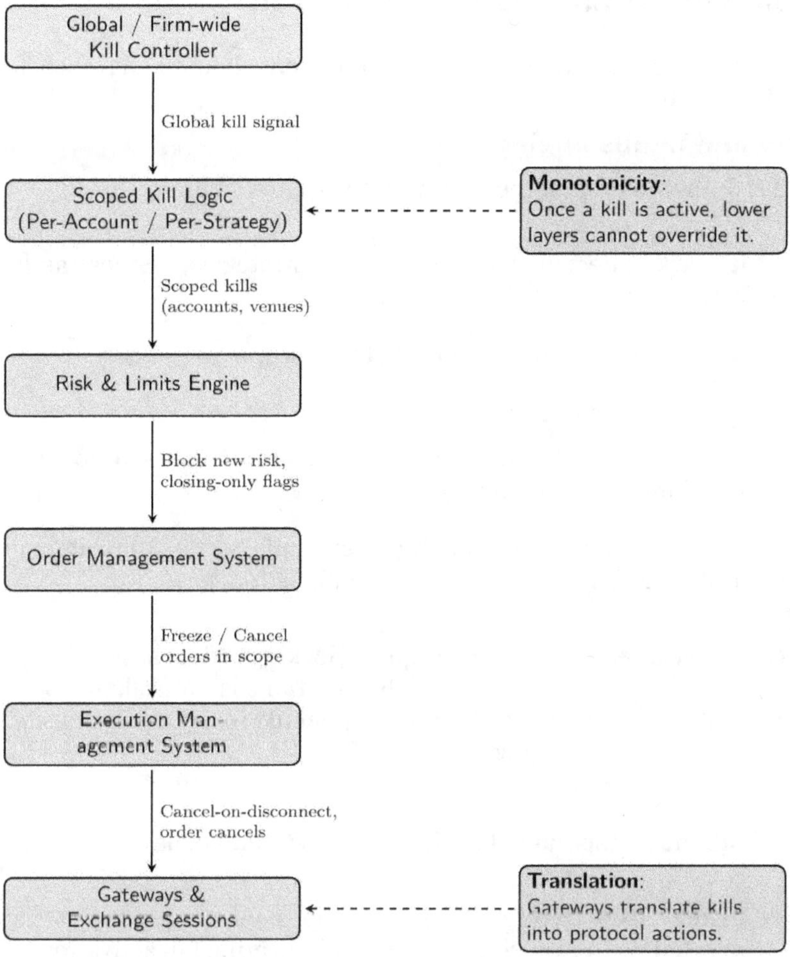

This diagram emphasizes that kill signals flow top-down and are monotonic: once a higher-level kill is in place, lower layers can become stricter but not more permissive.

Behavior of Each Layer Under Kill

Let us walk through how each core component should behave when a kill is activated.

Risk and Limits Engine

The risk engine is often the first layer to enforce a kill:

- It marks affected scopes (accounts, strategies, venues) as *kill-active.*
- New orders or modifications in those scopes are either:
  - Rejected outright, or
  - Restricted to closing-only (for example, allow sells to reduce long exposure, but block buys).
- It may tighten limits globally (for example, setting maximum utilization to zero) or locally for the affected scopes.

Because risk already has the concept of blocking orders based on exposure, extending it to block under kill conditions is natural. It also ensures that, as long as downstream components respect risk decisions, no new risk is taken during a kill.

Order Management System

The OMS must respond to kill signals with stateful behavior:

- **Freeze new orders**: for killed scopes, new order requests are rejected, with explicit reason codes indicating kill activation.
- **Process cancellations**: cancel requests for existing orders should still be accepted and processed, and may even be automatically generated as part of kill handling.
- **Track kill state per order**: orders and parent orders might be tagged with a kill status (for example, "canceled due to global kill" vs. "client-requested cancel"). This tagging is important for audit and for later automated restarts if appropriate.

The OMS remains the system of record: it records every kill-related decision as events in its log. That way, a later replay of OMS events will show precisely what the system did during the kill.

Execution Management System

The EMS is responsible for actively driving the market to the target safe state:

- It stops scheduling new child orders for affected parent orders.
- It sends cancel instructions for all currently working child orders in the relevant scopes and venues.
- It tracks which cancels have been acknowledged and which orders remain in a "pending cancellation" or uncertain state.

In addition, the EMS must adapt its algorithms:

- Execution algorithms should receive a clear kill signal and respond by terminating gracefully, canceling their orders, and emitting final state for the parent orders.
- Adaptive routing decisions should be disabled or constrained to avoid surprising behavior while the system is attempting to shut down.

The EMS's logs are critical for post-mortems: they reveal how quickly cancels were sent, which venues lagged in acknowledging them, and how much working exposure remained at each step.

Gateways and Exchange Sessions

At the edge, gateways translate kill intentions into protocol-specific actions:

- They may send explicit mass-cancel messages if supported by the venue (for example, cancel all orders for a session, symbol, or account).
- They may rely on configured cancel-on-disconnect behavior, possibly closing sessions as part of the kill.

- They track which orders are still believed to be live at the venue and continuously attempt to reconcile that with cancel responses and drop copies.

If a gateway is in doubt about the status of working orders (for example, due to a sequence gap or prolonged disconnection), it must raise the issue clearly so that risk and operations can treat the residual exposure conservatively.

Monotonic Kill Logic and Conflict Avoidance

A subtle but crucial design principle is *monotonicity*: once a kill has been activated at a given scope, no lower-scope or lower-layer component should be able to silently override it.

Avoiding Conflicting Decisions

Conflicts can arise if:

- A strategy attempts to restart trading locally after a brief self-imposed pause while a firm-level kill is still active.
- A venue-specific throttle or local safety control tries to resume order flow on a session that is still under a higher-level kill.
- Different parts of the system have inconsistent views of which scopes are in kill mode due to propagation delays or failures.

To avoid this:

- Kill status should be derivable from a single source of truth (for example, an internal control service or event log), not from ad hoc flags scattered across subsystems.
- Local components may introduce *additional* restrictions (for example, a strategy deciding to self-kill even when the global system is healthy), but they may not relax or ignore higher-level kills.
- Whenever the kill hierarchy is updated, events should be broadcast and acknowledged across relevant components, with conservative defaults (assume kill until proven otherwise) in the face of uncertainty.

Idempotent Kill Events

Because kill signals may be retried or echoed across layers, they should be designed to be idempotent:

- Receiving the same kill event twice should not cause duplicate or conflicting actions.
- Kill events should carry identifiers and scopes that allow components to recognize already-applied kills.
- Deactivation (un-kill) should be handled as a separate, explicitly controlled process, not as an automatic timeout unless that behavior is carefully justified and audited.

This parallels the idempotent processing you implemented for OMS order events; the same discipline applies here.

Observability: Knowing You Are Really Safe

During a crisis, partial knowledge is dangerous. Operators must be able to see, quickly and clearly, whether kill actions have taken full effect.

Dashboards and Status Indicators

Effective kill dashboards show:

- Current kill status by scope: which strategies, accounts, venues, or the firm as a whole are killed, in pending-kill, or active states.
- Counts of working orders and notional exposure before and after kill activation, broken down by venue and account.
- Progress of cancel waves: how many cancels have been sent, acknowledged, or are still awaiting confirmation.
- Any residual uncertainties: sessions with ambiguous status, suspected orphaned orders, or mismatches between internal and venue views.

Visual clarity matters. In high-stress situations, operators should not need to interpret cryptic codes or dig through logs; they should have obvious, up-to-date indicators.

Alerts and Logging

Automated alerts should fire when:

- A kill is activated or deactivated, with scope, trigger source, and reason.
- Expected cancellation progress stalls (for example, a venue is not acknowledging cancels within a configured time).
- Any component fails to receive or acknowledge a kill signal.

Logs need to capture:

- The exact timeline of kill activation, propagation, and completion.
- All decisions made by strategies, EMS, risk, and gateways in response to kill events.
- Any overrides or manual interventions during the incident.

This level of detail is essential for thorough post-incident analysis and for satisfying regulators that controls functioned as designed.

Testing, Drills, and Failure Modes

Kill switches that are only exercised on paper are almost as dangerous as having no kill switches at all. Real systems behave differently under load and partial failure, and assumptions that seem obvious in a design document can fail in subtle ways.

Regular Drills

Firms should schedule regular, controlled drills that:

- Activate various kill scopes (per-strategy, per-venue, firm-wide) in test or simulation environments, and occasionally in production during quiet periods with pre-agreed constraints.

- Measure how long it takes to reach target safe states, in terms of both time and residual working exposure.
- Validate that all layers (risk, OMS, EMS, gateways) respond correctly and that dashboards and alerts behave as expected.

Drills should be realistic: they should include in-flight orders, artificial delays in venue responses, and simulated partial network failures.

Planning for Partial Failures

The hardest scenarios are those in which the system cannot verify whether kill actions fully succeeded. Examples include:

- A gateway loses connectivity mid-cancel, and it is unclear which cancels reached the venue.
- An exchange itself experiences internal issues, resulting in inconsistent or delayed acknowledgments.
- Internal logs are temporarily unavailable, making it harder to reconcile OMS and EMS views of order state.

In these situations, the design should specify conservative fallback behavior, such as:

- Treating uncertain orders as potentially live and maintaining elevated risk flags until proven otherwise.
- Escalating to manual contact with venues or brokers to confirm cancellation status.
- Restricting any restart of trading until reconciliation is complete, at least for affected scopes.

These failure modes should be discussed and rehearsed in advance, not improvised amidst a live incident.

Restarting Safely After a Kill

Eventually, the firm will want to resume trading. Restarting should be as deliberate and controlled as killing, not a simple switch flip.

Prerequisites for Restart

Before lifting a kill, operators should verify:

- All targeted cancels have been acknowledged or otherwise definitively resolved.
- PnL and position views have been reconciled to the extent necessary for safe operation.
- The underlying cause of the kill (strategy bug, infrastructure fault, venue anomaly) has been addressed or mitigated.

Only then should the kill status be downgraded, ideally in stages:

- From firm-wide kill to closing-only mode for some accounts.
- From closing-only to normal operation for selected, lower-risk strategies or venues.

Each stage should be logged and, where feasible, peer-reviewed or approved by more than one person, especially for firm-wide restarts.

Event-Sourced View of the Incident

Because your system is built around event logs (OMS events, risk decisions, PnL updates), you can reconstruct the entire episode:

- When the kill was triggered and by whom.
- Which orders were live and which were canceled, and in what sequence.
- How exposure, PnL, and positions evolved from pre-incident to post-restart.

This event-sourced view is not just for compliance; it is a powerful tool for learning. After-action reviews can identify bottlenecks (for example, a particular venue that took too long to acknowledge cancels) and lead to improvements in configuration or even in venue selection.

Kill switches and safety controls are the culmination of the event-driven architecture we have been building. They bring together:

- The OMS's precise record of order state.
- The risk engine's authority to block new exposure.
- The EMS's ability to cancel and reroute working orders across venues.
- The gateways' direct control over exchange sessions and protocol-specific mass-cancel capabilities.

By designing kill mechanisms with clear scopes and triggers, enforcing monotonic, one-way propagation of kill signals, and treating kills and restarts as first-class events in your logs, you can ensure that even under extreme stress the system moves quickly toward a well-defined safe state while preserving state integrity and auditability.

In the final section of this chapter, we will turn to edge flow control and heartbeats, examining how rate limits and liveness detection support the day-to-day stability that, ideally, keeps kill switches firmly in the background.

6.7 Edge Flow Control and Heartbeats

The preceding sections described how core components—OMS, risk engine, EMS, gateways, and kill switches—cooperate to manage orders and exposure. All of these components ultimately converge at the *edge* of the trading system: the physical and logical connections to exchanges and other venues. At this edge, two practical concerns dominate:

- **Flow control**: sending orders, cancels, and other messages at rates that respect venue limits and keep latency predictable.

- **Liveness detection**: determining whether a session is truly alive or has silently failed, using heartbeats and related patterns.

Done well, edge flow control and heartbeat design make the system robust under stress and reduce the need for dramatic actions like global kill switches. Done poorly, they cause jitter, false disconnects, and unpredictable outages right when the market is most active.

This section focuses on these edge mechanics. We assume the existence of the EMS and gateways described earlier and concentrate on how they shape and monitor message traffic to venues.

Why Flow Control at the Edge Matters

Venues impose explicit and implicit rate limits on participants. Examples include:

- Maximum messages per second per session or per firm.
- Bursting rules (for example, short bursts above the nominal rate allowed, but sustained excess disallowed).
- Penalties or disconnections if limits are violated repeatedly.

At the same time, trading strategies, especially during volatile periods, may generate intense bursts of orders and cancels. If you connect these bursts directly to the venue without shaping, several bad things can happen:

- **Hard rejections**: the venue returns "throttle exceeded" or similar errors, leading to missed trading opportunities and extra complexity in the OMS and EMS.
- **Forced disconnects**: the venue tears down sessions for abuse, forcing expensive reconnections and resynchronizations.
- **Latency spikes**: even before formal limits are hit, overloaded gateways and networks cause round-trip times to increase unpredictably, confusing both execution algorithms and risk logic.

The purpose of flow control at the edge is therefore twofold:

1. To ensure that outbound traffic obeys venue rules, protecting sessions from disruption.
2. To smooth bursts in a way that preserves responsiveness while minimizing jitter and queue buildup.

Naïve Centralized Throttling and Its Pitfalls

A natural first attempt is a single centralized throttle: a component that measures the overall orders-per-second rate leaving the firm and enforces a global cap. This is simple but problematic in practice.

Lack of Per-Session Awareness

Venues enforce limits on a per-session or per-connection basis. A global throttle may keep the total rate under some number, but still allow uneven distribution across sessions:

- One session could receive a burst that exceeds its specific limit while others are almost idle.
- This session then suffers rejections or disconnects, even though the firm's overall rate looks fine.

Coordination with Algorithms and Risk

A single global cap also obscures context:

- It may slow down critical risk-reducing activity (such as cancel waves during a kill event) in favor of non-critical traffic.
- Execution algorithms may not know whether rejections stem from venue limits or from the global throttle, making adaptation harder.

In short, naïve, centralized throttling is too blunt an instrument for a system with many venues, sessions, and priorities. What is needed is more granular, context-aware flow control.

Token-Bucket and Leaky-Bucket Throttling

In practice, firms use simple yet powerful patterns such as token-bucket or leaky-bucket algorithms to shape traffic. While we will avoid formal equations, we can describe the intuition.

Conceptual Model

Imagine each session or resource (for example, "orders to Venue A on session S") has a virtual bucket:

- Tokens flow into the bucket at a steady configured rate (for example, 100 tokens per second).
- Each outbound message consumes a token.
- If the bucket is empty, messages must wait (or, in extreme cases, be rejected or re-routed).

This model naturally enforces an average rate: you cannot send messages faster than tokens accumulate over any sustained period. At the same time, if you allow the bucket to accumulate some maximum size, short bursts can be accommodated as long as the longer-term average complies.

Per-Session Buckets

By assigning one bucket per session:

- You ensure that each session respects the limits negotiated with the venue.
- You can tune different sessions differently. For example, a primary session might have a higher allowed rate than a backup, or

message types might be categorized (order entry vs. cancel) with distinct constraints.

The EMS and gateways coordinate to classify messages and charge them against the appropriate bucket before transmission.

Multi-Dimensional Limits

Real limits are often multi-dimensional. For example:

- A venue might limit both total message rate and cancel-to-order ratios.
- A firm might want additional controls at the strategy or account level.

You can model this by layering buckets:

- A per-session bucket for raw message rate.
- A per-account bucket for messages authored by a specific client.
- Possibly specialized buckets for cancels to smooth cancel storms.

An outbound message must have tokens available in all relevant buckets to proceed. Otherwise, it is delayed or rejected, and the EMS is notified so algorithms can adapt.

Adaptive Throttling Under Stress

Static rate settings are rarely perfect. Market conditions change, venues adjust limits, and the system's own capabilities evolve. Adaptive throttling adjusts behavior in response to observed feedback.

Feedback Signals

Useful signals include:

- **Venue rejects**: explicit "too fast" or "rate limit exceeded" messages.
- **Latency trends**: increasing round-trip or acknowledgment times, which may indicate congestion.
- **Gateway queue lengths**: growing internal queues between EMS and gateways, suggesting that send capacity is temporarily saturated.

Dynamic Adjustment

An adaptive throttle might:

- Temporarily reduce token refill rates for a session that triggers rate-limit rejects, then gradually increase them if conditions improve.
- Prioritize certain message types (for example, cancels and risk-reducing orders) when tokens are scarce, by reserving a portion of capacity for them.
- Redistribute traffic across multiple sessions to the same venue where supported.

The overarching goal is to respect external limits while making most effective use of available capacity, especially during stressed conditions when risk-reducing actions are most urgent.

Coordination Between EMS and Gateways

Flow control cannot live in isolation inside gateways; it must be coordinated with the EMS and higher layers.

Shared Understanding of Limits

The EMS needs to know:

- Current effective limits per session and per venue.

- Which sessions are currently constrained or degraded.
- How much "budget" remains for a strategy or account in the near term.

This information allows algorithms to adjust their behavior. For example:

- A TWAP engine might slow its schedule when it sees that the available message rate is limited.
- A liquidity-seeking strategy might temporarily shift volume to less-constrained venues.

Priorities and Preemption

The EMS and gateways also coordinate priorities:

- Messages associated with kill switches, risk-imposed cancels, or critical operational actions should preempt normal traffic.
- Limits can be structured so that a reserved fraction of capacity is always available for such high-priority messages.

This prevents a situation where benign trading activity starves the system of the ability to respond to emergencies because all capacity is consumed.

Heartbeats and Liveness as State Machines

Flow control ensures the system does not overwhelm the venue; liveness detection ensures the venue (and the path to it) are still functioning. Heartbeats are the primary tool for this.

Beyond Simple Timers

In many protocol descriptions, heartbeats are casually described as "messages sent every N seconds to check connectivity." In a production trading system, heartbeat handling should be treated as a *state machine*, not as a simple timer.

For each session, you can think of states such as:

- **Connected**: heartbeats and normal messages are flowing as expected.
- **Suspect**: heartbeats are delayed or missing, but not yet conclusively failed.
- **Disconnected**: the session is considered broken; trading via this path is no longer safe.

Transitions between these states are driven by events:

- Receipt of a heartbeat or any other message.
- Expiry of heartbeat timers or detection of consecutive misses.
- Low-level network events (socket errors, TCP resets).

Sensitivity and False Positives

Choosing heartbeat intervals and thresholds is a trade-off:

- If you are too aggressive (short intervals, few misses tolerated), normal jitter and small network hiccups will cause frequent false disconnects, needlessly disrupting trading.
- If you are too lax, genuine failures will be detected late, leaving the system trading blindly.

In practice:

- Different venues and regions may warrant different settings, reflecting network quality and protocol expectations.
- You may treat absence of *any* message (not just heartbeats) as evidence of trouble: in active markets, a sudden silence can be suspicious on its own.

The liveness state machine should be configurable but conservative: move to suspect and disconnected states decisively when evidence warrants, but avoid thrashing between states in marginal conditions.

Integrating Liveness with Safety Controls

Heartbeat-derived liveness states are not merely informational; they drive higher-level behavior.

Routing and Session Selection

When a session moves to *suspect* or *disconnected*:

- The EMS should stop routing new orders through it, preferring alternative sessions or venues if available.
- Existing working orders may need to be mass-canceled or treated as uncertain, triggering conservative risk assumptions.

In multi-session setups, the EMS may automatically fail over to backup sessions, provided that doing so does not violate client or regulatory constraints.

Interaction with Kill Switches

A session-level disconnect can be a trigger for scoped kill behavior:

- For accounts or strategies whose only accessible venue path is via the failed session, trading may need to be halted or restricted to closing-only.
- Cancel-on-disconnect policies at the venue may be relied upon or supplemented with explicit cancel waves upon reconnection.

The key is that liveness information feeds into the same safety apparatus described in the kill switch section, but at a more granular, session-focused level.

Minimizing Jitter and Latency Spikes

Flow control and heartbeat logic themselves can introduce jitter if not carefully designed. Some practices to minimize this include:

Smoothing Rather Than Bursting

Even when tokens are available, sending large bursts of messages in a single short window can:

- Overwhelm local queues and processing threads.
- Create microbursts on the network that contribute to packet loss and retransmissions.

Instead:

- Spread message sends more evenly over time, within the constraints of trading strategies.
- Coordinate scheduling of high-volume algorithms so they do not all fire at the same microsecond.

Avoiding Heartbeat Synchronization

If many sessions send heartbeats on identical schedules (for example, exactly every second on the second), this can create synchronized bursts of small packets, which is wasteful and may cause periodic jitter.

Mitigations include:

- Adding small random jitters to heartbeat send times within acceptable windows.
- Staggering heartbeat schedules across sessions.

The goal is to maintain timely liveness checks without amplifying load or creating artifacts in traffic patterns.

Metrics and Alerts for Edge Stability

Finally, edge flow control and heartbeat systems must be observable. Useful metrics include:

- Per-session send and receive rates, and their recent history.
- Token bucket utilizations: how close each session is to its configured limits.
- Queue lengths between EMS and gateways, and between gateways and the network.
- Heartbeat round-trip times, misses, and state transitions (connected, suspect, disconnected).
- Counts and causes of venue rejections related to throttling or protocol errors.

Alerts should highlight:

- Approaching rate limits or sustained high utilization, especially when risk-reducing messages might be needed.
- Repeated or unexplained transitions to suspect/disconnected states.
- Latency spikes that suggest congestion or resource exhaustion at the edge.

These signals allow operations and engineers to intervene early, tuning limits or investigating underlying causes before they escalate into outages or require activation of higher-level kill mechanisms.

Edge flow control and heartbeat design are the quiet guardians of a trading system's stability. Token-bucket-style throttling and its variants ensure that message rates stay within venue limits and that bursts are smoothed into manageable flows. Per-session awareness and adaptive behavior allow the system to make the most of available capacity while protecting against rejections and disconnects.

Heartbeats, treated as part of a liveness state machine rather than as trivial timers, provide timely and reliable signals about session health. Their outputs feed directly into routing decisions, risk assumptions, and, when needed, kill switches and cancel-on-disconnect policies.

By giving flow control and liveness detection the same architectural care afforded to OMS, risk, EMS, and PnL engines, you reduce the likelihood that edge instability will trigger larger crises. In an event-driven trading system, a well-behaved edge is what allows the rest of the stack to operate confidently at high speed, even under the stresses of real markets.

Chapter 7

Testing, Observability, Security, and Operations

Trading systems rarely fail in the lab; they fail in the wild, under real order flow, partial outages, and human mistakes. In this chapter, we turn your event-driven architecture into something you can trust at 9:30 a.m. on a volatile Monday: we'll learn how to replay the past tick-for-tick, break the system on purpose before the market does, see every critical event in real time, respond to incidents without panic, satisfy auditors without paralyzing engineers, and ship changes safely while the book is live.

7.1 Record/Replay and Backtesting

In earlier chapters we focused on getting events through the system correctly and on time: defining queues, managing state, and ensuring reliable processing under load. In this section we turn that same event-driven structure into a powerful tool for understanding and improving the system.

The core idea is simple but profound: **treat your live event stream as a first-class artifact**. Every message that enters or leaves your trading platform—market data ticks, order submissions, risk decisions, venue acknowledgments, fills, configuration changes—is not just something to process "right now." It is also raw material for:

- *Forensic debugging*: reconstructing what really happened during a production incident.
- *Realistic backtesting*: running strategies against production-like conditions, including quirks and imperfections.

To do that reliably, you need a pipeline that can *capture*, *store*, and *replay* event streams in a way that is deterministic enough that the same input sequence produces the same internal behaviour, at least for the aspects you care about (prices, orders, risk decisions, state transitions).

Treating the Event Stream as a First-Class Artifact

Think of your system as a function:

"*Event stream in* $\rightarrow$ *decisions and state changes out.*"

Most teams initially treat only the code and configuration as durable assets. Events are "in the air" for a few milliseconds on the wire and then gone. When something goes wrong, they rely on partial logs and metrics to guess what happened.

An event-oriented mindset inverts that priority:

- The incoming and outgoing event streams are primary data sources.
- Code and configuration are *ways of transforming* those streams.
- If you can replay the same event stream into a fixed version of the code and configuration, you should be able to reproduce the behaviour that occurred in production.

This requires two things:

1. A reliable way to **capture and store** the stream as it flows through the system.
2. A sufficiently **deterministic processing model** so that replaying the stream is meaningful.

Right after you adopt this view, it helps to visualize the overall path from exchanges to logs to replay.

Diagrammatic representation:

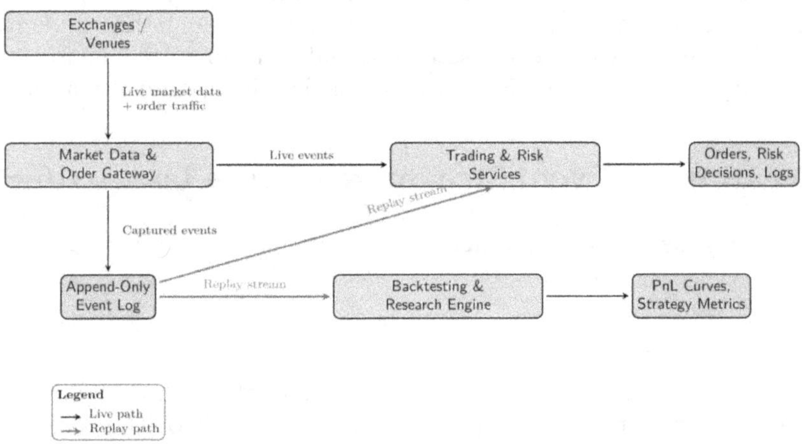

This diagram emphasizes two important properties:

- The event log is *append-only*: events are written in arrival order and never overwritten.
- The same log can feed both *production services* (for diagnosis) and *offline backtesting engines*.

The remainder of the section explains how to design this pipeline in detail.

Determinism: Making Replay Meaningful

If you replay yesterday's events into today's system, and the outcomes differ wildly, your log is not very helpful. Some differences are expected (you may fix bugs or change risk rules), but your goal is that:

> *Given the same sequence of external events and the same version of the code and configuration, the system should produce the same sequence of key decisions and state transitions.*

This does not require the system to be perfectly deterministic in every aspect. It *does* require that you carefully control or record the main sources of non-determinism:

Stable time semantics.

In a live system, many components ask, "What time is it?" and use that for:

- Timeouts and delays.
- Trading schedule changes (open/close auctions, breaks).
- Throttling decisions, such as "N orders per second per client."

If each service calls the operating system clock independently, replaying the same events later will yield different times and, therefore, different decisions.

A more replay-friendly pattern is:

- Treat *time* as another input event, carried alongside market data and orders.
- Use timestamps embedded in the captured events (e.g., exchange timestamps, gateway receive timestamps) to drive time-based logic in replay.

In practice, this often means that services consume a "clock stream" or that the event messages themselves carry authoritative timestamps that the business logic uses instead of the current wall-clock.

Idempotent handlers and explicit side effects.

Event handlers in a trading system may:

- Update in-memory or persisted state.
- Emit new events internally.
- Trigger external side effects: send an order to an exchange, email a risk officer, or adjust a margin requirement.

During replay we typically want to:

- *Reproduce* internal state transitions and internal events.
- *Suppress, neutralize, or redirect* external side effects so we do not resend old orders or emails.

Designing handlers to be *idempotent*—so that processing the same event twice has no extra effect beyond the first time—helps in both production and replay. It allows safe retries and simplifies the logic required to skip or annotate side effects during replay (for example, by writing them to a "shadow" bus instead of a real venue gateway).

Explicit external dependencies.

Many calculations pull in external data:

- Reference data: symbol definitions, corporate actions, tick sizes.
- Configuration: risk limits, strategy parameters, routing rules.
- Slow-moving feeds: volatility surfaces, yield curves.

If you fetch these on demand from some shared service without recording which version was used for each decision, replaying later may be impossible: the reference data has changed, but your captured market events have not.

To make replay trustworthy:

- Treat changes to reference data and configuration as *events* that are captured in the log.

- Tag market and order events with identifiers that allow you to recover or reconstruct the relevant reference snapshot.

In a fully disciplined setup, you can reconstruct the whole state of the system from the event log and a known code/configuration version.

Consistent serialization formats.

Finally, deterministic replay depends on being able to parse old messages. If you change message schemas freely, you may not be able to decode last month's events.

Practical measures include:

- Using schema-managed formats with explicit versioning.
- Avoiding incompatible changes to live schemas; add fields rather than reinterpreting old ones.
- Storing the schema version or message type alongside each event in the log.

Capturing Events at Ingress

With determinism principles in mind, we can design the capture side of the pipeline. The key is to record events *as early as possible* in their journey into and out of the system.

You typically have several ingress points:

- **Market data feeds** from exchanges and vendors.
- **Order entry** from internal clients, GUIs, and programmatic APIs.
- **Risk and compliance inputs**, such as credit limit updates.
- **Reference data updates** and configuration changes.

For each of these, you want a pattern like:

> Receive event $\rightarrow$ *append to durable log* $\rightarrow$ proceed to normal processing.

This is conceptually similar to a database write-ahead log: the log becomes the *ground truth* for what the system observed and when.

Write-ahead logging and dual-writes.

There are two common patterns for capturing events:

- Write-ahead logging: The gateway or service first writes the event to an append-only log (often on a dedicated logging cluster) and only then enqueues it into the main processing pipeline. This ensures that if the processing path crashes, the event is still in the log.
- Dual-writes: The gateway writes the event both to the processing message bus and to the capture log in parallel. This reduces the extra latency in the main path at the cost of more complex failure handling (what if one write succeeds and the other fails?).

In low-latency trading you must be explicit about where you are willing to pay a few more microseconds. Common compromises include:

- Capturing a slightly less detailed event on the ultra-fast path (e.g., only essential fields) and recording richer, derived events in a slower side channel.
- Making logging asynchronous but with strong back-pressure: the gateway can proceed as long as the logging lag stays within some small bound.

Latency-aware capture techniques.

To minimize capture overhead:

- Use pre-allocated buffers and avoid per-event memory allocations where possible.
- Batch writes to the log where acceptable: writing 100 events at once can be far cheaper than 100 individual writes.

- Keep serialization formats compact and cheap to encode; avoid expensive text formats in hot paths.
- Place capture components close to gateways in network terms, and often on the same host, to avoid extra round-trips.

The design goal is that *capture is always on*. Turning off capture "temporarily" in production is a sign that the capture path is too heavy.

Designing the Event Log

The event log is the backbone of record/replay. It does not have to be a single monolithic system, but it should behave like one conceptually.

Important characteristics include:

Append-only structure.

Events are appended in order. They are never updated in place. Corrections (for example, a fixed fill message) are themselves new events that reference the original. This ensures that during forensic analysis you can see the history of what was known, when.

Partitioning and topics.

You rarely want a single gigantic stream containing everything. More typical is:

- One or more topics per exchange or venue for market data.
- Separate topics for client orders, risk events, reference data updates, and configuration changes.
- Within each topic, partitioning by symbol, client, or some other key to support parallel processing.

Partitioning should preserve order *per key* where order matters, such as all events related to a specific order ID or instrument.

Retention policies.

For replay and backtesting you often want months or years of history. But storage is finite, and not all data is equally valuable.

You might, for example:

- Keep full-depth order book events for three months, then aggregate or down-sample for longer-term backtesting.
- Retain all order and fill events for as long as regulations require, often many years.
- Store detailed debug logs for a much shorter window, relying on more compact business-level events for long-term analysis.

Retention policies must be coordinated with compliance, risk, and research stakeholders so you do not accidentally delete the only record of an important scenario.

Schema evolution and discoverability.

Over time, messages change. New fields are added; optional fields become required; representations change. To ensure old data remains usable:

- Maintain a catalog that describes each topic: its schema versions, retention, and intended use.
- Provide tooling that allows quants and engineers to discover and browse streams without bypassing security or overloading production systems.

Building a Replay Engine

Once events are reliably captured, you need a replay engine: a component that can read from the event log and feed events into a target system (a service or a backtester) as if they were live.

A good replay engine allows you to:

- **Control playback speed.** Run in real time, faster than real time, or step-by-step.
- **Seek in time.** Jump to a specific time window, or to a specific event (e.g., just before an incident).

- **Filter and combine streams.** Select only particular symbols, clients, or venues, and merge multiple topics coherently.
- **Handle side effects.** Ensure that replay does not resend real orders or trigger real-world actions.

Time travel and playback speed.

In forensic debugging, you might want to:

- Start replay a few minutes before an incident.
- Run faster than real time to approach the incident quickly.
- Slow down or pause as you cross the critical moment, inspecting state as you go.

In backtesting, you might want to compress days of trading into minutes. To support this, the replay engine feeds events to the system under a virtual time model derived from event timestamps rather than the wall-clock. Services that respect this model can behave consistently whether they are in live or replay mode.

Neutralizing or redirecting side effects.

During replay, you do not want to actually submit orders to an exchange. But you *do* want your order-routing logic to think it sent those orders and handle the subsequent acknowledgments, rejects, and fills as usual.

Common techniques include:

- Running venues, clearing interfaces, and email gateways in a controlled "sandbox" environment that never reaches the real world.
- Replacing side-effecting adapters with stub components that log what *would* have been sent and immediately inject matching responses from the recorded log.
- Adding a "mode" flag (live vs. replay) to infrastructure components so that they route side effects appropriately without contaminating business logic with environment checks.

Injecting faults and parameter changes.

A powerful use of replay is to modify some internal aspect while keeping the external event stream fixed. For example:

- Change a strategy parameter and see how it would have behaved on last week's market.
- Inject extra latency in a downstream service during replay to mimic a slowdown and see whether risk protections still hold.
- Flip a feature flag at a certain replay time to evaluate a new routing rule.

Because the external inputs are fixed, differences in outcomes are attributable to your changes, not to market randomness.

From Replay to Realistic Backtesting

Traditional backtesting often uses idealized data:

- Clean price bars with no gaps.
- Instantaneous order acknowledgments and fills.
- Simplified assumptions about slippage, spreads, and throttling.

By contrast, replaying recorded production streams allows you to test strategies under more realistic conditions:

Handling partial and imperfect data.

Real market data has:

- Dropped packets.
- Sequence gaps and out-of-order messages.
- Occasional feed outages and restarts.

Your capture log should faithfully record these artefacts. A strategy that is robust in replay must deal with them, for example by:

- Detecting when order book state is unreliable and reducing exposure.
- Falling back to alternative feeds or conservative estimates when data is missing.

Reconstructing order book state.

If you record only top-of-book quotes, your ability to backtest depth-sensitive strategies is limited. If you record all book updates, you can reconstruct the full order book over time.

Even then, reconstruction must respect the exact semantics of the venue's feed:

- Apply sequence numbers strictly in order.
- Handle trade and cancel messages correctly.
- Deal with partial resets or truncations provided by the feed.

Backtesting engines should use the *same book-building logic* as production, ideally as a shared library, to avoid inconsistencies.

Mirroring fills, latencies, and throttling.

One of the biggest differences between simplistic and realistic backtests is latency and execution modelling.

With recorded streams, you can:

- Use the actual timestamps between your order submissions and exchange acknowledgments/fills in the captured log.
- Replicate venue-specific throttling rules, such as maximum messages per second or cancel-to-trade ratios, by replaying the system's historical interactions.
- Observe how your system behaved under bursty conditions, such as news events and auction openings, and test whether new strategies would aggravate or alleviate existing bottlenecks.

In a more advanced setup, you can also simulate the effect of new strategy orders on other strategies in the same system, using replay to coordinate multiple strategies' decisions over the same event stream.

Governance, Privacy, and Access to Recorded Streams

Event logs used for record/replay and backtesting contain sensitive information:

- Client identities and order details.
- Proprietary strategy behaviour.
- Potentially personally identifiable information in order annotations or user actions.

You need governance practices that balance usefulness and control.

Retention and deletion.

As with any historical trading data:

- Align retention with regulatory requirements for order and trade records.
- Consider shorter retention for highly sensitive or high-volume telemetry that is not required for compliance or research.
- Define clear deletion procedures for data that must not be retained indefinitely, documenting how that interacts with the integrity of replay and backtesting.

Privacy and minimization.

Avoid storing more personal or client-identifying data than necessary for your analytical goals. Techniques include:

- Pseudonymizing client IDs in derived research streams.
- Separating personally identifiable data from trading events, with strong access control on the former.
- Providing quants with curated, de-identified subsets of event logs for most work, reserving the full logs for restricted debugging uses.

Discoverability without chaos.

A well-designed catalog and access layer can:

- Expose which streams exist, their schemas, and time coverage.
- Allow authorized users to request extracts or controlled replay sessions.
- Prevent ad-hoc scraping of production logs that might overload infrastructure or violate policy.

Putting It All Together

Designing deterministic event capture and replay pipelines is not a side project; it is a natural extension of building an event-driven trading system in the first place.

When done well, you gain:

- **Forensic power**: the ability to replay incidents and see exactly what the system saw and did.
- **Testing realism**: backtests and what-if analyses that reflect the messiness of real markets, not just clean textbook data.
- **Faster iteration**: a common framework for quants and engineers to evaluate changes against real historical flows before risking live capital.

In the following sections, we will build on this foundation. Property-based and chaos testing will use the same replay infrastructure to generate stressful scenarios. Observability and SLOs will guide which events and decisions must be captured with the highest fidelity. Security and governance will ensure that the powerful record/replay capabilities are used safely and compliantly.

7.2 Property-Based, Chaos, and Resilience Testing

In the previous section we treated the event stream as a first-class artifact and built the machinery to record and replay it. That gave us the ability to *observe* what really happened and to *reproduce* it on demand.

In this section we turn that capability into an offensive weapon: instead of passively waiting for rare edge cases and failures to appear in production, we will *actively search for them.* We do this along two complementary axes:

- **Property-based testing**: systematically generating many different event sequences to see whether core financial and systems invariants ever break.
- **Chaos and resilience testing**: deliberately introducing failures in infrastructure and dependencies to ensure the system behaves acceptably under stress.

The common theme is that individual example-based tests—"send this order and expect that response"—are not enough in a trading environment. Markets are combinatorially complex: order types, instruments, time-of-day effects, latency patterns, venue behaviour, and human actions combine in ways you will not anticipate. Property-based and chaos testing are about exploring this vast space more thoroughly, using automation and your replay infrastructure.

From Example-Based to Property-Based Thinking

Most teams start with example-based tests. For instance:

- "If I submit a buy order above the best ask, I should receive an immediate fill."
- "If I submit an order that exceeds the client's position limit, the risk engine should reject it."

These tests are useful but brittle. They check exactly what you think of, under exactly the conditions you choose. They rarely explore boundary conditions you did not imagine, such as:

- Two orders arriving close together that jointly exceed a limit.
- Market data glitches that briefly invert the spread.
- Pathological sequences of cancels and replaces for the same order.

Property-based testing starts from a different question:

> Instead of asking "does the system behave correctly on this one example?", ask "what *properties* must always hold, no matter what valid input sequence it receives?"

Then you let a test framework generate many random or semi-random event sequences, trying to violate those properties. When a property fails, you have found a revealing corner case, often one you would never have written by hand.

Defining Invariants in a Trading Context

A *property* is a statement that should always be true if the system is behaving correctly. Many properties in trading and risk are natural to state because they capture basic financial common sense.

Some examples:

No negative balances.

For any account or client:

- The cash balance should never go below the allowed overdraft (often zero for trading accounts).
- If fees and commissions are applied, they should be consistently accounted for in how balances move.

A property-based test can generate sequences of deposits, withdrawals, trades, and fee applications and check that at no point does the system produce an impossible negative balance.

Position limits never exceeded.

Each client, desk, or strategy typically has position limits per instrument or asset class. A property:

> For every instrument and every account, the absolute position never exceeds the configured limit.

A generator can create random orders (buys, sells, cancels, partial fills) under various market conditions, and the test checks that limits are never breached. This has particular value around edge cases like:

- Rapid sequences of orders and cancels.
- Partial fills that arrive after a cancellation.
- Multiple services updating the same position independently.

P&L conservation under fee-free transformations.

You can specify transformations that, in theory, should leave P&L unchanged, such as:

- Splitting a single order into two consecutive orders with the same total size and price.
- Rebalancing between two instruments that perfectly track each other in a synthetic setup.

If your system shows different P&L for these equivalent scenarios, you may have a rounding, pricing, or booking bug.

Monotone sequence numbers and time ordering.

Event-driven systems often rely on sequence numbers or timestamps to reconstruct order. Properties include:

- For a given feed and key (such as symbol), sequence numbers are strictly increasing.

- For a given order ID, the system never observes a cancel *before* the corresponding new order.

A generator can produce scrambled or stressed sequences to ensure your logic robustly enforces these expectations.

Designing Generators for Event Sequences

Once you have properties, the next step is to generate test cases: sequences of events that resemble real usage but intentionally cover varied and extreme conditions.

In the context of trading, an event sequence might include:

- Market data updates: quotes, trades, order book changes.
- Order-related events: new orders, modifies, cancels, system rejections.
- External state changes: risk limit updates, connectivity drops, reference data updates.

Balancing realism and exploration.

If generated sequences are totally unrealistic (for example, prices randomly jumping between nonsensical values from one tick to the next), they will not teach you much about real behaviour. On the other hand, if they are *too* constrained, they may never explore interesting edge cases.

Useful generators often:

- Start from real distributions observed in your recorded event logs: typical price ranges, order sizes, inter-arrival times.
- Add controlled "stress knobs" that exaggerate certain phenomena, such as bursts of orders or fast price swings.
- Occasionally violate common patterns to simulate rare events like massive gaps or feed resets.

Composing simple generators.

You can think in terms of building blocks:

- A generator for a single limit order.
- A generator for a "session", such as opening auction, normal trading, closing auction.
- A generator for sequence anomalies, like out-of-order messages or duplicated messages.

By composing these blocks, you can create complex scenarios such as:

> "A normal morning session, followed by a news shock causing a burst of orders on a few symbols, interleaved with a brief exchange outage and recovery."

Integrating Property-Based Testing with Replay

The record/replay infrastructure from the previous section provides realistic raw material. Property-based testing complements this by pushing the system beyond what history has already shown.

You can combine the two:

- **Replay plus perturbation**: Start from a real day's event stream and inject additional synthetic orders, delays, or small data discrepancies generated by the property-based framework.
- **Sampled substreams**: Use replay to select representative segments (for example, a volatile 10-minute window) and then let generators vary only certain aspects within that window, such as client order behaviour.

This hybrid approach ensures that:

- The shape and concurrency of market data remain realistic (because they come from real logs).

- The system is still exposed to a wide variety of order flows and risk challenges beyond what actually happened historically.

Importantly, these tests run against the same services that process live traffic, using the same serialization formats, message buses, and risk engines. This reduces the "simulation gap" between test and production.

Interpreting Failures and Shrinking Test Cases

When a property-based test finds a failing case, the initial failing sequence may be long and complicated. Most frameworks support *shrinking*:

> Automatically simplifying the failing input sequence to a smaller, more understandable version that still fails.

This is crucial operationally:

- Engineers can more easily reason about a minimal sequence that breaks an invariant.
- The minimal sequence can be turned into a stable regression test for future runs.

In a trading system, a shrunk failing case might be:

- Just two or three orders and a particular pattern of partial fills that produce a negative balance.
- A small sequence of out-of-order market data messages that cause the book builder to misprice the best bid.

These minimal examples often reveal subtle coupling or assumptions between components that were not evident in higher-level design diagrams.

Chaos Testing: Intentionally Breaking the Infrastructure

Property-based testing attacks the *functional logic* of your system. Chaos and resilience testing attack its *operational environment*.

The premise of chaos testing is simple:

> Production systems will suffer network glitches, hardware failures, slow dependencies, and misconfigurations. You can discover how your system behaves under these conditions by *creating* them intentionally in a controlled way, rather than waiting for chance.

Typical Chaos Experiments in Trading Systems

Because trading is time-sensitive and highly regulated, you must be careful. But even with strict safety requirements, a wide range of experiments is possible, especially in non-production environments or in production during quiet periods with very tight control.

Common experiment types include:

Killing services.

Randomly or selectively terminating services such as:

- A single instance of a stateless gateway.
- One replica of a risk engine.
- A cache layer supplying reference data.

You then observe:

- Whether automatic failover occurs as expected.
- Whether traffic is rebalanced gracefully without violating SLOs.
- Whether stateful components recover cleanly when they restart.

Injecting latency and packet loss.

Introducing delays or drops on network paths, for example:

- Between strategy engines and market data feeds.
- Between order management systems and venues.
- Between the trading system and clearing or back-office services.

You monitor:

- How end-to-end order latency and rejection rates change.
- Whether circuit breakers trip correctly when latency becomes unsafe.
- Whether retry logic behaves sensibly or amplifies load.

Degrading external dependencies.

Many trading systems depend on external services, such as:

- Reference data providers.
- Historical data stores.
- Authentication and authorization services.

Chaos experiments can:

- Partially degrade these services (slower responses, higher error rate).
- Take them fully offline for a defined period.

The goal is to confirm that the trading system:

- Fails *closed* where required (for example, if risk data is unavailable).
- Falls back to safe defaults when possible (for example, using cached reference data).
- Surfaces clear, bounded alerts for operators.

Market-specific failure modes.

Some failure modes are unique to trading:

- An exchange goes offline while others remain open.
- A feed starts publishing crossed or locked markets (bid above ask or equal to ask).
- Two feeds for the same venue diverge temporarily.

Chaos testing can simulate these by:

- Mutating market data streams in replay environment.
- Rolling out feed simulators that produce deliberately inconsistent or broken data.

You then verify that your systems:

- Detect anomalies quickly.
- Adjust routing and quoting behaviour appropriately.
- Avoid sending obviously erroneous orders.

Running Chaos Experiments Safely

Chaos testing and trading systems mix uneasily if not planned with care. There are several safety principles you should follow.

Start in non-production environments.

Initial experiments should run against staging or replay-based test clusters that:

- Receive realistic traffic via replay from recorded streams.
- Exercise the same services and infrastructure components as production, whenever possible.

This allows you to tune fault injection tools and verify your assumptions about system behaviour before considering any production experiments.

Scope and schedule production experiments carefully.

If and when you run chaos tests in production:

- Limit them to low-risk periods (for example, outside main market hours, or during lower-liquidity windows) unless you are extremely confident.
- Define clear blast radius constraints: which components can be affected and how you will ensure client safety.
- Run with human oversight: designate an experiment conductor and an incident commander, even if you expect everything to go smoothly.

Use guardrails and kill switches.

Every chaos tool should include:

- A quick, obvious way to stop the experiment and restore normal behaviour.
- Built-in constraints (for example, never take down more than one instance of a given gateway at once).
- Logging and tagging of all injected faults so that incident timelines can distinguish between natural failures and those you induced.

Resilience as a Continuous Practice

Property-based and chaos tests are not one-off projects; they work best as *ongoing practices.*

Standard Failure Scenarios Library

Instead of running ad-hoc experiments, maintain a catalog of scenarios, each with:

- A clear description: "Single venue outage for 5 minutes during active market hours."
- Preconditions: which environments it applies to, required traffic levels.
- Expected behaviour: which protections and failovers should activate, what SLOs should still be met.

This library can include both property-based logical scenarios (for example, "mass cancellation flood from one client") and chaos scenarios (for example, "network partition between region A and B").

Pass/Fail Criteria Tied to Business Impact

Tests should not just ask "did something break?" but "did it break in a way that matters?" For each scenario, define measurable pass/fail criteria, such as:

- "The percentage of orders acknowledged within 5 milliseconds does not fall below X for more than Y seconds."
- "No trades occur at prices that violate configured price collars, even under data anomalies."
- "When reference data is unavailable, new orders from affected symbols are rejected with a clear error within Z milliseconds."

These criteria map technical resilience back to business risk and client experience.

Feedback into Design and Runbooks

Every failure found by property-based or chaos testing should lead to:

- A design or implementation change (to strengthen invariants or resilience mechanisms), *and*
- An improvement to operational documentation, such as:

- Runbooks describing how to detect and handle similar failures in production.

- Alerting rules and dashboards that highlight the symptoms discovered in testing.

This is how resilience testing and observability reinforce each other: tests reveal which signals matter; observability ensures those signals are visible during real incidents.

Bringing It Together with Record/Replay

Finally, note how tightly this section ties back to record/replay:

- Property-based generators can feed their event sequences through the same gateways and logs as production, increasing realism.
- Chaos tests in non-production can use replayed streams from real days, so that you are not testing resilience only against synthetic steady-state conditions.
- When a chaos experiment or property-based test uncovers a serious issue, you can store the exact failing event sequence and fault pattern in your log, then replay it later as a regression test.

Over time, your library of recorded failure scenarios becomes an asset in its own right, much like your live event streams: a catalog of ways the world can go wrong, and concrete proof that your system can withstand them.

In the next sections we will focus on *seeing* how the system behaves—logging, metrics, tracing, and SLOs—so that both everyday operations and the more adversarial tests described here can be interpreted quickly and accurately.

7.3 Logging, Metrics, Tracing, and SLO Management

In the previous sections we learned how to *replay* what happened and how to *attack* the system with property-based and chaos tests. Both of those practices depend on one more ingredient: the ability to *see* the system clearly while it runs.

That is the role of observability. In a low-latency trading system, observability is not just a convenience for developers. It is how you answer questions that matter to users and regulators, such as:

- Are orders being acknowledged and filled within acceptable time bounds?
- Are risk checks and limits being applied consistently?
- When something goes wrong, can we reconstruct who did what, and why?

This section describes how to build an observability stack that ties together:

- **Logging**: detailed records of what happened.
- **Metrics**: aggregated measurements of system and trading health.
- **Tracing**: end-to-end views of how a single request flows through services.
- **SLOs (Service Level Objectives)**: explicit reliability targets expressed in the language of users and regulators.

The goal is coherence: these pieces should fit together so that a question that starts from any angle—a client complaint, a strange metric, a regulator's query—can be followed through to a precise technical explanation.

Two Perspectives: Users and Regulators

Before diving into tooling, clarify whose questions you are trying to answer. In trading, two perspectives dominate.

User perspective.

Traders, quants, and clients care about symptoms they can see:

- How fast do my orders get acknowledgments and fills?
- How often are my orders rejected, and for what reasons?
- Do I ever see missing or duplicated fills?
- Does the system behave differently during busy markets?

User-focused observability emphasizes:

- End-to-end latency measurements.
- Success and failure rates for business actions.
- Availability of key workflows such as order entry, cancel/replace, and position queries.

Regulator and risk perspective.

Regulators and internal risk teams ask:

- Can you show a complete audit trail of orders and trades?
- Were risk checks applied as required by policy and law?
- Did your system ever trade through limits or price collars?
- If a client complains about an execution, can you reconstruct the sequence of events?

For them, observability means:

- Immutable logs of business events with clear identities and timestamps.
- Traceable decisions: who changed which configuration, and when.
- Evidence that controls (like kill switches and circuit breakers) operated correctly.

A coherent observability design serves both sets of questions without duplicating everything twice.

Logging: Recording What Happened

Logs are the most flexible observability tool. They can store rich, structured details about individual events. However, without discipline they become noisy and expensive.

Business vs. Technical Events

It is useful to distinguish:

Business events.

These represent meaningful steps in the trading process, such as:

- *OrderAccepted*: a new order from a client is validated and accepted.
- *OrderRejected*: an order is rejected, including the reason (risk, validation, venue error).
- *OrderRouted*: an order is sent to a specific venue or internal pool.
- *FillReceived*: a partial or full fill is received from a venue.
- *RiskCheckPerformed*: a risk module evaluated a proposed trade and allowed or blocked it.

For regulators and business users, these events are primary. They form the audit trail.

Technical events.

These track the health and behaviour of the system itself:

- Timeouts and retries when calling external services.
- Queue length warnings.
- Garbage collection pauses, CPU throttling, or memory pressure.
- Configuration reloads and deployment events.

These are more relevant for engineers and operations staff, but they often explain the root cause of business symptoms.

Log Schema and Correlation

To make logs useful for incident analysis and regulatory questions, you need consistent structure.

Important principles:

Use structured logs.

Rather than free-form text, logs should be structured records with named fields, such as:

- Timestamps (ideally in a consistent, unambiguous format).
- Event type (for example, OrderAccepted, RiskCheckFailed).
- Identifiers: order ID, client ID, strategy ID, correlation ID.
- Relevant attributes: symbol, side, quantity, price, reason codes.

Structured logs are easier to query and aggregate. They also survive schema evolution better if you plan field changes.

Correlation IDs and causality.

In an event-driven system, a single business action may trigger several services and queues. To trace it:

- Assign each incoming client order a global *correlation ID*.
- Propagate that ID through messages, logs, and traces as the order flows.
- When a service emits an event derived from earlier events, it should carry both its own event ID and a reference to the upstream correlation ID.

This makes it much easier to answer questions like, "What happened to order X after it entered the system?" by querying all logs with that correlation ID.

Log Levels, Sampling, and Data Protection

Logging everything at maximum verbosity can overwhelm storage and hinder performance. You need a strategy.

Log levels.

Common levels include:

- **Error**: something went wrong and needs attention.
- **Warning**: unusual condition worth tracking, but not necessarily a failure.
- **Info**: normal business events, such as order lifecycle steps.
- **Debug/Trace**: detailed internal information mainly for development.

In production, you typically:

- Always record key business events at info or higher.
- Record technical details at debug only when necessary, perhaps toggled via feature flags or dynamic configuration.
- Ensure that error logs are rare and actionable; if something noisy but benign is logged at error, downgrade it.

Sampling strategies.

For very high-volume flows (tick-level market data, internal heartbeats), logging every event may be unnecessary. Techniques include:

- Log summaries over time windows: "received 100,000 ticks for symbol X in the last second, max spread Y".
- Sample a fraction of events (for example, 1 in 1,000) for diagnostic visibility.
- Log full detail only when anomalies or thresholds are detected.

Redaction and privacy.

Logs often contain sensitive information. To manage this:

- Redact or hash fields that identify individuals if not strictly necessary for analysis.

- Separate highly sensitive data (like personal information) into restricted logs with tighter access controls.
- Ensure that logging does not violate regulatory constraints on data residency or retention.

Metrics: Quantifying Health and Performance

While logs tell individual stories, metrics summarize long-term behaviour. Metrics are numeric time series you can aggregate, visualize, and alert on.

In trading systems, you need metrics for both *technical health* and *trading health*.

Service Health Metrics

These ensure that infrastructure is functioning:

- CPU usage, memory usage, and garbage collection frequency.
- Queue lengths and message processing rates.
- Error and retry counts for calls to dependencies.
- Instance counts and restart rates for services.

These metrics help detect resource exhaustion, leaks, or misconfiguration before they manifest as trading problems.

Trading Health Metrics

These speak the language of traders and regulators:

Latency metrics.

Measure the time between critical events, such as:

- Client order submission to internal acknowledgment.
- Internal acknowledgment to venue acknowledgment.
- Venue acknowledgment to first fill and to final fill.
- Risk check request to risk check decision.

Record not just averages, but distributions:

- Percentiles (p50, p95, p99) to capture tail behaviour.
- Separate metrics for market hours vs. off-hours, and by venue or product.

Reliability metrics.

Track:

- Fraction of orders rejected, broken down by reason (risk, validation, venue error).
- Rate of failed or stale responses from venues.
- Frequency of failover events (for example, switching to a backup venue or feed).

These help spot systemic issues such as overly strict limits, bad configuration, or venue instability.

Throughput and volume metrics.

Measure:

- Orders per second per client, strategy, venue, or symbol group.
- Market data messages per second per feed.
- Aggregate traded volume per time interval.

These metrics inform capacity planning and protect against overload.

Designing Metrics for Scalability

Metrics cardinality—the number of distinct label combinations—is a common pitfall. If you label every metric by order ID or user ID, you will quickly overwhelm your monitoring system.

Good practice includes:

- Using low-cardinality labels (venue, asset class, broad client tier) for high-volume metrics.

- Reserving high-cardinality labels for sparse or sampled metrics, or for logs and traces instead.
- Ensuring naming conventions are consistent across services so that metrics can be aggregated meaningfully.

Tracing: Following a Single Request End-to-End

Logging and metrics are good at telling you "what generally happens." Tracing complements them by showing:

> "For this specific order, exactly which services did it pass through, and where did it spend time?"

In an event-driven trading system, tracing requires special care, because events may be:

- Asynchronous.
- Broadcast to multiple consumers.
- Processed in parallel and out of direct call-stack order.

Propagation of Trace Context

To trace across services:

- Attach a trace ID (and often a span ID) to the incoming request or event.
- Propagate this ID through all downstream events and RPC calls, including messages published on buses or queues.
- When a service handles an event, it creates a new span associated with the existing trace ID, records its start and end time, and associates relevant metadata (like symbol, venue, or action).

This allows a tracing system to reconstruct a timeline such as:

- 0 microseconds: Order received at gateway.

- 50 microseconds: Order decoded and validated.
- 120 microseconds: Risk engine call started.
- 250 microseconds: Risk engine responded with "allow".
- 270 microseconds: Order routed to venue.
- 600 microseconds: Venue acknowledgment received and sent back to client.

Choosing Spans in an Event-Driven System

You cannot trace everything; span creation has overhead. Focus on:

- Major stages in the critical path: decode, validation, risk, routing, venue IO.
- Cross-service boundaries where things often go wrong: calls across data centers or to external venues.
- Slow or stateful operations: interaction with databases, caches, and reference data services.

Traces can then answer questions like:

- "Are we spending more time in risk checks or in venue communication?"
- "Did this specific slow order get stuck in a queue, or did a downstream service stall?"

From Signals to Commitments: SLIs, SLOs, and Error Budgets

Logging, metrics, and tracing generate *signals*. To turn those into actionable commitments, we use three related concepts:

- **SLIs (Service Level Indicators)**: specific, measurable signals that represent quality from the user's point of view.

- **SLOs (Service Level Objectives)**: target ranges for SLIs over a defined time window.
- **Error budgets**: how much deviation from the SLO is acceptable before you must prioritize reliability work.

Defining Trading-Relevant SLIs

Good SLIs are:

- Closely tied to user experience or regulatory expectations.
- Expressed as simple, measurable quantities.

Examples for a trading platform include:

Order acknowledgment latency.

> "Percentage of client orders that receive an acknowledgment (accept or reject) within 5 milliseconds during regular market hours."

This is computed from metrics or traces that measure the time from gateway receipt to reply to the client.

Risk decision latency.

> "Percentage of risk check requests answered within 2 milliseconds under normal load."

This reflects responsiveness of your risk controls and is critical for high-frequency trading.

Fill reporting timeliness.

> "Percentage of fills that are reported back to the client within 10 milliseconds of venue acknowledgment."

Clients care about timely updates to their positions and P&L.

Regulatory completeness.

> “Percentage of orders and trades for which a complete audit trail (including risk decisions and configuration versions) is available within 24 hours.”

This captures your ability to satisfy regulator and internal review requests.

Setting SLOs and Error Budgets

An SLO is a target for an SLI over a period, such as:

> “99.9% of orders must be acknowledged within 5 milliseconds over a 30-day rolling window.”

The *error budget* is the complement:

- Over that 30-day window, up to 0.1% of orders may exceed 5 milliseconds before you consider the SLO violated.

Error budgets are useful because:

- They acknowledge that perfection is impossible in complex systems; occasional slow orders will occur.
- They provide a quantitative way to trade off feature development versus reliability improvements.

For example:

- If you are well within your error budget, you may accept a slightly risky deployment to ship a valuable feature.
- If you have burned through your budget early in the period, you pause risky changes and prioritize stability work.

Visualizing SLOs: A Concrete Dashboard

To make SLIs, SLOs, and error budgets tangible, teams often build dashboards that show:

- Latency percentiles over time, with SLO thresholds.
- Error rates for key operations.
- Cumulative error budget consumption.

A simple example for a critical order path might look like the following.

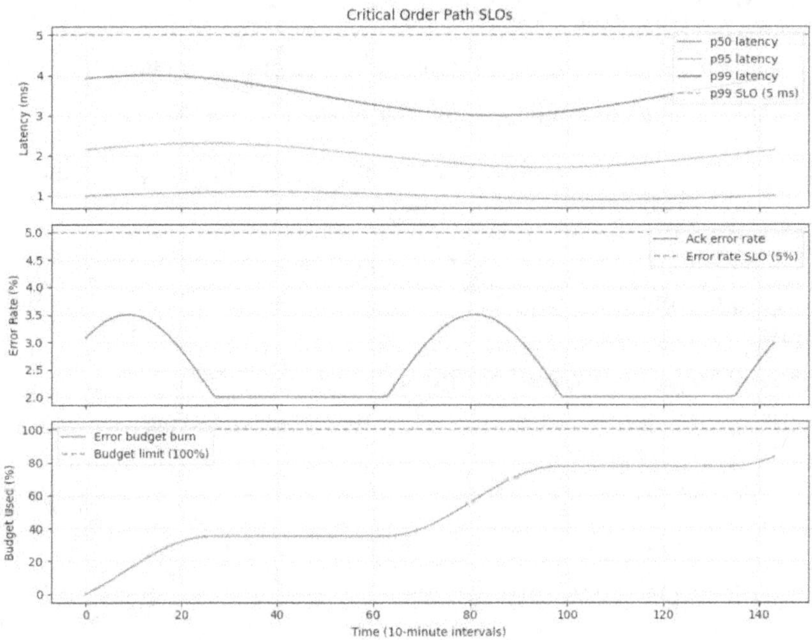

A dashboard like this lets an on-call engineer quickly answer:

- "Are we currently within our latency and error SLOs?"
- "Is the system degrading gradually or experiencing sharp spikes?"
- "How much error budget have we consumed, and how risky is it to make changes right now?"

Operationalizing Observability

Building the observability stack is not enough; you must integrate it into day-to-day operations.

Key practices include:

Dashboards that answer first questions.

When something looks wrong, the on-call engineer's first questions are usually:

- Is the problem localized to one venue, symbol, or client?
- Is it a spike in latency, an increase in errors, or both?
- Did any recent deployments or configuration changes coincide with the issue?

Dashboards should be designed to answer these quickly: obvious panels for per-venue latency, error rates by reason, and recent change events.

Consistent naming and tagging.

Metrics, logs, and traces should use consistent names for:

- Services and components.
- Venues, asset classes, and regions.
- Client tiers or strategy groups.

This consistency makes it much easier to build queries and alerts that span multiple systems.

Guardrails against telemetry overload.

More data is not always better. Observability can harm the system if:

- Logging volume saturates disks or networks.
- Metric cardinality overwhelms your monitoring backend.
- Tracing overhead slows down critical paths.

To prevent this:

- Regularly review telemetry cost and usefulness.
- Prune unused metrics and log fields.
- Use sampling, aggregation, and adaptive logging where appropriate.

Connecting Observability to Testing and Operations

Observability is not an island. It connects directly to the practices from earlier in the chapter:

- **Record/replay**: logs and traces inform what gets captured, and replay sessions often depend on being able to reconstruct events and their timings from logs and metrics.
- **Property-based and chaos testing**: SLIs and SLOs provide concrete pass/fail criteria for tests. Chaos experiments should be evaluated by their effect on user-visible metrics, not just internal status.
- **Incident response**: as we will see in the next section, alerts, runbooks, and postmortems all rely heavily on high-quality observability to make sense of what happened and to improve over time.

A coherent observability stack, grounded in clear SLOs, thus becomes the nervous system of the trading platform. It continuously tells you how the system is behaving from the outside, supports rapid diagnosis from the inside, and provides the evidence that regulators and risk managers require.

7.4 Alerting, Runbooks, and Incident Response

In the previous sections we built the raw capabilities for understanding the system: record/replay pipelines, adversarial testing, and an observability stack of logs, metrics, traces, and SLOs. Those capabilities are only fully valuable when they shape how you *operate* the system during trouble.

This section is about that operational layer. We will connect three ideas:

- **Alerting**: turning telemetry and SLOs into notifications that are specific, reliable, and rare enough that humans can act on them.
- **Runbooks**: pre-thought checklists and decision trees that tell people *what to do* when an alert fires.
- **Incident response and postmortems**: the process for managing real outages, learning from them, and improving both the system and the team.

The goal is simple: when your trading system misbehaves, everyone knows *who* will respond, *what* they will look at first, and *how* they will decide what to do, with minimal improvisation and panic.

From Observability to Alerting

Observability gives you many signals. If you turn all of them into alerts, you will drown your on-call staff, who will learn to ignore alarms. If you turn too few into alerts, you will miss early signs of serious problems.

Alerting is the art of selecting:

- *Which signals* should wake people up.
- *What thresholds and conditions* indicate real trouble.
- *Who* should be notified and how urgently.

Symptom-Driven Alerts

A foundational principle is to alert on *symptoms* visible to users rather than on every low-level anomaly.

For a trading platform, symptom alerts include:

- Order acknowledgment latency above a certain percentile threshold.
- Elevated order reject rates, especially for "internal error" reasons.
- Missing or delayed fills for a non-trivial fraction of orders.
- Inability to connect to a venue or a dramatic increase in venue-side errors.

In contrast, you typically do *not* want paging alerts for:

- A single host's CPU briefly peaking.
- One retry to a reference data service that quickly succeeds.
- Temporary blips in non-critical background jobs.

These may appear as warnings on dashboards and in logs, but only become alerts if they aggregate into user-visible degradation.

Using SLOs to Shape Alerting

The SLOs defined in the previous section give you a vocabulary for alerting. For each critical SLO, define one or more alerts such as:

- "If the 5-minute rolling p99 latency for order acknowledgments exceeds the 5 ms SLO threshold for more than 2 consecutive windows, raise a high-severity alert."
- "If the 30-minute error rate for order acknowledgments exceeds half of the allowed SLO error budget, raise a medium-severity alert."

This offers key benefits:

- Alerts are tied to user-visible impact, not arbitrary internal metrics.
- Alert thresholds are anchored in agreed business objectives, not guessed per service.
- Error budgets give you a way to gauge urgency: burning budget quickly is a strong signal that something needs immediate attention.

Reducing Noise: Correlation and Time Windows

Too many alerts create fatigue. Some techniques to keep noise down:

Multi-signal correlation.

Instead of alerting separately on every metric, combine related symptoms:

- Raise a single "Order Path Degradation" alert when you simultaneously see high latency *and* elevated error rates, or a strong drop in successful throughput.
- Attach the relevant metrics and traces to the alert so the on-call does not have to hunt for them.

Time-windowed detection.

Transient spikes happen. You can avoid alerting on noise by:

- Evaluating conditions over rolling windows (for example, 5 or 10 minutes).
- Requiring the condition to hold for a sustained period before notifying humans.

Context-aware routing.

Not everyone needs to be paged for everything:

- Venue-specific issues may page the connectivity/onboarding team and notify others via lower-urgency channels.

- Internal risk engine problems may page risk-platform engineers and inform trading desks with a status message.

Routing and severity should reflect both the technical importance and business impact of the signal.

Market Hours vs. Off-Hours

Trading systems live in a world with sharp time boundaries:

- During market hours, even minor degradations may be critical.
- Outside market hours, you can often accept slightly higher latency or partial unavailability for non-critical flows (for example, batch reporting).

Your alerting rules should account for this by:

- Tightening thresholds and paging more aggressively during active trading sessions.
- Relaxing certain alerts or changing them to notification-only outside those windows.

This respects both business priority and the sleep of your on-call team.

Runbooks: Making the First 15 Minutes Boring

If alerting answers "*when* should we react?" then runbooks answer "*what do we do next?*"

A good runbook aims to make the first 10–15 minutes of an incident almost routine. Instead of ad-hoc improvisation, responders follow a prepared plan that covers:

- Initial triage steps.
- Key dashboards and logs to inspect.
- Safe actions they can take without prior approval.

- Clear criteria for escalation and next steps.

Anatomy of a Good Runbook

Each runbook should be:

- **Specific:** Tied to a particular alert or symptom, e.g., "Order Acknowledgment Latency SLO Breach" or "Venue X Connectivity Loss."
- **Concise:** Readable and usable under stress; more like a checklist than a novel.
- **Linked:** Integrated with tools: from the alert, you can click directly into the relevant runbook and associated dashboards.

Common sections include:

Overview.

A short description of what the alert means in plain language, for example:

> "The system is taking too long to acknowledge client orders. Clients may perceive us as frozen or slow. Some orders may be missing trading opportunities."

Immediate checks.

A short checklist of quick observations, such as:

- Check the main order-path dashboard for latency, error rate, and throughput by venue.
- Verify whether the issue is localized to certain symbols, venues, or clients.
- Confirm whether any recent deployments or configuration changes occurred in the last 30 minutes.

Safe actions.

Actions that a responder can take without further approval, for example:

- Scale out a stateless service up to a known safe maximum.
- Shift traffic from a degraded venue to a backup, if that is an agreed policy.
- Apply a known, reversible configuration change that has been rehearsed.

Each action should include:

- The exact mechanism (for example, "use the deployment tool to select profile Y").
- Expected impact.
- Signals to watch for improvement or regression.

Escalation criteria.

Clear rules for when to call in more help or make bigger decisions, such as:

- "If p99 latency remains above threshold for more than 15 minutes after scaling, page the on-call for the risk engine and network teams."
- "If more than X% of orders are timing out at venue Y, consider invoking the venue kill-switch as described below."

Rollback or mitigation paths.

If recent changes are suspected, the runbook should:

- Describe how to roll back to a known-good version.
- Outline trade-offs of rollbacks (for example, losing a bugfix vs. restoring performance).

Examples of Trading-Specific Runbooks

Venue connectivity degradation.

A runbook for this scenario might cover:

- How to distinguish between your own connectivity issue and a venue-wide outage (for example, by checking alternative connections, venue status feeds, or peer reports).
- When to automatically or manually reroute orders to alternative venues or internal pools.
- When to temporarily halt trading in certain instruments to avoid unintended risk.

Backlog in internal queues.

Here, the runbook might instruct:

- Which queues to inspect first and how to estimate backlog clearance times.
- How to differentiate between CPU starvation, slow downstream services, and unexpected event bursts.
- Steps to apply rate limits or temporarily degrade non-critical features to keep the core order path healthy.

Misbehaving strategy.

A runbook aimed at strategy anomalies would describe:

- How to identify runaway or abnormal behaviour from metrics (for example, a sudden surge in order rate from one strategy).
- Procedures for throttling or disabling that strategy without impacting others, using feature flags, routing rules, or kill-switches.
- Communication steps with the strategy owner and risk team.

Keeping Runbooks Alive

Runbooks must evolve:

- Review and update them after each relevant incident or major deployment.

- Prune outdated steps and tools that no longer exist.
- Rehearse critical runbooks during game days or drills so that responders are familiar with them.

A stale, untested runbook is dangerous; it creates false confidence.

Incident Response: Managing the Real Thing

Even with good alerting and runbooks, serious incidents will occur. An *incident* is any situation where:

- Clients or internal users cannot rely on the system's normal behaviour, *and/or*
- There is a significant risk of regulatory or financial impact if the issue is not handled promptly.

Incident response is the process you follow from the moment you recognize such a situation until the system is stable and you understand what happened.

Declaring an Incident

The first step is to explicitly *declare* an incident. This may sound bureaucratic, but it has benefits:

- It clarifies that we are no longer in "normal operations" mode.
- It triggers standard practices: role assignments, communication channels, and tracking.

A typical declaration includes:

- A concise description of the problem as known so far.
- A preliminary severity level based on impact (for example, "high" if live trading is affected).
- The initial incident commander (IC), usually the first qualified responder on scene.

Roles and Responsibilities

Clear roles reduce confusion:

Incident Commander (IC).

The IC:

- Owns coordination and decision-making.
- Does *not* dive deep into debugging; instead, they track hypotheses, assign tasks, and keep the big picture.
- Decides when to escalate, roll back, or declare the incident over.

Subject-Matter Experts (SMEs).

These are engineers or operators with deep knowledge of particular components: order gateways, risk engines, networks, databases, and so on. They:

- Investigate specific areas, guided by the IC.
- Perform safe diagnostic steps and propose remediation actions.

Communications Lead.

Especially for larger incidents, one person should handle communication to:

- Internal stakeholders (trading desks, risk, management).
- External stakeholders if needed (clients, venues, regulators, following firm policies).

Centralizing communication avoids chaotic, conflicting messages.

Balancing Speed and Forensic Evidence

In trading, there is constant tension between:

- *Restoring service quickly* to minimize market and client impact.

- *Preserving evidence* needed for later investigation and regulatory reporting.

Some practices that help balance these aims:

Prefer reversible actions.

Whenever possible, take steps that can be safely undone:

- Scaling out or shifting load, rather than hard-restarting everything at once.
- Flipping feature flags, rather than deploying new binaries mid-incident.

Capture state before destructive changes.

If you must restart or reset components:

- Capture relevant logs, traces, and queue snapshots first.
- Note exact times of actions so they can be correlated with telemetry later.

Your record/replay infrastructure can help here; if critical events are flowing through append-only logs, you retain a base level of evidence even while restarting services.

Log the timeline.

During the incident, maintain a simple timeline:

- When was the incident declared?
- What assumptions or hypotheses were tested, and what did they show?
- What actions were taken (scale, reroute, rollback), and when?

This need not be perfect in real time, but even a rough log reduces confusion and greatly simplifies the later postmortem.

Postmortems: Turning Incidents into Improvements

Once the immediate crisis has passed and the system is stable, you face an important question:

> "How do we ensure that this incident *improves* our system and our practice, rather than being forgotten until it happens again?"

The main answer is a structured **postmortem**.

Blameless, but Not Toothless

A useful postmortem is:

- **Blameless:** It focuses on *what* happened and *why*, not on blaming individuals for making mistakes. In complex systems, errors are usually symptoms of deeper issues in process, tooling, or expectations.
- **Concrete:** It results in actionable items that change behaviour, architecture, or process.

Blamelessness does not mean ignoring responsibility; it means:

- Asking why the system made it easy to make a problematic change or miss a warning sign.
- Improving training, runbooks, tooling, or automation so that similar mistakes are less likely and less damaging.

Reconstructing the Incident

Using logs, metrics, traces, and the ad-hoc timeline from the incident, reconstruct:

- The exact sequence of key events, including market context if relevant.

- How symptoms first appeared (what users saw, which alerts fired).
- All major decisions and actions taken during response.

This reconstruction often reveals:

- Gaps between what on-call engineers *believed* was happening and what was actually happening.
- Missed early warning signs.
- Points where runbooks, dashboards, or alerts were missing or misleading.

Identifying Contributing Factors

You rarely want to stop at the proximate cause (for example, "a bug in service X caused a crash"). Look for contributing factors such as:

- Design weaknesses (single points of failure, lack of backpressure).
- Operational gaps (missing alerts, overly noisy alerts that were ignored).
- Process issues (inadequate review for risky changes, poor coordination across teams).
- Knowledge or training gaps (on-call staff not familiar with key runbooks or tools).

Each of these can become the focus of an improvement action.

Action Items and Follow-Up

A postmortem should end with a prioritized list of actions, including:

- Technical changes (code, configuration, infrastructure).
- Observability improvements (new or refined metrics, logs, traces, dashboards).

- Runbook and training updates.
- Adjustments to alerting rules or SLO definitions if they proved misaligned with real risk.

Crucially:

- Assign each action to an owner and a target completion date.
- Track progress and hold brief follow-ups to verify that the changes were actually implemented.

Without this rigor, postmortems risk becoming storytelling sessions rather than engines of improvement.

Bringing It All Together

Alerting, runbooks, and incident response form the operational layer of your trading system's reliability story:

- Observability and SLOs tell you *what matters* and *when it is off track.*
- Alerts map those deviations into concrete calls to action.
- Runbooks help responders act quickly and safely, especially under stress.
- Incident response processes coordinate people and decisions during real crises.
- Postmortems close the loop, feeding lessons back into design, tooling, and practice.

These are not separate from the technical foundations of queues, state, and event logs; they are how those foundations play out in the human world of traders, risk managers, and regulators. In the next section we will build on this further, looking at security, compliance, and data governance—ensuring that, even when operating under stress, your system remains not only reliable but also safe and compliant.

7.5 Security, Compliance, and Data Governance

Up to this point in the chapter we have focused on making the system *correct*, *observable*, and *operable* under stress. This section adds another dimension: the system must also be *secure* and *compliant* with regulatory expectations, while still allowing engineers and quants to move at a reasonable pace.

In trading, security and data governance are not optional add-ons. A compromised trading platform can leak positions, expose client identities, or even allow unauthorized trading that moves markets. At the same time, a security regime that blocks every experiment and requires manual approvals for every data access quickly becomes a competitive disadvantage.

Our goal is to embed three ideas into the platform's design:

- **Least privilege**: every user and service has only the permissions it needs, and no more.
- **Strong encryption**: data is protected in transit and at rest in a way that reflects its sensitivity and performance needs.
- **Auditable data practices**: key actions leave a durable, queryable trail that can support internal review and regulatory investigations.

We will approach this in a structured way: start with the threat model, then discuss identity and authorization, then encryption, and finally data governance and auditability, all with an eye on not crippling developer velocity.

Understanding the Threat Model

Security design should begin with a concrete threat model: who might attack the system, what they might want, and where they might come from.

Common threat sources in a trading environment include:

Internal misuse.

- A disgruntled employee with legitimate credentials misusing access.
- Well-intentioned staff accidentally accessing or modifying data they should not.

Compromised credentials and endpoints.

- Phishing or malware compromising trader or administrator accounts.
- Stolen API keys or certificates used to impersonate services.

External attackers.

- Attempted break-ins via your client APIs or web portals.
- Attacks on exposed gateways in colocation facilities.

Data integrity threats.

- Tampering with market or reference data feeds to distort prices or limits.
- Unauthorized changes to risk parameters or configuration that weaken controls.

Data exfiltration.

- Theft of client lists, trading strategies, positions, and historical orders.
- Leakage of personally identifiable information from logs or analytics stores.

With this mental map, we can design controls that address the most serious and realistic risks, rather than adding random security measures that look impressive but do little.

Identity and Least Privilege in an Event-Driven System

Least privilege means that each identity—human or machine—can do only what it legitimately must. In an event-driven architecture this touches:

- Who can produce and consume messages on each topic or queue.
- Who can read and write from order books, risk systems, and analytics stores.
- Who can deploy and configure services.

Service Identities and Mutual Authentication

Every service should have a clear identity. Avoid generic accounts like `trading_service` shared across many components. Instead:

- Assign each service or group of closely related instances its own identity (for example, certificate or token).
- Use mutual TLS (mTLS) between services: both client and server authenticate each other using certificates or strong tokens.
- Terminate TLS only at well-defined trust boundaries; do not rely on "secure" internal networks as sufficient protection.

This way, if one service is compromised, the attacker does not automatically gain the ability to impersonate every other service.

Authorization on Topics and Queues

In an event-driven system, the message bus is a central artery. Access control must be first-class:

- Define access policies per topic or queue: which identities may publish and which may subscribe.
- Separate *data* channels (like market data, order events, fills) from *control* channels (like configuration updates, risk limit changes).

- Treat control channels as particularly sensitive; only a small set of services and human operators should have write access.

For example:

- Strategy engines may subscribe to market data topics and publish to "proposed orders" topics.
- Only the risk engine may consume from "proposed orders" and publish "approved orders" to gateway-bound channels.
- Gateways may only accept from "approved orders" topics; they cannot be tricked into sending orders that bypass risk.

This enforces structural safety: even if a strategy process is compromised, it cannot directly send orders to the exchange without going through risk.

Role-Based Access Control for Humans

Human users—traders, quants, developers, operations staff—also need carefully designed roles.

Typical roles might include:

- **Trader**: can enter, modify, and cancel orders for specific accounts or desks; can view positions and P&L for those accounts.
- **Quant/Researcher**: can access de-identified or limited trading data sets for backtesting; cannot trade live or modify production configuration.
- **Developer**: can deploy to non-production environments, view logs, and run replay; limited or no ability to access production client data or modify risk settings.
- **Operations/Support**: can monitor system health dashboards, run operational runbooks, and execute certain controlled actions (failover, kill switches), often with additional approvals.

Guidelines for roles:

- Design roles around job functions, not individuals, and assign users to roles.
- Grant the minimum set of permissions needed for the role to perform its duties.
- Regularly review role assignments and permissions, especially when people change teams or leave.

Least privilege is not static. Processes must exist to ensure permissions stay appropriate over time.

Strong Encryption with Performance Awareness

Encryption is a basic expectation: data in transit and at rest should be protected against unauthorized reading or tampering. In trading, the challenge is that you often operate under tight latency budgets.

Encryption in Transit

All external connections—to clients, venues, reference data providers—must be encrypted using modern protocols (for example, TLS with current cipher suites). For internal traffic:

- Aim for end-to-end encryption between services, not just perimeter encryption.
- Use mTLS to combine encryption with strong mutual authentication.
- Terminate TLS only at well-secured intermediaries; avoid "plaintext" islands in the middle of your architecture.

Latency concerns often arise, especially around colocation gateways. In most modern environments:

- The overhead of properly tuned TLS is small compared with market microstructure latencies and exchange roundtrips.
- Prematurely dropping encryption on performance grounds is rarely justified; instead, profile and optimize the crypto stack.

If you have a truly extreme low-latency path, you might:

- Keep that path as narrow and constrained as possible.
- Compensate with stronger physical security and isolation.
- Still use integrity checks and authentication even if encryption is relaxed in very specific, tightly controlled links (for example, within a single locked rack).

Encryption at Rest

Data stored in databases, logs, and backups should be encrypted at rest:

- Use storage-level encryption for disks and object stores.
- Add application-level encryption for highly sensitive fields (such as PII or secret strategy parameters), so that even insiders with database access cannot easily read them.

Key management is critical:

- Keys must be stored and managed in dedicated key management systems, not scattered in configuration files or code.
- Keys should be rotated regularly and revoked promptly when compromise is suspected.
- Access to keys must follow least privilege: only services that need to decrypt a given data set should have the corresponding key or key access.

Encryption at rest does not replace access control. It protects against some physical and backup-related threats, but insiders or compromised applications with legitimate decryption capability can still exfiltrate data. You need both.

Data Governance: Knowing What You Have and How It Flows

Security is not only about blocking access; it is also about understanding your data: what it is, where it lives, and who uses it. This is the realm of data governance.

Classifying Data

A trading platform handles many kinds of data, each with different sensitivity and regulatory requirements. A simple classification might include:

Public or low sensitivity.

- Market prices and volumes (once publicly disseminated).
- Aggregate statistics that cannot be tied to clients or strategies.

Client confidential.

- Orders, positions, and P&L per client or account.
- Contact details and onboarding documentation.

Firm confidential.

- Proprietary strategy signals, parameters, and models.
- Internal risk limits and margin models.

Personal data.

- Names, email addresses, and identifiers of staff and clients.
- Any data subject to privacy regulations (for example, certain jurisdictions' data protection laws).

Each class should have:

- Defined storage and transmission rules.

- Retention and deletion policies.
- Access control and auditing expectations.

Data Lineage and Flow

Because the system is event-driven, data travels through many topics and services. You should be able to answer:

- Where does a given piece of data originate? (For example, a client order from a specific gateway.)
- Which services consume it, transform it, and produce derived data?
- Where is it ultimately stored (logs, databases, analytics warehouses)?

Maintaining a data catalog that maps topics, schemas, and consumers helps:

- Understand the impact of a data breach at a particular node.
- Apply consistent retention and access policies.
- Respond to regulatory queries, such as requests to provide or delete specific data.

Retention and Deletion Policies

Trading data is often subject to long regulatory retention requirements (for example, years of order and trade history). At the same time, storing everything forever is expensive and risky.

You need policies that reflect both:

- **Minimum retention**: to comply with laws and internal policies on order records, communications, and audit trails.
- **Maximum retention**: to limit exposure, especially for highly sensitive data like personal information or detailed logs that are not needed long-term.

In practice:

- Core order and trade history is kept for many years, with strong access control and durable storage.
- Detailed debug logs, traces, and raw market data may be kept for shorter periods, then either deleted or aggregated.
- Pseudonymized or aggregated data for research may be retained longer, as it poses less risk.

Retention policies should be implemented as automated processes, not manual clean-ups.

Audit Trails and Lineage for Compliance and Debugging

Regulators, risk managers, and internal compliance all demand one thing in common: a reliable account of who did what, when, and based on which information.

Immutable, Append-Only Logs of Key Decisions

Your event-driven architecture gives you a natural place to anchor audit trails: append-only logs.

For key decision points (orders, risk checks, configuration changes), design events that capture:

- What was requested: order details, parameter change, limit update.
- Who or what requested it: user identity, service identity, client.
- When it happened: high-precision timestamps with clear timezone semantics.
- Why it was allowed or denied: risk evaluation outcome, validation reasons, change ticket references.

These events should be:

- Written to append-only topics or stores that are protected against tampering.
- Versioned, so schema changes do not break older records.
- Indexed or catalogued so they can be queried by investigators and internal teams without guesswork.

Configuration and Code Lineage

Many serious incidents involve configuration or code changes. To support audit and debugging:

- Treat configuration as code: versioned, reviewed, and deployed via controlled pipelines, not hand-edited in production.
- For each order, risk decision, or trade, record (directly or indirectly) the code and configuration versions in effect at the time.
- Log administrative actions such as changing limits, toggling features, or invoking kill-switches, along with the operator identity and justification.

This link between events and versions enables powerful questions:

- "Did this incorrect trade occur before or after we deployed a new pricing model?"
- "Which configuration was used when this order exceeded its expected size?"

Maintaining Developer Velocity

All of the above controls are only sustainable if they do not grind development and research to a halt. Security and governance must be *ergonomic*: easy to do right, hard to do wrong.

Infrastructure as Code and Policy as Code

Rather than manual approvals and ad-hoc permissions:

- Define infrastructure (networks, queues, service identities, role bindings) in version-controlled templates.
- Encode security policies (for example, which role can access which topic) in machine-readable form.
- Use automated checks in your deployment pipelines to enforce policies (for example, rejecting a change that would grant an overly broad permission).

This has several benefits:

- Changes are reviewable and auditable.
- Reproducible environments can be created for testing and replay with the same security posture as production.
- Engineers interact with security via familiar tools (code review, continuous integration), not opaque manual processes.

Safe Data Access Patterns for Research

Quants and researchers need rich data to evaluate strategies. Naively granting them direct access to production databases or full event logs is risky. Better patterns include:

- **Curated research datasets**: regular extracts or replicas of trading data with:

- Sensitive identifiers pseudonymized or removed.
- Only fields necessary for research purposes.
- Enforced lag relative to live trading, if required by policy.

- **Replay sandboxes**: environments where quants can replay historical streams through strategy code without access to raw production credentials or control channels.
- **Self-service interfaces**: internal tools for requesting data extracts or replay sessions under well-defined rules, rather than one-off favors from operations.

The aim is to give researchers powerful capabilities while keeping core production data and controls under strict governance.

Avoiding Security Theater

Security theater refers to measures that look impressive but add little real protection. Examples include:

- Requiring frequent password changes without strengthening authentication mechanisms.
- Multi-step manual approvals for harmless, low-risk changes while leaving high-risk paths inadequately controlled.

To avoid this:

- Regularly revisit your control set in light of the threat model: which controls demonstrably reduce real risk?
- Ask front-line developers and operators where security processes feel painful but not protective; refine accordingly.
- Prefer strong, well-implemented core controls (least privilege, strong auth, dependable audit trails) over a long checklist of superficial requirements.

Security and Governance as Part of Reliability

Security, compliance, and data governance are not separate from reliability; they are part of it:

- A system that can be silently misconfigured or abused is not truly reliable, even if its queues and state machines behave perfectly.
- An audit trail that cannot be trusted or reconstructed undermines both regulatory standing and your ability to learn from incidents.
- Poorly governed data creates operational fragility: no one knows which data is authoritative, or who is allowed to change it.

By embedding least privilege, strong encryption, and auditable data practices into the event-driven fabric of your trading platform, you make security and compliance properties of the system, not add-ons. At the same time, by using automation, policy-as-code, and safe data access patterns, you preserve the flexibility and speed that modern trading requires.

In the final section of this chapter we will turn to deployment, orchestration, and capacity planning, tying together reliability, observability, and security into concrete practices for operating the platform day-to-day and as it grows.

7.6 Deployment, Orchestration, and Capacity Planning

By now we have designed systems that can be replayed, attacked with tests, observed, and operated securely. The final piece is how you *change* and *scale* those systems while markets are open and money is at risk.

In many industries, you can take a system down for a maintenance window and deploy at leisure. In trading, that luxury rarely exists. Releases happen while markets are live, and traffic patterns can change dramatically within seconds after news or at the open and close.

This section focuses on three connected disciplines:

- **Deployment**: how you ship new versions safely.
- **Orchestration**: how you manage many services and instances reliably.
- **Capacity planning**: how you ensure there is enough, but not wildly excessive, infrastructure to handle current and future load.

The theme is automation with guardrails: release and scaling mechanisms should be automatic enough to be trusted, but constrained enough that a mistake does not take down your trading platform during a volatile market.

Deployment Environments: Colocation, Cloud, and Hybrid

Before discussing concrete techniques, it is worth clarifying where your systems run, because this shapes your options.

Colocation Near Exchanges

For low-latency order routing and market making, firms often deploy in colocation (colo) facilities physically close to exchanges or major liquidity venues. Characteristics include:

- Extremely low network latency to one or more venues.
- Limited rack space and strict environmental controls.
- High expectations of physical security and network isolation.

In such environments:

- You may run bare-metal or lightly virtualized hosts optimized for predictable performance.
- Orchestration frameworks may be more constrained or customized.
- Deployment must be conservative: rolling out a broken gateway in colo can immediately harm trading.

Cloud and Data Centers

For strategy logic, risk engines, analytics, and backtesting, cloud or central data centers are increasingly common. They offer:

- Elastic capacity and managed services.
- Rich orchestration and deployment tooling.
- Easier integration with storage and batch compute.

Here, you can be more aggressive with automation and experimentation, as long as you respect connectivity and latency constraints back to colos and venues.

Hybrid Topologies

Most serious trading platforms are hybrid:

- Time-critical gateways and some strategy engines in colo.
- Risk, reference data, and orchestration control in regional data centers or cloud.
- Research and heavy analytics primarily in cloud.

Deployment and capacity planning must therefore take into account:

- Latency and bandwidth between regions.
- Failure domains: a local crash in one colo should not bring down global trading.
- Coordinated but not identical rollouts across environments.

Containerization and Orchestration Fundamentals

To manage many services consistently, you need a standard way to package and run them.

Packaging Services

Instead of installing dependencies directly on hosts, services are typically packaged as containers:

- Each container image includes the service binary, libraries, and runtime environment.
- The image is versioned and stored in a registry.
- Deployment involves pulling the appropriate image to hosts and starting containers with specific configuration.

This approach:

- Promotes consistency across environments (development, testing, production).
- Makes it easier to roll back: you can simply redeploy a previous image.
- Simplifies dependency management and reproducibility, which is important for audits and replay scenarios.

Orchestrators and Scheduling

An orchestration system (for example, a container orchestrator or an internal scheduler) manages:

- How many instances of each service should run.
- Where they should run (which hosts, racks, or regions).
- Health checks and automatic restarts.
- Rolling updates and rollbacks.

For a trading platform, key orchestration considerations include:

Placement constraints.

You often want strict rules around where instances run, such as:

- Certain services must be in specific colos or data centers.
- Instances must be spread across racks or failure domains to avoid correlated failures.
- Some workloads (like heavy analytics) should not share hosts with latency-sensitive gateways.

Health checks.

Health checks must reflect real readiness, not just process liveness. For example:

- A gateway is only "ready" when it has warmed up order books, established venue sessions, and passed basic connectivity tests.
- A risk engine is only "ready" when its state is loaded, its dependency caches are warm, and it has registered with routing services.

Your orchestrator should only send traffic to instances that have passed these checks.

Resource requests and limits.

Declaring how much CPU and memory each service needs helps prevent noisy neighbors and resource starvation. In trading:

- Latency-sensitive services may reserve dedicated cores or avoid shared noisy environments.
- Batch or low-priority services should have stricter limits to avoid interfering with real-time components.

Deployment Strategies for Live Markets

Changing code and configuration while markets are open is risky, but unavoidable. Structured deployment strategies help control that risk.

Rolling Updates

A rolling update replaces instances gradually:

- Take a small subset of instances out of service.
- Update them to the new version and verify health.
- Return them to service before proceeding to the next subset.

Advantages:

- No full outage; capacity remains available during the update.
- If a problem is detected early, you can stop the rollout with only a portion of instances affected.

Caveats for trading:

- Mixed-version clusters must be safe: ensure protocol compatibility and schema stability between old and new versions.
- State migration must be carefully handled so that partial upgrades do not corrupt shared state or order books.

Blue/Green Deployments

For critical components (for example, client gateways, risk engines) you may prefer blue/green deployments:

- Maintain two environments: *blue* (current production) and *green* (new version).
- Deploy the new version to green, warm it up, and run synthetic or replayed traffic through it.
- When ready, switch live traffic from blue to green, often via a routing or load-balancing change.

Benefits:

- Very fast rollback: you can switch back to blue if green misbehaves.
- Clear separation of environments simplifies debugging.

The cost is higher resource usage, since you must run both environments simultaneously, and careful management of data and state consistency between them.

Canary Releases

Canary releases introduce the new version to a small portion of traffic first:

- Start with, say, 1% of traffic routed to the new version.
- Monitor key SLOs (latency, error rates, trading outcomes).

- Gradually increase the share if metrics are acceptable; roll back if not.

In trading, "small portion of traffic" can be defined in various ways:

- A subset of symbols or asset classes.
- A specific venue or region.
- Internal-only users or paper-trading accounts.

Canaries are especially valuable for changes that affect complex behaviours, such as strategy logic or routing algorithms.

Configuration-First, Code-Second

Because changing binaries is riskier than changing configuration, many teams adopt:

- **Feature flags**: enable or disable features at runtime via configuration flags instead of code changes.
- **Parameterization**: expose limits, timeouts, and thresholds as config, not hard-coded values.

Deployment can then be separated into:

- Shipping code that supports new behaviour (but disabled by default).
- Gradually enabling that behaviour via configuration after the code has proven stable.

This lends itself well to safe experimentation and quick rollback: turning a flag off is usually safer and faster than rolling back a whole deployment.

Change Control During Trading Hours

Not all changes are equal, and not all times are equal. A disciplined change-management practice recognizes this.

Change Windows and Risk Levels

Define:

- **High-risk windows**: market open and close, major known news events, expiry days. Avoid non-essential changes here.
- **Lower-risk windows**: quieter periods within trading hours, or times when specific markets are closed.

Similarly, classify changes by risk:

- **High-risk changes**: core order-path code, risk logic, venue-specific adapters.
- **Medium-risk changes**: observability tooling, non-critical services with indirect impact.
- **Low-risk changes**: purely internal analytics, documentation, non-production environments.

Combine these to decide:

- Which changes may be deployed during which windows.
- What approval or additional testing is required before a change goes live.

Automated Pre-Deployment Checks

Before allowing a deployment to progress, automation can confirm:

- Tests have passed, including property-based and replay-based test suites where appropriate.
- Security and policy checks (for example, configuration diffs) are acceptable.

- The change has been reviewed by the relevant owners (risk, connectivity, etc.).

In more advanced setups, you can run:

- **Shadow traffic**: route a copy of production events to the new version in parallel, without affecting real outcomes, and compare results.
- **Smoke tests**: minimal end-to-end tests against critical paths immediately after deployment to catch glaring issues.

Capacity Planning: Staying Ahead of the Market

Capacity planning is the discipline of ensuring that your system has enough resources to handle traffic, with a safety margin, without over-provisioning so aggressively that you waste money and complexity.

Understanding Load Drivers

In trading, load is driven by multiple factors:

- **Market data volume**: number of price updates per second, which spikes during news and at the open and close.
- **Order flow**: number of new orders, cancels, and replaces from clients and strategies, which can be bursty.
- **Strategy complexity**: how much computation is required per event (for example, simple routing vs. complex optimization).
- **Risk checks and reference lookups**: frequency and complexity of calls to these systems.

Historical metrics are invaluable:

- Use past busy days to estimate typical and extreme loads.
- Identify which parts of the system saturate first: gateways, risk engines, databases, or networks.

Headroom Targets

Headroom is the buffer between current load and maximum safe capacity. For example:

- You might target that average CPU usage during normal trading does not exceed 50%, leaving room for spikes.
- Queue lengths and latencies should remain comfortably below thresholds, with spare throughput for bursts.

Headroom targets differ by component:

- Latency-critical services may maintain very high headroom.
- Batch analytics may run near capacity, scheduled outside critical windows.

These targets become SLOs for infrastructure: they guide scaling and capacity allocation.

Stress Testing and Scenario Planning

Beyond extrapolating from history, you should deliberately stress the system:

- Use replay to feed high-volume days (for example, during extreme volatility) into test clusters.
- Amplify certain streams (double quote volume, triple order rates) to see where bottlenecks emerge.
- Combine with chaos techniques: test how the system handles high load plus partial failures.

This yields:

- Empirical evidence of where you run out of capacity.
- Data to justify additional resources or optimization work.
- Confidence that the system can handle plausible future scenarios.

Scaling Strategies

Scaling can be:

Vertical.

- Give a service more powerful machines (more CPU, faster storage).
- Often useful for components that are hard to parallelize or where latency matters.

Horizontal.

- Add more instances and distribute load.
- Ideal for stateless or partitioned services (for example, per-symbol partitions).

In event-driven trading systems, horizontal scaling often leverages partitioned topics or queues:

- Each partition (for example, a group of symbols) is handled by a specific instance.
- You can increase partition count and instances together to get more throughput.

Scaling decisions should be automated where possible, but with constraints:

- **Auto-scaling**: triggers based on metrics like CPU usage, queue length, or latency.
- **Guardrails**: maximum and minimum instance counts; disabled auto-scaling for certain critical services where sudden churn is risky.

Release and Operations Hygiene

Beyond big-picture deployment and capacity planning, day-to-day practices make a huge difference in operational smoothness.

Feature Flags and Dark Launches

We touched on feature flags earlier. Operationally, they support:

- **Dark launches**: deploying features that are invisible to users or disabled by default, then gradually turning them on for subsets of users or flows.
- **Quick mitigations**: turning off problematic features without reverting entire releases.

Flags should be:

- Managed centrally, with audit trails of who changed what, when.
- Designed so that the "off" state is safe and well-tested.

Configuration Management

Configuration is a powerful lever; misconfigurations often cause major incidents. To control this:

- Keep configuration in version control.
- Apply the same review and testing standards to config changes as to code.
- Use staged rollouts of config (for example, test environments, then partial production, then full production), ideally using the same deployment mechanisms as code.

Runbooks for Scaling and Failover

Earlier we discussed runbooks for incidents. You should also have runbooks for:

- Planned scaling ahead of expected high-volume events (for example, macroeconomic announcements).

- Emergency failover between regions or colos.
- Graceful degradation: intentionally reducing non-essential functionality to preserve core trading during resource constraints.

These runbooks should be practiced in drills, not just written.

Bringing It All Together

Deployment, orchestration, and capacity planning are the operational expression of everything in this book:

- Your event-driven design informs how services are packaged and scaled.
- Record/replay powers safe deployments and realistic stress tests.
- Property-based and chaos tests validate behaviour under change and high load.
- Observability and SLOs tell you whether deployments are healthy and capacity is adequate.
- Security and governance ensure that changes and scaling respect permissions, encryption, and audit requirements.
- Alerting and incident response provide a safety net when changes go wrong.

When these disciplines work together, you can keep shipping improvements and responding to markets while maintaining a trading platform that is not only fast and profitable, but also reliable, safe, and understandable—even on the busiest days.

www.ingramcontent.com/pod-product-compliance
Lightning Source LLC
LaVergne TN
LVHW010916300926
849194LV00025B/242
* 9 7 9 8 8 9 6 6 5 2 2 2 9 *